EDITED BY **Bernard**
# Stiegler
WITH THE **INTERNATION COLLECTIVE**

# **BIFURCATE** 'THERE IS NO ALTERNATIVE'
TRANSLATED BY **DANIEL ROSS**

## CCC2 Irreversibility

Series Editors: Tom Cohen and Claire Colebrook

The second phase of 'the Anthropocene,' takes hold as tipping points speculated over in 'Anthropocene 1.0' click into place to retire the speculative bubble of "Anthropocene Talk". Temporalities are dispersed, the memes of 'globalization' revoked. A broad drift into a de facto era of managed extinction events dawns. With this acceleration from the speculative into the material orders, a factor without a means of expression emerges: climate panic.

EDITED BY **Bernard**
# Stiegler
WITH THE **INTERNATION COLLECTIVE**

# BIFURCATE 'THERE IS NO ALTERNATIVE'
TRANSLATED BY **DANIEL ROSS**

preceded by a letter from **JEAN-MARIE LE CLÉZIO**

with an afterword by **ALAIN SUPIOT**

and a lexicon by **ANNE ALOMBERT** and **MICHAŁ KRZYKAWSKI**

O

OPEN HUMANITIES PRESS

*London 2021*

First published in French: *Bifurquer: il n'y a pas d'alternative*, Collectif Internation, Coordonné par Bernard Stiegler, ©Les Liens Qui Libèrent, 2020

English translation first published by Open Humanities Press 2021

English Translation Copyright © 2021 Daniel Ross

Print ISBN  978-1-78542-122-8

PDF ISBN  978-1-78542-121-1

()

OPEN HUMANITIES PRESS

Open Humanities Press is an international, scholar-led open access publishing collective whose mission is to make leading works of contemporary critical thought freely available worldwide. More at http://openhumanitiespress.org

# Contents

# Letter from Jean-Marie Gustave Le Clézio
# to Bernard Stiegler

Thank you very much for inviting me to support Greta Thunberg's actions, and your own, so that future generations may live in a better world. I was born at a time when this concern was practically non-existent. Particularly for those of my generation, born during the Second World War, the question that arose was more of a social and political order. How was humanity (in Western Europe, but also in Japan, China and North America) going to survive this terrible post-war crisis and succeed in transforming it into an egalitarian and peaceful world? This did not mean that the equilibrium between human expenditure and natural assets was ignored, but that it occupied second place, since the search for individual well-being was the goal, and this implied solving all problems through technical progress. It is understandable: the children of my generation suffered from diseases that have today been eradicated in the developed world. We are survivors.

I say that, not to exonerate us from our responsibilities, nor to minimize our errors, but to better understand how far we have come since that time. After the war, I myself lived in West Africa, where everything seemed inexhaustible: the resources, nature, the ability to progress. We could feel a certain anxiety, an instinctive indignation, when, for example, we visited the home of a District Officer stationed in Obudu, near the border with Cameroon, and he showed us with vain pride his collection of skulls of mountain gorillas that he had shot. My father, a bush doctor in the same area, ironically told tourists on safari that the only dangerous animals in the region were mosquitos. Forty years later, Peter Matthiessen wrote a beautiful book, *African Silences*, in order to document the disaster. When young people today rise up to demand accountability, to demand action – and in this Greta is the great figure of our time – it is not only justified, it is urgent, and it can no longer await the promises of politicians.

The technocratic argument against decreasing emissions, intended to discredit the environmental movement as a whole, is that we cannot possibly 'go backwards', as if overdevelopment and the excessive consumption of resources did not themselves amount to a backwards step, impoverishing modern society. The other argument, which follows from the first, is that the development of the non-industrialized countries – those countries that supply most of the raw materials used by the rest of the world – depends on this overproduction, and any reduction of this production would imply that progress grinds to a halt, leading those countries into a backwards slide. Worse still, the cheerleaders of overdevelopment point to the threat that such a slide could affect rich countries, too, condemning them to return to the underdeveloped level of poor countries – offering as examples the GDP of Ghana or Vietnam, if not of the poorest countries on the planet, such as Haiti or Mozambique. The same arguments are also used by politicians to defend neo-colonial situations, by comparing the level of former colonies ('overseas' or 'mandated territories' such as the British Indian Ocean Territory or the French dependencies in the Pacific and Indian Oceans) to that of newly independent states, such as Mauritius or Vanuatu.

In this argument, no mention is ever made of the emotional or educational parameters that would improve the basis of these comparisons, that is, historical elements (the age of these new countries, their cruel colonial history, the ancient wisdom of their culture) and ethical elements – those parameters of happiness and sharing that appear in Amartya Sen's classification of states, and that place countries such as Ghana, Bolivia and Nepal well above the great imperialist systems.

The merit of Greta, and of all those who support her fight – let us remember the meaning of the word ecology, the science of the house, since after all the world is our only home – is to place ourselves before this emergency, this absolute necessity: to examine our values now, to make our choices without any further delay, to decide our own future and that of our children. This is called the truth, and everything else is just empty rhetoric, a destructive fantasy, a masquerade with no way out.

# Letter from Hans Ulrich Obrist and Bernard Stiegler to António Guterres

*11 November 2019, Paris*

Dear Secretary-General,

As you have pointed out on many occasions, international efforts to commit to a greenhouse gas reduction strategy compatible with the objectives set by the Paris Agreement have largely been inadequate, despite the forecasts documented by the IPCC and various other groups, organizations and scientific teams.

The gap between what is required and what is actually being done is often interpreted as a lack of (political and collective) will and as showing a rise of (political and collective) apathy. This state of affairs, in which we are bearing witness to a collective inability to change course, worries everyone: investors and populations alike, and in particular the younger generations, who are wondering what world they will inherit.

Given the state of emergency to which this state of affairs amounts, the transdisciplinary Internation/Geneva2020 Collective, on whose behalf we are writing to you, was formed at the Serpentine Galleries in London on 22 September 2018, on our initiative – Hans Ulrich Obrist and Bernard Stiegler. It is composed of fifty-two members from around the world, including scientists, mathematicians, lawyers, economists, philosophers, anthropologists, sociologists, doctors, artists, business leaders, activists and designers.

We argue that the general lack of will is symptomatic of a profound disorientation regarding the challenged posed by the contemporary epoch – the Anthropocene. The absence of a theoretical framework enabling us to properly understand these challenges hinders the implementation of actions capable of truly reversing the tendencies that threaten the biosphere. Our main thesis is that the Anthropocene era can be described as an Entropocene era, insofar as it is characterized above all by a process of the massive increase of entropy in all its forms (physical, biological and informational). The question of entropy has, however, been neglected by 'mainstream' economics. We therefore believe that a new macroeconomic model, designed to struggle against entropy, is required.

In order to investigate these problems scientifically and build democratic solutions, we believe that new research methods must also be developed, which we call contributory research. In a manner similar to what you have described as 'inclusive multilateralism', contributory research aims to foster close associations between researchers from different disciplines and territorial stakeholders (inhabitants, businesses, associations, elected officials and public administrations) in new territorialized research and experimentation networks. In this way, territories could experiment with economic activities and technological tools that are at the same time sustainable, solvent and desirable. The objective of these networks would be to enable local societies to develop reproducible solutions, through processes of rapid knowledge transfer and with transposable models.

Adopting a *territorialized* approach of this type might provide an opportunity to reread the reflections recorded by the anthropologist Marcel Mauss in various manuscripts written in 1920 and later published under the title *La nation*. Mauss recommended that the development of internationalism should not come at the expense of the territorial and cultural specificities of nations. He thus outlined the concept of the *internation*, a dynamic through which nations would be called upon to cooperate without erasing their local dimensions.

A century after the founding of the League of Nations, it is by referring to this work that we believe that such an internation could be constituted in order to form the institutional framework of a new inclusive multilateralism. Its function would be to encourage, launch, support and evaluate experimental operations that could be initiated on the basis of a call for tenders, inviting stakeholders from candidate territories to collectively engage, and to do so in a network of contributory research approaches and territorial laboratories.

In order to establish a set of specifications for these territorial laboratory initiatives and the networks they will require, the Internation/ Geneva 2020 Collective has defined a set of theoretical questions and thematic axes capable of structuring such an approach.

Part of this work, in its general outline, will be debated next December at the Centre Pompidou (Paris). Representatives of the movement initiated by Greta Thunberg, *Youth for Climate*, will be invited. We will also publish this work, both on the internation.world website and in the form of a book that will be published in French by *Les Liens qui Libèrent*.

We would like to be able to present this work to you and your staff, and to present it publicly in Geneva, if possible by means of a press conference assembling various stakeholders (a team from the UN, representatives of the political and economic world, citizens' movements, academics). Given the importance of these issues, and in the hope of sparking an international debate, we would be very grateful if this event could be held in the historic premises of the Palais des Nations around the centenary of the League of Nations, which will be celebrated on 10 January 2020.

In thanking you for your action and for the attention given to this initiative, we ask that you believe, Mr. Secretary-General, in our very respectful devotion.

*For the Internation/Geneva 2020 Collective,*
*Hans Ulrich Obrist*
*Director, Serpentine Galleries*
*Bernard Stiegler*
*President, Institut de Recherche et d'Innovation*

# Foreword

The pandemic that has paralysed the world in just a few weeks is now making *evident* the extraordinary and appalling vulnerability of the current 'development model', and the potential multiplication of the combined systemic risks that are accumulating within it. It *proves* that, wherever in the world we happen to be, this model has a death sentence hanging over it, if we do not change it. If there are, to this day (9 April 2020), still people who wonder why the world economy is being held up for a health crisis 'that causes fewer deaths than do car accidents' – which shows that they do not understand that if the number of deaths in France and Italy is limited, it is precisely *because* drastic measures have *finally* been taken – this testifies to the fact that a large part of the problem that threatens us all is the *stupidity on which this developmental model is fundamentally based.*[1]

This is the case because it imposes mechanistic models on living realities (nature and human beings), poisoning them. Failure to understand that the problem is not whether the pandemic causes greater or fewer deaths than road accidents is a failure to understand that, in life, exponential dynamics are the rule, as Charles Darwin wrote in 1859:

> There is no exception to the rule that every organic being naturally increases at so high a rate, that if not destroyed, the earth would soon be covered by the progeny of a single pair.[2]

The so-called 'Spanish flu' that emerged in North America and claimed some 50 million victims, or even double that figure according to some estimates, was globalized by what was then the First *World* War. It would probably not have been such a disaster without the mechanical acceleration (by ship and other forms of troop movements) of the spread of the virus. Covid-19, for its part, was transported and saw its spread accelerated by the *world economic war* that our 'developmental model' has become, particularly since the 'conservative revolution'.

This is why this developmental model is in reality a *model of destruction* – and this destruction, long regarded as 'creative', has been accomplished over the past two decades through the *global civil war* now being waged with the computational weapons of mass destruction that arise with reticular and disruptive innovation. When President Macron declared, 'We are at war', he should have added, 'and have been for decades', and, more precisely, ever since the advent of this 'conservative revolution' that has *systematically and systemically* destroyed the social constructions which had in the past two centuries limited, relatively speaking, the anti-social effects of economic struggle.[3]

The collective work that produced this book is based on the claim that this destructive development model is reaching its ultimate limits, and that its toxicity, which is increasingly massive, manifest and multidimensional (medical, environmental, mental, epistemological, economic – accumulating pockets of insolvency, which become veritable oceans), is generated above all by the fact that the current industrial economy, as Nicholas Georgescu-Roegen said contra Joseph Schumpeter as early as 1971, is based in every sector on an obsolete physical model – a mechanism that ignores the *constraints of locality* in biology and the *entropic tendency* in reticulated computational information. A fundamental aspect of this *structural scientific archaism* is that it a priori eliminates the *irreducibly local* dimension of biological and human phenomena – in order to justify a globalization process that has been weakening and ultimately ruining entire regions of the world for decades, and that is bound to lead to the multiplication of catastrophes such as the one we are currently experiencing, which will increasingly *combine with* climate problems, resource depletion, the exacerbation of tensions over access to resources, mental and social regression, financial disaster and so on.

It is to establish a precise diagnosis and advocate a general method in order to exit from this state of fact without law that this book has been written – just before the pandemic – and presented in broad outline in Geneva on 10 January 2020. The proposals set out in this work respond in advance to the question of a post-pandemic world – and with a view to rebuilding, not a war economy, but an economy of transition towards a global economic peace based on a *new economic pact* and giving concrete form to a *peace treaty.*

■ ■ ■

After 2008, and after the restoration over the following decade of a process of financialization that was not only just as absurd (where the banks were recapitalized without in any way requiring them to adopt new investment policies) but in fact *intensified to an extreme degree by digital disruption*, it is doubtful whether, in order to *build* a post-health-crisis world, it is still possible to trust corporations and banks with regard to their willingness and ability to modify their investment policies – because, behind these economic powers, there are shareholders who hold them in check by keeping a gun pointed constantly at their heads. This is why, if it is obvious that the primary issue is the reconstruction of functional economic and political localities, which alone (and for scientific reasons) are capable of struggling against entropy, and the reconstruction of variously reticulated *open* localities, then the *transitional operator* in this regard must be the gradual implementation of new binding accounting standards, that is, a form of accounting that functionally *penalizes* entropy at the micro-, meso- and macro-economic levels.

This resolute transformation of accounting standards can and must occur by setting up networked territorial economic innovation workshops around the world, created in order to constitute polarities and reticularities of contributory economics, all guided by the absolute priority of struggling against entropy – these pathways being by nature diverse. This is what will be developed in what follows, and it is why this book proposes that territorial laboratories be set up without delay, linked together through an authority to be called the internation.

In addition, the fundamental issue concerning *accountancy directives* in the age of algorithms is the *technology of calculability*, which must become a *technology of incalculability*: a new foundation of theoretical computer science is essential – and, on this basis, a *contributory reticulation* must be put in place. Today's data economy is based on a form of theoretical computer science that is utterly subservient to the neoliberal model as defined by Friedrich Hayek and Herbert Simon at the Mont Pelerin Society, giving to information the function of reducing everything to market calculations – thus eliminating the possibility of taking the incalculable into account, even though it is the incalculable that always lies at the origin of bifurcations – opportunities to branch off in new directions, whether positive or negative. This point, which is only touched upon in this book (see Chapter 10), is now the subject of an informal online working group that aims to publish specific proposals in the coming months – proposals that should feed into a new European Union policy on basic research in the field of theoretical computer science, in turn fuelling a new industrial reticulation policy.

## Notes

1    And this is why Greece and Croatia, for example, which took immediate containment measures, are, for the moment at least, in a far less critical situation.

2    Charles Darwin, *On the Origin of Species* (Oxford: Oxford University Press, 2008), p. 52.

3    John L. Pfaltz, 'Entropy in Social Networks' (2012), available at: <https://arxiv.org/pdf/1212.2917.pdf>, no page numbers: 'under continuous change/transformation, all networks tend to "break down" and become less complex. It is a kind of entropy.'

# Introduction – Decarbonization and Deproletarianization: Gagner sa vie in the Twenty-First Century

*Bernard Stiegler with Paolo Vignola and Mitra Azar*

## On the Pharmacology of Locality

### 1   Overview

This book is the fruit of sixteen months of work carried out by the Internation Collective (see internation.world), which aims to respond to two speeches delivered by António Guterres, Secretary-General of the United Nations, the first on 10 September 2018 at the UN and the second on 24 January 2019 in Davos, Switzerland, as well as to the appeals made on several occasions by Greta Thunberg. COP25, held in Madrid in December 2019, showed to what degree neither the IPCC, nor António Guterres, nor Greta Thunberg, nor the youth movements she has sparked throughout the world, are being listened to by the political and economic powers – while public opinion, with the exception of the younger generation, seems to have lost its voice in relation to these appeals, despite the increase in the environmental vote, for example in Europe.

It is the view of the Internation Collective that, in addition to all the particular conflicts of interest with the general interest that clearly exist on the side of both governments and corporations, thanks to which they fail to live up to their responsibilities – which, in the current situation, seems to us to amount to a moral, political *and economic* failing – this state of affairs is due primarily to the fact that the implementation of truly decisive and effective measures to combat climate change, and, more generally, the disorders tied to the excesses of the Anthropocene era, depends on profoundly changing the scientific models that have dominated the industrial economy since the late eighteenth century. These models all have a fundamentally Newtonian construction in the sense that they all ignore the question of entropy. Integrating these issues (and the toxic aspects of development are all expressions of these issues) presupposes modifying the microeconomic and macroeconomic axioms, theorems, methods, instruments and organizations of the global industrial economy – an industrial economy characterized by the fact that, as technology, it integrates *scientific formalisms* with knowledge and with technical production methods. The need for a change of economic organization, due to the toxicity generated by the current industrial economy, was highlighted during COP23 by the researchers who signed the appeal published on 13 November 2017 in *BioScience*, in particular in their twelfth point.[1]

Humanity as a whole, represented on the largest scale by the UN, has the challenge of formalizing, and bringing into play at the level of the planetary economy, new theoretical models equal to the real situation – a global threat caused by the global economy in its encounter with the biosphere, which could in the near future turn into a kind of 'necrosphere' thanks to the irrational and unreasonable exploitation of what, since Vernadsky, has also been called the technosphere. Can such a discourse be heard any more than have the warnings constantly issued since 1992, which, despite the unfolding of countless biospheric catastrophes, of which the 2019 fires provide some of the most appalling images, have remained without effect?

It may be that such a discourse can be heard, and without delay, if it turns this challenge into an opportunity to create new forms of economic activity – industrial as well as artisanal and agricultural, along with service industries – based on the struggle against entropy. These more solvent forms of economic activity must, with a transitional and in-depth approach, progressively redefine investment, work and employment, by taking advantage of the automation currently underway – not so that it will be possible for technology to solve every problem, but so that it can strengthen the capabilities of individuals and groups in the struggle against entropy, and, in so doing, enable them to *earn their living* [*gagner leur vie*], to *regain their life*, both individually and collectively.

From ten different angles, corresponding to ten chapters, this work proposes:

- a diagnosis of the present situation;

- a theoretical formalization of its causes, consequences and possible transformations;

- a method of large-scale social experimentation, based on the *rapid transfer* of the results of contributory research – fundamental research, applied research and action research – in the form of contributory economic models;

- the sharing of results and experiments by consolidating them on a global scale through a specific organization

inspired by the concept of the internation, outlined by
Marcel Mauss in 1920.

The ten angles are: 1) epistemology; 2) territorial dynamics; 3) contributory economics; 4) contributory research; 5) internation and
nations; 6) internation as institution; 7) ethics in the Anthropocene
era; 8) contributory design; 9) addiction and the dopaminergic system;
10) global political economy of carbon (fire) and silicon (information).

## 2    The Internation Collective and the Association
of Friends of the Thunberg Generation

Composed of scientists, economists, epistemologists, philosophers,
sociologists, lawyers, artists, doctors, engineers, designers and citizens actively engaged in these issues, the Internation Collective was
formed in order to confront these questions of axioms, theorems,
methods, instruments and organizations of the global industrial economy in the context of automation. It aims to progressively transform
macroeconomic norms, starting from an experimentally-driven transitional process. The goal of this process is to set up an alternative
industrial macroeconomy through which all[2] aspects related to the
Anthropocene's encounter with its own limits would be addressed in
a functional and systemic way.

The name 'Internation Collective' was adopted in November 2019
– the collective having been formed in London on 22 September 2018.
'Internation' is a neologism put forward by Marcel Mauss in 1920,[3]
during the time of the creation of the institution that would on 10
January 1920 come to be named the League of Nations, at the Palais
Wilson in Geneva (then called the Hôtel National). On 10 January
2020,[4] the work presented in the following chapters will be presented
publicly in Geneva at a press conference preceded by a day of work
and exchange with two international youth movements, Youth for
Climate and Extinction Rebellion. The press conference will be held
on behalf of the Internation Collective, but also on behalf of those
invited to the event and wanting to be present at the table, whether
they have been invited to take part in these discussions on behalf
of institutions, associations or informal groups, or are there in their
own capacity.

The work being done with members of Youth for Climate and
Extinction Rebellion – two movements striving to push political and
economic powers to take the action required by the extremely critical
situation in which the biosphere finds itself, both of which are essentially led by the younger generation – is being carried out within the

framework of the Association of Friends of the Thunberg Generation, whose project was presented at the Centre Pompidou on 17 December 2019, created from a proposal to transform the Ars Industrialis association. The vocation of the Association of Friends of the Thunberg Generation will be described in an appendix (see the Appendix on the Mission of the Association of Friends of the Thunberg Generation, p. 303). To put it in one sentence, it aims to open up an ongoing dialogue with the youth movements struggling to cope with the climate emergency, starting from Greta Thunberg's demand to 'listen to the scientists', and in order to formulate carefully considered proposals from various standpoints, enriched by generational differences.

The materials contained in the following chapters have been written collectively. They are addressed first of all to the UN and expand on points that were raised in a letter addressed to António Guterres, Secretary-General of the United Nations (see p. 11). They were partially presented and discussed during a symposium held at the Centre Pompidou on 17–18 December 2019, as part of the Entretiens du nouveau monde industriel that IRI (Institut de Recherche et d'Innovation) organizes there each year.[5]

## 3   The UN context

The Internation Collective met for the first time on 22 September 2018 at the Serpentine Galleries in London, after its director Hans Ulrich Obrist suggested that a debate be organized on the question of work in the twenty-first century – and in reference to a program of social experimentation and contributory research (see Chapter 4) launched in Seine-Saint-Denis in 2016 under the name of Territoire Apprenant Contributif (Contributory Learning Territory – see recherchecontributiv.org). Its aim was to explore the question of the future of work, and it was conducted within the framework of the Marathon (see https://www.serpentinegalleries.org/exhibitions-events/work-marathon), an initiative of Hans Ulrich Obrist held each autumn at the Serpentine Galleries.

The Collective has set itself the task of submitting proposals to the United Nations in order to rethink work in the twenty-first century on a new theoretical and practical basis, in the context of an essential transformation of the industrial economy, which at the end of the Anthropocene era is confronted with its own toxic effects. In other words, it is a question of facing up to the injunctions regularly formulated by the scientific world with regard to the immediate future of humanity and life on Earth.

This meeting was followed by several seminars held in various locations, including a session held in February 2019 based on the symposium, Le travail au XXIè siècle, organized by Alain Supiot at the Collège de France as part of the centenary of the ILO, the proceedings of which have now been published.[6] A two-day seminar was also held at Maison Suger in early July 2019, within the framework of the Collège d'études Mondiales of the Fondation Maison des Sciences de l'Homme, which included the participation of members of Youth for Climate (see https://youthforclimate.fr).

The first scientific work analysing the threats to the biosphere posed by the industrial development of human societies emerged within the United Nations context in 1972, with the first Earth Summit held that year in Stockholm, leading to the establishment of the United Nations Environment Program (UNEP). Since then, such work has continued to develop and strengthen, with almost every new assessment confirming and extending the significance of the toxic consequences of the current form of industrial development – up to and including the most recent IPCC reports, to which the Secretary-General of the United Nations has frequently referred, especially since the autumn of 2018. These reports are highly alarming.

In the same year as the Stockholm summit, the famous Meadows report, a commission given to MIT by the Club of Rome, was published as *The Limits to Growth*. A year earlier, Nicholas Georgescu-Roegen's *The Entropy Law and the Economic Process* was published by Harvard University Press. In 1976, Arnold Toynbee's *Mankind and Mother Earth* appeared, followed in 1979 by René Passet's *L'économique et le vivant*.

Long before all these works, an article by Alfred J. Lotka was printed in a 1945 issue of the journal *Human Biology*, entitled 'The Law of Evolution as a Maximal Principle'.[7] This article, and Lotka's earlier work (synthesized, in a way, in the 1945 article), are widely discussed in the work presented here. Lotka was a mathematician and biologist who studied the question of entropy in the field of life as early as the 1920s, and his reflections came to the notable attention of Vladimir Vernadsky, who referred to them, together with those of Alfred Whitehead, in the final chapter of *The Biosphere* (1926).

## 4    Conceiving the role of work in the Anthropocene
     with Alfred Lotka

As has already been mentioned, the proposals of the Internation Collective presented below were inspired by a social experiment currently ongoing in the department of Seine-Saint-Denis. This

experimental Contributory Learning Territory is devoted to the reinvention of work in the context of a contributory economy. As we will
see repeatedly, the future of work, forming more or less the heart of
all these analyses, is *fundamentally and functionally* tied to climate
and environmental issues.

In *Le travail au XXIè siècle*, Alain Supiot writes that

> through its work, *Homo faber* aims in principle to adapt
> its vital milieu to its needs, or in other words, to create a
> cosmos from out of chaos, a humanly liveable world from
> out of worldlessness [*immonde*]. But conversely, its work
> can, whether voluntarily or not, also destroy or devastate
> its vital milieu, and make it humanly unliveable. The ques-
> tion of work and the ecological question are thus inextri-
> cably linked.[8]

Unlike employment, from which it is therefore strictly distinguished,
just as it is distinguished from labour or toil (*ponos* in Greek), work
(*ergon* in Greek)[9] is here conceived above all as a production of
knowledge.[10]

In 1945, however, Lotka showed that, for that technical form of life
known as human life, the condition of the struggle against entropy is
the production of *knowledge*. If the organogenesis in which the *evolution of life in general* consists produces endosomatic organs that are
spontaneously ordered by biological constraints, nevertheless, in the
specifically human form of life, organogenesis is also exosomatic. In
what Lotka calls exosomatic evolution, artificial organs are produced
by the *cooperation* of human groups, and this always involves knowledge, through which their negentropic capabilities are intensified,
over against their entropic tendencies.[11]

With respect to cooperation, and with respect to the development
of the 'division of labour' as the acquisition of constantly renewed
knowledge, recent palaeo-anthropology in North America and
Australia has shown that these were the condition of survival of
*Homo sapiens*, and before that the condition of hominization itself.[12]
In his recent work, Richard Sennett has brought these questions into
the context of the contemporary world.[13]

Exosomatic organs are bivalent: they are what Socrates called
*pharmaka* – at once poisons and remedies (and this is why, by its
work, *Homo faber* can as easily produce a *kosmos* as devastate its
milieu). The practice of exosomatic organs must therefore be *prescribed* by theories as well as by the empirical knowledge supplied by
experience. Georgescu-Roegen takes up Lotka's perspective, arguing
that it is the function of the *economy* to limit entropy and increase

negentropy. For Georgescu-Roegen, this means that economics must no longer be based exclusively on Newtonian physics, but must integrate both thermodynamics, as the question of entropy, and biology, as the question of negentropy.

Here, however, we must reiterate that in Lotka's view, beyond a strictly biological question, it is possible for the economy to limit the entropy of exosomatic organs and increase their negentropy only on the condition that it *valorizes* knowledge. It is in order to avoid being trapped in a biological model whose inadequacy was described by Lotka that we thus refer to anthropy and neganthropy,[14] positing that what produces neganthropy is knowledge in all its forms.[15]

Once the vital function of knowledge has been recognized, it becomes necessary to analyse the consequences of the fact that, from the beginning of the Anthropocene era – if we allow that this can be dated from the industrial revolution[16] – work has been transformed into employment, and the *knowledge that had been implemented by work has now been progressively transformed into machinic formalisms*.[17] This has resulted in a structural impoverishment of employment, ever more clearly proletarianized, something that was already of concern to Adam Smith, and which will occupy the centre of Marxist theory.

Today, we know that above all, this impoverishment consists in:

- an entropic development of employment, with, as we know, disastrous consequences for the environment;

- a loss of meaning, which lies at the origin of what is now called 'suffering at work', but which is also the origin, more generally, of demotivation and the crisis of 'human resources';

- the replacement of proletarianized employees by automatons (whether robotic or algorithmic, as highlighted by an MIT report taken up by Oxford), proletarianized jobs tending to disappear, and the activity of pure labour (*ponos*) without work (*ergon*) being transferred to automated machines.

The level of employment, however, which is crucial to the developmental model known as the *perpetual growth economy,* is for this reason *systemically oriented to decline,* with the result that the overall *solvency* of the model is necessarily and irreversibly compromised. 'Irreversibly' – unless there is a change of macroeconomic model, and of its functions and variables. It is to propose achievable and experimental pathways to such a change, which must occur *as a matter of*

*urgency*, that the Internation Collective is advocating a specific experimental approach called 'contributory research', which was proposed
in 2014 in France by the Conseil National du Numérique, as part of
the *Jules Ferry 3.0* report.[18]

## 5    Detoxifying the industrial economy:
         the contributory economy

The program of the Contributory Learning Territory was developed
in Seine-Saint-Denis on the basis of this observation of a systemic
downward tendency of proletarianized employment and the subsequent need for the productivity gains achieved by automation to be
redistributed via work performed and remunerated outside employment. For this reason, it conducts experiments in the development of
an economy of contribution.

Work outside employment means a knowledge activity that is yet
to be economically and socially valued. We maintain that in the context of the Anthropocene era, it is necessary to invest in the development of this kind of work, in order to foster the emergence of new
knowledge – of how to live, make and conceive differently – capable
of *detoxifying the industrial economy*.

The goal of the contributory economy, as a macroeconomic model
based on microeconomic and mesoeconomic territorial activities,
is thus to revalorize knowledge of all kinds – from that of mothers
raising their children in the epoch of touchscreens (an issue worked
on by the contributory clinic of the Plaine Commune Contributory
Learning Territory) to the most formalized and mathematized forms
of knowledge, disrupted by 'black boxes', as well as the work-knowledge [*savoir-faire*] of the manual or intellectual worker in the age
of automation.

In this conception of the contributory economy, which remuner-
ates work through a contributory income inspired by the French
model for intermittent workers in the performing arts, employment,
which becomes intermittent, is functionally deproletarianized. This
also means that new ways of organizing work – inspired first by free
software, but also by action research methods practised by institutional psychiatry, or those studied by Gregory Bateson (such as the
Alcoholics Anonymous association) – are implemented through specific systems and institutions. (Starting from the case of Seine-Saint-
Denis, Management Institutes of the Contributory Economy – MICE
– have been conceived and designed, a description of which will be
found in Chapter 3.)

Here, the *decarbonization of the economy therefore passes through the deproletarianization of industry.* Of course, not all jobs will be involved in this evolution. But it will crucially involve all those that could tend to decrease the entropic human footprint – the human form of entropy production also being called, in the 2014 IPCC report,[19] 'anthropogenic forcing', referred to more generally, for example in geography, as anthropization.

This is why, in what follows, we will use the term *anthropy* in order to qualify the *specifically human form of entropy.* The increase of anthropy (in thermodynamic, biological and informational forms) is the specific feature of the Anthropocene era. Conceived in this way, and having now developed to such an extent that its own conditions of possibility are inevitably compromised, the issue at stake with anthropy is to *reconstitute neganthropic potentials.* What defines knowledge *as* knowledge, moreover, is precisely its neganthropic character.

## 6    The revaluation of work is the revaluation of knowledge

Inasmuch as it makes it possible to struggle against this anthropy, knowledge may be empirical, such as the knowledge of the hand in the sense described by Richard Sennett or Matthew Crawford, or, again, in the sense of Winnicott's 'good enough mother', who does the work of raising her child, that is, cultivating a knowledge *of* her child and thus transmitting knowledge *to* her child, which is called parental education.[20] Empirical knowledge can be an art (*ars*) in the sense of the artisan or the craftsman, but also in the sense of the artist, or even in the sense of the sportsperson.

Conceptual knowledge may be scientific, or technical, or technological. As for the social knowledge of everyday life – hospitality, companionship, neighbourly relations, festive practices, rules of life constituting mores – they are ruined and destroyed by marketing, user manuals, the reduction of usages to utility, which comes to replace those social practices still containing specific forms of knowledge amounting to 'mores' or 'morals' as collective care, and hence as solidarity. Such practices are the basis of what Henri Bergson called obligation, which is the condition of social life, and which, if destroyed, is bound to lead to generalized incivility.

We could continue for a long time delineating everything that (empirical, conceptual, social) knowledge *could* be: the task is *inherently interminable*, because knowledge, like inventiveness, creativity or discovery, is infinite in principle and in potential, albeit always coming to completion in actualization, the whole issue of reason being to know how to make the most of this difference between potential and act (in Aristotle's sense of *dunamis* and *energeia*, the root of the latter being *ergon*).

We should stress here that decarbonization, like deproletarianization, does not just concern work and employment activities in production or services: the challenge is also the detoxification of consumers, that is, the deproletarianization of ways of life.[21] Here, an immense educational project opens up, whose terms and stakes are profoundly new, and which cannot wait for the reformation of educational institutions (which find themselves in an increasingly parlous state), but must on the contrary foster social dynamics of civil society that nourish and transform educational institutions. And the latter once again raises the question of what was developed in the twentieth century under the banner of popular education, and of the relationships between democracy and education in John Dewey's sense.

Here, we posit in principle that *all* knowledge, of whatever kind – empirical, parental, artistic, sporting, scientific, academic or social, in all of the senses that can be given to this last adjective – *knows* something of the world in that it *adds* something to this world: it knows that this world is *unfinished*, and that we must continue to make it unfold towards a future, to create the advent of something new. This adding something, through which *the world happens through knowledge*, contributes to human worlds in a way that is neganthropic (and anti-anthropic, this notion being based on that of anti-entropy that will be developed in Chapter 1). Without this contribution, these worlds would collapse into anthropy: knowledge, whatever its form, is what, in the spontaneous tendency of the universe as a whole to move towards disorder, maintains or constitutes an order.

*Deprived* of such knowledge, employment can become toxic and 'devastate' its milieu, as Supiot highlights. It is precisely in such *deprivation*, however, that proletarianization consists. And *here lies the deepest origin of the Anthropocene era* that is now reaching its limits – the IPCC reports precisely describe such limits from the climatological perspective, but the challenge posed by the warming of the biosphere does not, unfortunately, exhaust the subject of the limits of the Anthropocene, which will undoubtedly mark all the most salient features of the remainder of the twenty-first century, including, hopefully, in terms of responses to these limits, and as the overcoming of the Anthropocene era by the Neganthropocene era.

At the origin of thermodynamic anthropization lies the toxic anthropization of human life, itself produced by the anthropization of knowledge. By defining knowledge above all as neganthropic potential (in the wake of Alfred Whitehead and Georges Canguilhem), the elements of a response to António Guterres and Greta Thunberg presented here consist, above all, in *reconsidering the very purpose of the economy in general* – in particular when the latter, having become industrial, functionally and systemically mobilizes scientific knowledge.

It is this specific relationship of the industrial economy to scientific knowledge that Chapter 1, 'Anthropocene, Exosomatization and Negentropy' – co-authored by Maël Montévil, Giuseppe Longo, Carlos Sonnenschein, Ana Soto and Bernard Stiegler – tries to describe. On the basis of this chapter, it is shown that, in a context where the Anthropocene is reaching its limits, the economy must be redefined above all as *collective action in the struggle against entropy and against anthropy,* given that the various disturbances afflicting the current stage of the Anthropocene *all* consist in an increase of (1) thermodynamic entropy, as the dissipation of energy, (2) biological entropy, as the reduction of biodiversity, and (3) informational entropy, as the reduction of knowledge to data and computation – and, correspondingly, as loss of credit, as mistrust, as generalized mimetism and as the domination of what has been called the 'post-truth era' at the very moment when, more than ever, what Alfred Whitehead called the function of reason should be brought back to the heart of what amounts to an extreme state of emergency.

## 7    Struggling against anthropy

If it is obvious that the economy consists above all in the production, sharing and exchange of value, and if, since the advent of the industrial economy, the so-called consumer economy has fundamentally consisted in the production of various forms of value beyond its meaning in subsistence economies (which it has done by devaluing traditional values, and through the valuing, *by the economy,* of scientific discoveries and technical inventions via a process of innovation whose primary functional element is marketing inasmuch as it 'creates needs'), then in the current stage of the Anthropocene:

- this value has been devalued, which amounts to an extreme form of *disenchantment,* in the sense that Max Weber gives to this word[22] – but far beyond what he himself could have anticipated;

- the 'value of values' ever more clearly becomes that which allows this era to *overcome its limits* – and to thus enter into a new era.

Overcoming these limits can only mean struggling against entropy, and against its main source: anthropy. Struggling against entropy is what living things do: negative entropy has been referred to in this sense ever since Erwin Schrödinger formulated it as a concept in 1944 in Dublin – during lectures subsequently published as *What is Life?*.[23]

As we have already indicated, in 1971, thirty-seven years after his encounter with Joseph Schumpeter at Harvard, Nicholas Georgescu-Roegen showed that the industrial economy does not take entropy into account, and is thereby necessarily *condemned* to destroy its own conditions of possibility.[24] Arnold Toynbee will develop similar arguments by taking up Vladimir Vernadsky's analysis, in a chapter of *Mankind and Mother Earth* entitled 'The Biosphere'.[25]

Negative entropy, which controls the organizational process of living things throughout their evolution, can, however, only ever occur in a temporary and local way. We argue that this is also true of what we call negative anthropy, or neganthropy, and we posit that every society is a neganthropic locality belonging to a larger locality of the same type, up until the largest locality on Earth, which is the biosphere itself as an *absolute singularity* in the known sidereal universe.

Conversely and consequently, when globalization (as a toxic and unsustainable completion of the transformation of the biosphere into a technosphere) systematically eliminates local specificities, this leads to a massive increase in entropic and anthropic processes. This is why the present initiative, aimed towards the United Nations, also consists, for our collective, in reviving the notion of the 'internation' put forward by Marcel Mauss in 1920.

## 8    The notion of the internation and the scales of locality

We argue that reconsideration of the notion of the 'internation' must start from a negentropic standpoint, by producing neganthropic value and by taking into consideration what, inspired by the theory of anti-entropy developed by Francis Bailly, Giuseppe Longo and Maël Montévil, we will therefore call anti-anthropy. Anti-anthropy is distinguished from neganthropy in that it diachronizes a synchronic neganthropic order. These (neganthropic and anti-anthropic) values are produced by *locality* as such, which they characterize and, in so doing, *delimit*.

The way in which Mauss described nations in 1920 must be re-evaluated according to these notions, which he did not himself have at his disposal: nations, like all other forms of those localities called human societies (from the clan to the negentropic locality to which the biosphere itself as a whole amounts on the scale of the solar system), are cases of organizations that we call neganthropic in order to distinguish them from the negentropy constituted by life in general. The use of such a vocabulary is a way of heeding the 'pharmacological' issue at stake in exosomatic organs as theorized by Lotka. Any economy worthy of the name must reduce the various forms of toxicity produced by these organs to a minimum, through a form of organization appropriate for both knowledge (and therefore education) and exchange (and therefore economy) – knowledge itself being based on exchanges, of which the editorial economy, in all its forms, is a fundamental condition, along with scientific institutions. We will see how this is something about which, like Bergson and Mauss, Albert Einstein was concerned, and was so within the context of the League of Nations.[26]

In 1920, in the context of the creation of the League of Nations and the debate this provoked among socialists (of which he was one), Mauss posited that nations must not be diluted into internationalism, contrary to the reaction of most Marxist supporters of the October Revolution of 1917: for Mauss, it was a matter of facilitating the 'concert' of nations through the constitution of an internation. We can see this as a prescient warning that any negation of nations is bound to lead to an exacerbation of nationalisms. But we can also see it as wishful thinking, pious wishes – especially after the failure of the League of Nations. If this is true, then this wish and its piety (as belief in the *superiority of the peaceful interest* of men) must today be reconsidered from the standpoint of an economy conceived above all as the struggle against entropy, and therefore as the valorization of open locality, which for this reason must be founded (this economy and these localities) on a new epistemology of economics and the disciplines it involves (especially mathematics, physics, biology and theoretical computer science), taking the stakes of entropy fully into account.

Taking the stakes of entropy into account means learning to count otherwise, by translating these stakes into *formal* terms, in particular in the processes of certification, traceability and accounting that constitute every industrial economy, and by translating them into legal and institutional terms. It is a question of taking account of these issues at various scales, and hence of reconstituting them – not as barriers but as *crossing points* and *negotiations of economies of scale,* as required by an economy of negentropy, and by extraterritorial monetization. All kinds of possibilities are being raised in the work currently being undertaken in accounting by, in particular, economists,[27] jurists[28] and philosophers[29] – for example, in Europe, with the setting up of what are called 'satellite accounts' (see §55).

## 9    Economic war and peace

A century after the institution of the League of Nations, a century after Mauss's reflections, the *immediate* concern is not the avoidance of global conflict – even if, over the last decade, such worries are once again on the rise, a long way from the 'optimism' that characterized the end of the twentieth century. The main concern in terms of conflict has become economic war, which is ruinous for environments – social, moral and mental, as well as physical. It is in this context that the most archaic nationalisms are once again on the march throughout the world – and, along with them, processes of remilitarization, and thus new threats of war, the difference from the context in which the two world wars of the twentieth century erupted being the subsequent spread of atomic weapons. In other words, the situation is immeasurably more serious than it was at the time of the League of Nations.

Why, in that case, does it seem that nothing can be done to change this state of affairs? We argue in Chapter 1 that this is first of all an epistemic and epistemological question: the question *'quid juris?'*, as Kant introduces it at the beginning of *Critique of Pure Reason*, must be posed anew, and this requires – and in a state of extreme urgency – setting up and supporting appropriate contributory research processes, supported by a scientific institution that must be created for this purpose, and that would constitute the institutional basis of an internation.

In 1945, the League of Nations became the United Nations, precisely because of the failure to contain the exacerbated nationalisms of Germany, Italy and Japan – with all of the consequences we know so well, while the world had in the meantime divided into two blocs. Now that

- internationalization is carried out by the market,

- the Anthropocene has been defined, the question of the struggle against entropy thus imposing itself at the core of economics,

it is time to *rethink this century-long history from the perspective of a critique of the globalized economy that structurally and functionally ignores local diversities and specificities* insofar as, as neganthropy, they generate *noodiversity* (that is, infinitely varied and precious knowledge) – just as negentropic life generates biodiversity.

Note here that initiatives as different as those emerging from the territorialist school instigated in Italy by Alberto Magnaghi,[30] and those of the 'transition towns' inspired by Rob Hopkins in the United Kingdom,[31] above all amount to discourses and practices conducted on and through locality – as do, in slightly different ways, the reaffirmations of 'ancestral knowledge' in South America (for example, in the Ecuadorian constitution, or in Eduardo Viveiros de Castro's perspectivism[32]), and of the indigenous peoples of North America (in Canada[33]), reopening the prior question of the *status of locality in social, economic and noetic life.*[34]

At the same time, it should be recalled that:

- *politeia*, as it comes from the Greek experience of the *polis*, and inasmuch as it has always consisted in affirming the prevalence of political decision over economic decision, is always the *privilege of a place*, whether it is called a city (*polis*, *civitas* or republic in the sense of the Renaissance, then of Kant), monarchy, empire, nation or union (federation or confederation as in the United States, India, Brazil and so on);

- the 'people' and their 'independence' are constituted by their territorial right to self-determination, and this is something that no cosmopolitanism can afford to ignore (starting with Kant's).

At the end of the twentieth century, globalization spread rapidly across the entire planet by using the vector of technology to standardize usage, no longer taking any account of the specificities of what Bertrand Gille and Niklas Luhmann called social systems, thereby ignoring the singular social practices that new exosomatic organs also make possible. In this way, globalization has *eliminated all local scales* – from the domestic *nano-locality* to the national or even continental (regional in the Anglo-Saxon sense of a geographical unit) *macro-locality.* It has thus imposed a standardized and monolithic conception of the market, which attempts to set itself up as a computational hegemony itself based on the elimination of everything that is not calculable.

In this way, globalization has ruined biospheric metalocality, which can remain a singularity in the universe (as a living environment) only on the condition of protecting its biodiversity, and, when it tends to become technospheric, its noodiversity: such is the reality of the Anthropocene era that is presently reaching its extreme limits. And this is why nationalist extremism is rearing its head almost everywhere, even becoming, or again becoming, the leading political force.

## 10  Urban localities and human commerce
   in computational becoming

As for the city – not only in the sense of the small locality of Totnes described by Hopkins, but the metropolis or megalopolis, constituting what, after the work of Saskia Sassen, it has become customary to refer to as the global city – it is also, as Sassen has shown, the site of a complex reinvention of locality and citizenship:

> The space constituted by the worldwide grid of global cities [...] is perhaps one of the most strategic spaces for the formation of new types of politics, identities, and communities, including transnational ones. This is a space that is place-centered in that it is embedded in particular and strategic sites, and transterritorial in that it connects sites that are not geographically proximate [...]. The centrality of place in a context of global processes engenders a transnational economic and political opening...[35]

In this respect, the global city and networks of global cities are not just 'learning territories' in the sense put forward by Pierre Veltz in 1994:[36] since that time, digital networks have developed at such a rate and on such a scale that urban localities have been profoundly transformed: 'The whole issue of context and of its surroundings, as part of locality, is profoundly affected [by digital networks]'.[37] As a result, new types of borders are appearing, which are not just national or territorial, while at the same time we see the formation of 'a global law [...] that must be [...] distinguished from both national law and international law.'[38] This is above all a contract law that disintegrates those notions of law that emerged from Greco-Roman antiquity, fundamentally tied to the questions *'quid juris?'* and *'quid facti?'* as Kant revisits them and *inasmuch as they concern both science and law.* The fact remains that these local urban economies and organizations, which are reticulated and in this way becoming global, are thus far more like 'Trojan horses' that aid in the penetration of those criteriologies of value emerging from the global market as it continues to ignore questions of entropy, than the converse.

With the erasure of localities insofar as they are negentropic and neganthropic, the global market has also destroyed commerce – in the sense of the distinction between commerce and the market proposed by Armand Hatchuel, Olivier Favereau and Franck Aggeri.[39] Here, it is important to underline that the notion of the *global market* is based on an utterly fallacious *a priori* assumption that rational behaviour is a calculation, that is, a 'ratio', all economic agents then being defined

as those who make calculations with respect to utterly decontextu-
alized and delocalized particular interests, supporting, after consolidation, a universal rationality that has more to do with what Adorno
called rationalization than with what Whitehead called reason. It is
this that leads to what Supiot has called governance by numbers.[40]

To conceive the economy in this way inevitably leads to the negation of politics, as democracy disintegrates into marketing, generating
among the populations of the whole world a feeling of being dispossessed of their future and of submitting to a functionally blind computational becoming. This is all the more the case as this computational-
ist hegemony, of which 'platforms' have become the operators, now
in fact controls the reticulation of these global cities. From this, we
are led to expect a coming catastrophe, and on a timescale so short
that it could strike with unprecedented violence at today's youngest
generations by the time they become adults (and we can then see that
the benefit of abandoning finality in the name of efficiency is *absolutely illusory*).

## 11   The address to António Guterres: a way out of the coming hell

On 10 September 2018, ten days before the first meeting of the
Internation Collective in London, António Guterres delivered a
speech in New York to the UN General Assembly in which he called
upon nations to take the urgent measures that the latest IPCC reports
concluded are necessary. Four months later, on 24 January 2019, he
made similar remarks to the heads of the global corporations meeting
at the World Economic Forum in Davos – at which Greta Thunberg
also appeared, after taking the initiative in August 2018 to speak on
behalf of her generation by initiating a 'global climate strike'.

The Internation Collective then decided to send to António
Guterres, as Secretary-General of the United Nations, the letter that is
reproduced at the beginning of this book (see p. 11), announcing the
proposals set out in the following chapters. In this letter, we proposed
to António Guterres and the UN:

- on the one hand, a *diagnosis* of what blocks any concerted
  effort by public and economic authorities to overcome the
  catastrophes now variously anticipated and described;

- on the other hand, a *method* for overcoming these blockages
  – this method taking note, first, of the sustainable development objectives adopted by the UN in 2015, second, of
  the imperative need for an *integrated* way of tackling the

immense challenges posed by climate change but also by
its consequences on migration, and third, of the upheavals
brought by digital technology – as António Guterres highlighted on 24 January in Davos.[41]

We should reiterate that if neither the member states nor global
or transnational companies act in the way demanded by António
Guterres and Greta Thunberg, this is the result not just of particular
conflicts of interest, faced with the need to give priority to the public
good at the level of the biosphere: it is *first of all* because of a lack, at
the scale of nations and corporations, of concepts and methods ade-
quate to the task of facing up to this 'reversal of all values' that is the
ordeal of the Anthropocene in the post-truth era.

What this suggests is that a *colossal research effort* must be undertaken in order to meet these challenges, despite the fact that the IPCC
says that what must be taken without delay is action, and that there is
no longer any time for a preliminary research process in which reflection would precede action. This apparent contradiction, however, is
not something we shy away from, and we have already argued in this
way: turning this contradiction into a new prospect is both the goal
and the very method of contributory research.

## 12   Territorial laboratories and contributory research: plan of the work

Years of research have already been conducted in an effort to overcome dominant forms of thought that remain profoundly tied to the
paradigm that has led to what the IPCC has announced will be, if it
does not change course, an inevitable disaster. Beyond that, contributory research[42] consists in the development of laboratory territories
bringing together, and involving on a daily basis, inhabitants, associations, institutions, businesses and administrations. For these learning communities, it is a question of dealing in a very practical way
with the immediate challenges of the Anthropocene, such as toxic
processes of all kinds, while at the same time testing and formalizing new theoretical models, which must be generic and transposable,
while at the same time being capable of taking localities into account.

This is why our proposal to the United Nations (via the Secretary-
General) is for a large-scale launch, in all regions of the world, of
laboratory territories designed to carry out contributory research.
This would require opening a call for tender endowed with sufficient
means, calling for applications on the basis of a set of specifications

and in relation to which the work we present here is intended as a starting point.

As already indicated, the first thesis consists in positing that the causes of the main blockage in current economic development are *above all epistemological*. This is set out in Chapter 1.

The integration of the issues and formalisms linked to entropy requires territorialized approaches, for reasons explained above. The challenge is thus to find ways of shifting from the microeconomic level to the macroeconomic level by passing through regional (meso-economic) strata and sectors. Territorial and urban dynamics, on the one hand, and the specificities of contributory economies that value work and deproletarianize employment, on the other hand, constitute the respective issues at stake in Chapters 2 and 3.

The contributory research method, inspired in part by what the German artist Joseph Beuys called 'social sculpture', is discussed in Chapter 4. As proposed here, that is, in the framework of an experimental approach to be implemented on a global scale, this requires the constitution of a scientific institution that should be the starting point for an internation – as explained in Chapters 5 and 6.

Such an experimental, theoretical and contributory research practice requires instruments of deliberation, cooperation and exchange, for which new practices of computer design and engineering are required. This presupposes a redefinition of those questions we call ethical, by, on the one hand, starting from the notion of *ethōs* – which is also to say, of locality – and by, on the other hand, redefining *ethōs* in the global and now technospheric context. These analyses are discussed in Chapters 7 and 8.

The challenge of climate change is clearly identified, qualified and quantified as the question of carbon metabolism in a society based on thermodynamic technology, and to begin with the steam engine – from the study of which thermodynamic *theory* emerged. The question of silicon technologies – which today have become competitors of proletarianized employees and automated decision-making systems – is just as crucial in the struggle against crossing the threshold limits of the Anthropocene era.

Since the beginning of the twenty-first century, and in the context of a trade war and the rise of smartphones and so-called social networks, these silicon technologies have been socialized in the form of a systemically addictive exploitation of dopaminergic reward circuits. Chapters 9 and 10 discuss these issues, laying out the fundamental basis of a *politics of detoxification* based on deproletarianization and on forging new relationships with these highly toxic exosomatic systems that carbon and silicon technologies have become, the question being to know how to reorient them towards curative economic practices.

## 13   Aporetic questions and problems of locality

Introducing the issue of the struggle against anthropy is a way of emphasizing the irreducible character of locality. In the case of the exosomatic form of life, however, locality can itself become toxic: since exosomatic organs are irreducibly bivalent, they can harm individuals and collectives, who then suffer from their entropic effects. Any crisis situation stems directly or indirectly from such a 'disadjustment' in which the exosomatic *'pharmakon'* can thus reverse its sign and become a 'poison' rather than a 'remedy'. Locality then tends to withdraw and to close in upon itself – that is, to fall into decline.

As for the possible toxicity of organs that are in principle beneficial, the early twenty-first century presents itself as a veritable accumulation of such sign-reversals by which the remedy suddenly turns out to be poisonous. In every respect, the Anthropocene appears to be precisely such a reversal on the scale of the entire planet, and it is now clear to what extent such value-reversals can lead to violence. This is all the more the case since most of the time, when an exosomatic system or device that has more or less established its positivity reverses its sign, it happens that the victims of this bivalence turn upon another victim, an 'expiatory' victim: a *'pharmakos'*,[43] as the ancient Greeks and the Scriptures of monotheism say, that is, a scapegoat. Locality then constitutes itself essentially as a symptomatology of exclusion.

Given that locality is nowadays lived in some way by default, claims for it are therefore often made in terms of a closed and sterile assertion of identity – the scapegoat making it possible to *conceal the challenges* involved in a true revaluation of localities based on the sharing and exchange of new knowledge, inaugurating a new relationship to technologies and, more generally, to the *milieu* this forms (an exosomatic milieu that, in Chapter 10, Daniel Ross calls an element). Locality then becomes the fantasized projection of a given identity, and not the process of a perpetually open identification, one that is still to come and adoptive, that is, metabolizing its alterity.

A locality is not an identity. On the contrary, it is a process of alteration, composed of multiple smaller localities, and included within larger localities. The fundamental question is that of the metabolism that is locality qua neganthropic process – including at its highest level, the biosphere as a whole, which has now become a technosphere.

The metabolism through which localities enter into relationships and exchange alterities is the economy, which is not reducible to the exchange of subsistence or consumer goods, and which always constitutes what Paul Valéry called a political economy of spirit value[44] – the most sublimated level of what Freud more generally called the libidinal economy.[45] This economy is conditioned in its forms by the historical configurations of the exosomatization process.

The process of exosomatization continuously *disorients* the exosomatic form of life. First and foremost, locality is the *taking-place* [*avoir lieu*] from which an orientation emerges, that is, a meaning – an end, arising from a point of view shared by the community, thus constituting knowledge, or rather, a bundle of types of knowledge, always already on the way to diffracting towards an open and diverse future. Such a point of view is a potential for bifurcation, that is, for the emergence of a difference qua place – where a phase shift occurs in that relationship to matter which we call metabolization, generating a dimensionality that is both singular and collective. Conceived in this way, locality is the engine of difference itself: it is not constituted by its identity (it does not have one: it arises from the originary default that strikes exosomatization – and strikes it as mystery[46]), but by its potential for differentiation.

This is true of locality in all epochs and everywhere around the world. The fact that the Baruya are organized into tribes that themselves belong to an ethnic group, the tribe itself being composed of clans,[47] means that it is in the *differential constituted by these scales of locality* that local processes of individuation can arise – these different scales being cosmologically inscribed in localities that exceed ethnicity, and this *exceeding* being the object of what we here call noesis qua noodiversity. Locality, in other words, is always expressed in points of view that are themselves local in relation to the process of unification that the locality forms.

Locality is therefore *relational* and functions as the place of activation of another dimension in a field – which is itself the product of another differential produced by another locality on another dimension of the field. Difference is primary, that is, fundamentally tied to another difference, rather than to the existence of a pre-constituted identity. To re-evaluate localities, conceived as sources of neganthropy and anti-anthropy (metastabilized processes in the form of social structures and emergent singularities always capable of calling into question any constituted order), it is necessary to rethink automated calculation and algorithms on the basis of a new understanding of information theory and computer science. This is outlined in terms of its most general principles in Chapter 7, and as a *technodiversity constitutive of cosmotechnics.*[48]

Currently, relationships between psychic individuals are generated automatically, and this leads – through 'user profiling', 'echo chambers' and 'nudging' – to the literal *annihilation* of these *psychic localities* that are *individuals themselves*, who find themselves replaced by what Félix Guattari called dividuals, in the sense in which 'patterns' are statistically extracted in a manner already in a way foreshadowed by Robert Musil in *The Man Without Qualities*, at a moment when in Italy, German and Japan a catastrophe was brewing.

Here, it is knowledge qua memory (sets of collective retentions and protentions) that is very seriously compromised by 'user profiling', 'echo chambers' and 'nudging', society thus becoming systemically *amnesic*. It is not, however, a question of advocating the protection of an 'authentic' individual or collective memory that would be kept away from or sheltered from calculation: it is a question of the neganthropic and anti-anthropic socialization of artificial retention, which, as exosomatization, constitutes every form of society, as the totem reflected on by Emile Durkheim,[49] or as works in the sense of Ignace Meyerson.[50] Today, digital retention must be theorized in a new way so as to be put at the service of the metabolization of localities, rather than their purely computational and extractive abstraction.

It is in this sense that Management Institutes of the Contributory Economy (MICE) are based above all on deliberative platforms constituted *by starting from the local level*, and on the basis of projects forming micro-reticular exchange structures and aiming towards macro-reticular exchange structures.

## 14   The future according to Bergson

Faced with the mortal and (in the strict sense) apocalyptic challenges of the end of the Anthropocene era announced by the vast majority of the scientific community, human beings must reconstruct knowledge by rediscovering old knowledge, even ancestral knowledge, and by producing new knowledge in all fields. Inventiveness, creativity and discovery are today, as always, the only guarantees of the future of humanity – and of life in general.

Contributory research posits that everyone can and must take part in such a production of new wealth, and the contributory economy posits that this requires a reasoned, tested and deliberate macroeconomic change, based on taking into account scientific work in many fields, in the service of a new economic rationality to combat anthropy, opening up an age founded on cooperation and economic peace rather than on a form of destruction that has long ceased to be 'creative': the Anthropocene era is the revelation of the primarily destructive character of the 'creative destruction' that according to Joseph Schumpeter describes consumerist capitalism.

If there are never any guarantees of the future other than those brought by inventiveness, creativity and discovery, then what is now changing, and in a disorienting way, is the fact that a global economy of extraordinary efficiency, which has made it possible to feed, clothe and house billions of people, more or less badly, turns out to have *also* been extraordinarily toxic – so toxic that it threatens to put an end to what Toynbee called 'the great human adventure'.[51] Here, and in order to learn the lessons they teach, we must reread three quite extraordinary – extra-lucid – little sentences that were published by Henri Bergson in 1932:

> Mankind lies groaning, half crushed beneath the weight of its own progress. Men do not sufficiently realize that their future is in their own hands. Theirs is the task of determining first of all whether they want to go on living or not.[52]

## Notes

1    William J. Ripple et al., 'World Scientists' Warning to Humanity: A Second Notice', *BioScience* 67 (2017), pp. 1026–28, available at: <https://academic.oup.com/bioscience/article/67/12/1026/4605229>. Here is the twelfth point, posited as a condition for any change of course: 'revising our economy to reduce wealth inequality and ensure that prices, taxation, and incentive systems take into account the real costs which consumption patterns impose on our environment'.

2    By accumulating a diversity of experiments and doing so according to local specificities: see below.

3    Marcel Mauss, *La nation ou le sens du social*, corrected edition (Paris: Presses Universitaires de France, 2018).

4    This date, 10 January 2020, is thus the centenary of the birth of the League of Nations, established in Geneva, first at the Hôtel National, which has since become the Palais Wilson in honour of Woodrow Wilson (the League of Nations having been established at the instigation of President Wilson, in the context of the Treaty of Versailles signed in 1919), then, from 1936, in the current Palais des Nations in Geneva. On 24 October 1945, the League of Nations became the United Nations, headquartered in New York – the phrase 'united nations' being attributed to Franklin D. Roosevelt.

5     In addition to members of the Internation Collective, participants in-
      cluded Richard Sennett (Columbia University, MIT, London School
      of Economics), Jean-Marie Le Clézio (Nobel prize winner for litera-
      ture), Samuel Jubé (IEA de Nantes, Grenoble école de management),
      Valérie Charolles (Institut Mines Télécom), Alexandre Rambaud
      (Agroparistech, Université Paris-Dauphine), Dominique Bourg
      (UNIL), and Damien Carême (MEP). The recordings of the inter-
      ventions are available here: <https://enmi-conf.org/wp/enmi19>.

6     Alain Supiot (ed.), *Le travail au XXIè siècle* (Ivry-sur-Seine:
      Atelier, 2019).

7     Alfred J. Lotka, 'The Law of Evolution as a Maximal Principle',
      *Human Biology* 17:3 (1945), pp. 167–94.

8     Supiot, *Le travail au XXIè siècle*, p. 19.

9     On these points, see Jean-Pierre Vernant, *Myth and Thought among
      the Greeks*, trans. Janet Lloyd with Jeff Fort (New York: Zone
      Books, 2006).

10    See Bernard Stiegler, 'L'*ergon* dans l'ère Anthropocène et la nouvelle
      question de la richesse', in Supiot, *Le travail au XXIè siècle*, p. 73.

11    See Lotka, 'The Law of Evolution as a Maximal Principle', p. 192.

12    See in particular the work of Kim Sterelny and Michael Tomasello.

13    See Richard Sennett, *Together: The Rituals, Pleasures and Politics of
      Cooperation* (New Haven and London: Yale University Press, 2012).

14    It has often been said that Georgescu-Roegen advocates a bio-eco-
      nomics, in the sense that economics would thus be modelled on biol-
      ogy. Such a view is highly paradoxical, if it is true that (1) it relies
      on Lotka's work, and (2) what Lotka showed is precisely the insuf-
      ficiency of biology. It is for this reason that we posit the necessity of
      constituting a neganthropology, that is, an economics that integrates
      the new problems, for both physics and biology, posed by exosomat-
      ic evolution.

15    And here we should refer to the definitions of knowledge and its
      function in human life found in Whitehead's *The Function of Reason*
      and Canguilhem's *Knowledge of Life*.

16    On the controversies concerning the dating of the Anthropocene,
      see Bernard Stiegler, *Qu'appelle-t-on panser? 2: La leçon de Greta
      Thunberg* (Paris: Les Liens qui Libèrent, 2020), §§31–32 and 63ff.

17    For a detailed exposition of this process, see Bernard Stiegler,
      *Automatic Society, Volume 1: The Future of Work*, trans. Daniel Ross
      (Cambridge: Polity Press, 2016).

18   Conseil National du Numérique, *Jules Ferry 3.0. Bâtir une école créative et juste dans un monde numérique* (October 2014), available at: <https://cnnumerique.fr/files/2017-10/Rapport_CNNum_Education_oct14.pdf>.

19   IPCC, *Climate Change 2014: Synthesis Report*, available at: <https://www.ipcc.ch/site/assets/uploads/2018/02/SYR_AR5_FINAL_full_fr.pdf>.

20   Richard Sennett, *The Craftsman* (New Haven and London: Yale University Press, 2008); Matthew B. Crawford, *Shop Class as Soulcraft: An Inquiry into the Value of Work* (New York: Penguin, 2009); Donald A. Winnicott, *Playing and Reality* (London: Routledge, 1971).

21   This is also the issue at stake in Mark Hunyadi, *La tyrannie des modes de vie: sur le paradoxe moral de notre temps* (Lormont: Le Borde de l'Eau, 2015). Unfortunately, more recent works by this philosopher show that he has not understood the distinction made by Freud from 1920 onwards between drive and libido, nor therefore what in 1923 Freud called libidinal economy. This leads Hunyadi to posit that consumerist capitalism would be a libidinal economy, even though it is the complete opposite: consumerism is a *destruction* of the libidinal economy, or the libido, as the *power of binding* and social obligation (in Bergson's sense) is replaced by the submission of the drives to the dopaminergic system (see the works of Gerald Moore and below). *Everyday knowledge* – which constitutes this libidinal economy and which forms at the scale of the *domestic nano-economy* that is in this way always *both domestic and political* – is thus systemically short-circuited and discredited by the 'lifestyles' prescribed by ever more viral and mimetic user manuals and marketing campaigns. This is why Silicon Valley prefers to define desire with Girard rather than with Freud.

22   Max Weber, *The Protestant Ethic and the Spirit of Capitalism*, trans. Talcott Parsons (London and New York: Routledge, 1992).

23   Erwin Schrödinger, *What is Life?*, in *What is Life?, with Mind and Matter and Autobiographical Sketches* (Cambridge: Cambridge University Press, 1992).

24   In this regard, Henri Bergson wrote in 1932, that 'the possession of a car, [which] is for so many men the supreme ambition [...], may after some time no longer be so desired'. Henri Bergson, *The Two Sources of Morality and Religion*, trans. R. Ashley Audra and Cloudesley Brereton, with W. Horsfall Carter (Westport: Greenwood Press, 1974), p. 292, translation modified.

25 Vladimir I. Vernadsky, *The Biosphere*, trans. D. B. Langmuir (New York: Copernicus, 1998); Arnold J. Toynbee, *Mankind and Mother Earth* (Oxford: Oxford University Press, 1976).

26 See Albert Einstein, *Ideas and Opinions*, trans. Sonja Bargmann (New York and Avenel: Wing Books, 1954), pp. 83–85.

27 For example, Alexandre Rambaud.

28 For example, Samuel Jubé.

29 For example, Valérie Charolles.

30 Alberto Magnaghi, *The Urban Village: A Charter for Democracy and Local Self-Sustainable Development*, trans. David Kerr (London and New York: Zed Books, 2005).

31 On Rob Hopkins and the experience of Transition Town Totnes, see: <https://www.dailymotion.com/video/xxoc9a>.

32 Eduardo Viveiros de Castro, *Cannibal Metaphysics*, trans. Peter Skafish (Minneapolis: Univocal, 2014).

33 Naomi Klein, *No Is Not Enough: Resisting Trump's Shock Politics and Winning the World We Need* (Chicago: Haymarket, 2017).

34 In this context, David Djaïz, *Slow démocratie* (Paris: Allary, 2019), is a major contribution.

35 Saskia Sassen, *A Sociology of Globalization* (New York and London: Columbia University Press, 2007), pp. 127–28.

36 Pierre Veltz, *Des territoires pour apprendre et innover* (Paris: Aube, 1994).

37 Sassen, *A Sociology of Globalization*, p. 213.

38 Ibid., p. 216.

39 Armand Hatchuel, Olivier Favereau and Franck Aggeri (eds), *L'activité marchande sans le marché?* (Paris: Presses des Mines, 2013).

40 Alain Supiot, *La gouvernance par les nombres* (Paris: Fayard, 2015).

41 In his address to the World Economic Forum in Davos on 24 January 2019, António Guterres stressed above all the increasingly integrated nature of global challenges, while responses are becoming more and more fragmented. His conclusion: 'it's a recipe for disaster'. Available at: <https://www.weforum.org/agenda/2019/01/these-are-the-global-priorities-and-risks-for-the-future-according-to-antonio-guterres/>.

42   Both in the work carried out on the Contributory Learning Territory located in Seine-Saint-Denis and in the work proposed by the Internation Collective.

43   See Bernard Stiegler, *Pharmacologie du Front national* (Paris: Flammarion, 2013).

44   Paul Valéry, 'Freedom of the Mind', in Jackson Mathews (ed.), *The Collected Works of Paul Valéry, Volume 10: History and Politics*, trans. Denise Folliot and Jackson Mathews (New York: Bollingen, 1962), p. 190.

45   Sigmund Freud, *The Ego and the Id*, in Volume 19 of James Strachey (ed. and trans.), *The Standard Edition of the Complete Psychological Works of Sigmund Freud* (London: Hogarth Press, 1953–74).

46   What is here called mystery, which echoes the 'mysteries of Eleusis', is what, under various names – including the mystical bifurcation that in Bergson is connected to mechanics, and as the 'mystical foundation of authority' – remains *incalculable* and in this way improbable and unprogrammable, or what Rainer Maria Rilke and Gilles Deleuze call (in different ways) the open.

47   Maurice Godelier, *The Metamorphoses of Kinship*, trans. Nora Scott (London and New York: Verso, 2011), pp. 45–50.

48   Here, a dialogue should be initiated with Augustin Berque's 'mesology'.

49   See the introduction of Emile Durkheim, *The Elementary Forms of the Religious Life*, trans. Joseph Ward Swain (New York: Free Press, 1965).

50   And here we should return to Watsuji Tetsuro's *Fūdo* (translated as *A Climate*) and to the interpretation of it proposed by Berque.

51   Arnold J. Toynbee, *A Study of History: Abridgement of Volumes I–VI* (New York and London: Oxford University Press, 1946), p. 200.

52   Bergson, *The Two Sources of Morality and Religion*, p. 306.

# 1 Anthropocene, Exosomatization and Negentropy

*Maël Montévil, Bernard Stiegler, Giuseppe Longo,*
*Ana Soto, Carlos Sonnenschein*

## 15 Industrial economy, scientific knowledge, technology and the Anthropocene era

The industrial economy took shape in the period from the late eighteenth century to the nineteenth century – first in Western Europe, then in North America. In addition to technical production, it led to technological production: mobilizing science to produce industrial goods. As Marx showed in 1857, *capitalism turns knowledge and its economic valuation into its primary element.*

Newtonian physics and the metaphysics that accompanies it lie at the origin of the epistemic (in Michel Foucault's sense) and epistemological (in Gaston Bachelard's sense) framework of this great transformation – which is the condition of what Karl Polanyi himself called the 'great transformation'.[1] In this transformation, *otium* (productive leisure time) submits to *negotium* (worldly affairs). Meanwhile, mathematics is applied through ever more powerful and performative calculating machines – referred to after the Second World War as computers.

After precursors such as Nicholas Georgescu-Roegen, himself inspired by Alfred Lotka, we will argue in this book that political economy, in what is now called the Anthropocene era (thematized in 2000 by Paul Crutzen, and whose characteristics were described by Vladimir Vernadsky as early as 1926), is a challenge that requires a fundamental re-examination of these epistemic and epistemological frameworks.[2]

With the work of Charles Darwin, living things came to be seen as part of a constantly evolving historical process.[3] In humans, knowledge is part of this process, which is *performative* in the dual sense of this word: both in the sense of efficiency and in the sense of prescription.[4] This process becomes exosomatic, that is, extra-corporeal, as Lotka shows,[5] shaping and reshaping ways of life, particularly in order to limit the negative effects of technical innovations.

## 16  Relations between knowledge and technics: historical overview from an industrial perspective

In the context of the industrial revolution, science, economics and especially trade were seen as the new basis of legitimacy, security, justice and peace. Hume, for example, argued that the gold standard spontaneously adjusts the balance of payments between states. The underlying scientific paradigm was Newtonian – in which deterministic mathematical laws are seen as the ultimate form of knowledge.

From the Newtonian perspective, equilibrium and optimization arise spontaneously from the relationships between parts of a system. Scientific work is therefore dedicated to describing spontaneous and optimal equilibriums. From such a perspective, the scientific formalization of economics and production favours the withdrawal of all rational supervision once the desired dynamic is in place, and it can be posited in principle that any outside intervention in the spontaneous functioning of the system would disrupt the properties of these equilibriums. In this sense, scientific and technological developments make progress through the optimization of processes and the providence of spontaneous equilibriums.

Such analyses, however, neglect *by construction* the *context* of a situation, even when this context is the *condition of possibility* of this situation: this formalization ignores localities. Moreover, following the same logic, both in science and industry, and on the basis of the axioms of modern philosophy, singular situations (co-implicating a primordial diversity of singular factors) are reduced to a combination of simple elements that can be known and controlled. For example, the production undertaken by a single craftsman or craftswoman can be decomposed into simple tasks carried out by several skilled workers, then eventually by machines: this is what Adam Smith described in *The Wealth of Nations*,[6] an enterprise that will be continued in the nineteenth century by Andrew Ure, Charles Babbage and Frederick Taylor, and applied systemically in the twentieth and twenty-first centuries.[7]

Such a method leads to the progressive loss of the knowledge possessed by workers as it is transferred to the technological system. This tendency was described for the first time by Adam Smith, and seventy-two years later by Karl Marx, who called it proletarianization. This loss of knowledge is the essential element of a more general process that we here refer to as denoetization,[8] that is, the loss of the ability to think (*noesis*). Technique becomes technology, and like the former it is a *pharmakon*: as with a drug, it can lead to results that may either be toxic or curative.

## 17    The life sciences and entropy theory –
## from the nineteenth to the twentieth century

Contemporaneously with these events, new scientific ideas emerge with the truly revolutionary perspectives on life opened up by Jean-Baptiste Lamarck and then by Darwin: *On the Origin of Species* establishes a new and irreversible evolutionary understanding of what will become biology (the science baptized with this name was projected as early as Lamarck, who coined the term). This framework will be interpreted by some as another instantiation of the Newtonian scientific model; others will emphasize the originality of a scientific theory based on *historical* reasoning in the natural sciences, in contrast with physical theories that study universal and permanent laws.

From the evolutionary perspective, from which biology strictly speaking will emerge, the living world is no longer a static manifestation of the divine order: current life forms come from a long process of historical becoming. This change of perspective leads to questions about the development of humanity and the role played in this process by human intelligence and the freedom in which it consists, for better and for worse: hence the development of eugenics and social Darwinism – contrary to Darwin's vision, which embraced the idea of a singularity of human societies – while, as we will see, Lotka posited that the human (that is, technical) form of life establishes an orthogenic and not simply biological form of evolution and selection.

The nineteenth century also saw the emergence of another scientific framework, this time in the field of physics: the industrial revolution brought the development of heat engines, which raised theoretical questions that would lead to the birth of thermodynamics. In this way, physicists were led to the concept of entropy, and to the realization that it is bound to increase in isolated systems – such is the second law of thermodynamics. In physics, energy is in principle conserved, but the fact that entropy increases means that this energy becomes less usable for performing macroscopic tasks.

In a nutshell, the increase of entropy in a physical system is the process that consists in passing from less probable macroscopic states to more probable macroscopic states. It follows that the increase of entropy is the disappearance of improbable initial states, and their replacement by more probable characteristics, which has the effect of erasing the past. For example, a drop of ink would tend to disperse in water until it reaches a uniform situation, which will erase the initial position of the drop. This framework challenges the reversibility of classical mechanics – the latter having no objective arrow of time – and leads in cosmological terms to the heat death of the universe.

The concept of entropy is tied to Poincaré's discovery of chaotic dynamics and to the refutation of Laplace's idea that mathematical determinism implies predictability. It therefore refutes the general notion of the mathematical predictability and controllability of natural phenomena. In particular, Poincare's work was focused on the solar system, showing that its long-term stability cannot be established. These scientific developments lead to the idea of a precarious cosmos.

Determinism in Laplace's sense, however, found a second wind in the twentieth century with mathematical logic and later computer science. These developments took place as industrial production was being transformed into a capitalism of consumption, organized around standardized mass production. The media, itself becoming 'mass', was increasingly designed so as to trigger standardized consumer responses.[9] The tendency of denoetization that began with the proletarianization of producers is thus extended to consumers as such – for example, the processed foods produced by the agro-food industry lead to an increasing loss of the knowledge of how to cook, contributing to the pandemics of non-communicable diseases such as obesity and diabetes.

## 18   The twentieth century and information theory

In this context, the vague notion of information becomes central. In 1948, Claude Shannon proposed a formalized and calculable concept of information in order to understand and optimize the transmission of written or audio messages in noisy communication channels[10] – according to principles that would lead to what is known as signal compression, which today allows, for example, high-definition video to be transmitted over telecommunications networks. A very different concept was proposed by Andrei Kolmogorov during the 1960s to describe the difficulty of generating a given sequence of characters for computer programs.

Shannon's theory posits that information is what reduces ambiguity, hence it is what is improbable once a probabilistic model has been set up. This idea becomes absurd when it is used to study the meaning of a message *beyond* the question of difficulties of (noisy) transmission, which was Shannon's original motivation. For example, sequences such as 'qqqq...' carry maximum information in Shannon's sense because 'q' is the least probable letter, whereas a random sequence, for example, 'ldznck...', has maximum information in Kolmogorov's sense – it cannot be effectively compressed. These two limit cases carry more information in their respective senses than a fragment of Corneille of the same length.

Despite this confrontation of two perspectives making obvious the self-contradictory character and thus the theoretical fragility of this notion,[11] the dominant opinion in current cognitive science – itself dominating common as well as scientific representations in digital capitalism – is that intelligence is information processing, that is, a probabilistic or digital calculation, depending on the point of view being privileged, the two frameworks often being mixed together. Similarly, information plays a key role in molecular biology, despite the absence of a theoretical account of the notion. Finally, by ignoring early critiques by authors such as Poincaré,[12] economics has, via Herbert Simon and Friedrich Hayek, been conceptualized as a process of spontaneous mathematical optimization by 'rational' agents equipped with an ability to process information – possibly biased for biological reasons – in cognitive economic approaches.

At the beginning of the twenty-first century, the use of computers expanded into various forms (such as personal computers, smartphones and tablets). Their connection to networks deepened and transformed the role of the media. Private interests began to compete to attract and hold the attention of users through calculation (anticipated to a lesser extent by twentieth-century analogue mass media, but at that time what is analysed and controlled is not yet individual behaviour).

With digital network technologies, the services provided to users depend on the data they produce, service providers using this data to capture and hold the attention of other users – the whole system being based on the exploitation of network effects. These transformations are leading to a new wave of automation: algorithms such as those utilized in social networks formalize and automate activities that were hitherto structurally alien to the formal economy.

These changes lead to new losses of knowledge and to a form of denoetization caused by a *destructive* form of capturing attention, seriously undermining the capacity for attention. Since the dominant view in the cognitive sciences is that intelligence is information processing, many scientists consider algorithms to be artificial intelligence, thus ignoring the conditions of possibility of human intelligence, such as attention-formation. At the same time, management and commercial platforms break people down into tables of skills, interests and behaviours, and these are fed into algorithms, allowing targeted political and commercial marketing, and shaping training and recruitment policies.

## 19    Digital denoetization as the 'end of theory'
in the Anthropocene era

The same tendency exists in science:

- knowledge tends to be balkanized into ever more specialized research fields;

- scientific research thus tends to be reduced to the deployment of new technological systems for capturing and processing information;

- operational definitions replace theoretical definitions.

Theorization, however, is the condition of science: it constitutes a
synthetic activity that requires reassessment, based on experience of
concepts used, history of a field, empirical observation and the perspectives of other fields – whether by analogy or by the development
of theoretical articulations – in coherence with and in opposition to
earlier theoretical models.[13]

With the emergency of data mining, Chris Anderson believed he
could declare 'the end of theory'.[14] This perspective was criticized as
soon as it was uttered, and eventually in the same magazine, notably
by Kevin Kelly.[15] Nevertheless, the twilight of scientific theorizing
seems to come mainly from another direction. Following the general
tendency of society, the loss of the ability to theorize is first of all the
result of the transformation of human activities. These include institutional restructuring and the increasing weight of scientific marketing,
both in scientific publications and in terms of the criteria utilized for
financial decisions.

The decline in theorizing and the scientific denoetization to which
it leads also stem from an inadequate critical assessment of digital
technologies and the consequences they bear for scientific activities –
whether in terms of bibliometrics and scientometrics[16] or of statistical
software used by experimental researchers.[17] As a result:

- the academic and scientific appropriation of these technologies is lacking (such an appropriation presupposes theoretical modelling exposed to peer review, and thus to contest
  and debate);

- their toxic consequences (in Socrates's sense when he points
  out the toxicity of writing as practised in his time by the
  sophists) are not mastered;

- these technologies are not implemented in accordance with scientific ends (except for certain purely mathematical questions that have been dealt with in detail).

Today, at the beginning of the twenty-first century, we are also witnessing a growing awareness of the consequences of human activity for the rest of the planet, leading to the definition of a new era: the Anthropocene. The Anthropocene is characterized by the tendency of human activity to destroy the conditions of possibility of human existence – both at the level of biological organizations (organisms, ecosystems) and at the level of the capacity to think (noesis). In this context, the ability to generate knowledge in order to mitigate the toxicity of technological innovations, and transform them, is profoundly weakened, to the extent that the problem of this toxicity is mostly repressed as such by governments and societies – at the risk of being recognized too late.

## 20   Thermodynamic entropy and biological negentropy

From the standpoint of physics, energy and mineral resources such as metals are quantities that are conserved. And yet we clearly see that these resources are becoming scarce. How is this possible? It is the crucial concept of entropy that allows us to understand this apparent paradox.

Entropy is a *property of configurations*, and, more precisely, of the evolution of these configurations, which distinguishes it from the question of quantities of matter or energy. It is directly tied to our ability or inability to make use of these resources. Mineral deposits, for example, are *exploitable* because they can be found at sufficiently high concentrations, which is highly improbable (improbable with respect to the statistically dominant state of the distribution of this material on the planet). In other words, we can exploit these deposits because the entropy of the distribution of these metals on Earth is not maximally spread.

Such configurations are generated by geological and atmospheric mechanisms that are far from equilibrium processes, such as volcanoes, and through a combination of circumstances occurring on geological time scales[18] – and human activities further concentrate these metals through mechanical and chemical work. All these processes lowering the entropy of the distribution of metals come at the cost of a higher dispersion of energy in the form of heat, whether it is the energy of the sun in the atmosphere or the energy (whether from fossil fuels or otherwise) used to refine metals. What we generally call 'consuming energy' actually means dispersing energy as heat, that is, producing entropy.

Nevertheless, a simple accounting of entropy is not enough: the measurement of entropy, which is a concentration/dispersion ratio with regard to configurations, is meaningful only within the processual character of the universe and, on Earth, of the biosphere. We can imagine possibilities such as destroying life in order to minimize the production of entropy on Earth – which is obviously absurd. For a precise grasp of contemporary issues, it is on the contrary necessary to specify the articulation of entropy and life, first with regard to the diverse forms of living things, and second with regard to the specific case of human societies.

From a thermodynamic standpoint, biological situations (or configurations) are not at a maximum level of entropy, but nor do they tend towards a maximum level of entropy. The low and sometimes even decreasing entropy of biological objects seems to contradict the second law of thermodynamics, which stipulates that entropy does not diminish in an isolated system. Biological situations, however, including the biosphere as a whole, are not isolated systems: they are open, and they functionalize interrelated flows of energy, matter and entropy.

At the level of the biosphere, the Sun is the main provider of the free energy (low entropy) used by photosynthetic organisms. Consequently, biological situations do not contradict the second law. But this is possible only insofar as biological organizations – and by extension social organizations – are necessarily local, locally deferring the increase of entropy through a local and organic (organized) differentiation of space, and dependent on coupling with their environment. In organisms, the relationship between the interior and the exterior is materialized and organized by semi-permeable membranes.

How can we further understand biological situations and the way they relate to thermodynamics? Here, a brief discussion of the epistemology of the application of mathematics is necessary in order to understand natural or social phenomena. Prediction requires theoretically distinguishing the situation that will be realized from other possible situations. The maximization of entropy is therefore one macroscopic state among other possible states: the state that maximizes entropy. Functions fulfilling this role in physics are called potentials. There exists a diversity of potentials in the field of equilibrium thermodynamics, which are different variants of free energy, involving entropy, and whose relevance depends on the coupling between the system being studied and its exterior.

For example, the function that makes it possible to predict the final situation of an isolated system is not the same as the function that describes a system that exchanges heat with its environment, such as a cup of tea exchanging energy with the room in which it is located. But in the case of systems that are far from thermodynamic equilibrium – situations that require flows with the outside in order to last, such as organisms, or a heated apartment – there is no consensus on the theoretical existence of such a function or family of functions.

Prigogine's fundamental idea is that the rate of production of entropy (that is, the rate of energy dissipation) could play the theoretical role of a potential – it would be spontaneously optimized. This idea is valid, however, only in (very) particular systems.[19] The absence of a function playing the role of potential for general far-from-equilibrium systems means that our ability to understand and predict such systems by calculation, as in the usual kinds of physical theories, is not theoretically justified. The epistemological status of mathematization can thus no longer be the same[20] across these two different cases.

This is why the method of economic analysis that we defend here organically articulates mathematics (notably indicators) with deliberation in a locality, instead of using a mathematical framework taken as universal and permanent (see Chapter 3). From a less technical standpoint, Schrödinger introduces the idea that the problem in biology is not to understand order by starting from disorder, as in many physical situations such as the formation of ice with its crystalline structure, but rather to understand order starting from order.[21] To grasp this idea, he proposed studying negative entropy, an idea that was later developed further by Brillouin, who called this negative entropy 'negentropy'.

Negative entropy, however, as a decrease in the dissipation of energy, does not purely and simply coincide with the existence of biological organizations. Entropy can be lowered simply by reducing the temperature, while biological organisms remain organisms only between certain minimum and maximum temperatures. A major glaciation would lower the entropy of the Earth (by inversely releasing it in the form of heat in the rest of the universe), but it would also destroy life.

Furthermore, the functional parts of biological organizations often involve a local *increase* of entropy in order to be functional. For example, the diffusion of a compound from the place it is produced to the rest of the cell is a process of producing physical entropy. Nevertheless, this process allows the compound to reach the places where it can play its functional role. It follows that the theoretical articulation between entropy and biological organization requires a careful analysis that goes beyond the framework of a simple opposition between entropy (considered as disorder) and negentropy (considered as order).

## 21  Biodiversity, anthropic situations in the Anthropocene and anti-entropic novelty

Biological organizations keep themselves far from maximum entropy configurations by functionalizing the flows coming from their external milieu so as to maintain themselves. They actively maintain themselves through the interaction between their parts, and between these organizations and their milieus. This necessary coupling between organism and environment takes place in ecosystems that are themselves anchored within larger levels – up to the level of the biosphere, which is their upper limit.

The viability of living things derives from the systemic properties of these different levels, but these are not spontaneous situations, such as fires, volcanoes or hurricanes, and we cannot simply relate the organization that is life and organic matter to the order we find in countless configurations in the universe, and particularly on Earth. The way in which biological organizations maintain themselves stems from the *history* that gave rise to them, including the different contexts in which the members of a lineage have lived.

The way in which biological organization is maintained is therefore fundamentally historical: it unfolds from the natural *history* of the species, the ecosystem or the individual. In the context of the Anthropocene era, this historicity implies a particular vulnerability to rapid anthropic changes that simultaneously disrupt biological organizations as a whole at various levels in the biosphere. Examples are the effect of climate change on ecosystems or the effect of endocrine disruptors on organisms.[22] Moreover, living things continue to change over time by generating new structures and functions. Biologists focus less on individual species than on the conservation of biodiversity, and especially on the conservation of the burgeoning process of evolution that we can call biodiversification. This process is itself subject to anthropic disruptions, preventing life from reorganizing itself.

In a word, biological organizations are precarious because the existence and nature of their parts are fundamentally contingent. It is for this reason that these parts must be actively and constantly maintained. It is not sustainable for an organism to stop feeding, drinking or breathing without irreversibly sinking into entropy: without dying.

Organizations maintain themselves according to behaviours and operations that emanate from their articulation with their past contexts, but which can be reorganized over time – reorganizations that are forms of learning. These two processes – maintenance and reorganization – are disrupted in various ways by the changes introduced by human activities, in particular since the dawn of the Anthropocene (that is, the industrial era). The presentation of knowledge set out in this chapter, which represents the current state of knowledge in biology, also makes clear how, in our view, these questions have still not been sufficiently theorized, particularly with regard to the relationships between entropy, negentropy, the anthropy typical of the Anthropocene and what we will at the end of this chapter refer to as neganthropy.

To go further in the analysis of the living dynamics not just of maintenance but of reorganization, there is a concept complementary to that of entropy (and to that of negative entropy, which is mathematically and *relatively* opposed to it – as a relationship between more or less ordered states over the course of a process): the concept of anti-entropy, which refers to biological organizations (organs, functions, etc.).[23] For this concept, and unlike (digital) information, which is a one-dimensional notion (the alphanumeric strings of Shannon and Kolmogorov), the geometry, space and time of life are essential. A living organism produces entropy by transforming energy, it maintains its anti-entropy by constantly creating and renewing its organization, and it produces anti-entropy by generating *organizational novelty*.

The concept of anti-entropy aims to account for biological organizations in their historicity. Current life-forms maintain themselves both through the activation of functional innovations that appeared in the past (anti-entropy) and through the production of functional innovations (production of anti-entropy) arising from the individual or the group (population, ecosystem and so on). Not only are such innovations unpredictable, but their very nature cannot be predicted. As a result, probability theory is insufficient for describing life and its evolution. (This also means, as we will see, that there is also a factual anti-anthropy of the new in the sense understood by both Arthur Rimbaud and Henri Bergson[24] – this 'new' being improbable in the sense of Maurice Blanchot.[25])

This anti-entropic novelty is specific in that it contributes to the ability of biological objects to persist over time by contributing to their organization in a given context (which this organization may affect). Entropy depends on the coupling of a system with its exterior. Likewise, anti-entropy is relative to an organization, and not all objects are organized. For example, considered on its own, the heart has no function: it is only at the level of the organism that it has a function. Consequently, all discussions of anti-entropy relate to a given organized object, that is, a specific locality – open both to an external environment on which it feeds and to its possibilities of reorganization.[26]

## 22   Noodiversity and anti-anthropy

As Lotka pointed out, from the perspective of their organization, and thus of their organs, the specific character of human societies lies in the importance of inorganic objects in their social structures (their organizations), such as tools, written texts and computers. These objects are fashioned and maintained by human activity. Lotka referred to the constitution of such objects – theoretically analogous to endosomatic organs but external to organic bodies – as *exosomatization*. This process thoroughly conditions the evolution of the ways that human beings live.

Exosomatic productions are the fruits of economic activity, and their evolution, which in the beginning is undetectable, does not become obvious until the sudden acceleration of technical evolution brought by the industrial revolution gives rise to so-called historical consciousness and constitutes the Anthropocene era. Lotka highlights that, as exosomatic productions, the new objects that arise in the course of the evolution of societies, and which constitute their artificial organs, are not spontaneously beneficial for either social organizations or psychic organizations. Rather, they are *pharmaka*, as the Greeks said, that is, poisons that can become remedies, and vice versa. Lotka develops this point of view in 1945 while considering the awful suffering inflicted on human beings during the Second World War.

Inorganic organs are, then, exosomatic productions resulting from work. In order for them to fulfil a functional role, and in order to limit the destabilization that they necessarily introduce,[27] developmental and physiological evolution and plasticity must play a major role in the course of the process of exosomatization. For example, reading enlists the plasticity of several areas of the brain that rely on the writing system.[28]

These purely biological and physiological responses, however, are not enough to turn a potential poison into an actual remedy: noetic activities, which are always collective, and therefore always social, and linked to social *organizations*, are necessary for the achievement of the process of exosomatization. Socratic philosophy, for example, which can be interpreted as a reaction to writing and to the way it is used by the sophists (with potentially catastrophic consequences for the city, the *polis*), will lead to the founding of Plato's academy – and will for a long time constitute the basis of power across various transformations of knowledge effected on this basis.

In the contemporary context, exosomatization has become thoroughly technological (and not just technical). It is today driven by marketing, but for a technology to have found its market does not imply that it should be considered beneficial. It is just as necessary to find the positive modalities of which this technology is in fact the bearer, and the practices and social prescriptions that will limit its toxicity, which we will call its anthropy, and intensify its curativity, which we will call its neganthropy.

This is particularly necessary in the current context characterized by climate change, loss of biodiversity and the generalization of denoetization: the Anthropocene era and the anthropic excesses described by the IPCC, which could totally destroy humanity and life in the biosphere, are highlighted by the fact that when the exosomatization process is driven by a market that has become hegemonic, it proves to be not just toxic but literally *deadly*.

For a new exosomatic production to become beneficial, and limit its toxicity (in this sense 'economizing' it), additional work is always necessary, in any epoch of anthropological evolution. Only by understanding work in this way can we identify the exosomatic innovations (whether technical or technological) actually required by and compatible with a desirable future for a locality – even if this locality is the biosphere itself. This is the work of *noesis*, that is, of thinking, in *all* its forms, and as practical as well as theoretical, familial, artisanal, sporting and artistic knowledge, and thus theoretical, juridical and spiritual knowledge in the broadest sense. This belongs to what we therefore call *noodiversity* and *noodiversification*.

From such a perspective, to raise a child is to think, and this thinking is also caring (and in this way it constitutes what we call a noetic treatment or dressing, *pansement*), which will turn the singularity of this child into a potential for noodiversity.[29] Today, technological evolution prevents more and more parents from thinking, and therefore from taking care of their children by educating them (by providing them with those noetic forms of care, those dressings, *pansements*, that we call cultures). From the perspective of exosomatization inasmuch as it requires such forms of thought and care, knowledge in all its forms, both practical and theoretical, plays a crucial role: it makes it possible to prescribe functional variants and social practices for the innovations introduced by exosomatization. Knowledge is thus articulated with *ethōs* (as the site of exosomatization), and, in this way, with ethics (as will be discussed in Chapter 6).

Computers, which are today heavily involved in this curative and toxic process, can be defined as automatic rewriting systems. With the increase in computing speeds and the growth of databases, the ability of computers to process information and perform categorizations also increases dramatically. Nevertheless, the tasks they are capable of performing are not equivalent to the novel innovations produced by human work. This work produces meaning that is neither contained in the initial data nor in the combination of data resulting from algorithmic methods. This is why, as we will see in Chapter 3:

- it is essential to distinguish between work and employment;

- work outside employment must be economically valued within what we describe as an economy of contribution – consisting in producing neganthropy, and sometimes anti-anthropy, that is, in limiting or even reversing (anti-anthropically) the anthropic dimensions of any activity undertaken by *Anthropos.*

## 23   Principles, rights and facts

Stemming from Galileo's theoretical work, the principle of inertia describes a situation that on Earth is highly exotic: it posits that if no force is exerted on an object (for example, no friction or gravitation), then any object will maintain its speed. This principle obviously cannot be derived from data, but was posited by Galileo as an asymptotic (limit) principle making it possible to understand all other movements and to analyse what can affect them, such as friction and gravitation. It is also the first principle of Newtonian physics.

Similarly, equal rights among citizens or the equality of the sexes are political principles that break with previous – or existing and factual – situations, and reshape social organizations according to a new right, a new rule or state of law [*état de droit*] that cannot be inferred from previous situations. These examples are historically important in their respective fields, but this type of process is, in a sense, an ordinary part of human activity.

Such processes, in which *droit* ('law', in both the scientific sense and the juridical sense, and 'right' in the political sense) is distinguished from facts, define work by opposing it to proletarianized employment (that is, labour, where work ≠ labour in English, *Werk* ≠ *Arbeit* in German, and *ergon* ≠ *ponos* in ancient Greek): the first is also the perpetual possibility of the invention of a new configuration of meaning. Unfortunately, the current tendency is not towards the development of work in this sense, but rather towards a convergence between algorithms and human activities that accentuates this proletarianization, that is, the loss of the ability to work in the sense of working to turn anthropy into neganthropy.

Currently, the convergence between algorithms and human activities as this is systematically and systemically exploited by platforms that are from every perspective massively anthropic means that work is sterilized through being standardized – through being transformed into generic information processing. Such a state of fact is eminently capable of being changed – and this task should be placed at the centre of a new conception of design (see Chapter 7).

The scientific consensus is that the current path of civilization leads to its destruction. It does so, notably, by reducing and eliminating anti-entropy and anti-anthropy (as the extension of anti-entropy to social organizations), with information technology itself reduced to calculation thanks to a one-dimensional flattening that generates what Ludwig von Bertalanffy describes as closed systems – that is, systems that destroy their own dynamics. It thus seems clear that the 'creative destruction' conceptualized by Joseph Schumpeter has become destructive destruction – as was shown in 1971 by Schumpeter's former assistant, Georgescu-Roegen.[30]

Work, unlike mere labour, invents new tools and prescribes new practices, which generate new usages, that is, ways of life in the sense of habits, customs and cultures (these usages are cultivated, they do not merely involve instructions or 'user manuals'), thus constructing *new configurations of meaning* for human and ecosystemic interactions. Hence work is something other than probabilistic alphanumeric combinatorics in a set of predetermined possibilities (computerized data processing). This is why a reinvention of work (and with it of the economy, both psychic and political) is necessary at all levels of society, if we are to confront the current crisis and strive to overcome it. For this reason, and as explained in the Introduction, we consider it necessary to extend and transpose the concepts of entropy, negentropy and anti-entropy into the concepts of anthropy, neganthropy and anti-anthropy, in order to specify the dual character (as *pharmakon*, both poison and remedy) of the exosomatic organ and its practices and usages in economics, understood through the relationship entropy/negentropy and so as to overcome the Anthropocene era (which is an Entropocene) in favour of what we call the Neganthropocene.[31]

## Notes

1 Karl Polanyi, *The Great Transformation: The Political and Economic Origins of Our Time* (London: Victor Gollancz, 1945).

2 Nicholas Georgescu-Roegen, 'The Entropy Law and the Economic Problem', in Herman E. Daly and Kenneth N. Townsend (eds), *Valuing the Earth: Economics, Ecology, Ethics* (Cambridge, Massachusetts and London: MIT Press, 1993); Vladimir I. Vernadsky, *The Biosphere*, trans. D. B. Langmuir (New York: Copernicus, 1998).

3 Charles Darwin, *On the Origin of Species* (Oxford: Oxford University Press, 2008).

4 Emphasized in J. L. Austin, *How to Do Things with Words*, 2nd edition (Oxford: Oxford University Press, 1975).

5 In particular, in Alfred J. Lotka, 'The Law of Evolution as a Maximal Principle', *Human Biology* 17:3 (1945), pp. 167–94.

6 The book begins with such a description via the famous example of a pin factory.

7 Andrew Ure, *The Philosophy of Manufactures: or, An Exposition of the Scientific, Moral, and Commercial Economy of the Factory System of Great Britain* (London: Charles Knight, 1835); Charles Babbage, *On the Economy of Machinery and Manufactures* (London: Charles Knight, 1832); Frederick Winslow Taylor, *The Principles of Scientific Management* (New York and London: Harper and Brothers, 1919). On Google's Taylorism, see Nicholas Carr, 'Is Google Making Us Stupid?', *The Atlantic* (July-August 2008), available at: <https://www.theatlantic.com/magazine/archive/2008/07/is-google-making-us-stupid/306868/>.

8 See also Bernard Stiegler, *Qu'appelle-t-on panser? 1. L'immense régression* (Paris: Les Liens qui Libèrent, 2018).

9 Edward Bernays, *Propaganda* (New York: Routledge, 1928).

10 Claude E. Shannon, 'A Mathematical Theory of Communication', *Bell System Technical Journal* 27 (1948), pp. 379–423.

11 See Giuseppe Longo et al., 'Is Information a Proper Observable for Biological Organization?', *Progress in Biophysics and Molecular Biology* 109 (2012), pp. 108–14.

12 See, for example, the letter from Henri Poincaré to Léon Walras, available at: <http://henri-poincare.ahp-numerique.fr/items/show/295>.

13  Hence some scientific journals are founded against this tendency. See, for example, Mariano Bizzarri et al., 'Why Organisms?', *Organisms: Journal of Biological Sciences* 1 (2017), pp. 1–2.

14  Chris Anderson, 'The End of Theory: The Data Deluge Makes the Scientific Method Obsolete', *Wired* (23 June 2008), available at: <http://archive.wired.com/science/discoveries/magazine/16-07/pb_theory>.

15  Kevin Kelly, 'The AI Cargo Cult: The Myth of a Superhuman AI', *Wired* (25 April 2017), available at: <https://www.wired.com/2017/04/the-myth-of-a-superhuman-ai/>.

16  Donald Geman and Stuart Geman, 'Opinion: Science in the Age of Selfies', *Proceedings of the National Academy of Sciences* 113 (2016), pp. 9384–9387, available at: <https://www.pnas.org/content/pnas/113/34/9384.full.pdf>.

17  Ronald L. Wasserstein and Nicole A. Lazar, 'The ASA Statement on $p$-Values: Context, Process, and Purpose', *American Statistician* 70 (2016), pp. 129–33, available at: <https://amstat.tandfonline.com/doi/full/10.1080/00031305.2016.1154108#.XoLa_C-r3jA>.

18  Heinrich D. Holland and Karl K. Turekian (eds), *Treatise on Geochemistry, Volume 13: Geochemistry of Mineral Deposits*, 2nd edition (Oxford: Elsevier, 2014).

19  Gregoire Nicolis and Ilya Prigogine, *Self-Organization in Non-Equilibrium Systems* (New York: Wiley, 1977).

20  See Giuseppe Longo and Maël Montévil, *Perspectives on Organisms: Biological Time, Symmetries and Singularities* (Dordrecht: Springer, 2014), and Stuart A. Kauffman, *A World Beyond Physics: The Emergence and Evolution of Life* (New York: Oxford University Press, 2019).

21  Erwin Schrödinger, *What is Life?*, in *What is Life?, with Mind and Matter and Autobiographical Sketches* (Cambridge: Cambridge University Press, 1992).

22  Maël Montévil, 'Entropies and the Anthropocene Crisis', *AI and Society*, forthcoming.

23  Francis Bailly and Giuseppe Longo, 'Biological Organization and Anti-Entropy', *Journal of Biological Systems* 17 (2009), pp. 63–96, and Longo and Montévil, *Perspectives on Organisms*.

24  This also means that anti-anthropy constitutes the open (in the sense of Rainer Maria Rilke as well as Gilles Deleuze) – the open that arises from a neganthropy struggling against anthropy. This open, in ancient Greek, is called *noesis*.

25   Maurice Blanchot, *The Infinite Conversation*, trans. Susan Hanson (Minneapolis and London: University of Minnesota Press, 1993), p. 41.

26   Montévil, 'Entropies and the Anthropocene Crisis'.

27   This is what has on various occasions been described as the doubly epokhal redoubling. See, for example, Bernard Stiegler, *The Age of Disruption: Technology and Madness in Computational Capitalism*, trans. Daniel Ross (Cambridge: Polity Press, 2019).

28   Maryanne Wolf, *Proust and the Squid: The Story and Science of the Reading Brain* (New York: Harper, 2007).

29   And this potential always in some way amounts to the transformation of what presents itself as fragility into an unexpected and improbable strength: this is how the dyslexic Leonardo da Vinci, the deaf Thomas Edison and the epileptic Fyodor Dostoyevsky became for humanity what the Greeks called heroes.

30   Georgescu-Roegen, 'The Entropy Law and the Economic Problem'.

31   See Bernard Stiegler, *The Neganthropocene*, trans. Daniel Ross (London: Open Humanities Press, 2018).

## 2 Localities, Territories and Urbanities in the Age of Platforms and Faced with the Challenges of the Anthropocene Era

*Giacomo Gilmozzi, Olivier Landau, Bernard Stiegler,*
*David M. Berry, Sara Baranzoni, Pierre Clergue, Anne Alombert*

### 24 A new age of urbanity, a new urban revolution

We saw in the previous chapter that locality becomes a central object of science in the struggle against that anthropy that has poisoned the Anthropocene era. Locality, however, has become predominantly urban, and it is well known that the modern process of urbanization, which began with the industrial revolution and intensified during the twentieth century as the formation of metropolises and 'global cities', is a key element in the real battle to limit the effects of climate change.

This is why, even if a number of experiments with 'territories in transition' (in the sense referred to with this label; see transition-network.org, founded by Rob Hopkins) are being developed in rural, semi-rural or small or medium-sized urban areas, the question of locality introduced previously arises first and foremost in urban territories. Moreover, it is now clear that the marketing of 'smart cities' has to a large extent consisted in promoting algorithmic governance of the city by means of collecting the data and traces of its inhabitants. Is this the model we should follow?

Contrary to such an approach, we posit that this 'storytelling' is above all a commercial discourse based on an immeasurable worsening of proletarianization to a uniquely dangerous point, and in all respects – and it must be investigated while keeping in mind the recent Amnesty International report[1] on the enormous threat to every form of freedom (political, economic, artistic, scientific, existential) posed by the current development of digital technologies, monopolized by a few actors who have become literally irresponsible. On the other hand, the enormous transformation presently underway, generated by new modes of distributed production – made possible by digitally-controlled machines, the 'Internet of Things', 'ubiquitous computing' and everything to which this gives rise in the various fields of the urban environment – leads to a true overhaul of urban development and to a call for an overhaul of democracy in general, and in particular in the milieu of the city. As we will see at the end of this chapter, this involves the opening of a formidable project with educational and academic institutions at all levels – and through an accelerated contributory research training operation for the personnel in charge of education.

Here, we advocate contributory approaches to urban research in order to grasp the profound dynamics of what we consider to be the possibility of a new *urban genius*, where the inhabitants would once again become the primary source of territorial intelligence, in the context of a contributory economy that deproletarianizes the inhabitants, but also their elected representatives and their administrations, today totally destitute, and very often manipulated by merchants of new services and other illusory promises. With this new urban genius, based on this new urban research, technology would be reconfigured and redesigned starting from contributory territorial practices themselves.

We lay out the same hypothesis with respect to what we could call digital urbanity as we do with the contributory economy in general: *the efficiency of automation* must allow the *release of energies and time*, so that they may be put at the service of *urban deliberation*, at all scales and in the spirt of cooperation that contributory technologies make possible. It is equally a matter of struggling against the incapacitation (by proletarianization) to which automation can give rise, both in production and in consumption.

## 25  Reconsidering the digital city according to two alternative scenarios

The new urbanity is based on a systemic increase and valuing of negentropy at the scale of individual and collective urban behaviour, as well as on shared urban knowledge, debated at the various scales of urban locality. Such a vision presupposes a profound reconsideration of the history of urbanity as it relates to techniques and technologies – in particular since the industrial revolution, which fundamentally changed urban dynamics – inasmuch as it has led to the development of functionalities that are unique to each stage of that history.

Digital and contributory technologies themselves represent a new functional horizon. These functionalities can be conceived according to two contrasting scenarios:

- in one, the automated city becomes literally *inurbane*, that is, it destroys urbanity in the original sense of the word, because it short-circuits urbanity itself through an *immature implementation of technology and automated functions, destroying urban relations* – that is, civil, and in that way 'civilized', relations.

- in the other, the city reinvents intelligence in the eighteenth-century sense of this word, when it referred first and foremost to sociability, such that it enables the whole to be greater than the sum of its parts.

Understood from a very general perspective, digital urban technologies amount to a change of the technical system, and one that generates a brutal disadjustment in relation to the already-established social systems (juridical, political, economic, educational, commercial, administrative and so on). As a result, these social systems are *destabilized*. In this respect, the current epoch is characterized – far beyond the urban question alone – by what is now called disruption, where technological advances outpace social advances (in a broad sense of the word 'social', encompassing social systems in the sense of both Gille and Luhmann).

Disruption is a fact, and it is hardly credible to pretend to avoid it. But the approach envisaged here is to create an 'alternative disruption', as a kind of 'disruption of disruption'. As it is currently used, in the service of business models coming mainly from North America, and sometimes Asia (Japan and South Korea in particular), the current basis of disruption is not sustainable, given that it produces insolvency, incivility and inurbanity.

The digital urbanity to come will be based on a state of affairs that is already partially established: that of the reorganization of production (in particular, material goods) and the deployment of digital urban technologies – forming what Thomas Berns and Antoinette Rouvroy have called 'algorithmic governmentality'. But this technological state of fact is yet to result in a *state of law capable of itself establishing a new, recognized and deliberate state of fact* – and in this way engendering a new urban dynamic. This recognition, this deliberation, this dynamic, which are indispensable and urgent, are possibly only if the following two conditions are met:

- to take the measure of long-term urban dynamics in their relationship to industrialization in particular, and, through that, to develop a historical consciousness of urbanity (among the inhabitants as well as economic stakeholders, administrators and elected officials);

- to identify the specific characteristics of productive technologies and disruptive urban technologies that bring to its extremities what is often referred to today as hyper-industrial society – by Pierre Veltz, for example[2] – and in so doing generate a new age of urbanity.

## 26   Beyond the opposition between the machine and the living: urbanization as the process of exosomatic organogenesis

It is a question of starting from these specificities in order to initiate a new model of urban development that would also involve a new urban economic model. However, this requires reconsideration of the *urban function* in general, and of how this is modified by new *algorithmic* urban functions.

It has often been suggested, usually in a metaphorical way, that the city is a kind of organism, and that the urban milieu is a kind of connective tissue. Italo Calvino pointed out that it is possible to have two seemingly-opposed visions of the city: the city as machine and the city as organism.[3] Today, this *machinization of the city* is no longer a metaphor: it is effected through the implementation of *automated functionalities* that are deployed via digital urban technologies.

The mechanized city, however, must *also* become an 'organic' city, in the sense that it is dynamic only when it grows like a living thing. It is obviously not a matter of choosing the machine city over the organism city, or vice versa. It's a matter of turning the machine city (and the city has always been a kind of machine, as has been shown many times) into a new urban dynamic, that is, an organic dynamic – in a sense that we are able to understand via Calvino, and to understand how structures that are apparently purely functional are in reality extensive new dimensions of the living organism, which is therefore always also an urban locality in a way that exceeds a mechanistic functionalist approach.

The question of the relationship between the living and the machine is very old – Descartes reduces life itself to the status of the machine. This question can and must be overcome today, particularly after the work of Alfred Lotka already mentioned in the Introduction and Chapter 1, and through an understanding of the human living thing as a process of exosomatic organogenesis. The organogenesis of plant and animal organisms is endosomatic, in the sense that the evolution of life consists for plants and animals in a diversification of organic functions, implemented by organs that are themselves parts of living organisms. But man is an exosomatic living organism, and, living in society, he builds and institutes exosomatic organisms of higher dimensions within which human groups live.

In what follows (here and in the chapters devoted to the internation), the human individuals that we are will be called *simple exorganisms*, and the collective individuals that human groups form will be called *collective exorganisms* – a boat and its crew, a factory, a supermarket, a city, the United Nations... As we will see in Chapter 5, *two types of complex exorganisms* must be distinguished:

- those that assume a function within a larger complex exorganism, as a factory does within a country;

- those that have metafunctions in relation to law, whether these are legal in the juridical sense (including as religious canon law) or lawful according to the canon of scientific truth of evidence, that is, defining both what is forbidden and what establishes regimes of truth, as Michel Foucault called them.

Some complex exorganisms are small and short-lived, such as a boat and its crew, assembled for the duration of a voyage. Others are vast and last for centuries or even millennia, and this is true in particular of cities, and more generally of higher complex exorganisms (and a city is 'higher' in this way to the extent that it is endowed with its own legal authority). Cities are themselves aggregates and localizations of complex exorganisms within which simple exorganisms cooperate.

In late eighteenth-century England, urban dynamics were reshaped around those *industrial lower complex exorganisms* that were manufacturing plants, which were then emerging – and of which Andrew Ure was, after Adam Smith, one of the first thinkers, calling them factories.[4] In the twentieth century, transnational industrial complex exorganisms appeared: for a long time, one of the best known and most powerful was IBM. In the twenty-first century, planetary complex exorganisms have arisen, tending to install functional monopolies at the scale of the biosphere.

## 27   Technologies of scalability and economies of scale in reticulated urban localities

These evolutions are directly tied to questions of the relations of scale resulting from economies of scale that are themselves conditioned by technologies of scalability. The data economy amounts, precisely, to the systematic implementation of *digital technologies of scalability*, allowing the simultaneous processing of vast amounts of data on a global scale, and the achievement of unprecedented economies of scale that are both disruptive and predatory.

Such a conception of scalability thus comes at the cost of a rapid dissolution of localities, which are absorbed and reduced to *patterns* to be algorithmically extracted from their populations – a kind of value extraction that leads to a drastic reduction of their specific capabilities, that is, of their negentropic potentials. Territories retic-ulated in this way find themselves subject to extra-territorial logics that lead to their incapacitation, which is to say, to the *systemic* loss of those forms of knowledge that constitute what we are here call-ing urbanity. To achieve digital urbanity – that is, to overcome this process of standardization and incapacitation, which also leads to structural economic insolvency by undermining purchasing power – it is necessary to rethink urban development and the urban future as a local process of exosomatization and as the fruitful arrangement of local and extra-territorial exorganisms, and, within this process, as the production of new forms of value by the inhabitants, understood in the broad sense (in the sense that every stakeholder who intervenes in the territory counts as an inhabitant).

Metaphorical references to either the machine or the organism to characterize the city or the metropolis are often in opposition to one another, because the spatial and the material, which are dead, would be on the side of functions forming a whole such as is the case for a machine, while the social and the inhabitants would be its *more than material* life, a life that would thus be more than functional – ideal, cultural and temporal, in this way furnishing the vital energies essen-tial to urban dynamism.

The concepts of exosomatization and exorganism expose the super-ficiality of such an opposition. Materializations themselves induce temporal dynamics, while also arising from such dynamics. As for imagination, intelligence, intuition and reason – both individual and collective – they are themselves functions of what Kant called the faculties (of knowing, desiring and judging). Such faculties are delib-erative. Space, constituted by an organogenetic process of spatializa-tion, is what records the past while at the same time making available future habitable possibilities, as the collective dynamics of the inhab-itants of this space, and, precisely, as urbanity. This is what Calvino makes it possible for us to understand.

Digital technologies and their disruptive effects, however, rely on the fact that their operation has de-spatializing effects, which are at the same time de-temporalizing, as operations become virtual, tend-ing to disappear into algorithmic governmentality and in this way escaping all deliberation. This is what David M. Berry calls infraso-matization, a concept that will be explored at the end of this chapter. This state of fact renders inaccessible and inconceivable a state of law capable of constituting a true digital urbanity – given that the latter must be deliberative.

This is why the contributory research program proposed here consists in *locally consolidating an urban awareness of new digital functions.* It aims to make the latter into *objects of capacitation* rather than incapacitation – by conceiving and designing services and functions that *systematically* invite and strengthen the deliberative capacities of the various groups that together form the inhabitants of a territory. By taking up Lotka's concepts, it is possible to posit the following:

- Inhabitants themselves are first and foremost exorganic beings (simple exorganisms), that is, beings endowed with artificial organs that are not appendages added onto them but rather *constitute* them as human individuals – and, when they live in an exorganic milieu, as urban individuals, in a milieu itself composed of specific artificial organs such as arteries, sewage and distribution networks, and now digital networks, along with many other urban functions that mostly find themselves reconfigured by this new reticulation.

- By assembling together, inhabitants form *exorganic communities*, themselves forming exorganisms, including the urban exorganism itself, that is, lasting entities existing as arrangements of functions and exorganic agents – whether they are neighbourhoods, workshops, factories, associations, markets, loyal customers, institutions, reticulated organizations of all kinds and, of course, ethnic, religious, political and generational communities, and so on.

- As we have already mentioned, and as Lotka shows,[5] the *acceleration* of exosomatization – or what we today call innovation, and even more so disruption – can generate serious problems and reverse the expected benefits of exosomatization by creating disturbances and difficulties, leading to destruction when the knowledge required by technology ceases to be acquired.[6]

- Digital technology is the contemporary *pharmakon* – and this is how Socrates already described alphabetical writing, then still quite recent. To be a remedy instead of a poison, any new *pharmakon* requires the definition of shared knowledge, amounting to the many kinds of therapies and therapeutics allowing *exosomatization to be put at the service of care.* This program has the aim of closely articulating the dynamics of capacitation, implemented in the context of the contributory economy program, with the urban environment and its new functions – which clearly form the new architecture and new infrastructure of the economy of tomorrow.

- This also presupposes the conception of new contributory platforms, whose principles will be outlined in Chapter 7, where contributory fields are reserved for deliberation and preserved from computation – in a functional relationship to a new form of social networking, itself structurally localized. Such reserves aim to put the results of automated calculation undertaken in all domains at the service of decision-making.

To argue these points, however, we must briefly return to the archaeology and history of the urbanization process, which begins with sedentarization – which some specialists consider to be the true starting point of the Anthropocene, a perspective that we will not discuss here.

## 28   The city, social representation and the industrial and economic organization of society

Over the past three decades, the impact of digital technology on production has become a constant concern, in terms of its organization and the types of goods produced, and their social consequences. The effects of the introduction of digital technology in the city ('smart cities', mobility platforms, Building Information Modelling, and so on) is a topic that has received regular coverage in the media. But it is less common for consideration to be given to the profound links between production and the transformations it brings to the city, if not a challenge to its very existence.

Cities first appeared in the Neolithic period with the development of agricultural techniques and animal husbandry that made it possible for human groups to settle in one place. Much later, the invention of writing would overturn the spatial and institutional organization of the Greek city-state, centred around those early forms of public space that were the *agora* and the *bouleuterion*.[7]

As Max Weber[8] showed, the Middle Ages saw the emergence of a more powerful economic organization of the production of material goods. And as Jean Gimpel highlighted, a major energetic revolution accompanied the massive deployment of mills and the development of mechanics.[9] These new means of production transformed construction techniques, giving rise to the *cathedral builders* and the social reorganization of the city: mentoring and teaching techniques (apprenticeships, and apprentices touring around France, for example) then appeared – and continue in France to this day through the Compagnons du Devoir. This must be recalled at a time when the introduction of Building Information Modelling is leading to profound changes in construction, its methods, trades and working conditions, and ultimately to changes in the city as a whole and its relations to its inhabitants.

The social city is organized according to workforce needs and developmental models: work arrangements evolve according to the times, technical developments and political and economic choices. Hence the feudal *master*, by guaranteeing the protection of the serf who works for him, makes it possible for the slavery of antiquity to be replaced by serfdom. The development of artisanship and trade structures the town, transforming it into a city. Mills economize costs and reduce the need for manual labour in the countryside. The city requires an available workforce and serfs were therefore encouraged to leave the countryside, thanks to which they were able to acquire a further degree of freedom.

In the nineteenth century, the industrialization of production (mechanization, the intensification of the industrial division of labour and industrial paternalism), the development of the steel industry, *networks* of transport, energy and telecommunications (railways, gas, electricity, telegraphy, etc.) transform the relationships between cities (places of production and consumption) and profoundly reshape urban morphogenesis.

The production processes heralding the advent of Taylorism in factories lead to the separation of manufacturing and commercialization as craftsmen and women had arranged these in the city since the sixteenth century. Neighbourhoods and housing are accordingly redistributed between workers, employees and the bourgeoisie. During the same period, the invention of department stores sets in train the development of the service sector and consumer society – which reaches its peak in the second half of the last century.

The twentieth century, characterized by the oil and car industries along with the culture industries, in turn gives rise to specific types of urban development and planning, such as neighbourhoods segmented according to activity (life, work, leisure and transport), the development of road and highway networks, supermarkets, shopping centres and hypermarkets, and the setting up of radio and television broadcasting networks. These technical evolutions, the new needs of industrialists, but also a new vision of the social development of society, all lead to the introduction of a functionalist conceptualization of city organization, along with new professions such as the urban planner, sometimes perceived as technocratic. One result is the Athens

Charter, the main instigator of which was Le Corbusier. Initially, this reflects the impact of the Taylorist organization of production. After 1945, it integrates the Keynesian-Fordist model of consumerist social organization into Europe.

This urban model, strongly tied to the Taylorist proletarianization of employment, is today associated with many problems, such as ghettoization, the ejection of those with precarious employment (the allocation of public or private housing being strongly linked to permanent employment), and a host of others. But it is from this model that the 'neoliberal' city is derived, particularly in the United States and Asia. The city centre is made up of office buildings, shopping centres and parks, while housing is pushed to the outskirts, dictated by the financial means of the inhabitants. Over the last thirty years, these developments have been embedded in the process of the globalization of trade, leading to the rise of global cities[10] occupying strategic functions and organizing flows on a worldwide scale[11] – although 'hyper-liberal cities' are now appearing, mainly in Silicon Valley, and limited to the headquarters of companies with a global impact, as will be explained further below.

## 29   The new urban morphogenesis

An almost diametrically opposed movement, however, is today foreseeable, which could usher in a new age of urban morphogenesis, and which needs to be taken into account in a very precise way – after the first phase of *factory-less industries* that led to the relocation of manufacturing to countries with low labour costs, particularly in Asia. Today, the relocation of production closer to the catchment area of consumption is being given more serious consideration.

This reindustrialization is being prepared with models that require little or no wage labour: massively automated factories '4.0', FabLab or TechShop workshops, office services, and so on, all requiring customers themselves to finalize their orders. The city must therefore rapidly consider how to integrate these new production units – these workshops open to customers, constituting a new artisanship – into its organization and infrastructure. This necessitates reflection on the work of Richard Sennett, Matthew Crawford and Pierre Veltz, as well as the Maker movement and the Do-It-Yourself movement.

With the development of digital technologies and platforms, supported by exospheric infrastructure (orbiting the Earth), a new industrial revolution is once again transforming the production and organization of work, as well as modes of urban construction, transport, planning, management and life. Digital or platform capitalism is characterized by the permanent and planetary interconnection of individuals, whose activities are systemically traced and processed by the intensive computation of algorithms, allowing them to be controlled by exospheric giants for the purpose of value extraction. This data economy is expressed spatially by what marketing refers to as 'smart cities', a term that serves to mask the subjection of territories to extraterritorial logics short-circuiting local political authorities and the practices of inhabitants. This new urban morphogenesis occurs, for example, around Highway 101, which is the backbone of Silicon Valley, along which towns are being converted into 'headquarter cities': Cupertino, with Apple's futuristic new headquarters, 492 metres in diameter; Mountain View, where Google's new headquarters is conceived as a true city, integrating numerous activities for employees who can 'live and work' there at any hour of the day; Menlo Park, where Facebook's headquarters is 'an amusement park for engineers',[12] and so on.

When Amazon was looking for a site for its second headquarters, the town of Stonecrest, as Frank Pasquale notes, 'even offered to cannibalize itself, to give Bezos the chance to become mayor of a 345 acre annex that would be known as "Amazon, Georgia"'.[13] Although technically the infrastructure of these digital technology companies is fully distributed across the globe, the fact remains that these corporations are highly centralized, with Silicon Valley headquarters serving as nerve centres. It is there that everything is decided in real time, regardless of whatever dot on the map may be under discussion. Research, design offices, strategy and governance: all are co-located in these headquarters cities, from which pyramid management 'steers' the infrastructure and factories that they have disseminated across the globe.

## 30  The new division of labour and the battle for or against control of the new urban genius

These industrial models, which for the moment mainly involve digital companies, propose a new 'fabless' approach, and pave the way for a reorganization of production by bringing it as close as possible to the consumer. Automation, and especially the development of CNC machines and additive manufacturing (3D printers), linked to computer-aided design (CAD) and client software accessible to the general public, are transforming production and its commercialization.

The *division of labour* can be structured around two scenarios:

- large regional production plants (factories 4.0) capable of manufacturing a wide variety of parts, for many brands – independent of major manufacturers, in line with the concept of fabless manufacturing;

- small local units carrying out the production of goods, dependent on the contribution of the consumer (adaptation to need, customization, finishing, assembly, and so on).

According to such scenarios, whether these are large factories or small units, they will have little need for paid employment as we know it today: either they will be fully automated or the remaining manual tasks will be performed by the customer. These new production sites – which will not be far from the resident, who becomes a producer-consumer ('prosumer') – will be located right in city neighbourhoods. Likewise, 'factories 4.0' will seek to be located within their catchment area and their size will depend on territorial needs.

If the model that is currently taking shape continues to develop around centralized companies as per the GAFAM (Google, Apple, Facebook, Amazon, Microsoft) model, cities could become pseudopods (possessing exosomatic tentacles), producing/selling 'headquarter cities' for global brands. And if, as we have been considering, this model of commodity production is taking on a new 'fabless' variation, then this implies a *new battle with regard to the social and industrial development of the city and the territory*.

'Fabless' models and digital industries amount to a generalization of the economic model of the agro-food industries, as Alain Supiot has often pointed out. Adapted to industry in general, they would lead to *design, marketing* and *choice of materials* for the creation of commodities all remaining the exclusive property of global brands – such as IKEA.

In this battle, and to capture the heart of the city, these industrialists will utilize franchising. Local 'new artisans' will manage small production units on behalf of these brands. Hence, like chicken or pig breeders, they will be totally dependent both upstream (design of 3D models [CAO] and manufacturing materials) and downstream (marketing and exclusive commercialization [consumer commercial sites and centralized payment]). The 'owners' of these local production units located in the heart of the city will take on all the risk for the benefit of global brands, following the example that has been set in agriculture for several decades (battery farms, but also in cereals).

Major industrial brands have long sought to develop a model where the risks and costs of production would be reduced almost to zero.

This objective could lead the morphology of cities to be redrawn in such a way that they would become totally dependent on the models of these large corporations. Proposed items would be modifiable at the margins by the client (via consumer-based CAO software) but developed at the global headquarters. This currently emerging possibility would constitute a 'relocalization' of automated commodity production designed in 'delocalized headquarters cities' – but this locality would then be totally under the control of control technologies, amounting to a *dis-society of hyper-control*.[14]

The impact of this organization of production on the organization of the city and its (digital) urbanity is what is at stake today. Behind the issue of dismantling GAFAM, which is fuelling political debates in the United States, it is also industrial organization that is in question. If vertical concentration is limited, and if the role of the creator/ designer can be recognized outside the brand, that is, the manufacturer, it may be possible for new spaces to be developed that give a place to local initiatives.

Thus, in France, Leroy Merlin's TechShop model[15] differs from the one described above with regard to IKEA. Leroy Merlin encourages TechShop users to obtain their materials from his stores, but leaves them free with respect to prototyping and creation. This approach is in line with the FabLab[16] approach initiated by MIT, but in the context of the market and commercialization of the Merlin offering.

Following the worldwide success of the software production mode initiated by 'free software' communities, this suggests that the FabLab mode of object production could be a positive option for the relocalization of production. Nevertheless, this model is not sufficient: it has the same weaknesses as the free software model, because it fails to take account of regional social data,[17] that is, the profound transformation of the economic model that it implies, calling into question the Fordist-Keynesian model of full employment. We are therefore forced to reflect further on how to remunerate productive work undertaken outside employment.

### 31   Towards collective territorial agreements and new forms of urban intelligence: challenges of contributory urbanity

It is desirable to move towards new territorialized social contracts, taking the reduction of salaried employment into account, but so too the development of highly localized work outside employment. This relocalization of commodity production also requires a new approach to the economic, social and ecological equilibrium of the territory. Depending on the options chosen by the territory, it is conceivable that this time spent working outside employment could promote the power of inhabitants to act[18] on their locality.

From this perspective, territorial social contracts would offer social redistribution according to a model that is independent of employment, one that would recognize *capabilizing*[19] autonomous work undertaken during periods that are productive but not part of employment. The idea of an unconditional universal basic income (UBI) has been proposed as a way of responding to these challenges. Ars Industrialis – which since 27 February 2020 has become the Association of Friends of the Thunberg Generation – has, as part of the contributory learning program at Plaine Commune, been preparing to experiment with a conditional contributory income, recognizing work outside employment and linked to intermittent periods of employment (which is not incompatible with UBI).

The contemporary urban revolution is not limited to the 'smart cities' model. It is characterized by deeper industrial changes, the challenges of which, concealed by 'storytelling', are still too little analysed:

- the digitalization of all services, products, objects and materials (smartphones, GPS systems, sensors, RFID chips, connected objects and 'interactive concrete') leads to a mnemotechnical trend in all urban infrastructure, transforming the city itself into an 'augmented space';

- urban programming and architectural design, housing construction and the management of urban flows are being transformed by robotization, as well as modelling, simulation and virtual reality technologies (Building Information Management and Building Information Modelling technologies);

- automated commodity production tends to be relocated close to consumers, who are entrusted with the tasks of finalizing production in FabLabs, TechShops or other production units linked to massively automated factories 4.0.

These industrial transformations, which are occurring in the context of a major climatic and environmental crisis, need to be analysed from the standpoint of their environmental, urban planning, anthropological and societal challenges.

These transformations contain the risk of turning the city into a machine (through standardizing automation of construction and urban management, segmentation and hyper-specialization of tasks, 'technological solutionism'[20]), and consequently of standardizing urban life (data capture and user profiling, destructive exploitation of attention and destruction of local knowledge, 'functional sovereignty'[21] of platforms), thereby eliminating diversity and the singularities of urban civilizations and the political sovereignty of territories. Nevertheless, these transformations *also* open up significant potential for the constitution of *new forms of urban intelligence.*

It is becoming essential for cities and territories to consider the contributory/productive dimension of their inhabitants and the economic agents they involve. Cities and territories should, therefore, at their own initiative, and under *their* control, install new tools making possible the analysis of flows, through which it will be possible to reconsider the values entailed for various territorial stakeholders. It should thus be possible to *locally* review the contributory/productive investment policies of the whole set of stakeholders operating on a territory. This is one of the challenges of Management Institutes of the Contributory Economy (MICE), discussed in the next chapter. Such an approach, moreover, presupposes a critical awareness of urban technologies – for which the concept of infrasomatization is particularly useful.

## 32   Platformization of the city: infrasomatization and the impairment of minding[22] and democracy

As far back as 1981, Steve Jobs, then CEO of Apple, famously called computers 'bicycles for the mind', implying that they augmented the cognitive capacities of the user, making them faster, sharper and more knowledgeable. More recently, writers such as Nicholas Carr have started worrying that the same technological tools could also undermine or fragment the possibility of thought. Today, ubiquitous computing and reticular digital technologies structure and govern the environment and the society in which we live, limiting thought and undermining the possibility of certain noetic practices – in particular, through the hypertrophy of the understanding (in Kant's sense). This evolution of the organization of social functions, which Bernard Stiegler describes as 'automatic society',[23] short-circuits not just social relations and political institutions, but also psychic and social individuation (in Simondon's sense).

Today, the automated 'interpretability' of voluntary or involuntary actions has become omnipresent, and for some constitutes a new market. It is largely determined by data capture and processing by industry platforms. This infrastructure generates and processes most of this data using increasingly sophisticated and secret algorithms. To describe their impact on humans, David M. Berry has developed the concept of *infrasomatization*.

This concept introduces a third term between those that have been used to describe organogenetic processes until now – endosomatic, when it relates to life in general, and exosomatic, which is specific to man. As David M. Berry points out: 'the specific reticular nature of digital technologies creates new non-human and potentially unpredictable entropic effects'.[24] Infrasomatization is a kind of computerization or informatization, both a 'softwarization' and an automatization of the human milieu. It can be seen as a *social structuring technology* that inscribes new social forms – or anti-social forms – within the very bodies and minds of humans, and, consequently, in the functioning of their institutions.

Today, it is mainly through smartphones and tablets that we see the manifestation of these infrasomatizations. Having become indispensable (exosomatic) prostheses for most of us, these terminals create a loop between our bodies, our brains and platform servers, in this way partially cutting us off from the world outside this loop. This occurs in such a way that the opening of thinking is mediated and compressed, as consciousness is bypassed and short-circuited by the intensive computation effected by algorithms on platform servers.

This loop, made possible by a reticulation that is partially open to the outside, prevents human brains from being aware of what derives from algorithms and what from their own thinking. Without humans being able to perceive it, therefore, and thus without being able to bring it to consciousness, the algorithms of intensive computing alter thinking and lead to denoetization, that is, hyper-proletarianization. Human reason is functionally weakened, if not annihilated, and humans become highly susceptible to persuasion and propaganda created by troll factories and other industries of lies and manipulation.

Infrasomatization can be mobilized to support specific instances of thought, rationality and action – in a form of reasoning that is, however, self-defeating insofar as reason must be intrinsically deliberative (synthetic, in the senses of Aristotle and Kant). Reason is thus increasingly replaced by a purely computational analytical power that amounts to the hypertrophy of the understanding (in the Kantian sense of the words reason and understanding), creating the conditions for a conception and above all a management of common space and time that is inherently and functionally anti-democratic.

By replacing local synthetic rationalities with a computational function in social spheres, the process of infrasomatization leads to the suppression of the deliberative capacity that once constituted the functional independence of social life. These conditions create a data intensive economy based on the technological computational possibility of processing such data – in a way that fails to take account of the role of technics in calculation and its effects, in particular in terms of feedback loops and performativity. Consequently, this calculation is *anti-scientific.*

So then, if the ability of citizens to think is impaired, how is it possible for a city to be called 'intelligent' – that is, *without its inhabitants?* These tendencies require the elaboration of a critique and ethics of data-processing, particularly from the standpoint of an imperative that would be not only negentropic, but anti-entropic, and ultimately anti-anthropic, both in the sense specified in the previous chapter and in the sense referred to by the IPCC when they discuss 'anthropogenic forcing', that is, the increase in the rate of entropy due to human activity. How could such a *struggle against anthropy* possibly do without the *intelligence of the inhabitants of the Anthropocene era?*

## 33  Smartness and speculation

The constellations of services with infrasomatizing effects can be mobilized into de facto monopolies in specific imbrications: an approach that takes the infrasomatizing effects of service ecosystems into account is a better way of understanding the functioning of these computing structures than the neutral notion of 'platform', which tends to use a self-description, and consequently hides more than it reveals.

As described by Robert Mitchell and Orit Halpern, the 'smartness' of the smart city 'is a function of its extensive use of informatics infrastructure'.[25] Data streams are collected through sensors and analysed by learning algorithms, then organized and used for optimizing urban interaction by creating different predictive models. Barely visible if not invisible to the eyes of citizens, these digital infrastructures impose, by normalizing this situation, an extraterritorial logic that bypasses local political authorities and the local practices of the inhabitants. The truth of this from revelations from industry insiders and those conducting research on behavioural nudging and manipulation has been widely documented and serves to prompt public calls for more regulation over these systems.[26]

In the *industrial* 'smart city' approach, the citizen is viewed as the agent who, within a system of loops, feeds the machine-learning techniques of urban digital infrastructure, at the cost of eliminating individual rationality in favour of tele-guidance that takes up past actions in order to inspire future actions. As a result, smartness 'reconfigures a human population not just as that which uses infrastructure, but as itself an infrastructure'.[27] The current digital business models are mainly based on two broad principles:

1   rapidly gaining a leadership position in imposing standards;

2   exploiting recovered data and speculating on it through services offered.

In her critical study of *actual* attempts to build 'smart cities', Halpern has also convincingly unveiled their *fundamentally speculative* nature. In spite of the good intentions and genuine hopes their designers may possess, they rest on the same dynamics as the derivatives that have restructured the financial world of the last two decades. They function as promises, designed to raise – largely unjustified – hopes, soon to be abandoned in favour of more promising prospects.

This drift towards ever-elusive futures, which the initiators of these projects often find unmanageable (the impact of communication facilitates speculative motivations), drives a fundamentally speculative economy. At the same time, and aggravating this situation, this speculative economy makes it possible to finance major corporate R&D projects via speculation and public offerings. This dynamic explores and tests a wide range of possibilities, but its achievements are limited and barely visible, and the impact difficult for the inhabitants and administrators to assess. The 'smartness mandate'[28] that rules in parallel the design of smart cities and the social logic of financial derivatives rewards forms of governance, orientation and control whose result is to disorient and mislead our collective decisions.

## 34   Technological sovereignty, political vacuum and new urban genius

The smartification of the city currently underway can be described as a *platformization* of the urban milieu. We argue that in order to pass from a 'smart' data-mine-city to a Real Smart City, inhabitants should *actually* be 'capacitated' (in Amartya Sen's sense when he refers to capabilities) by critical technological practices and not just subjected to technology. *Technological sovereignty* implies that citizens should be able to contribute to the analysis and prescription of the functioning of the technological infrastructure that surrounds them, and that they should be able to question and orient its aims. Chapter 8 returns to this point in relation to contributory design.

In Europe more than elsewhere, there has been a calamitous political vacuum regarding the question of digital technology – industrial policy having been replaced by mimicry in a way that is both ridiculous and disastrous. This is all the more paradoxical given that Europe was at the origin of the World Wide Web. Given the Anthropocene crisis, it is now more than ever up to political institutions to create, at all levels, the conditions for technical change that would be in line with a solvent and sustainable social and economic project. It is only on this condition that a coherent trajectory for technological sovereignty could be defined, corresponding to a democratically-elaborated political will. It is indeed a question, here, for inhabitants and for public administrations (that is, higher complex exorganisms), of reappropriating technology, data and digital infrastructure (data sovereignty).

A holistic approach is required. It must take account of data governance, along with the ownership, transparency and criteria of infrastructure, as well as the right to an explanation.[29] It is not enough to make changes to the legal system. It is necessary to go beyond this, and to seek to understand and challenge the way in which 'smart' infrastructure recasts certain regulatory or legal limitations as ineffective measures. These disruptive situations profoundly affect local economies, creating new forms of structural poverty and inequality:

> Absent major action on the national scale or clever strategic coordination between cities on the international scale, it will be extremely difficult to reverse this already worrying trend.[30]

Unlike the 'smartness' strategies described above, the digital technologies implemented by these counter-strategies in fact offer, with certain modifications (to be specified in what follows and in Chapter 8), the opportunity to facilitate economic and political projects based on giving inhabitants the ability to develop knowledge. Digital urbanity projects based on the intelligence of the inhabitants could emerge, favouring a contributory urban economy that generates a new 'urban genius' [genie urbain]: an arrangement of, on the one hand, urban exosomatic and infrasomatic organs, and, on the other hand, inhabitants who again become contributors, which is also to say, citizens, capable of developing their own urban planning by enhancing their local potentials within the framework of an open but singular economy, and knowing how to value its singularity (that is, its neganthropy).

## 35   Urban intelligence or automated surveillance?

The key argument of the 'smart city' marketing concept is that urban management will be improved by the *maximum centralization* of data captured on the territory, to be displayed on an 'urban dashboard'.[31]

For the sales engineers of the companies offering these solutions, the aim is to promote, to local decision-makers, the effectiveness of a better understanding of the 'functioning' of their city, to be achieved by 'monitoring' it in real time and with algorithmic means to support decision-making.

The underlying idea is that all the city's problems are purely technical, and that they can be more effectively solved using the arithmetic of 'big data' or 'artificial intelligence' than by administrations and inhabitants. In this way, debates, democratic deliberations, collective learning and administrative decision-making procedures are all tacitly evacuated. The initiators of these 'smartness' modes of city management claim *automated computation* will be able to deal with all the problems that will arise in the city of tomorrow: climate change, security, mobility, employment, food. This is what Evgeny Morozov has dubbed *technological solutionism*.

As might be expected, the first implementations of so-called smart systems have turned out to be anything but capacitating for the population. Nor do they make urban management and city life any easier. Most of the time, the benefit comes down to strengthened and automated surveillance for infrastructure and security. Rio de Janeiro's Operation Room (IBM) and New York's Domain Awareness Systems (Microsoft), which clearly fall within this pure logic of security, are also part of an attempt to globalize this model on the basis of a militarized conception of the city: the massive use of predictive algorithms goes along with the consequent militarization of urban areas, exacerbation of social problems, and the creation of socio-economic silos and invisible urban frontiers.

Cities must oppose these corporations, whose sole objective is to develop new captive and ongoing markets. Whether voluntary or not, these systems create new barriers and a new segregated city geography. They destroy the historical mixture and creativity of urban centres that enabled them to invent new ways of life for the majority of the population. All those already well-known and increasingly unbearable scourges of a development that has become inurbane are thereby reinforced.

## 36  Contributory economy, contributory research and local platforms

A new urban revolution is taking place with the digital city, which must be turned into a new civility functionally linked to the contributory economy of the city. Whereas, as Cathy O'Neil has shown,[32] the algorithmic governance of 'big data' curtails the possibility of bifurcation, this new urban territorial revolution can and must, on the contrary, open up new and unprecedented opportunities to struggle against the anthropy that is poisoning the Anthropocene era. This presupposes, on the one hand, taking the *pharmacological* dimension of all technics constantly and functionally into account, and, on the other hand, designing and creating neganthropic infrastructure capable of facilitating processes of interpretation, deliberation and collective decision-making.

The Institut de Recherche et d'Innovation (IRI) – in collaboration with the Digital Studies Network (see https://digital-studies.org/wp/en/), the consortium of the European Real Smart City project (see http://realsms.eu/about/), local institutions, associations and residents of what has been dubbed the Contributory Learning Territory (located in Seine-Saint-Denis, in the northern suburbs of Paris) – is trying to lay the foundations of an alternative model of urban dynamics giving inhabitants an active role in the design and making of their environment on the basis of the profound transformations taking place in the fields of urban planning, architecture, construction and building management.

This approach aims more generally to develop investments in contributory economic models based on valuing knowledge and the locality from which it emerges, and to do so via contributory platforms (very different from the so-called 'collaborative' models exploited by structurally and functionally extra-territorialized platforms). This experiment is based on two pillars:

- The first is *contributory research*, which brings researchers from various academic fields and territorial actors together to work in research and experimentation networks on the basis of the principles set out in Chapter 1 regarding the need to systemically and functionally value the struggle against anthropy. Contributory research makes it possible to perform rapid experiments on the territory, involving the development of new economic activities while at the same time elaborating the new concepts they require (for example, in the fields of accounting, labour law, production and engineering methods), along with digital instruments for building new local ecosystems and learning communities. The aim is also to identify generic principles that would be applicable at various scales, and that facilitate cooperation with other localities. The principles, concepts and methods of contributory research are detailed in Chapter 4.

- The second is the *contributory economy* (whose principles are detailed in Chapter 3). The new urban genius and engineering required by the critical situation of the biosphere demands a new economic form – the contributory economy – to struggle against the anthropy generated by proletarianization, by economically valuing capabilization processes (processes of deproletarianization) and collective knowledge practices (involving work knowledge, life knowledge and theoretical knowledge). This economy and the experimentation underway in the Contributory Learning Territory are described in more detail in the next chapter.

## 37 Communities of territorial knowledge networked by noetization

The efficiency gains enabled by automation should allow the freeing of time for urban deliberation, which is necessary for deproletarianization and the regaining of knowledge, in the spirit of cooperation as theorized by Richard Sennett.[33] Reticulated digital technology, which is structurally contributory, does make this possible, provided that it is designed and implemented with this objective in mind: we will return to this point in detail in Chapter 8.

The Italian Territorialist School has developed the concept of *self-sustaining local development*, in order to emphasize the balance that must be maintained between directing development to fundamental human needs (such as *social sustainability*, which cannot be reduced to material needs alone) and enhancing the environmental quality of the territory (for the benefit of the territory itself as well as the rest of the planet). This approach to spatial planning is not a regressive form of localism: it is form of bottom-up 're-worlding'. In this sense, the concept of *open locality* proposed here relates to the Territorialist School's concept of *inter-local solidarities*, allowing flexible and non-hierarchical links between the sustainable and diversified ways of life present in different localities. It thus opens the way to a multiplicity of development styles contrary to the universal flattening by neoliberal market logics that erase all singularity, and it reconstitutes what was referred to above as *noodiversity* in the sense of an economy struggling against anthropy.

Jose Ramos and Michel Bauwens (from the P2P Foundation) call this *cosmo-localization*,[34] that is, the creation of a *cosmo-local production system* in which what is 'light', that is, 'soft' (like knowledge), is shared globally as the commons of 'open design', and what is 'heavy', that is, 'hard', like territorial hardware, is produced locally by territorial economic production units. We will see in Chapters 5 and 6 how this intersects with the conception of an *experimental internation* based on the ideas of Marcel Mauss, but also related to the theme of an *International of Science*, evoked by Albert Einstein.[35]

In slightly different language, Ramos and Bauwens refer to developing a

> meaningful (virtualized) knowledge commons of high quality, open source, circular and community owned designs [thanks to which] local production creates a virtual organizations [*sic*] power to produce high quality goods.[36]


## 38   Energy sobriety and equality: sustainable and resilient cities in an uncertain future

If silicon lies at the heart of digital infrastructure, as we will see in Chapter 10, then in everyday life and construction the main materials that are put to use are concrete, paper, wood, brick, plastic, glass and steel. Ubiquitous in global cities and in today's increasingly standardized 'lifestyle', these materials lend themselves well to construction due to their physical properties (such as changeability from liquid to solid states). They are thus quite easy to model with, and require less human work force – and its *savoir faire.*

These materials, however, are mostly extracted and then transported to more or less distant construction sites: a model that involves high levels of energy consumption. These globalized techniques represent one of the most entropic factors in human life on Earth. And as the OECD indicates in *Global Material Resources Outlook to 2020*:

> The economic activities that drive materials use have a range of environmental consequences. Some of these consequences can be attributed directly to resource provision (e.g. greenhouse gas (GHG) emissions from extraction and processing of primary materials), while others are indirectly linked to resource use (e.g. air pollution caused by combustion of fossil fuels).[37]

This is what the economist Éloi Laurent calls global physical trade.[38] Today's construction industry generates around 10% of total greenhouse gas emissions – and this figure rises to 30% if we also take the operating energy of buildings into account.

The model of automated construction as it is proposed today will in all likelihood only aggravate the environmental problem. On the one hand, it is still based on a Newtonian framework that ignores the laws of thermodynamics. On the other hand, it is leading to increasingly standardized urban landscapes while at the same time creating models that are economically and ecologically costly and that lead to the disappearance of the singular characteristics of cities. Digital technologies for urban and architectural design, engineering, visualization and project management, such as BIM (Building Information Modelling and Management), open up new opportunities and pose new challenges. They can either aggravate the situation or, on the contrary, alleviate it.

A 'real smart city' must break social and technical deadlocks by opening the way to experimentation with new technical, industrial and social models, involving the invention of new ways of dwelling in (*habitare*) and living in (*habitus*) its socio-technical *habitat*. To redefine local technics, the right to make mistakes in the pursuit of bifurcations is essential. The real smart city will be born from a new, more profound understanding of the negentropic and neganthropic techniques of the past, potentiated by emerging technological capabilities that will themselves stimulate the valorization of knowledge and thus be capable of serving deproletarianization.

The challenge is to redefine digital construction techniques coupling 3D printing, cobots and BIM with pre-industrial construction techniques allowing the re-evaluation of raw materials such as earth (including clay), stone and wood, as well as short circuits and virtuous recycling metabolisms. In this sense, the design of cities will be in direct relation to locally available materials (including in the form of waste), and will avoid the exploitation of distant resources (overconsumption of sand, iron and so on) in ways that generate anthropogenic forcings on the other side of the world.

## 39   BIM, CIM (City Information Modelling) and contributory design

Social scientists have long stressed the importance of involving inhabitants in the co-production and co-design of services. In Belgium, for example, the architect Lucien Kroll has promoted participatory architecture, a practice also developed in France by Patrick Bouchain. Today's new urban design tools, such as BIM and now CIM (City Information Modelling), offer a vision of new urban futures where resident contribution and deliberation become possible – provided that the parties involved in this development of the construction *industry* agree to open up the technologies they implement.

Mobilized from such a perspective, these technologies, which are increasingly important in construction, would make it possible to integrate at (almost) every moment the contributions of associations, professionals and inhabitants of the territory. Building Information Modelling and City Information Modelling are multiscalar and allow a holistic understanding of the urban, while creating the conditions for the territory to make a real contribution to the genesis of its future (we will see in Chapter 8 that this requires a generative approach in the sense of Chiara Giaccardi and Mauro Magatti): BIM and CIM should become the *building blocks* of an *infrastructure of transindividuation* that goes beyond the proletarianization effects of infrasomatization described above.

Practised with a view to neganthropic development, these platforms should lead to the creation of new techniques for transforming locally available materials. Within the framework of contributory research, the processes of citizen creation can be transferable and shareable by networked territories, in the sense of Pierre Veltz (1996) but also of Robert Hopkins (see https://transitionnetwork.org/people/rob_hopkins/). The emergence of similar experiments in bottom-up globalization would allow *multiscalar* (rural as well as urban) territorial networks to be constructed in order to achieve neganthropic objectives and increase the resilience of cities confronted with large technological enterprises.

■ ■ ■

*The urban modelling initiative carried out by contributory research workshops on urbanity within the framework of the Contributory Learning Territory of Seine-Saint-Denis (in collaboration with the Rectorate of Créteil and the CO3 EU, H2020 project – see www.recherchecontributive.org and www.projectco3.eu)*

This contributory research project aims to identify and develop the potential offered by urban technologies resulting from digitalization, in order to initiate a process of the appropriation of urban digital technologies by territories and their inhabitants, leading to the production of new urban knowledge. Based on the observation that BIM and CIM technologies stem from a much broader grammatization process allowing new forms of urban and architectural modelling as well as construction and site management, this program, which is associated with two architectural firms, uses the Minecraft video game and its open source version

Minetest as instruments for simulating and visualizing the future potential of the city, based on GIS data (geographical information systems) and BIM, under the umbrella of the work undertaken in this territory in connection with the Olympic Village and construction sites in Greater Paris.

These technologies are thus being put into practice in the territory's middle and high schools in order to transform the disruption caused by urban modelling and planning technologies into a future for and by the inhabitants. The use by students of games such as Minecraft, under the guidance of their teachers and across a wide variety of academic disciplines, has the aim of gradually leading to the evolution of professional digital tools (including the SketchUp software and software suites connected with BIM technology). These approaches are inspired by the initiative launched in Rennes under the name Rennescraft by the artist Thomas François, who is also a partner in these contributory workshops on urbanity.

■ ■ ■

## 40   Recapitulation on the morphogenesis of the industrial city

There are very strong interactions between technical evolutions, production processes and the morphology of those higher complex exorganisms that are cities – and which are always more or less rapidly changing. The profound links between production and organizations are directly reflected in the morphology of the city. In this respect, we are undoubtedly living through an exceptional moment of bifurcation, in relation to which, as we have already said, there are divergent options. These social reorganizations of work affect how housing is structured, how production and commercial units are organized, governance tools are institutionalized (guilds, urban administrations, trade unions, etc.), as well as the place of religious elements, institutional buildings, the life of the city (shows, games, sports, etc.), luxury facilities, and so on: the set of elements that together make up the higher complex exorganism that is the city.[39]

Cities were fundamentally transformed in the mid-nineteenth century. Shortly after the repression of the workers' revolts of 1848 and the seizure of power by Louis Napoleon Bonaparte, Baron Haussmann very rapidly redesigned Paris so as to make the city 'compatible' with the industrial challenges of the day. The steel industry, transport and especially the railway had, over the previous thirty years, already been greatly developed. It was a matter of creating large markets for national industry (steel-producing ironworkers) so that it could compete with German and British industries. Haussmann insisted on utilizing metallic structures for all new buildings (opera house, railway stations, etc.) and transport infrastructure (railway lines, tramway, metro, etc.).

By comparison, today's challenges are not just about steel and fossil fuels but about data management (but also, in some economies, about 'rare earth' materials). The data of the city and its inhabitants represents a major potential production investment that constitutes – together with sensors, GPS systems, GIS and everything that falls under what we have called infrasomatization – the horizon of the smart city and the reason for the interest of large technological conglomerations in these subjects (in particular the Google subsidiary Sidewalk Labs in Toronto, where the setbacks caused by this program were revealed in 2019).

For Haussmann, it was a question of reorganizing the city in order to integrate technical progress such as rail and transport, doubtless already with the idea of individual transport, even though the automobile had yet to appear. It was also a question of lighting (oil, gas and electricity were at that time in competition), which, together with rail, established the concept of the network. Today, the network has become not just central, but almost literally a nervous system, with the internet being a data network for production processes as well as for urban functioning.

In the mid-nineteenth century, the exploitation of manual workers who had recently arrived from the countryside, and who had often reluctantly become wage labourers,[40] generated new 'demands' and organizations to support them (the trade union movement); these too find their place in the structuring of the city. Housing, which is obviously the primary component of the city, changes rapidly with production techniques and workforce needs, and in particular, as we have seen, when manufacturing and commercialization (marketing) are separated.

Could the paternalism of certain nineteenth-century industrialists not be seen as a continuity inherited from feudalism (taking responsibility for the protection of *its* serfs)? This more or less generous paternalism is materialized, on the side of the ironmasters, by the organization of housing in cottage settlements, where the industrialists would in their own shops recover a portion of the wages paid. Fourierist industrialists would themselves develop projects for utopian social cities built around production workshops (Godin in Guise, Menier in Nosiel, etc.).

After the Second World War, Keynesianism transformed these different models of 'philanthropic' social housing into the public or para-public social housing of the 'welfare state'. Cities such as Johannesburg have been completely transformed by this objective. The historic centre of the city (adjacent to the old gold mines) has been abandoned for a new city centre, Sandton, centred on the Sandton City shopping mall built around 'Nelson Mandela Square'.

## 41   Infrasomatization and BIM as possibilities of a digital feudalism

BIM was briefly evoked through the discussion of the importance of the evolution of construction techniques linked to production: techniques that in the Middle Ages were artisanal, in the nineteenth century industrial, and today have become digital and automated. BIM is a new stage of infrasomatization, and it leads to the inscription of data into every element of building, by constituting a sort of living memory referring to catalogues. For the time being, BIM is mainly seen as a tool for facilitating project management. The next step is the automation of the building site under development, particularly by means of 'chipping' the elements (building blocks, windows, doors, etc.), or increasing the autonomy of robots, as has happened in the manufacture of cars, planes and ships.

But the ambition behind BIM is greater still: its objective is to manage buildings from design to demolition. A residential building, however, does not function like a ship, not even like a cruise ship, and still less does a city. If these 'transport/leisure' places do count as complex exorganisms, nevertheless they follow very different organizational models from those of a city. Their social organization fundamentally contradicts that of the city: even in the least democratic cities, the mayor cannot be compared to a pilot or a captain (the only master on board apart from God).

One way or another, the resident of a digital city will interact with BIM. But this interaction can be conceived according to two quite different scenarios:

- either residents will be driven by the digital environment and conform to the resulting form of organization but without being able to challenge it;

- or they will be able to contribute – in particular through the acquisition of new urban knowledge, productive activities, deliberations – to the evolution of their living milieu in its locality, and thus participate in the formation of a new urban intelligence.

In this second hypothesis, it is likely that 'BIMed' urban materials and buildings will constitute the platforms of territories, and that these territorial platforms will interact with planetary platforms. This issue is highly topical at a moment when Sidewalk Labs is trying to design the neighbourhoods of tomorrow in Toronto,[41] but also in New York and many other metropolises.

The very nature of the digital economy means that it involves contributions from the various agents of the integrated services offered on these platforms. The platform economy undoubtedly amounts to an expansion of the digital economy, which has hitherto been confined to technology companies such as GAFAM. Traditional, unidirectional value chains are no longer enough for an analysis of the flows and uses coming from all these users (customers, communities, businesses), who create value for these platforms by enriching them with content or by finalizing the manufacture of objects, as we have seen. Thus, little by little, two-sided value-chains develop, then multisided, in order to analyse these flows and especially the values created by different agents. The flows generated by these platforms are becoming as complex as those observed in the city.

Taking these flows and the values constituted by user contributions into account forms the basis of the economic models behind GAFAM. These companies pool the different values created and monetize them only at certain points. In this way, they make services available that allow their users – companies or individuals – to contribute and create new use values, to be exploited by these platforms for their own benefit. Generally speaking, access to such services is mostly free for the user, and these services are wrongly believed to be the bearers of potential new knowledge – yet they do not, properly speaking, involve practices at all, but uses. It is possible to see some analogies with the management of the city and the services offered to its inhabitants.

For more than twenty years now, these technology companies have gradually built up these *ecosystems*. The latter retain users, who are themselves contributors, and lock them into logics from which they find it difficult to escape – users who are as much other companies as they are individuals. These ecosystems were originally built on the basis of a response to identified needs tied to the digital evolution of society: the search engine for Google; the management of music for Apple; digital management of book inventories for booksellers, then stock management in general, for Amazon. Today, their power in terms of user numbers and the volume of data processed amounts to *functional sovereignty*, as Frank Pasquale writes, or *efficient sovereignty*, as Bernard Stiegler proposes.

Facebook is considering the creation of a currency and the constitution of a 'court' *capable of handling content disputes*, according to Nick Clegg, the company's public affairs chief. If they succeed in these plans, it would obviously strengthen the platform's *power to certify*, and thus strengthen its chances of instituting such a sovereignty. Both this currency and this 'court' could be described as planetary counter-institutions based on a model not dissimilar to that of sharecropping in feudal times.

In the economic model installed by these platforms, access to the content, data and metadata they collect, but also the contribution made by users to the manufacturing of objects, constitutes the monetizable *harvest* of these platforms. This harvest is possible thanks to the services and tools made available to contributor/producer businesses and users. Under certain conditions, like the serfs of the Middle Ages, these contributor/producer/sharecroppers have access to the tools, infrastructure and services shared by these platforms, being able to use them and possibly also to derive income from them.

Facebook's plan to mint its own currency so as to facilitate these exchanges puts this company, if not in the situation of a state or nation, at least in a position of almost feudal sovereignty with respect to its contributing communities and businesses. From the moment that digital techniques, in an economic context strongly influenced by these platforms, are rolled out at the city, local or territorial level, questions about the organization and functioning of the city and the territory are raised in completely new terms.

### Notes

1   Amnesty International, *Surveillance Giants: How the Business Model of Google and Facebook Threatens Human Rights* (London: Amnesty International, 2019), available at: <https://www.amnesty.org/download/Documents/POL3014042019ENGLISH.PDF>.

2   See Pierre Veltz, *La Société hyper-industrielle. Le nouveau capitalisme productif* (Paris: Seuil, 2017). Veltz is also the first to conceive learning territories: see Veltz, *Des territoires pour apprendre et innover* (La Tour-d'Aigues: Aube, 1994).

3   Italo Calvino, 'The Gods of the City', trans. Ellen Shapiro, *Monumentality and the City*, issue of *Harvard Architecture Review* 4 (1984), p. 7: 'it is the comparison with a living organism in the

evolution of species that tells us something important about the city: how, in passing from one era to another, living species adapt their organs to new functions or disappear, just as cities do. And it must not be forgotten that in the history of evolution each species carries with it characteristics which seem to be relics of another time insofar as they no longer correspond to vital necessities [...]. The city may therefore have characteristics and elements that seem left out of consideration today because they are inessential or contradictory to the force and continuity of its daily function.'

4       Andrew Ure, *The Philosophy of Manufactures: or, An Exposition of the Scientific, Moral, and Commercial Economy of the Factory System in Great Britain* (London: Charles Knight, 1835).

5       Lotka, 'The Law of Evolution as a Maximal Principle', p. 188.

6       As was pointed out in the Introduction, in Lotka's time this destruction led to two world wars (after each of which he wrote, respectively, his texts of 1922 and 1945, in which his main ideas are synthesized and formulated), while we ourselves are living in the midst of the economic war that disruption has become, which in this way becomes highly destructive.

7       Jean-Pierre Vernant, *Myth and Thought among the Greeks*, trans. Janet Lloyd with Jeff Fort (New York: Zone Books, 2006).

8       Max Weber, *The Protestant Ethic and the Spirit of Capitalism*, trans. Talcott Parsons (London and New York: Routledge, 1992).

9       Jean Gimpel, *The Medieval Machine: The Industrial Revolution of the Middle Ages* (Harmondsworth: Penguin, 1977).

10      Saskia Sassen, *A Sociology of Globalization* (New York and London: W. W. Norton & Co., 2007), ch. 4.

11      Manufacturing is transferred to countries with low labour costs. Serge Tchuruk, head of Alcatel-Alsthom, declared on 26 June 2001: 'We want to be a factory-free company quite soon', and introduced the term 'fabless'. This led to the closure of most of the 120 factories in his group, replaced by subcontracting agreements.

12      Benjamin Ferran, 'Comment Facebook menace la presse', *Le Figaro* (8 September 2017).

13      Frank Pasquale, 'From Territorial to Functional Sovereignty: The Case of Amazon', *Law and Political Economy* (6 December 2017), available at: <https://lpeblog.org/2017/12/06/from-territorial-to-functional-sovereignty-the-case-of-amazon/>.

14      On the dissociety generated by the dissociation of functions, see Bernard Stiegler, *The Re-Enchantment of the World: The Value of*

*Spirit Against Industrial Populism*, trans. Trevor Arthur (London: Bloomsbury, 2014).

15   TechShop is an initiative of Jim Newton in the United States. It is a third kind of place, similar to a FabLab but commercial and open to 'makers'. They closed down in the United States, but the concept has been taken up and developed by Leroy Merlin, and he has opened several in the Paris region and in Lille.

16   See: <http://fab.cba.mit.edu/about/charter/>.

17   Sébastien Broca, *Utopie du logiciel libre. Du bricolage informatique à la reinvention sociale* (Neuvy-en-Champagne: Passager clandestin, 2013).

18   See Amartya Sen, *Development as Freedom* (New York: Alfred A. Knopf, 2000).

19   See ibid.

20   Evgeny Morozov, *To Save Everything, Click Here: The Folly of Technological Solutionism* (New York: Public Affairs, 2014).

21   Pasquale, 'From Territorial to Functional Sovereignty'.

22   With the term 'minding', David M. Berry understands the socio-cultural and historical practices of learning, educating oneself and strengthening the capacity for autonomy, and therefore of thinking for oneself. See David M. Berry, 'Smartness et le tournant de l'explicabilité', in Bernard Stiegler (ed.), *L'intelligence des villes et la nouvelle révolution urbaine* (Paris: FYP, forthcoming).

23   Bernard Stiegler, *Automatic Society, Volume 1: The Future of Work*, trans. Daniel Ross (Cambridge: Polity Press, 2016).

24   Berry, 'Smartness et le tournant de l'explicabilité'.

25   Robert Mitchell and Orit Halpern, 'Smartness, Populations, and Infrastructure', in Stiegler, *L'intelligence des villes et la nouvelle révolution urbaine*.

26   Shoshana Zuboff, *The Age of Surveillance Capitalism: The Fight for a Human Future at the New Frontier of Power* (New York: Public Affairs, 2019), and Roger McNamee, *Zucked: Waking up to the Facebook Catastrophe* (London: HarperCollins, 2019).

27   Mitchell and Halpern, 'Smartness, Populations, and Infrastructure'.

28   Orit Halpern, Robert Mitchell and Bernard Dionysius Geoghegan, 'The Smartness Mandate: Notes Toward a Critique', *Grey Room* 68 (2017), pp. 106–29, available at: <http://www.greyroom.org/media/files/grey68_pp106-129_greymatter_final.pdf>.

29   Berry, 'Smartness et le tournant de l'explicabilité'.

30   Evgeny Morozov and Francesca Bria, *Rethinking the Smart City: Democratizing Urban Technology* (New York: Rosa Luxemburg Stiftung, 2018), available at: <http://www.rosalux-nyc.org/wp-content/files_mf/morozovandbria_eng_final55.pdf>, p. 23.

31   See Shannon Mattern, 'Mission Control: A History of the Urban Dashboard', *Places* (March 2015), available at: <https://placesjournal.org/article/mission-control-a-history-of-the-urban-dashboard/>.

32   Cathy O'Neil, *Weapons of Math Destruction: How Big Data Increases Inequality and Threatens Democracy* (London: Penguin, 2017).

33   Richard Sennett, *Building and Dwelling: Ethics for the City* (London: Allen Lane, 2018).

34   See Jose Ramos and Michel Bauwens, 'Jose Ramos on Cosmo-Localization for the Anthropocene Transition' (15 August 2017), available at: <https://blog.p2pfoundation.net/jose-ramos-on-cosmo-localization-for-the-anthropocene-transition/2017/08/15>.

35   Albert Einstein, 'The International of Science', *Ideas and Opinions*, trans. Sonja Bargmann (New York and Avenel: Wing Books, 1954).

36   'Cosmo-Localization', entry in the P2PF Wiki, available at: <https://wiki.p2pfoundation.net/Cosmo-Localization>.

37   OECD, *Global Materials Resources Outlook to 2060: Economic Drivers and Environmental Consequences* (Paris: OECD Publishing, 2018), p. 184.

38   See Éloi Laurent, 'Travail et commerce de la terre: le mirage de l'"économie de l'apesanteur"', in Alain Supiot (ed.), *Le Travail au XXIe siècle* (Paris: Atelier, 2019), p. 105.

39   In this picture, we should not forget the place that, until the nineteenth century, animals occupied in the city, where they were essential for production and for organization (transport) up until fossil fuels began to be used – while automation caused them to disappear from the productive function (for example, mining) during the twentieth century.

40   Robert Castel, *From Manual Workers to Wage Laborers: Transformation of the Social Question*, trans. Richard Boyd (New Brunswick and London: Transaction Publishers, 2003).

41   See Grégoire Allix, 'A Toronto, le projet de « Google City » sort du bois', *Le Monde* (17 August 2018), available at: <https://www.lemonde.fr/smart-cities/article/2018/08/17/a-toronto-le-projet-de-google-city-sort-du-bois_5343459_4811534.html>.

# 3   Contributory Economy, Territorial Capacitation Processes and New Accounting Methods

*Clément Morlat, Olivier Landau, Théo Sentis, Franck Cormerais, Anne Alombert, Michał Krzykawski*

## I   The Economy of Contribution

### 42   Introduction

It must be stated firmly: responding to the challenges of the Anthropocene is *impossible* within the framework of the current macroeconomic model as it has been globalized over the last fifty years. This position is not ideological, but the result of a rational analysis. The challenge of the Anthropocene is to reduce entropy rates, and this requires the development of a *new macroeconomic model* based on contemporary scientific understanding. The current macroeconomic model, however, ignores the challenges posed by different forms of entropy. It is based on indicators (standard of living, gross domestic product, debt levels, productivity, monetary value, interest rates and so on) that today threaten the future of the biosphere, and thus the survival of those who inhabit it.

The current macroeconomic model fails to preserve the natural, psychic and cultural resources that are essential for establishing truly economic ways of living. As the work of Nicholas Georgescu-Roegen[1] shows, however, it is *in precisely this sense* that human life must be economic, if it is to be sustainable into the future: unlike other animal species, whose life and survival depend on their natural organs, human groups, which produce and exchange artificial organs, do not evolve just according to the laws of biology. They transform and are transformed by artificial organs, whose development was described by Alfred Lotka as exosomatic evolution (see Chapter 1 and §§22–23), and this also profoundly modifies human milieus and social organizations. Such artificial organs can both enrich the human world (provided that they are socialized through a diversity of knowledge and practices) and destroy it (by standardizing practices and depleting natural and psychic resources): they are producers both of negentropy (diversification and novelty) and entropy (standardization and resource-depletion).

In the era of industrial capitalism, however, the trajectory of the evolution of artificial organs, whether as production apparatus or epistemological instruments, changed, becoming subject solely to the imperatives of the market. The dominant economic model thus disregarded the biophysical limits and conditions of exosomatic evolution. The result has been a generalized increase in entropy rates not just at the thermodynamic level (concentration of anthropic energy in atmospheric greenhouse gases) and the biological level (destruction of biodiversity), but also at the informational level (post-truth) and the psycho-social level (destruction of collective knowledge, widespread addiction and psychic ill-being).

Proletarianization, mechanical formalization and finally the generalized algorithmic automation of production have together led to a destruction of all forms of knowledge. Nineteenth-century industrial capitalism destroyed work-knowledge [savoir-faire] by turning workers into proletarians, in the sense defined by Karl Marx.[2] In the twentieth century, this proletarianization was extended to practical and theoretical knowledge: the knowledge of everyday life has been destroyed by the culture industries and by permanent innovation based on marketing, and intellectual knowledge is now disintegrated by software substitution, including in scientific activities.[3]

This amounts to a situation of generalized proletarianization: the liquidation of knowledge in all its forms and the dissolution of work into employment,[4] as 'work without quality'[5] and labour force. It is economically unsustainable: whereas the first two waves of automation – machinism in the nineteenth century and Taylorism in the twentieth century – did create jobs, algorithmic automation destroys far more jobs than it creates. Such a situation sends the Fordist-Keynesian model into crisis, a model that had hitherto made it possible to organize employment and consumption by redistributing part of the productivity gains through wages – as Keynes himself envisaged in his 'Economic Possibilities for Our Grandchildren'.[6]

## 43   Rethinking work beyond employment

Faced with the process of proletarianization, we must revalorize work, which should itself be redefined through a new concept that is emerging in many contemporary works. As shown by André Gorz in the 1980s, work, which became work-employment in the course of industrial modernity, that is, a job that one *has* rather than work that one *does*, has, for the overwhelming majority of worker-employees, and especially blue-collar workers, lost its function as a place of identification or a time for personal fulfilment.[7] The exponential development of automation that has occurred since then has only aggravated and generalized this situation, with the rise of what David Graeber defines as 'bullshit jobs'.[8] Today, these are no longer just the concern of blue-collar workers but of office workers, who sell their time executing tasks that seem to them to be both meaningless and useless.

Employment activities that are today automated can be so only because they are based on the repetition of programmed tasks that are standardized and routine, and which can therefore be formalized and implemented in (mechanical or algorithmic) automatisms. On the other hand, work activities cannot be automated: they are based on the transmission, sharing and transformation of knowledge (see Chapter 4) by living individuals who practise it – knowledge that is always local, collective and singular.

Starting from the distinction between *ergon* and *ponos*, as explained by Jean-Pierre Vernant,[9] work must here be understood in the sense of *a* work and in a sense distinguished from labour, insofar as work involves not only an expenditure of physical force or energy transformed into exchange value, but an investment of the individual or group in the production of a work. Such a concept of work has everything to do with the concept of 'craftsmanship' developed by Richard Sennett (to go beyond the Arendtian distinction between *Homo faber* and *animal laborans*[10]), which refers not only to skilled manual work, but to 'an enduring, basic human impulse, the desire to do a job well for its own sake'.[11] Such work activities (whether a trade or a craft), which concern computer programmers as well as doctors, artists or parents bringing up their children, obviously require the acquisition of skills (routines and automatisms), but above all a capacity for innovation, invention or creation, that is, the ability to disautomatize automatisms so as to produce novelty, through what Sennett describes as 'intuitive leaps', which we propose to conceive here as bifurcations in circuits of transindividuation.

By working, individuals collectively and intergenerationally connect together: they co-individuate and transindividuate by transmitting knowledge, and develop singular capabilities through which they participate in the transformation of knowledge itself by causing it to bifurcate in new directions. These improbable bifurcations (which cannot be generated simply through performing calculations) come to enrich reality in a way that is not reducible to simple algorithms, and make it possible to struggle against the entropic effects of massive standardization, by producing diversification of behaviours and practices, and by transforming rules and institutions. In this sense, work can be considered an anti-entropic activity (a notion defined in Chapter 1, to which is added the notion of anti-anthropy: producing cultural and social singularities and historical novelties), that is, producing negentropy.

It is, therefore, a matter of developing an economic and accounting model capable of recognizing the positive value of these bifurcations as the production of negentropic knowledge. This approach, which presumes a theoretical model enabling the qualification and quantification of the various forms of entropy, negentropy and anti-entropy, is part of a transitional context, and, as has already been indicated, is based on a method called contributory research (defined in Chapter 4).

## 44  Rethinking wealth: the practical (and anti-anthropic) value of knowledge

By transforming, in the course of their experiences of work, the practices and institutions that regulate their existence in their technical milieus, and by in this way practising knowledge, human beings produce new forms of life through which they take care of themselves, those close to them, and their environments. The practice of any form of knowledge is what allows technical (exosomatic) living things to make their artificial organs the bearers more of neganthropy than of anthropy (see Chapter 1). This is why the lives of human beings are in principle organized so as to ensure they acquire and increase knowledge, which is transmitted from generation to generation through institutions that make this transmission possible (educational, academic and scientific institutions).

Knowledge has a practical or anti-anthropic value: work activities produce a wealth that is irreducible to the production of value as thought by classical economics (as use value or exchange value). In other words, the value produced by work activities and through the practice of knowledge cannot be understood in terms of use value and exchange value. This is so because:

- contrary to information, knowledge does not lose value over time, does not wear out as it is practised, but on the contrary grows richer as it is transmitted; it is in this sense *durable*;

- knowledge is structurally shareable and shared by peers and across the generations, growing richer through being practised, and its value does not increase as a function of its scarcity.

In this sense, knowledge is valuable on its own terms, to the extent that it does not wear out over time but is instead constantly renewed – provided that it is transmitted and collectively practised.

It is this practical (or anti-anthropic) value of knowledge that the economist Amartya Sen proposes to conceive through the concepts of an 'economics of well-being' and a 'human development index', by showing that the development of 'capabilities' (the power of inhabitants to act) leads to an increase in the life expectancy of individuals and in the resilience of populations.[12] Combining these works with those of Gilbert Simondon,[13] it appears that such 'capabilities' are never just individual potentials, and can be constituted only through processes of individuation that are always both psychic and collective, and which we call processes of capacitation.

It is such capacitation processes that need to be implemented within the framework of a new macroeconomic model based on the struggle against entropy. Such a model should enable the time saved by automation to be redistributed, thus granting citizens the means of developing work activities and the possibility of practising knowledge that produces economic and industrial activity that is sustainable for the biosphere and desirable for populations. Such an economic model itself requires the implementation of new indicators, capable of taking account of negentropic activities (of renewing exploited resources, preserving biodiversity and producing social and cultural diversity).

## 45   Defining contributory income

Contributory income is an idea conceived in the context of the confrontation of industrial countries with both the tendency towards a decrease of employment, particularly due to automation, and the pressure of the toxic effects of the Anthropocene era. Experimental research is currently being conducted in Seine-Saint-Denis, and constitutes the founding element of an economy of contribution in the context of industrial countries. Its implementation outside this context would require adaptations taking account of the specificity of the economies and social organizations involved.

The aim of contributory income is to remunerate work outside of employment. It is modelled on the French scheme for intermittent entertainment workers, which provides technicians and artists in cinema and the performing arts with a resource outside of their intermittent periods of employment, up to a certain percentage of their wage income for the year,[14] and on the condition that their right to continued participation in the scheme depends on at least 507 hours of paid employment from the tenth month of payment of the allowance. Contributory income is also a way of organizing work inspired by the free software movement, inasmuch as both involve knowledge-producing communities.

Contributory income is an extension of these models to activities beyond just the performing arts and audiovisual production. For example, the sectors targeted in the Seine-Saint-Denis experiment are child care, food (agriculture and cooking), recycling, construction, car mechanics and energy. These activities have been identified on the basis of the actual potential of the territory, rather than *a priori*, or in other words through a combination of: 1) existing knowledge, or knowledge that can be developed and valorized; 2) economic opportunities; 3) appropriate capacitation mechanisms; and 4) financial investment capacities (territorial or extra-territorial).

Contributory income is therefore conditional: it is not a 'universal income'. Universal income replaces the logic of wage labour, and there are endless debates about its amount, but it does not, as such, have the objective of reducing entropy. Contributory income fosters the local establishment of dynamic solidarities. The condition for obtaining this income is what we call 'contributory' practice, which forms part of the socially useful activity of which the economy of contribution is composed.

Contributory income brings with it the emergence of the figure of the contributor, which complements that already well-established figure of the taxpayer-contributor. The notion of contribution comes from the legal world: it is the action of contributing to a *common expense*. Contributory income is action relating to a *common creation*, that is, a common investment – in terms of both work and capital. This income forms an element in a context of collective creation facilitated by the digital environment. It corresponds to a new way of envisaging production and the distribution of wealth.

Contributory income, then, is not a guaranteed minimum income. Nor is it a form of welfare income: it is an investment income implemented by public authorities as a way of providing the means for the development of capabilities. Contributory income guarantees the continuity of resources for people carrying out activities in which cooperation and exchange are important, within collectives that are in one way or another working to reduce entropy – in the context of associational activities, public services or market exchanges. Contributory income will be adapted to the development of laboratory ('FabLab') logics that arise in the territory. It is a replacement for unpaid work. It will contribute functionally to the creation of positive externalities on the territories where it is developed.

Contributory income is part of a more general logic of restructuring social transfers and the industrial economy of a given territory. It is also part of a vast movement to index income to productivity and set up an individual training account. More directly, the financing of contributory income is organized in relation to both a national shared investment and local MICE (Management Institute of the Contributory Economy).

This joint contribution body (MICE) manages funds to help create a governance representative of the stakeholders in the territory. It must ensure the transparency of the new circuits of value around a local accounting system organized through a common collective creation account. Collective territorial agreements, negotiated with local stakeholders, determine the rules of application of the contributory income/intermittent employment couple, as well as income and remuneration levels.

### 46   The progressive implementation of contributory income

Contributory income is not a liberal work incentive (workfare) intended as a substitute for the welfare state. Rather, it is part of a third, emerging logic, a form of 'creative welfare' that combines the solid foundation of social insurance with the dynamics of a broadening of the free spaces necessary for collective production. Within the territory, the implementation of this income depends on compliance with traceability label issued for the contribution and awarded by the MICE. This label, the 'anti-entropic quality of the territorial contribution', is the expression of a dynamic solidarity.

Open and shared accounting tools will make it possible for authorized public servants to certify contributions. A distributed database will manage anti-forgery registration lists around a decentralized history of transactions made since the opening of the distributed system, and this will make it possible for the choices of a territory to be subject to social control. The accounting of the contribution will thus allow a rebalancing between positive and negative quantities in the collective creation account. This account is a tool for the valorization of externalities created *in situ*.

## II   Territorial Experimentation

### 47   Methodological specification with respect to the general applicability of the method

A methodology combining contributory research and local experimentation must be implemented so that the bifurcations mentioned in Chapters 1 and 2, and in §43 – bifurcations that can under no circumstances arise from anticipatory calculations carried out by algorithms, automata, statistics or, more generally, procedural models – can come to enrich the lives of inhabitants and make it possible to struggle against the entropic effects of massive standardization. This can be achieved only by producing a diversification of behaviours and practices, and, as already indicated, a transformation of rules and institutions.

The contributory economy has no fixed model, but it develops *principles* whose conditions of application evolve according to local situations and the knowledge possessed by inhabitants. Hence, the bifurcations organized by this economy are deeply implanted at a local level, while the territory is thereby allowed to remain open: open to other territories, and at the level of the nation, the inter-nation and the technosphere, while retaining control of its neganthropic future. In this way, it aims to take simultaneous control of the negative impacts of the carbon economy and the silicon economy (see Chapter 10).

The experiments proposed here, within the framework of this contributory research, put inhabitants at the centre of the construction of their economic model. They methodologically adopt the principles of the contributory economy in a manner dictated by their locality and the realities of their daily life. In the course of *capacitating* themselves, that is, regenerating their power to act, inhabitants build their own anti-entropic ecosystem, embodying a life lived in common.

It is according to these principles that in France, at the request of the Plaine Commune territorial public establishment (EPT) – encompassing an area numbering some 430,000 inhabitants in the northern suburbs of Paris, Seine-Saint-Denis department – teams from the Institut de Recherche et d'Innovation (IRI) have spent ten years undertaking an experimental program called the Contributory Learning Territory (see recherchecontributive.org).

*Learning* territories are those that create the conditions for their inhabitants to practise the knowledge necessary for new activities to be undertaken in the service of the struggle against entropy. *Inhabitants* refers to the resident populations, associations, economic actors, institutions and administrations. Inhabitants contribute to rethinking the economy in the face of the realities of automation and the reduction of jobs. In this new context, they allow the territory's economic actors to reorganize their economy, as well as allowing the related functions of institutions, associations and public services to contribute to these reorganizations. In this way, project sites are set up (called *ateliers*, workshops) that initiate new institutional frameworks guaranteeing the emergence of anti-entropic activities, in turn renewing the solvency of the territory by generating new knowledge, and thus new wealth.

The successful emergence of such territories is obviously not a given – processes of the transmission, sharing and production of knowledge have been seriously altered, having been turned, as we have seen, into processes of proletarianization. This is why any sustainable and solvent approach to experimenting with the contributory economy model requires the implementation of laboratory territories (of which the Contributory Learning Territory of Seine-Saint-Denis is the first instance, which can, however, be assimilated to territories in transition), where this economy is itself based on contributory research methodology (see Chapter 4). This is obviously neither a recipe to be followed nor some vague outline, but a method aimed at initiating the deployment of the economy of contribution in a way that best suits the singularity of the territory, and this method operates across four stages: the field survey, the setting up of capacitation projects, scripting, and labelling.

## 48   The field survey

The implementation of the method begins with a field survey aimed at understanding what appears as 'already there', and which, depending on the case, will need to be *valorized* or *taken care of*. By exchanging with territorial stakeholders (residents, associations, businesses, public actors), the practices and elements of already-cultivated knowledge, as well as the major needs of the territory – current and future – can be identified. It is a matter of forming points of support for the synergies to be developed between stakeholders.

The only possible starting point is the potential that exists in the location itself. This approach can prove difficult, since such potentials, being far from the 'mainstream', are often literally suppressed or repressed, or else channelled through an apparatus that tends to sterilize them. Furthermore, these potentials can enter into competition with one another, and thus into conflict. Finally, the solicitation of territorial actors, of residents (including those who are 'illegal' or in a situation of civil insecurity, for example with respect to their rights as residents), cannot be conducted in the form of a simple survey gathering information, opinions or energies: it requires an input, a diagnostic proposal that concerns more than just the local situation itself, and in this respect is already a performative operation that from the outset initiates a dialogue on the basis of theses proposed by the investigative 'surveyors'. In this regard, the method mobilized by John Dewey is both valuable and insufficient.

The primary aim of this investigation is, of course, to bring these 'potentials' to light, but also to bring to light actions already undertaken (sometimes in a very advanced way), to analyse them, and, finally, sketch a map of the *links* between the territorial stakeholders, highlighting the way in which the activity of an actor is able to positively and/or negatively influence other actors, and vice versa. In this way, particularly important territorial problems will be brought to the surface, as well as a network of actors *affected* by them (for example, in areas such as mobility, recycling, food and so on).

## 49   Implementing capacitation projects

Having identified problems through the field survey, *capacitation projects* are launched. These involve local mechanisms that allow the arrangement of meetings between those wishing to engage in a project aimed at transforming the territory. A community of knowledge can then be created, bearing inventive capacities for new economic activities in the territory.

These projects are micro-laboratories of contributory research: the formation of such knowledge communities demands an approach of this kind, which will be described in more detail in the next chapter. Inspired by action research, it aims to bring together academic researchers and territorial stakeholders (residents, associations, institutions, businesses, public services) in order to confront the (theoretical) research questions on which the former are working and the (practical) problems encountered by the latter. In essence, it is a question of setting up a dialogue based on the experience possessed by each actor of the problem to be addressed, and of thus stimulating the emergence, through mutual learning, of *good practices based on new forms of knowledge*.

To support the work of developing these good practices and this knowledge, researchers build upon the work carried out in these projects, and carry out a *value analysis* highlighting two levels:

- what is collectively desirable: the emergence of local development aims tied with the problem being addressed, which, in order to eventuate, requires the formation and transmission of knowledge; value analysis is thus mobilized in order to translate the potential for collective creation for all those who are ready for it into work carried out according to *descriptive criteria necessary for the knowledge to be developed*;

- the benefits that each stakeholder specifically expects, leading to the establishment of *indicators of new expected practices.*

These two analytical stages make it possible to weave the relationship between the individual and the collective – which is the condition for the establishment of relations of solidarity and trust between actors.

## 50   Scripting, then labelling by MICE

The progress of capacitation projects incidentally feeds the work of value analysis. Once this process is sufficiently advanced, a work of scripting takes over. Scripting consists in creating a narrative from the criteria and indicators by imagining a thematic scenario that could be supported by the economy of contribution, and that could therefore be produced and organized around an alternation between periods of capacitation, supported by contributory income, and intermittent contributory employment, carried out in labelled employer organizations.

This forward-looking scenario thus presents activity proposals involving the identified synergies, modalities of capacitation and types of intermittent contributory employment. It must allow functional articulation between the three dimensions of the economy of contribution, of which the scenario should be an instantiation:

- the existence of a potential leading to the formation and local sharing of individual and collective knowledge, which is also a work investment;

- the existence of a financial investor (public or private, or from an association) who can offer one or more intermittent jobs corresponding to the knowledge developed, as an activity struggling against anthropy (labelled by the MICE – see below);

- the existence of a contributory income, which is a national collective investment financing the formation of knowledge (in the current state of the Contributory Learning Territory in Seine-Saint-Denis this income has not yet been allocated, but simulation processes have been set up pending the legal registration of the experiment, as required by French law).

A scenario is therefore gradually stabilized, in a contributory way and as a research activity. The final adoption of this scenario, however, does not take place until it has been proclaimed by the governing structure of the economy of contribution, called the MICE.

The MICE:

- labels the activities described in each of the scenarios submitted to it (within the framework of the Contributory Learning Territory: contributory clinic, contributory urbanity, urban agriculture and food, mechanical recycling, waste recycling, contributory energy and so on);

- grants accreditation, in the context of these activities, to a network of public and private employer organizations that may benefit from intermittent employment;

- supports periods of the capacitation of inhabitants contributing to these activities through the payment of a contributory income, where the conditions under which this can be obtained and the amount are defined by *collective territorial agreements*.

## III   Effects on Other Economies, From the Microeconomic to the Macroeconomic Level: Elements of Contributory Accounting

### 51   System of information, deliberation and meta-deliberation for the governance of a territorial commons

The experimentation described in the previous section amounts to basing an economy of contribution on a model that functionally articulates the *economy of the commons* with the market economy. Indeed, the workshops of the capacitation network, in close connection with the activities of the contributory ecosystem embodied in the MICE, are a territorial *resource* mobilized by *communities* of knowledge development and practice that define the specific *rules of governance* for this resource. The whole that is this resource, together with this community of practitioners and the rules they construct, is in itself, a commons: a commons involved in the production of knowledge and its mobilization for neganthropic usages.

This approach is directly inspired by that of Elinor Ostrom,[15] for whom the communities constituting the commons are above all communities of knowledge. It also calls for new metrics, based on a critique of the existing metrics of a 'weightless economy', and in the sense proposed by the economist Éloi Laurent in *Le travail au XXIè siècle*.[16] The *communities of contributory work that the practice of knowledge constitutes* are based on social arrangements and systems of rules that are themselves the result of the collective practice of knowledge. Through these arrangements, stakeholders form themselves into contributory and capacitating communities taking care of the set of objects that make up the commons they have built together through the capacitation network and the MICE.

The governance of this territorial commons occurs at the interface of the network of capacitation workshops and the MICE: this constitutes the level of a *capacitation meta-workshop*. Relations are formalized during the different thematic workshops ranging from the development of knowledge to new practices enabling microeconomic synergies, and these relations are interpreted and qualified within the meta-workshop, but in this case from the perspective of a *mesoeconomic synergy*, and set within the *macroeconomic context*. The objective of this qualifying interpretation is to determine whether the knowledge developed to improve the interactions between stakeholders involved with the capacitation workshops (for example, in the fields of health, food and agriculture) can also be mobilized to improve relations between activity sectors and institutional sectors around more general questions (for example, addressing the issue of care on a territorial scale).

In other words, it is a matter of assessing whether the operating scenarios of the various capacitation workshops can be combined into a territorial scenario of neganthropic usages. And, as with the thematic workshops, it is deliberation that forms the basis of this combination. To put it another way, a territorial deliberation arranges and synthesizes thematic deliberations, amounting to a '*meta-deliberation*' controlling the *governance process of the commons*.

An *ad hoc* territorial *information system* feeds into this governance by assuring both the *conservation* and *articulation*:

- of *microeconomic data structures* built around each capacitation workshop (qualitative criteria derived from developed knowledge, quantitative indicators of use and exchange values describing the synergies between all the activities occurring at the workshop);

- of *mesoeconomic data structures* built specifically for the governance of the commons (qualitative criteria derived from developed knowledge or from the development of knowledge to synergize the activities associated with different workshops from a territorial perspective, quantitative indicators of use and exchange values describing the expectations of the coordination of the various scenarios for capacitation in the territory).

This information system is a support for the dialogical relationship between several levels of capacitation. The congruence of micro- and meso-data structures (the same mode of organizing indicators of use and exchange value around knowledge criteria, at all levels) is sought in order to facilitate the interpretation of the effect that the development of knowledge in a workshop can have for another workshop, or for the territory as a whole. This is in no way for the purpose of aggregating the assessments of use value carried out in the various workshops. The information system is not intended to automate the structuring of data, nor, therefore, to base a territorial analysis of value on a single method of calculation.

## 52   Wealth, calculation and accounting

Within the meta-workshop, microeconomic data structures are interpreted in order to feed into territorial deliberation – or, as just discussed, meta-deliberation. More specifically, they are intended to inspire the participants in this meta-workshop (who may be representatives of thematic workshops, or other stakeholders, with meso- or macro-economic influences) to *build social and participatory indicators in order to aid deliberation.*

Conversely, mesoeconomic data structures inspire the construction of indicators to aid in the deliberation carried out within thematic capacitation workshops. These indicators *specify and document the judgments concerning use value made by a stakeholder.* By constructing these indicators, the stakeholder who participates in a workshop communicates with other participants, but also – thanks to the support of the territorial information system – with the participants of other workshops. At the same time, this participant has access to indicators built by other stakeholders in the same workshop and relative to the same knowledge, but also relative to other knowledge developed in other workshops.

*Indicators aiding in deliberation therefore allow stakeholders to distinguish and combine in their decision-making, and thus to grammatize:* 1) *the value judgments that other contributors to the commons make with respect to what knowledge-practice enables* in terms of new synergistic uses necessary for governing what is held in common; and 2) *a value judgment that is specific to that particular stakeholder and that relates to what he or she expects from their contribution in common*, that is, the advantages and constraints that these new uses are likely to confer to and impose on that stakeholder.

Resulting from the dialogical interaction between the various thematic workshops and meta-deliberations, *the territorial deliberation process* as a whole *always relates to both*: 1) *issues of common interest*, with regard to which specific problems of territorial life are clarified, and then feed into *collective choices*; and 2) *issues of greater individual interest* that motivate stakeholders in their personal and professional lives. The direct consequence is that stakeholders whose decision-making involves methods of value analysis specific to the exercise of their activity – geared, for example, to the management of public goods and services, local market valuation, globalized market finance or the gift economy – must all be able to interact and deliberate, in order to: 1) agree on the definition of a collective method of governance, that is, of the organization and management (particularly, economically) of the commons; and 2) adapt their own methods to take account of the requirements stemming from their inclusion in the commons.[17]

As a result, *multiple methods of value analysis coexist*:[18] this coexistence of different approaches to value analysis determines a *territorial locality of valuation*. The *calculation of contributory income* within the MICE is based on a 'meta-method' that makes it possible to bring these approaches coherently together so that stakeholders will wish either to finance contributory income or to benefit from it. More generally, *value analysis* in an economy of contribution is founded on the *dynamic analytical cross-linking of several 'cost centres', 'profit centres' and 'knowledge centres'*. It is based on:

1  micro- and meso-data structures, whose interpretation makes it possible to produce

2  indicators aiding with territorial deliberation, which makes it possible to feed into

3  a *common accounting of wealth creation* (adequacy of knowledge to neganthropic synergies, cost of participation/ management of anti-anthropic capacitation), an accounting that must then be put *into dialogue with*

4  the *accounts associated with other economies* (of capitalization, risk, public goods and services, capabilities and so on).

The system composed of these data structures, this deliberative process and this organization of accounts is called *contributory accounting*.

## 53   Valuation scales and contributory income

The economy of contribution is not based on envisaging a direct and immediate link between the accountancy of wealth (as knowledge) and the account-keeping of the stakeholders who try to benefit from this wealth. Among the institutional embodiments of this economy, contributory income[19] is probably the most visible benefit with regard to the modalities of changes of scale (from the local to the national).

In the economy of contribution as defined in the preceding paragraphs, when this income is allocated to an inhabitant who, in the context of their work of practising knowledge in a capacitation workshop, constructs an indicator to aid in deliberation,[20] the work fostered by this allocation of income has an influence on all levels of the economy. Moreover, it can respond to multiple motivations. Indeed, the contributory income distributed to the (nanoeconomic) inhabitant who participates in this (microeconomic) workshop at the same time involves:

- an allocation of dynamic solidarity as described in the first part (macroeconomy);

- an incentive-based redistribution of the accounting products generated by (mesoeconomic) industrial reorganization and recorded in the (macroeconomic) national public accounts;

- a productive investment on the part of stakeholders (from nano-, micro-, meso- and macro-economies) capable of developing these synergies.

## 54   A new model to confront misgrowth

One of the peculiarities of the economy of contribution model is that it does not measure the wealth of a nation 'at the end of the value chain' and with regard to the monetary standard. The aim of this model is to make wealth that has been produced in common – knowledge – the 'centre of gravity' of a multitude of 'satellite' approaches to value analysis and accounting. These approaches are undertaken in concert at all levels of national economic space, and all of them are calibrated by a collective view – constructed by deliberation at the territorial scale – focused on the adequacy of knowledge for a neganthropic reorganization of these territories. The multiple monetary representations of value, as well as the various forms of calculation that precede them, and of the different forms of accounting that make it possible to render an account of them, are not disconnected from the structuring of data in the localities of knowledge-practice from which they arose.

This is why, as we have already indicated, the shift from one level to another of national economic analysis (from the nanoeconomic – domestic – level to the macroeconomic level[21]) is not envisaged through a transmission from one level to another of data relating to one and the same issue, as is currently the case for the calculation of GDP (or public statistics in general), but through a dialogical interpretation and a specific form of structuring, and through a formalization, at each level, of data relating to multiple issues and that has been produced following formalizations carried out at all other levels.[22]

It is also and perhaps above all necessary to use existing knowledge-practice, and dialogue between several levels of interpretation, to grasp the nanoeconomic, microeconomic, mesoeconomic and macroeconomic determinants of the future development of knowledge, that is, to evaluate the quality of capacitation systems so as to take stock of the growth dynamics of knowledge in terms of its adequacy for reorganizing neoliberal industrial economies.[23]

In fact, investment in the work of knowledge-practice cannot be satisfied with the current frameworks dedicated to macroeconomic analysis. These frameworks are static, whereas the economy of contribution requires accounting in a shifting frame. This framework must communicate with other economies by relying on innovative systems that make possible a dialogical relationship between micro- and meso-economic analyses, in order to institutionalize a multiscalar value analysis.

What matters is above all that this allows analytical objects and analytical concepts to be redefined in the short space of time required for the evaluation process (and not only over the longer-term institutionalization of systems). This requirement is necessary for modelling the analytical relationship between the two central organizing concepts of the economy of contribution, which are entropy and knowledge, which is also to say, entropy and wealth.[24]

The relationship between entropy and knowledge must be seen in relation to an open locality, and with regard to the evolution of the limits imposed on human societies by the Anthropocene era. The need to take the measure of the adequacy of knowledge for the reorganization of economies, therefore, does not refer to a performative measure useful only for the governance of a territory: it aims to qualify the knowledge produced and the reorganizations that result from it, on the particular territory but in relation to the global stakes – which calls for the setting up of a worldwide dialogue on the territorial accounting of the economy of contribution as a basis for the contributory accounting of the internation.[25]

The valorization of that to which wealth gives access – that is, to what is enabled through knowledge – must indeed be based on a perpetual renewal of the representation of wealth, with regard to the dynamics of thermodynamic, biological and informational entropization. More specifically, from an economic perspective, it is a matter of seeing how capacitation allows a reduction of informational entropy within the territorial economy, and how this reduction of entropy promotes synergies between territorial activities – in particular industrial synergies, which can be interpreted as being negentropic from a thermodynamic, biological and psychosocial standpoint.

Investing in the work of knowledge-practice means investing directly in informational negentropy and *valuing* this negentropy for the fact that it itself has neganthropic implications: this is the primary function of contributory income. But this alone is not enough. *It is also necessary, in valorizing neganthropy, to devalue anthropy.* More importantly, *value analysis in an economy of contribution should not be limited just to articulating current representations of value* – even in the most negentropic way. The practice of knowledge aims above all at a *new relationship to investment,* pertaining to the vocation to invest in an activity, and not to be legitimated in terms of 'value' in the sense that contemporary economics gives to this word.

## 55  Conclusion: valorizing localities within a new macroeconomy adopting the accounting perspectives opened up by the European Union and the United Nations

Capacitation processes, which involve the transmission, sharing and transformation of knowledge, always occur under local conditions. Even if they always involve delocalization – on a market, in libraries, on scientific networks, in schools and universities, or through other types of exchanges – practical and theoretical knowledge varies according to epochs and techno-geographical milieus: it evolves over time according to technical mutations that transform the spatiotemporal conditions of existence for individuals and societies. The processes of transindividuation in which knowledge consists amount to spatial and temporal localities giving rise to singular and diversified events (which we have described as anti-anthropic bifurcations).

An economy that values the production of anti-anthropy through the practice of knowledge presupposes the valuing of localities, as well as exchanges at all scales, ranging from the domestic (nanoeconomic) level to the biospheric (macroeconomic) level. This is why a contributory economy must contribute to the reinvention of the international level in relation to an internation – as described in more detail in Chapters 5 and 6 – that does not deny localities, but on the contrary mobilizes them for the sake of the whole that is the planetarized economy.

Such an evolution can get underway only through territorialized and reticulated contributory research experiments, within the framework of an internation that is itself experimental and transitional, and which could just as easily consist in an experimentation and appropriation of the possibilities of European accounting.[26] The choice of a local adaptation of the European SEC 2010 standard is in this respect not insignificant. Taking note of the spirit and the letter of the Eurostat text,[27] which institutes this system by signalling the possibility for a member state of the European Union to construct as many satellite accounts as necessary for the analysis of its political economy, the economy of contribution is based on building a *mesoeconomic satellite account of deliberation.*

This account, organized in the same way as other satellite accounts, will record monetary data extracted from the central framework of national accounting, and non-monetary data aimed at precisely depicting its own function: analysis of the influence of the development of knowledge (anti-anthropy) on the reorganization of the territory (neganthropy). The account of each member state of the European Union applying the ESA 2010 system will be consolidated according to specific methods within a common framework that aims to describe the economy of the European Union and its interactions with other macroeconomies.

More broadly, ESA 2010 is a local EU version of the principles of the United Nations System of National Accounts, ESA 2008, jointly produced by Eurostat, the OECD, the World Bank and the United Nations. And as future French national accounts communicate with the EU-wide ESA 2010, so too the latter communicates with the UN's ESA 2008. In an ideal neganthropic scenario, deliberative satellite accounts could be established at the levels of national, regional (continental) and global accounts, and communicate with each other and with other satellite accounts at each of these levels, in order to provide a real prospect of internation accounting.

## Notes

1 Nicholas Georgescu-Roegen, *The Entropy Law and the Economic Process* (Cambridge, Massachusetts: Harvard University Press, 1971), and Georgescu-Roegen, *Energy and Economic Myths: Institutional and Analytical Economic Essays* (New York: Pergamon, 1976).

2 Karl Marx and Friedrich Engels, *The Communist Manifesto*, trans. Samuel Moore (London: Penguin, 1967).

3 Bernard Stiegler, *Automatic Society, Volume 1: The Future of Work*, trans. Daniel Ross (Cambridge: Polity Press, 2016).

4 Alain Supiot, *Le travail n'est pas une marchandise. Contenu et sens du travail au XXIe siècle* (Paris: Collège de France, 2019).

5 Richard Sennett, *The Corrosion of Character: The Personal Consequences of Work in the New Capitalism* (New York: W. W. Norton, 1998).

6 John Maynard Keynes, 'Economic Possibilities for Our Grandchildren', *Essays in Persuasion* (Houndmills, Basingstoke: Palgrave Macmillan, 2010). This text, which deserves detailed analysis, is also very confused, and it is striking that it ignores the questions and problems that will be raised under the name of the Anthropocene.

7 André Gorz *Farewell to the Working Class: An Essay on Post-Industrial Socialism*, trans. Michael Sonenscher (London and Sydney: Pluto Press, 1982).

8 David Graeber, *Bullshit Jobs: A Theory* (New York: Simon & Schuster, 2018).

9 Jean-Pierre Vernant, *Myth and Thought among the Greeks*, trans. Janet Lloyd with Jeff Fort (New York: Zone Books, 2006).

10 Hannah Arendt, *The Human Condition*, 2nd edition (Chicago and London: University of Chicago Press, 1998).

11 Richard Sennett, *The Craftsman* (New Haven and London: Yale University Press, 2008), p. 9.

12 Amartya Sen, *Commodities and Capabilities* (New Delhi: Oxford University Press, 1999).

13 Gilbert Simondon, *Individuation in Light of Notions of Form and Information*, trans. Taylor Adkins (Minneapolis and London: University of Minnesota Press, 2020).

14 Originally, the remuneration for periods of non-employment was a percentage of compensation applied to the general unemployment

scheme, calculated on the basis of the minimum wage for the position occupied, negotiated through collective bargaining for the sector.

15 See Charlotte Hess, 'Communs de la connaissance, communs globaux et connaissance des communs', in Benjamin Coriat (ed.), *Le retour des communs. La crise de l'idéologie propriétaire* (Paris: Les Liens qui Libèrent, 2015).

16 Éloi Laurent, 'Travail et commerce de la terre: le mirage de l'économie en apesanteur', in Alain Supiot (ed.), *Le travail au XXIè siècle* (Paris: Atelier, 2019), p. 105.

17 If, brought together in a deliberative situation, *all the participants collectively describe the wealth that is composed of knowledge, which is the yardstick when calculating value* (building data structures specific to collective deliberation), then in the exercise of their activity, *each one mobilizes these common knowledge yardsticks in a singular way,* and considers specific 'analytical objects' so as to make individual decisions (based on data structures that are always singular).

18 A *local market player* is interested in knowledge insofar as it allows new work skills, new products to be exchanged, partnerships around capacitation activities and so on. He or she interprets the influence of knowledge through analytical objects such as financial *capital* (and sometimes human and natural capital), the value of which is directly tied to *market calculations of profit,* which is another analytical object. This capital overlaps – but not completely – the analytical objects considered by the commons:

- A *globalized market player* considers the effects of the development of knowledge on the valuation of *risk* associated with transactions and securitizations that influence the 'fair value' (IFRS) of the entities it controls, and this risk therefore necessarily comes into play when *calculating prospects for financial gain.* The territorial synergies envisaged in common thanks to the development of knowledge influence this risk and the legibility of the effects of these synergies on the risk can therefore encourage the involvement of this stakeholder in the governance of the commons;

- A *public actor* considers the effects of the development of knowledge on the management and delivery of *public goods and services,* the development of which influences the *calculation of social and societal costs.* These public goods and services relate at the same time to the management of the commons, microeconomic multistakeholder strategies for the preservation of (human, natural and financial) capital, and a local contribution to the control of systemic financial risk;

- An *inhabitant of a territory* involved in the economy of contribution considers the effects of the development of knowledge on the *capabilities* that he or she can develop to transform his or her daily life, while *calculating the cost of his or her contributory activity* with respect to the monetary resources at his or her disposal, the immediate benefits in terms of quality of life and standard of living, and the potential for future investment in gift, market, financial and public economies.

19   Because it is: 1) *deliberate* (in order to establish levels of the adequacy of capacitation with respect to the need for new neganthropic uses); 2) *contractualized* (within the MICE, which structures the whole composed of territorial agreements, labels, contributory work contracts, workshop contribution agreements, laws of contributory income, and so on); and 3) *influencing other economies in a way that is subject to accounting* (public meso- and macro-accounts, private micro-, macro- and nano-accounts); and doing so through 4) stakeholders concerned with stakes at multiple levels (from nano- to macro-levels).

20   This indicator is used during deliberations aimed at calibrating actions to be undertaken by a micro-entity to limit its impact on local ecosystems, and its interpretation can also help to inspire the meso-economic conception of a more ecologically sustainable territorial synergy, including, for example, a circular reorganization of industrial processes whose effects in terms of $CO_2$ emissions can be tackled by aggregation at the macroeconomic level.

21   Hence also, necessarily, from one to another of the analytical temporalities that usually characterize them.

22   The question of the preservation of life, in particular, cannot be addressed simply through an aggregation of microeconomic data aimed at producing aggregate statistics on the state of the global ecosystem as represented in macroeconomic analyses (SDGs, national accounts, etc.).

23   In order to recognize the potential for future influence over these reorganizations and to invest in strengthening this potential, in particular, but not exclusively (far from it), through their impact on macroeconomic statistics.

24   And where a further step necessary for the analysis of value is to consider the relationship between the work of knowledge-practice and the neganthropic reorganization of territorial activities. In

short, a new 'map' – a new structure of information systems – is not enough: value analysis also requires a new 'compass'.

25 Nor does this necessity refer to a static analysis of the suitability or otherwise of a capacitation system, with regard to the adequacy of knowledge to the challenges identified and addressed – which is what 'sustainability' is usually understood as meaning – but to a discursive analysis of problems relating to levels of reality driven by extreme dynamics, and of which humans have but a partial knowledge, and will never have more than a partial knowledge.

26 The definition of the object of national account-keeping is less trivial than neoclassical economists believe. The latter tend to base accounting conventions on the traditional representations of the economy, whose limits we have already discussed. The quality of the representations on which these conventions are based must therefore be guaranteed, just as much as the optimality of the structure and process of accounting. Beyond a substantive 'expert' rationality, geared towards the rigour of figures, it is necessary to promote a procedural rationality, geared towards transparency and ensuring that contributions are representative, in the negotiation of accounting conventions. The figure, then, becomes a social fact up for discussion. On this point, see Marie-Andrée Caron, 'Apport de la comptabilité environnementale à la mutation de l'entreprise', chair in social responsibility and sustainable development, ESG, UQAM, 2012.

27 Eurostat, the European statistical system – ESA 2010, European Commission.

# 4 Contributory Research and Social Sculpture of the Self

*Noel Fitzpatrick, Anne Alombert, Colette Tron,*
*Glenn Loughran, Yves Citton, Bernard Stiegler*

## 56 Primary aims of contributory research

Contributory research can be considered to be a form of social sculpture (that is, of the contribution of psychic individuals to collective individuation in Gilbert Simondon's sense, collective individuation being here that of a community of knowledge), based on a culture and a sculpture of the self, in the sense that the ancient Greeks (along with, on that basis, Michel Foucault) referred to *tekhnē tou biou*: technics of the self.[1]

In this approach, culture, arts and knowledge can all be viewed as *transindividual* processes (producing what Simondon called the transindividual, that is, shared signification) through which groups, and individuals within these groups, *cultivate themselves* (as one cultivates a garden), 'sculpting' themselves by sharing and through common *practices*, as well as by bringing these practices into confrontation with each other. It is in this sense that the artist Joseph Beuys spoke of social sculpture.[2] One could also speak – and perhaps more correctly – of a form of gardening: culture is understood here as a kind of 'permaculture' (that is, of *permanent culture*), forming a local ecosystem, based in this case not on biodiversity, but on noodiversity (see §§9 and 22) – that is, on the cultural diversity generated by exosomatization.

In the context of the *acceleration of technological innovation* that has now become 'disruptive' innovation, which defines the most recent period of the Anthropocene – after the accelerations of exosomatization that were represented initially by the *'Trente Glorieuses'*, then by the opening of the World Wide Web and the reticulated and generalized digitalization that was its result – the speed of penetration of the new technologies emerging from that permanent innovation characteristic of economic war leads to a *structural lateness of knowledge in all its forms* in relation to technological evolution. This lateness – which was already examined and anticipated as the great problem of the future by Lotka in 1945 – leads to a *permanent disadjustment* that proves to be less and less bearable for societies, which find themselves literally *dis-integrated* (a society is a process of integration of its members within social systems, themselves composed of what we have called lower complex exorganisms [see §82], which themselves constitute functions of the division of labour in the sense of Emile Durkheim, that is, inasmuch as it generates what he called the organic solidarity of the social group[3]).

Because it causes this delay and therefore this *structural deficiency* of knowledge, which is also to say its *discredit*, economic war and the resulting acceleration of the process of exosomatization (more commonly known as the process of production) intensify the *toxicity* of exosomatic organs. It is with a view to struggling against this state of fact that an economy of contribution has been conceived that serves decarbonization insofar as it depends on the revaluation of knowledge – and therefore on deproletarianization. It is precisely in this sense that the economy of contribution, which is conceived as a process of deproletarianization, and in this way as an *economy of detoxification* struggling against anthropy, requires research itself to become contributory: research methods in the sciences (physical sciences, life sciences, earth sciences, human and social sciences), in technological research, in design and in the arts, must become inclusive in this sense, that is, integrative and open, and in this way produce neganthropy and anti-anthropy (see §8).

Conceived in this way, contributory research methods are based on the constitution of research communities *integrating* the diverse forms of knowledge, *both practical and theoretical* – of everyday life, civility, crafts, trades and professions, thus extending well beyond the world of academic research, artistic research, technological research and industrial research. Moreover, this is how, faced with the Anthropocene event, a new *ecology of educational subjectivity* can be formed, taking account of its technical conditions and related evolutions, that is, of the development of exosomatization, by fighting against its toxicity and by cultivating its curative potential for new psychic and collective individuation.

## 57   On the need to set up networks of laboratory territories

The disintegration brought about by the acceleration of technological evolution combines its toxic effects with the effects of specialization on the organization of research, accentuating the search for efficiency while weakening finalities – both theoretical (formal coherence beyond specialization), as we saw in Chapter 1, and practical (coherence of social cohesion and psychic cohesion, solvency and sustainability). In the social field, this is reflected in an ever-widening gap between design, production, distribution and consumption (see

Chapters 2 and 8). This results in a transformation and ultimately a fundamental deterioration of the conditions of psychic and collective individuation, leading to collective disindividuation and social disintegration, atomizing all forms of relations by subjecting them to 'top-down' statistical calculations carried out at the scale of the technosphere, erasing localities and thus liquidating the very criteria of the 'superiority' (of higher complex exorganisms) through which various forms of legitimacy are constituted and maintained.

Conversely, contributory research aims to set up territorialized laboratories forming networks of localities. This will contribute to the collective and 'bottom-up' creation of the new criteria needed to struggle against anthropy in the Anthropocene era – leading to the constitution of collective creation accounts and to the new forms of accounting mentioned in the previous chapter. It will also allow a rapid transfer of research results to the various *levels of territoriality* that form societies. Just as transfer centres or clusters have been set up over recent decades in order to accelerate the appropriation of academic research by economic actors, and in particular small and medium business (see, for example, the Université de technologie de Compiègne), so too these *learning territories* are intended to give rise to rapid transfer processes, but in this case involving *territorial societies undertaking research work together with inhabitants.*

## 58 Contributory research and digital studies

Between the nineteenth and twenty-first centuries, technical conditions became technological conditions, leading to the generalization of proletarianization (loss of knowledge, externalized and fixed in artifacts): integrating scientific formalisms not mastered by the users of technologies stemming from this new stage of exosomatization, technologies have led to the proletarianization initially of workers, then of consumers, then of middle management, then of the tertiary sector, then of executives,[4] and finally of scientists themselves (via 'black boxes'). Inasmuch as it profoundly reshapes urban fabrics and social connections, the infrasomatization discussed in Chapter 2 is the most advanced stage of proletarianization – and it (dys)functionally proletarianizes both citizens and the politicians who represent them.

The key question to be addressed by contributory research is that of generalized proletarianization. This is in turn tied to the question of a *new relationship with technology, based on the goal of deproletarianization*, that is, a relationship in which the inhabitants of territories are not merely users of technological systems and public or private organizations and services, but rather enter into a relationship with technology based on studying it collectively, both practically and theoretically, so that these researcher-inhabitants can understand, prescribe, transform and practise it. Territorial laboratories are for this reason called upon to reinvent industrial design in all sectors.

The term 'contributory research' was first used within the framework of the French Conseil National du Numérique, in its report entitled *Jules Ferry 3.0*,[5] with the aim of closely linking academic research on the digital with teaching practices used in schools. The report concluded that, to the extent that digital technologies transform the activity of the mind as well as social relations and scientific practice in all their dimensions, a new epistemic and epistemological organization of research and teaching institutions is required.[6]

Shortly before this report was published, Bernard Stiegler had proposed contributory research to the office of the then Minister of National Education, Vincent Peillon: having posited that, before distributing computer equipment and software in schools, it was necessary to study their effects in depth and in a transdisciplinary way, and to launch large-scale research programs for this purpose, the response received was that neither the minister nor teachers have time to wait, in the face of a veritable invasion of smartphones, tables, social networks and new media into classrooms and schoolyards. It was in order to respond to this problem (and this state of fact) that it was proposed to set up research laboratories, for example on mathematics teaching, with, on the one hand, researchers in the epistemology of mathematics, exploring the consequences of algorithmic calculations on the structure of axioms, theorems and theories, and, on the other hand, in institutions, classes and their teachers – in this way territorializing research. The result was the proposals made by the Conseil National du Numérique, the primary objectives of which were:

- to launch a transdisciplinary research process addressing all academic disciplines, dedicated to the study of digital technologies (on the model of the Digital Studies Network[7]), by systematically and territorially integrating this with educational institutions (along with students and parents, or parents' representatives);

- to organize a rapid transfer of technological and scientific advances (across the disciplines, from mathematical physics to legal, economic and artistic studies, and including cultural practices in the broadest sense – which obviously includes sport) to societies, at all levels of territoriality, and first of all at the most local level, where for structural reasons such research is always carried out, then consolidated at less local levels.

In a disruptive period, all types of knowledge, technics and art have to be thought again from scratch – while revisiting in return, and after the disruptive shock, earlier forms of knowledge and social practice. In order to do so, we need to provide therapeutic prescriptions for disruptive technologies, which initially appear to be toxic. The perspective opened up by contributory research aims to revisit the notion of 'social sculpture' as it was coined by Joseph Beuys during the 1970s, and to do so within the contemporary technological context and the framework of digital studies.

## 59   Disruption, algorithmic governmentality as 'anti-social sculpture', and noetic permaculture

If, from the perspective of the art market, the term 'social sculpture' could conceivably seem dated, it would nevertheless be absurd, from the standpoint of art history, or of art in general, to say of an artist that he or she is 'dated' – unless, precisely, one does not recognize him or her *as* an artist. Similarly, forms of knowledge in general do not 'date': they are not like commodities that can become obsolete or go past their expiry date. Knowledge is cumulative, and every form of knowledge is representative of a historicity that is irreducible, and consequently knowledge constantly finds itself revived and reactivated in new forms – the advent of Einstein does not mean that Newton has reached his expiry date, but rather that his work returns and is resituated. This is what is at stake in what Socrates called anamnesis, and what Husserl called *Rückfrage*.

As for Joseph Beuys himself, who coined the concept of 'social sculpture', he is sometimes considered controversial: on the one hand, because of his links with Rudolf Steiner's anthroposophy; on the other hand, because the very term 'sculpture' sometimes leads to a confusion in which a separation would seem to be reconstituted between an active master-sculptor and a passive material on which this sculpting action would be exerted. It is for this reason that we refer to gardening and noetic permaculture.

Anyone familiar with the work of Joseph Beuys knows that views of this kind contradict his own proposals. The fact remains that we obviously need to clarify the issues at stake with the terms 'social' and 'sculpture' (which is also to say, what is meant by 'social sculpture of the self' and 'social plastic'). More precisely, it is a matter of reconsidering the proposal for a 'social sculpture' – inasmuch as, in Beuys's approach in the early 1970s, *artistic practice* and *political economy* were tied strongly together – in relation to contemporary modes of the technical and technological mediation of the world. It was *in this sense* that Beuys referred to 'social plasticity',[8] where modelling and social transformation become a total work, considering every individual as an artist, themselves constituting, *together with other individuals*, a 'creative power'.

This creative power to work [*oeuvrer*], that is, to open up [*ouvrir*], and therefore to constitute neganthropic and anti-anthropic localities, is collective individuation as such, as noetic (perma)culture. It thus participates in 'social sculpting' that configures the forms and functions of the world in which these cultivator-sculptors live, cultivator-sculptors that we should all once again become, and we should do so from, essentially, the perspective of the Anthropocene era – where there is widespread participation in both the production of symbols and *production in general*: as we know, Beuys claimed that the creation of the German Green Party (*Die Grünen*) was a work of art.

## 60   Sculpting, gardening and cultivating memory in the twenty-first century

In the history of philosophy, the use of the word 'sculpture' should be traced back through Martin Heidegger to Aristotle. It is related to the term '*tekhnē*', which can itself be translated as both *technics* and *art*, and where sculpting means forming: giving form to matter – the analysis here occurring in the context of what will later be called (by commentators on Aristotle) the theory of the four causes,[9] distinguishing between the material cause, the efficient cause (that is, technics), the formal cause and the final cause. It should be noted here that matter (*hylē*) is for Aristotle a *dunamis*, that is, a potential, while shaping matter (as a conjunction of the *efficient* or technical cause, the *formal* or theoretical, first of all as contemplative, cause, and the *final* cause, in the sense of its completion, which Aristotle calls *entelekheia*) is its *passage into actuality*, that is, its *energeia*. The passage from *dunamis* to *energeia* is the basis of Aristotelian ontology, that is, of its conception of what can be and what must be.

If we now consider social behaviour, and therefore the forms of motility of noetic living things, as cases of *dunamis*, then we can better understand how the concept of social sculpture is close to *Bildung* (formation, training, education), the notion of noetic culture and education as it will be conceived by the heirs of Immanuel Kant – from Fichte and Schelling to Nietzsche, via Schiller, and as a shaping or putting into form in the sense of individuation, culture (if not of worship, *culte*) and gardening.

The behaviour of psychic individuals – of which a society is composed as a set of collective individuals themselves forming social systems and complex exorganisms – is formed through education as a 'sculpture' of *retentions* (habits or memories) and *protentions* (expectations or desires). This does not mean, of course, that individuals are objects, putty in the hands of their educators: this question was widely explored, for example by Wilhelm Dilthey, in the twentieth century. Those who are educated are so precisely with a view to allowing them to develop, *by themselves*, their potential as subjects who are not just particular, but singular – and as participants, *from their singularity* (like artists), in a process of collective individuation called knowledge. This is what Kant called maturity.

Since at least the Upper Palaeolithic (the time of cave painting, the oldest examples of which are perhaps 70,000 years old, according to a recent discovery in Australia, said to be the 'cradle' of shamanism), the retentions and protentions of individuals have been sculpted and gardened by social organizations (rituals and institutions, whether political, religious, philosophical, academic or educational) through the practice of knowledge (knowledge of how to make and do, how to contemplate – *theorein* – and how to live) or arts (*ars*, art and craft techniques, arts of living, creative and performing arts, techniques of the self and spirituality – *noesis, nous* – in the *tekhnē tou biou*). This knowledge and these arts, which are *always* techniques (even though, today, contemporary art has great difficulty in seizing hold of technologies, an issue that forms part of what we call organology), are *neganthropic practices through which individuals take care of their environment, constituting their commons*, and learn to live together by sharing common retentions and protentions – through the memory of a singular past and the projection of an unforeseeable future, the arrangement of memory and milieu constituting what Watsuji Tetsuro called *fūdo*.[10]

In the disruptive period, the social organizations through which individuals transmit, practise and transform their knowledge and their arts, trades and techniques, seem to be structurally and constantly overtaken by radical and permanent innovation, leaving individuals and groups *devoid of knowledge, that is, links*. The practices constituting *common knowledge* as well as academic knowledge become obsolete, replaced by marketing injunctions implemented via algorithmic technologies functioning in real time – and, more precisely, up to two thirds of the speed of light in the centralized memories of so-called 'intensive' computing, which extracts *patterns* that are called 'big data'.

Indeed, the current functioning of the digital technical system that serves the consumerist data economy leads to the capture and control not just of attention, but also of the retentions and protentions of users of digital devices, connected objects and 'social' networks, and by the automatic generation of their profiles. Algorithmic environments suggest programmable and standardized behaviours that solicit and direct their drives towards consumer products: the constitution of mimetic and consumerist crowds and the depletion of libidinal energy[11] thus lead to the production of a *psychosocial anthropy from which nothing but the worst can arise.*

## 61   Anti-social sculpture and the data economy as platformization

The development of new ways of recording and reproducing knowledge (through technologies of grammatization), beyond those constituted by writing (which lay at the origin of the Western *epistēmē*), gave rise after the Renaissance and the printing press to technologies of mechanical grammatization (in the nineteenth century), analogue grammatization (in the nineteenth and twentieth centuries) and digital grammatization (in the twentieth and twenty-first centuries). It is through these reproductions of movement (first of all, the gestures of workers) and of the knowledge tied to movement (including as a moving image and as mobility now directed by GPS) that the various stages of industrial society emerged.

Industrial exosomatization – which constitutes the Anthropocene era – was first concretized as modes of production based on the machine, then, after Taylorism, with the consumerist economy based on the culture industries, that is, on the control of behaviour by capturing attention and controlling collective retentions and protentions, and finally, as a data economy based on the control of individual retentions and protentions via smartphones, algorithms and statistics, referred to as algorithmic governmentality, platform capitalism, or surveillance capitalism, where statistical computation constitutes societies of hyper-control (well beyond what Gilles Deleuze, after William Burroughs, called control societies).

These grammatization technologies have transformed both the practice and the status of knowledge, and, consequently, the social organizations that this knowledge supported – and that in turn supported it. As Theodor Adorno and Max Horkheimer described, the culture industries, as 'mass media' based on analogue technologies, have 'shaped' consumerist behaviour in line with the investments and economies of scale effected by industrial production. Based on digital technology, that is, on the application of calculation to any event functionally transformed for that purpose into data, and above all *incited* as data, the reticular computational industries have, via social media and smartphones, led to algorithmic governmentality, as Thomas Berns and Antoinette Rouvroy have described it.

This transformation has given rise to the stage of generalized proletarianization, where work-knowledge, life-knowledge and theoretical knowledge have all been massively short-circuited by what eventually led to a kind of 'anti-social sculpture' – that is, to that which Beuys was fighting to prevent from becoming generalized. This occurred because what had initially amounted to the fundamental principles of an editorial and hypertextual digital network called the World Wide Web was systematically and rapidly destroyed by what gradually came to replace it: platforms. And especially Facebook. While web pages and websites were at first open to a wide variety of formats, intended to be read by noetic (human) readers before being read by machines, this has been progressively replaced in the data economy with processes that generate pre-formatted data for the sole purpose of being calculable by and transformable into 'big data', that is, patterns drawn from higher level data. In this way, web pages and websites whose metadata allowed automated linking without eliminating the reading paths traced by HTML then XML links, and which were shared by reader-writers, came to be replaced by Facebook pages and other hyper-standardized formats, while 'tweet threads' and other technologies based on mimetic processes, and 'peer review' based on 'likes', have ended up producing the precise opposite of what Tim Berners-Lee and Robert Cailliau had imagined at CERN when, in 1989, they launched the software suite that would become known as 'the web' – and transformed the face of the world.

## 62   Six reasons to reinvent knowledge and deproletarianize: towards a new noetic contract

That reticular digital technologies have become anti-social is a fact – a state of fact. Once again taking up this initial program for the web is, however, not only possible, but essential, and this necessity must become a principle – a state of law. And first of all in Europe: it is in Europe that the web was conceived, and where the president of the European Commission aims to reduce carbon emissions, and therefore, in our view, must also reduce proletarianization.

The acceleration of anthropic (entropic and human-originated) tendencies by current platforms[12] cannot last: it precipitates the catastrophe that the Anthropocene has become. This is why it is strategic to relaunch fundamental and applied research in the field of theoretical computer science as well as in computer engineering and design. To do this, it is necessary to practise contributory research, that is, to start from local social and territorialized practices, producing new forms of knowledge generated by the appropriation of these technologies, and transforming these technologies in return.

In other words, the study of the specificities of knowledge tied to digital technologies must be placed at the heart of contributory research. This is so for six reasons:

- the shift from a conception of entropy based on standard information theory to a conception that integrates the notion of negative entropy – which Schrödinger conceived so as to account for the specificity of the biological domain, and which eventually necessitates the introduction of the concept of anti-entropy (see Chapter 1) – requires the redefinition of the theoretical basis of computer science;

- Lotka introduces into this new standpoint the question of exosomatization, and makes it possible to formalize in theoretical terms the pharmacology of exosomatic organs insofar as they are always potentially both toxic and curative;

- on this basis, taking account of the problems caused by exosomatization (and by its acceleration, tied both to economic war and to the efficiency of computational technologies) makes it possible to conceive a new 'noetic contract', so to speak, inasmuch as contributory research, which is structurally transdisciplinary, approaches the vital problems posed by the current period of the Anthropocene era on the basis of a common aim, which is the optimization of the exosomatic condition of human societies so as to reduce not only their carbon footprint, but, as we have seen, their anthropic tendencies in all areas, reflected first of all by the loss of knowledge and vast processes of proletarianization;

- contributory research, which always involves doctoral or post-doctoral research activity, is fundamentally experimental research in two senses: 1) it practises technologies that it critiques, prescribes and transforms, which has elsewhere been referred to as practical organology; 2) it undertakes these practices on territories whose inhabitants are put in the position of being non-academic researchers (at least in the usual sense of the word 'academic' today), but urban or rural researchers, in this or that field of communal life – that is, of life in complex exorganisms that themselves form what we call commons;

- such territorialized research, based on the contribution of all its partners to the development of practical or theoretical knowledge, and conducted on the basis of theses (with respect to anthropy and the possibilities of limiting it) and hypotheses (with respect to possible scenarios for the concretization of these theses through territorialized collective actions, and beyond these territories themselves), is above all a matter of *work*, in the sense that to work first of all means to open, that is, to add to the world what it had not previously contained – this addition amounting to a care taken of this world at a more or less local level, and in networks with other territories of care, and therefore in exchanges with them;

- here, working does not necessarily mean being employed to do a job, and it is because he placed work at the heart of what he called social sculpture that Beuys spoke of human creative power and human capacity invested in work.

## 63  Designing our existence and digital studies

In order for a social sculpture of the self to emerge in digital society, it is necessary to *establish*, at various scales of territoriality (from rural or urban locality to the locality of the biosphere that has been transformed into a technosphere), territorial capacities for prescribing and modelling individual and collective practices of the digital systems that are today composed of traces, memories and psychosocial relations, and for making the media that underlies all of this once again into supports of knowledge. To forge and conceive society through individual and collective contributions is the path towards contributory design, described in 2007 in *Le 'design' de nos existences*,[13] which reopens, in the blind and suicidal development of the technosphere, the possibility of giving rise to future bifurcations. The objective of digital studies (which does not just study the digital, but reconsiders the history of knowledge as a whole from the standpoint of the role that technics has always played as a milieu of tertiary retentions) is to theorize and therefore to prescribe the conditions in which digital technologies completely reshape the construction of disciplinary knowledge (disciplinary epistemologies) as well as everyday knowledge and artistic knowledge (social sciences and aesthetics).

Contributory research, as we have just described it, is largely based on the contributory potential of reticular digital technologies. As will be seen in Chapter 7, this involves distinguishing fields of calculable data that algorithms can compute in order to aid collective decision-making from non-calculable data and non-computable subjects of deliberation. In a territorial laboratory of contributory research, researchers from different disciplines work with the inhabitants of the territory to develop such platforms. These contributory platforms facilitate the regular publication of research results, along with public debate about these results – particularly within MICE, as described in Chapter 3.

Contributory research is based on practice and deliberation – artistic practice itself being understood as a form of knowledge production. Art conceived as such a social culture of the self, as gardening, is 'socially engaged'. But no art that has been recognized as such by posterity would have been possible without, at the time, such 'social engagement' – over time becoming characteristic of the form of society constituted by the social element.

The various forms of art's engagement in the social element have changed profoundly over time – and have done so at least since the ornate caves of the Upper Palaeolithic. Art will be variously magical, basilical, imperial, tragic, religious and eventually political, then modern – up to contemporary art. We will not try to characterize these periods here. We will point out, though, that in each period art was engaged in a significant way in the processes of differentiation between lower complex exorganisms and higher complex exorganisms (see Chapter 2).

In the contemporary period, then, art, along with scientific and academic research and social critique, constitutes a dimension of what could be called public activism in the epoch of network communications – where activism is understood as the passage to actuality (*energeia*) of a social potentiality itself conceived as *dunamis* (see §6). The aim of an 'eventwork' (in Brian Holmes's sense; see https://brian-holmes.wordpress.com/2012/02/17/eventwork/) consists in articulating artistic research with other research – including political economy, and as contributory economy – in order to address contemporary challenges. The notion of eventwork thus names the relationship between the event and work by insisting on the social transformation and collective individuation involved in work activities, and on the bifurcations that can be produced by these activities.

64   Artistic engagement in contributory research – in the wake
     of the new patrons, and of François Hers, Robert Smithson,
     Black Mountain College and Alcoholics Anonymous, in the
     reticular digital context

In such a context, the role of the artist is not to create artworks or
objects that spectators can contemplate, but to create new *situations*
in which the public can engage. To do work here means to open new
ways of doing, living and thinking – as Nietzsche invited the 'artist philosopher' to do. The artist of the Anthropocene, an era that is
reaching its limits, is a relational actor in the world, who produces
situations and opens improbable bifurcations, rather than an autonomous actor in the world who produces objects (cf., the concept of the
artist qua proposer). It is a way of thinking and caring [*panser*] – in
an Anthropocene reaching its limits – what François Hers called the
new patrons of art, as well as of reviving both what Robert Smithson
opened up in 'land art' in terms of anti-anthropy and the Black
Mountain College inspired by John Dewey.[14]

   Digital technologies represent a new stage of the process of exosomatization based on hypomnesic tertiary retentions, which have
become thoroughly computational. It is not just a matter of a change
of system or technology as occurred in the past (as described by
Bertrand Gille, for example, in *The History of Techniques*, or by
Maurice Daumas in *A History of Technology and Invention*): it is a
mutation in the very nature of exosomatization, including its direction, its conditions of solvency and durability, and so on.

   This mutation generates massive, undifferentiated proletarianization that dis-integrates all forms of knowledge, and does so by isolating and specializing them more than ever, subjecting them in this
way to the matrix of the hyper-industrial division of labour, some of
the limits of which were already described by Durkheim. Moreover,
this mutation also dis-integrates, for every social framework, the most
elementary modes of life – from daily dental care[15] to the observation
of exoplanets, via parental and institutional education, military and
financial decision-making, relationships with others and with oneself, and so on.

   This colossal transformation today requires the formation of a new
era of knowledge, and tight cooperation between forms of knowledge
– their *reintegration*, which must follow, by thinking and by taking
care [*pansant*], the terrible disintegration that has brought humanity to the brink. It is to confront these challenges that contributory
research has been conceived. And it is for this reason that it is greatly
inspired by the work of Donald Winnicott, who, during an emergency

situation in the Second World War, took care of infants separated from their mothers and fathers, just as, during the same period, François Tosquelles had to take care of psychiatric patients at the Saint-Alban hospital who had been condemned by the Vichy regime to die of hunger, and just as Gregory Bateson theorized the therapy invented by Alcoholics Anonymous to initiate contributory processes of detoxification.[16]

## Notes

1   Michel Foucault, 'Technologies of the Self', in Paul Rabinow (ed.), *The Essential Works of Michel Foucault, 1954–1984, Volume One: Ethics*, trans. Robert Hurley et al. (London: Allen Lane, The Penguin Press, 1997).

2   See Volker Harlan (ed.), *What is Art? Conversation with Joseph Beuys*, trans. Matthew Barton and Shelley Sacks (West Hoathly: Clairview, 2004).

3   Emile Durkheim, *The Division of Labour in Society*, trans. W. D. Halls (Houndmills, Basingstoke: Macmillan, 1984).

4   As was anticipated in Karl Marx, *Grundrisse: Foundations of the Critique of Political Economy (Rough Draft)*, trans. Martin Nicolaus (London: Penguin, 1973).

5   Conseil National du Numérique, *Jules Ferry 3.0. Bâtir une école créative et juste dans un monde numérique* (October 2014), available at: <https://eduscol.education.fr/sti/sites/eduscol.education.fr.sti/files/actualites/5006/5006-rapport-cnnum-education-oct14.pdf>.

6   This perspective was first developed in *Le Journal du Dimanche*, in reaction to the announcement, by the Prime Minister Jean-Marc Ayrault and the Minister for Innovation and the Digital Economy Fleur Pellerin, of a 20 billion euros investment plan for fibre optics in France. See Camille Neveux, interview with Bernard Stiegler, '"Entrer dans la troisième époque du Web"', *Le Journal du Dimanche* (11 May 2013), available at: <https://www.lejdd.fr/Economie/La-France-dans-dix-ans-Entrer-dans-la-troisieme-epoque-du-Web-606814-3139082>.

7   See Bernard Stiegler (ed.), *Digital Studies. Technologies de la connaissance et organologie des savoirs* (Paris: FYP, 2014).

8   Joseph Beuys', 'Introduction', in Caroline Tisdall, *Joseph Beuys* (New York: The Solomon R. Guggenheim Museum, 1979), p. 7.

9   Aristotle, *Physics*, Book II, 194b17–20.

10   Watsuji Tetsuro, *A Climate: A Philosophical Study*, trans. Geoffrey Bownas (Japan: Government Printing Bureau, 1961).

11   In Freud's sense in Sigmund Freud, 'The Ego and the Id', in Volume 19 of James Strachey (ed. and trans.), *The Standard Edition of the Complete Psychological Works of Sigmund Freud* (London: Hogarth, 1953–74).

12   John L. Pfaltz, 'Entropy in Social Networks' (2012), available at: <https://arxiv.org/pdf/1212.2917.pdf>.

13   Bernard Stiegler (ed.), *Le 'design' de nos existences à l'époque de l'innovation ascendante* (Paris: Fayard, 2008).

14   François Hers, *Letter to a Friend About the New Patrons*, trans. Emmelene Landon (Dijon: Les presses du réel, 2016); Jack Flam (ed.), *Robert Smithson: The Collected Writings* (Berkeley, Los Angeles and London: University of California Press, 1996); Vincent Katz (ed.), *Black Mountain College: Experiment in Art* (Cambridge, Massachusetts: MIT Press, 2013).

15   Evgeny Morozov, *To Save Everything, Click Here: The Folly of Technological Solutionism* (New York: Public Affairs, 2014).

16   Donald A. Winnicott, *Playing and Reality* (London: Routledge, 1971); François Tosquelles, *Trait-d'union, Journal de Saint-Alban: Éditoriaux, articles, notes (1950–1962)* (Paris: Éditions d'une, 2015); Gregory Bateson, 'The Cybernetics of "Self": A Theory of Alcoholism', *Steps to an Ecology of Mind* (Frogmore: Paladin, 1973).

# 5    Internation and Nations

*Michał Krzykawski, Edoardo Toffoletto, Bernard Stiegler*

## 65    Introduction and reminders

In this book, we reflect on the need to take account of the various levels and scales of locality – from rural or urban locality to the locality of the biosphere as a whole that has become a technosphere as a whole – while positing that localities, in their struggle against anthropy, should, at their various scales, experiment with contributory research approaches, and with forms of social creativity that will make it possible to generate concerted transitional proposals aimed at overcoming the limits of the Anthropocene era. We will now argue that such a concerted effort should occur within an institutional system that is itself experimental and transitional, which we call an *internation*, taking up, as already mentioned, a proposal by Marcel Mauss. The internation would thus be a kind of crucible in which a new form of *noetic superiority* could develop, constituting what we will call a process of the individuation of reference, forming a higher complex exorganism of reference – in a sense that will be clarified in §69.

We posed in Chapter 2, and as an initial thesis in §27, that the *legitimacy* of collective decision beyond the particular interest, and as an expression of the public good, is what distinguishes higher complex exorganisms in general, which constitute public authorities, from lower complex exorganisms, which are mainly devoted to ensuring subsistence – as units of production, distribution and exchange. The objective of this fifth chapter is to set theoretical milestones for the emergence of the internation as a higher complex exorganism *of reference*. Only the constitution of such an international exorganism, drawing on the achievements of *all* scientific disciplines, can make it possible to develop, in a short space of time, a rational method with which to confront the true problem of the Anthropocene, which is the generalized increase of entropy in all its forms. This amounts to leaving behind the dominant macroeconomic model through a process of concerted territorial experimentations based on the contributory research described in the previous chapter.

We borrow the concept of the internation from Marcel Mauss, who introduced it in 1920.[1] This, however, involves more than just a simple reworking of the concept – of which Mauss gave only the barest outlines. The theoretical challenge consists in reinventing the internation by taking into account thermodynamic, organic and exosomatic constraints that Mauss could not have known, but which today are unavoidable if we are to seriously address the problem of the Anthropocene. It is precisely these constraints that lead us to re-examine the questions, however thorny and historically loaded they may be, of the nation, the nation-state, superiority and sovereignty, as well as the question of locality, which must be revalorized so as to make it a pillar of a new political economy – beyond all forms of localism and nationalism, which can lead only to global chaos, and which are nothing but reactions of closure and ill-being induced by the globalized production of entropy.

## 66   Chapter summary

This chapter unfolds in two stages.

The first stage will be a matter of redeveloping the concept of the internation in the current geopolitical context, which is primarily technological. Rather than defining the internation, we will attempt to determine the conditions under which it can emerge and take shape through local experimentation. It is only at local reticulated and associated scales that it is possible to struggle against the entropic tendencies characteristic of our epoch. If these tendencies are intertwined, it is because they are *all* results of the obsolete and blind macroeconomic model that systemically destroys the ecosystems of the biosphere, just as it destroys political, social and cultural ecosystems.

With the second stage – which starts from a historical path that makes it possible to reveal the foundations of superiority, so as to transform them according to the needs of the twenty-first century, and to do so on the basis of the scientific knowledge inherited from the twentieth century – the question of a new supranationality will be posed. While it cannot do without the national level in order to maintain itself as a superiority of reference, it is nevertheless necessary to consider this national level in a different light: the national level, as an open system that in principle opposes homogenization and excludes any form of withdrawal into itself, must be reconsidered as the *synthetic and local level of a set of localities* that will be understood as nation-locality.

In the next chapter, a third stage will be developed, in which we will try to rethink what, shortly after the Great War, Albert Einstein called the 'International of Science'. The experimental internation, as a supranational level of reference, can emerge only from *scientific engagement* freed from all submission to the anthropic macroeconomic model that has led to the present situation. This response must, on the basis of the unconditional requirements of scientificity as regards the administration of proof, be nourished by the controversies without which no science worthy of the name can develop: this evident fact must become the very germ of the internation.

A fourth stage will be developed in Chapter 6, which is thus a kind of addendum to the present chapter. In that chapter, the consideration of thermodynamic, organic and exosomatic constraints will lead to rethinking institutions from the perspective opened up by what we are calling the internation. The climate crisis, which is not just a question of global warming, is above all an institutional crisis, and at all levels, insofar as institutions have proven incapable of struggling against entropy or have contributed to its increase – themselves generating their own forms of anthropy. And their deficiency has become more serious with the disruption produced by platforms.

Faced with this institutional crisis, we outline here the principles of a new theory of institutions, which feeds into the contributory economy, as well as the contributory urbanity founded on the intelligence of urban dwellers, and as an alternative to the noetic misery and poverty of 'smart cities' – the *vocation* of institutions in the internation consisting in organizing, articulating, negotiating and adjusting the biological, social and technical systems that define humanity.

## First Stage of the Internation: Nations and the Internation

### 67  Nations, globalization, internationalism and the internation

The rise of populism and the return of nationalism that marked the second decade of the twenty-first century are *reactions* to a form of technological acceleration that is utterly subject to the blind and entropic macroeconomic model, and to the psycho-social and political repercussions to which it gives rise. After four decades characterized by one-sided praise of globalization – which this acceleration has suddenly turned into disappointment and exposed as manifestly dangerous, shifting from the ultra-liberalism of the conservative revolution to massively transhumanist libertarianism – this globalization, having reduced the world to a market, has ended up worldless and befouled [*immonde*].

The distinction between globalization and worlding [*mondialisation*] is not just a linguistic subtlety. A worlding worthy of the name brings out, from the diversity of worlds, a desired and open common world. Globalization that reduces all relations to questions of competition, themselves utterly controlled by calculation, flattens worlds by denying the anti-anthropic promises they bear within them as forms of the ability to bifurcate.

The internation, projected here as an institutional, transitional and global experiment, based above all on the confrontation of scientific arguments, takes as its essential thesis the need to rethink localities, and nations as levels of such localities. As we have seen, the notion of the internation was proposed by Mauss in the context of the creation of the League of Nations and in response to the scepticism of proletarian internationalism, which was at that time focused around the October Revolution of 1917. More than the detail of the legal and institutional aspects of the League of Nations, Mauss admired the spirit in which President Woodrow Wilson initiated the proposal to create it (whose name takes up one of Immanuel Kant's proposals in 'Idea for a Universal History with a Cosmopolitan Purpose'[2]) – without, however, being able to involve the United States due to his term of office ending in 1921.

The implication of the Wilsonian spirit praised by Mauss was that

> the international system should be based not on the balance of power but on ethnic self-determination, that their security should depend not on military alliances but on collective security, and that their diplomacy should no longer be conducted secretly by experts but on the basis of 'open agreements, openly arrived at'.[3]

The idea of the nation, from the perspective formed by the idea of the internation outlined by Mauss, which thus expresses the principle of ethnic self-determination, and which remains embedded in the political thought of the nineteenth century, must obviously be reformulated, recontextualized and critiqued in order to be brought into the twenty-first century and with regard to the struggle against anthropy in which this century must consist.

In Mauss's time (and after the First World War), the primary interest expressed with the neologism *internation* lay in its intention to combat nationalism: Mauss's optimism saw in the birth of the League of Nations an institutional framework in which neither nationalist closure nor undifferentiated liberal or proletarian internationalism would prevail. For us, this interest consists above all in the idea of preserving the diversity of the levels of locality, of which the nation is historically a political synthesis, within which, over a long period of time, the superiority required for the unification of complex exorganisms has developed.

According to Mauss, if the internation is opposed to nationalism, which ideologically and economically isolates the nation, it nevertheless does not deny the nation – and in this it is as opposed to the 'a-nation'[4] as much as it is to nationalism. The concept of the internation was therefore intended as a pillar of a form of internationalism aimed not at erasing nations but at uniting them, by conceiving them in a new way.

## 68  Internation and technosphere

To properly understand the notion of the internation, we must focus on the 'inter', that is, on the modality by which these socio-political entities that are then called nations interact with each other. If it is easy for us to understand this critique of the autarkic closure of nationalism, less obvious is Mauss's crusade against the dominant internationalism or globalism, which produces the 'a-nation', that is, the repression of national singularities in order to increase the unity of the global level. Mauss teaches us, however, that no global unity can last if it is based on eliminating national differences.

The question of the internation, seen retrospectively and from a twenty-first century perspective, must be posed first and foremost as a technological question, insofar as both geopolitics and international relations are conditioned by technological development – in particular, inasmuch as technology is driven by digital giants and the 'high tech' industry. In this unprecedented context, the vocation of the internation is not just to reinvent the interrelations between nation-localities but also to recognize that they are now conditioned by the techno-logical-cum-techno-spherical system – forming what Vernadsky already called the technosphere.

It is therefore not simply the biosphere that constitutes the milieu of interactions between geopolitical exorganisms but the technosphere, and it is in relation to the latter that questions of global sustainability and global solvency must now be raised. This amounts to responding to and for the biosphere through a new rationality that knows how to articulate the *biological* and the *technological*, well beyond technocratic solutionism and the impoverished vision of technological 'singularity' promoted by transhumanist libertarians.

Intrinsically tied to the internation as the horizon of this new rationality, the nation is a level on a scale of localities, and this level retains a privilege insofar as it still today synthesizes the unity of the territorial noetic diversities of which it forms the horizon:[5] if this national-local scale retains a privileged position, it is not only because of the historical reasons to which we will return in §§72–73. It is also and first of all because it is composed of a set of localities that it has the ability to synthesize at a higher local level.

Conversely, the revalorization of locality that we advocate here as an economy of the struggle against anthropy requires *rethinking the general principles of the nation in functional relation to the general principles of the internation* – principles that will be outlined in Chapter 6 as new conditions for reticulations between localities, where the national level assumes the function of interfacing between, on the one hand, microeconomic and micropolitical levels, and, on the other hand, macroeconomic and macropolitical levels. Hence, the idea of the internation is presented as the possibility of an institution organizing political localities, both noetic and technological, at all levels, from the nano-level of the citizen-individual to the meta-level of the internation itself, constituting in this way what we describe in §§74ff. as a higher complex exorganism *of reference*, itself composed of nation-localities as higher locally sovereign exorganisms at this level, where the sovereignty of reference constituted by the internation is the opening of sovereignties to alterities with which they compose the technosphere, threatened today with major poisoning and needing to find the pathway to new forms of cooperation from a neganthropic perspective.

## 69  Sovereignty on the scale of localities in the technosphere

From such a point of view, sovereignty is exorganologically conditioned by the internation qua noetic community of global neganthropic knowledge, which belongs to a scale of locality higher than the national-local scale (the locality of the biosphere as a whole), but which posits in principle that it can maintain its superiority only when it respects the sovereignty of its nation-localities precisely as noetic localities constitutive of a primordial noodiversity. In other words, whatever the scale of its locality, sovereignty must deal with what is higher or superior than it, while this superiority can exercise its authority only *through* its local differentiations. Always already other than itself, it is reducible neither to a local 'essence' (origin of an identity) nor to the facile organic image of a whole made up of parts: exosomatic organs require an approach other than any form of bio-economics or bio-politics, the latter always being tempted to draw inspiration from social Darwinism.

If we may risk an analogy, we can posit that, just as the biosphere is a locality within the solar system, so too local forms of sovereignty (national or otherwise: indigenous peoples are not nationalities, even though they today define themselves as nations, but in an ancient sense of this word) are localities in the internation at the level of the biosphere-cum-technosphere, and as the site of articulation of multi-polar and multilateral forms of political life, in the technospheric and planetary geopolitical system, a site *that functionally promotes noodi-versity*, that is, the diversity of knowledge, along with the technodi-versity that is its material support.[6] Noodiversity is the starting point of the internation: it is only through the *cultivation of the diversity of knowledge* – all forms of which are universalizable, but which, on the other hand, can be cultivated only locally – that it is possible to limit the anthropy produced by exosomatic evolution. It is precisely for this reason that the internation, as a higher complex exorganism of reference, must *protect* this diversity of local knowledge against any attempt to homogenize it, that is, against all entropic and anthropic tendencies, while producing negentropy, anti-entropy, neganthropy and anti-anthropy, which can only be done locally.

It is only within this conceptual framework that it is possible both to free the notions of nation and locality from far-right, nationalist or fascist fantasies (which can perfectly well become realities, and as nightmares, however fantastical they may be) and to go beyond the neoliberal and extractivist implications of the slogan 'think global, act local' – which precisely means *short-circuiting democratic sover-eignties*, and which ends up becoming a sterile and now toxic banality, impudently exploited by management as well as by marketing.

## 70   Institutional entropy and the re-worlding of the technosphere: questions of social physics

This perspective makes it possible to overcome the false problem of the opposition between worlding [*mondialisation*] and localities. As António Guterres has pointed out, only humanity *as a whole* can respond to the global crises that lie ahead. But this is possible only if globalization is replaced with an authentic worlding of the techno-sphere – as the world-becoming [*devenir monde*] of what would other-wise become befouled [*immonde*].

If the internation is the framework for the interaction between com-plex exorganisms, which express diverse localities, then the solu-tion to global crises, although necessarily global, is only concret-ized locally, and therefore always différantly: by noodiversifying. For example, in order to implement the transition to alternative and renewable energy, each political locality, which is first and foremost an exosomatic biological locality, can only respond to this issue in a singular way, according to what takes best advantage of the poten-tialities of its territory – if it would not occur to anyone to invest in hydroelectric power in a desert, it is worth considering investing in solar energy there.

But the singularity of a political locality also lies, first of all, at the institutional level. After thirty years of one-sided praise of globalization and the rhetoric of the 'end of history' (Fukuyama), it has become urgent – and vital – to recognize the local character of institutions. The struggle against institutional entropy is the exact opposite of a global and nonsensical homogenization of political institutions. On the contrary, this fantasy does nothing but disastrously accelerate institutional entropy.

Institutional entropy has accelerated and worsened over the course of the world's becoming capitalist. The exosomatic evolution of the last three centuries, initiated by the first industrial revolution of the second half of the eighteenth century and characterized by the development of mechanics, was structured by an intimate relationship between economics and modern physics, as we saw in Chapter 1. It is this theoretical and sociological tie that allows Philip Mirowski to define industrial economics as 'social physics'.

The liberal economic model has always advocated the practice of free trade in a 'free' and homogeneous space, that is, devoid of geopolitical divisions. Adam Smith himself, however, emphasized to what degree this image of society, derived from a pure and simple transposition of Newtonian mechanics into the social and political field, is a chimera, such mechanics being itself based on a Cartesian conception of an infinite and homogeneous space – constituting here a theatre of socio-economic relations where the market replaces society. Such a space is governed by an invariant, the token of which happens to be the notion of energy – an intrinsic condition for the establishment of such a space, where objects and their interactions are all quantifiable with the help of mathematical instruments, from money to data and via algorithms, exospheric satellite infrastructure and GPS.

The theoretical foundation of free trade – which removes all institutional barriers, be they national, customary, fiscal, monetary, linguistic, etc., and which overcomes all physical obstacles, by reducing distances, penetrating mountains, crossing oceans and deserts along containerized routes and the air routes of cargo planes, which are large emitters of carbon dioxide – conceives geopolitical cleavages as physical obstacles, as frictions that hamper the free circulation of objects and symbols.

Mathematically speaking, the formula for economic value is derived from the formula for physical force. From this point of view, any obstacle disperses force – and therefore economic value. The limit of this perspective is that it fails to take entropy into account, and holds to the absolute conservation of energy, that is, capital, where force = value. Furthermore, it defines work as force, and not as knowledge.

By allocating capital where it can make the greatest profit, regardless of the distance between producer and consumer, the theory of this kind of limitless global free trade fails to take account of the (environmentally, psychosocially or geopolitically) entropic impacts of the movement of commodities. Conversely, we conceive here the possibility of the internation as a higher complex exorganism of reference in which commerce between localities (both symbolic and economic) is functionally designed to intensify neganthropic exchanges – that is, such that delocalization is an agent that increases potentialities and defers anthropy by noodiversifying it.

It should be recalled, here, that locality is not simply a spatial concept. It does not just designate a delimited territory on this or that scale. The various levels of locality constitute in the nation-locality a fractal diaspora – where the nation-state is the sovereign exorganism within which sub-national localities materially and symbolically exchange, where these sub-national localities may very well co-belong to other sovereign exorganisms. Here, the sub-national refers to the micro-level, with nation-states constituting the macro-level as the local articulation (at the national level of locality) of the meso-levels, with the internation being the meta-level of locality.

As a new horizon of the anticipation of the future in the Anthropocene era, the internation operates across all levels by *affecting* them and, in so doing, by *mobilizing* them as the *motive formed by this new perspective* in the biosphere, which itself forms in the solar system the largest locality of all living localities, having been transformed over the last three million years into a technosphere, and now having to struggle against anthropy – in the Anthropocene era – by reconstituting new kinds of open neganthropic localities.

## 71  States of fact in contradiction
    and the projection of a new state of law

At a time when nationalisms and populisms seem, almost everywhere throughout the world, to dominate the public sphere, it is necessary to say why and how localities, including national localities, have a future – and are an inescapably *political* condition for the articulation between nanoeconomies, microeconomies, mesoeconomies and macroeconomies, all reticulated at the level of the technosphere. A radically different approach to the nation, as well as to other forms of locality, is necessary in order to overcome both: 1) the globalizing impasse that is the end of the Anthropocene; and 2) the nationalist-localist tendencies that form local impasses corresponding symmetrically to the global impasse – of which Trumpism and Bolsonarism are the models for all the closed localisms now emerging everywhere.

That the modern idea of the nation, especially as nation-state, is challenged by the contemporary state of the world – often described as post-national – and that the nation-state has become ineffective in that world, are undeniable facts. The fact that existing nations, which in the past constituted a territorial level of locality synthesizing smaller localities, cannot be erased and ignored, and must be reinvented beyond the nation-state model of the nineteenth century, in particular as a new arrangement between scales in the era of the technosphere surrounded by its satellite-belt exosphere, and as the condition of any political legitimacy, is another contemporary state of fact – equally evident. These two states of fact amount to a *contradiction* that calls for the establishment of a *new state of law*. This new state of law can be based only on a revaluation of locality in its various forms, within the various forms of knowledge, and of which the nation-state will have long been the territorialized reality, itself based on the right to self-determination of peoples, claimed by them with the advent of the bourgeoisie, and in order to free itself from pre-modern forms of domination – both secular and religious.

The challenge for an internation conceived on the basis of these considerations is to redefine the nation as a relevant level of articulation between the nano-, micro-, meso- and macro-economic scales, in relation to the economic, political and noetic life of societies – beyond the mortifying and sterile fantasy of national 'identity'. The nation must be redefined as a form and level of historical social organization, one that made possible the establishment of civil liberties, the redistribution of wealth, and the negotiation, at the level of this national locality, of the economic and technological processes characteristic of the nineteenth and twentieth centuries.

The reinvention of this level in the new technospheric context is what all forms of 'nation-state' politics have failed to accomplish since the turn taken after the Thirty Glorious Years. The salvation of any political legitimacy, like the reinvention of the democratic exigency, involves the reinvention of a national territorial locality. The latter must not become an obstacle to the higher interests of the technosphere, but should, on the contrary, become the operative level of an open revalorization of locality as the condition of all noodiversity, all solidarity and any peaceful future faced with the challenges of the Anthropocene era reaching its limits.

In 1920, Mauss did not hesitate to assert that 'nations are the most recent and the most perfect forms of life in society'.[7] Such an assertion can with hindsight only appear to us to amount to staggering imprudence – after the glorification of the Italian, German and Japanese nations, but also after Croatia and Serbia, which marked the twentieth century, and, today, the USA or China, or India, Burma, and so on, which mark the twenty-first century. It should be noted, however, that Mauss, *as an anthropologist,* was attempting to designate a state of fact that tended to constitute a state of law in a context that was already characterized by the upheavals characteristic of the Anthropocene era – since, basically, *the nation-state was the historically dominant form of social organization in the Anthropocene era, establishing this era as such,* and doing so at least until the end of the Second World War: the Philadelphia Convention is addressed to nation-states.

## 72  The aporia of locality

The term 'nation' was claimed by nationalist and populist movements, while the slogan 'regaining control' (state *control* being a typical trap of the Western metaphysics of *mastery*[8]) was the key idea that led the UK into Brexit. The regressive and illusory tendencies generated by the states of fact described above – and largely caused, in the case of Brexit, by true *negligence* on the part of the European Commission, which was largely premised on the destruction of European democracies[9] – haunt what must be understood as an *aporia of locality.*

How can locality be established *by surpassing itself,* like Baron Munchausen? And what role can the national level, sole guarantor today of political and civic effectiveness,[10] now play in this establishment? The challenge here is not simply to *oppose* reactionary or reactive (in the sense of Deleuze reading Nietzsche) movements that seize upon the issue of locality, or simply to reject their nationalism:[11] the challenge is to *relate the question of the nation to that of the organization of scales of locality* – the complete opposite of the fantasy of identity, but without ignoring the issues involved in territorial integrity, inasmuch as it can and must be *integrative.*

Alberto Magnaghi, for example, can in this way write 'of the need to encourage the growth of local societies intent on constructing virtuous relations with their own built environment by reinterpreting local territorial values'. He continues:

> From this point of view, the local project is the political manifestation of a need, a requirement or an idea in response

> to the challenge of neo-liberalist economic globalization
> and to overcome the current ambivalent twofold reaction
> to it: on the one hand, the self-excluding resistance of local
> communities defending their own identity through closure,
> refusal to innovate or entertain outside relations; and, on
> the other, the competitive content of local systems and cities
> exploiting and denaturing their own environmental, territo-
> rial and human heritage in the anxious race to gain an upper
> position by slavishly following the exogenous rules of the
> world market.[12]

Or again:

> In the local project the density of social and economic inter-
> actions being pursued is what is required to create a suffi-
> ciently closed system compared with the potential destruc-
> turing due to pressure from globalization. At the same time
> there is a need to build the necessary openness so as not to
> fall into the isolation of 'sad localisms', unable to react to
> the context. If a local system is too 'closed' or too 'open',
> for opposite reasons it will be destructured, either through
> exclusion or exploitation and standardization.[13]

It is necessary to go beyond the classical and universalist critique of
nationalism, and the pseudo-'defence of democracy' ultimately based
on the supremacy of the market, by distinguishing ourselves from the
so-called post-nationalist liberal positions or so-called internationalist radical leftist positions that ignore the primordial question of locality and the struggle against anthropy considered from the exosomatic
standpoint put forward by Lotka.

On the cusp of the third decade of the twenty-first century, locality and territoriality must therefore be reinvented, and the nation, as
a historically configured form of collective life, is an essential level
in this reinvention – and the only legitimate one – *provided that this
level is itself profoundly reinvented, which is possible and credible only
if it is set at the heart of the territorial economy, and transforms the
international economy* – and does so on the basis of a fundamental
revaluation of all 'knowledge-forms' (to take up an expression used
by Jean-François Lyotard in *The Postmodern Condition*) that passes
through the technodiversity discussed in Chapter 7 – and first and
foremost as the design of *deliberative digital platforms* that are in this
respect neganthropic.

Reconceptualized as remaining, in the global macroeconomic and
technological context, a *sine qua non* of political governmentality,

and not just computational and commercial governmentality, the nation becomes, in the Anthropocene era, the operator of the legitimate establishment of relations of scale between localities (from the psychic locality that is an individual in itself to the biosphere as the locality of life in the known universe), provided that:

- this key element is re-inscribed in a process of scalar reticulation that gives rights to smaller localities and so comes to inscribe these rights and inscribe itself in the broadest of localities: the biosphere as the largest of the commons in the sense established by the theory of the commons;[14]

- nations and their various networks of scalar reticulations, engaged in experimental economic approaches that valorize the struggle against anthropy, cooperate and collaborate within an organization that is itself experimental, and that we call the internation.

What we discover at the end of the second half of the twentieth century is that globalized capitalism and territorialized democracy are undergoing a divorce.[15] In this divorce, the conflict that has arisen is between the industrial economy and national politics. It is only by reconsidering political economy in terms of the question of the struggle against anthropy that it is possible to overcome this extremely dangerous state of fact.

## 73   Spirits, matter, localities, *fūdo*

Reconceptualized as nation-localities, nation-states, which form the member states of the United Nations, are also *localizations of the spirit* in the sense of *esprit* described by the Polish-born French psychologist Ignace Meyerson, who placed the exosomatic openness that constitutes what he called works at the heart of the individuation of the spirit: 'The spirit of man is in his works.'[16] Here, we must understand work [*oeuvre*] in the sense of a work [*ouvrage*]. For Meyerson, as for Augustin Berque and Watsuji Tetsuro,[17] the works that weave an inhabited territory constitute a spirit. Here, spirit is not opposed to matter: on the contrary, its activity consists in producing objective forms that matter through being defined and recognized (by diverse means) as works.

Language, science and customs are cases of the objectification of the spirit through its works – and form a neganthropic locality. The spiritual reality localized in a nation does not exist outside the locally arranged noetic acts that make this reality possible: Meyerson argues that if this objectification, typical of the spirit as specific to the human, appears to be universal, the way in which it functions is always specifically attached to a given place, for the works of the human mind are inseparable from the geographical, historical, institutional and socio-cultural context and situation.[18]

What constitutes a nation-locality is everyday life that is shareable, subject to transformation, and in this way constitutes *communities of experience and thus of knowledge of all kinds.* As a specific site of spiritual objectification, however, a nation-locality exists at different scales, and therefore cannot be homogeneous either physically or noetically (spatially or temporally). One never belongs to a single nation-locality. An individual belongs to several localities that can be localized within the locality-nation and beyond it, and as a plurality of nation-localities, for example as multilingualism, or as an international community of knowledge – work knowledge, artistic knowledge, sports knowledge, theoretical knowledge, spiritual knowledge. In ancient Greece, the Olympic Games, with poetry, thus constituted the culture of Greece beyond the level of the cities.

The feeling of belonging to a nation-locality emerges in a place where individual and collective action – imbued with more or less local customs, traditions and forms of knowledge, and open to the new and the other – occurs as the pursuit of a psychic and collective transformation of the inhabitants of the place. This is the issue at stake in what Simone Weil described in terms that can seem frightening – but which must be read – such as rootedness and uprootedness.[19] In this regard, the feeling of belonging to a locality-nation is never taken for granted, and is in no way a national *identity.* It is an *identification,* which is not an identity (which would be stable), but a metastable and constantly changing process of individuation.[20]

Such individuation (always both psychic and collective) is a *work,* more or less difficult, before which the perpetual temptation is to flee – and to seek scapegoats. What is therefore called the *identity of a place,* which manifests itself much more by its difference than by its identity – by its character, that is, its *ēthos* – must always be *staged.* This putting on stage is always dangerous and 'pharmacological': a place can surpass itself only through a power to fiction (which Etienne Balibar and Immanuel Wallerstein call 'fictive ethnicity'[21]), itself always susceptible to becoming the dogmatic basis for a temptation to flee the work that is the collective individuation imposed by exosomatization.

What we define as nation-locality should be heard as an echo of the concept of *fūdo,* developed by the Japanese philosopher Watsuji Tetsuro, and of the concept of ecumene, developed by the French geographer Augustin Berque. Much more precise attention than these thinkers gave must be paid, however, to the way in which the *fūdo* constituting the ecumene is exosomatically anthropized, as well as neganthropized, and to the conditions in which technics and works, in Meyerson's (and Jean-Pierre Vernant's) sense, can be used for anti-anthropic ends, and, in so doing, can maintain the neganthropy without which there can be neither sustainable noetic locality nor any resilience of the biosphere-cum-technosphere.

We know from historical experience that the geographico-philosophical notion of place, whether *fūdo* or ecumene, can be made to serve nationalist discourses, from National Socialism to the Japanese ultra-nationalist government of 1942. It is for precisely this reason that it is essential to reconceptualize the irreducible question of place by starting from the questions raised in this regard by physics, biology and anthropology (from Mauss to Leroi-Gourhan, via the 'entropology'[22] of Lévi-Strauss).

With the experimental constitution of an internation to accompany, in a transitional way, the experiments on laboratory territories proposed above, it is a matter of developing a new political economy bringing these territories into contact with the rest of the economic world. The internation is thus a space for the negotiation and consolidation (both conceptually and as a form of accounting) of the conditions of negentropic economic change. It is based on an economic revaluation of all forms of knowledge, and on the arrangement of scales according to theoretical models implemented in accounting instruments (see Chapter 3).

Reinvented starting from localities, nations can enter into metamorphosis, and, consequently, transform their outdated historical condition as national forms, structures and institutions, in order to become sovereign bodies that nevertheless recognize the superiority of the internation as a higher complex exorganism of reference, and align with it in their conjoined struggles against entropy. This 'superiority' of the higher complex exorganism, however, which is also and more commonly called sovereignty, is not self-evident, these two notions being historically loaded just as is the notion of the nation. It is for this reason that a historical sojourn is necessary in order to discover the foundations of these notions, and to know in what way to transform them.

## Second Stage of the Internation: Sovereignty, Superiority and Supremacy - Complex Exorganisms of Reference

### 74 The foundations of 'superiority'

Throughout history, and even in prehistory,[23] the foundations of 'superiority' have not ceased to evolve – the 'Western' basis of this distinction being established around the seventh century B.C.E., between Greece and Judea, and coinciding with the appearance of the book, both as a formulation of the secular law of the city and as the sacred writing of divine law. These theologico-political bases, themselves constituting an onto-theology, will define what is entailed by sovereignty, and will do so by defining what constitutes autonomy. After the fall of the Roman Empire, the superiority of higher complex exorganisms (which became feudal and then monarchical) was established in the West, and continued practically up until the Renaissance, through the recognition of the primacy and supremacy of papal authority.

With the Renaissance, that is, with the appearance of humanism and the Reformation, and then with modern philosophy – which unfolds at the moment when accounting records are becoming widespread, along with money,[24] while the relationship to texts is totally transformed[25] – the path to modernity is opened up. This modernity, especially when it is translated into industrial modernization, was to a large extent installed with what will lead to the establishment, in most of Europe, and then throughout the world, of the form of society and government called the nation-state.

The sovereignty of the nation-state was essentially stabilized after the French Revolution, under the influence of what was called Enlightenment philosophy.[26] The notion of the nation is much older (the word refers to the heathens, then the lineages, then the co-natives of a single place). It is on the basis of the discourse on 'the right of peoples to self-determination' – the people forming a nation of co-natives of the same place – that the *law of nations effects a fundamental redefinition of sovereignty* by postulating that everyone is capable of accessing reason (and as such are all equal). And it is on this new basis that the 'national movement', which in the nineteenth century transformed the whole of Europe, understands (in various ways) the *new superiority* that was thereby affirmed, and affirmed as the sovereignty of the people[27] – Napoleon claiming to *embody* this sovereignty solely in himself.

The 'national' movement that transformed all of nineteenth-century Europe shaped the way that societies appropriated industrial development and technology – this appropriation constituting what the historian Bertrand Gille will call an 'adjustment' between, on the one hand, the technical system, which was still largely local, but which had begun to enter permanent evolution (through what will later be called permanent innovation), and, on the other hand, the social systems, themselves synchronized and governed by the state, which therefore gives itself, for this reason, new institutions[28] that *constitute* its superiority as the sovereignty of public authority. The apparatus of the modern state was prepared in the eighteenth century on the basis of the glorification of knowledge and education against dogma and tradition. Its development will be concretized by the unification of territories such as Italy or Germany that had hitherto been highly fragmented – these unifications taking place around languages, literatures, knowledge, and of course, the new class that was then on the rise, *newly knowledgeable,* emerging from the 'Republic of Letters' and called the bourgeoisie (Diderot being in this an exemplary figure).

Defining a new territoriality whose religious markers had begun to fade, this national unification around a state that is becoming secular promotes techno-industrialization, which in turn reinforces this unification. The resulting state of affairs (railways, distribution networks, the telegraph and the press) is *imposed* in a way as the *fruit* of such unifications: these fruits are called progress. Colonialism also gives rise, especially in France, to an unprecedented form of nationalism and (good) 'national conscience', of which Jules Ferry was one of the creators, legitimizing this approach by referring to Condorcet and the Enlightenment – in other words, the sources of progress.[29]

The nation-state was the *European* form of industrial economic development. It is in this that its fate is fundamentally tied to a modernity that is more economic and social than philosophical – the modern philosophy of the seventeenth century laying the axiomatic, conceptual and theoretical foundations of nineteenth-century modernization, in particular via modern physics, and on the basis of the Cartesian program of the mastery and possession of nature, which is today profoundly in question, and which was borne and concretized by the industrial economy, both liberal/capitalist and planned/communist, thereby constituting the conceptual basis of what is now recognized as the Anthropocene era.[30]

## 75   Welfare, supremacy and the 'Trente Glorieuses'

In the twentieth century, John Maynard Keynes and Franklin D. Roosevelt produced a new version of the nation-state, Anglo-Saxon and North American, as a federal state promoting and guaranteeing welfare, that is, a public good *superior* to particular interests and imposed upon them as the very law of solidarity in the federal nation – which is *no longer a nation of natives but of migrants*, whose unification took place before Roosevelt to a great extent through Hollywood, the first major film to be produced there, *Birth of a Nation*, being explicitly racist, and affirming the *supremacy* of the white race, which will be partly corrected but not erased by *Gone with the Wind*. Roosevelt's new approach responded, at the same time, to: 1) the internationalism proclaimed by the Bolshevik revolution at the end of the First World War; 2) the nationalist and fascist drift of the nation-state, of which Italy, Germany and Japan will in one way or another reveal the cost and the dangers of the 'national-state' invention;[31] 3) the profound irrationality of the law of the disembedded market, as described by Karl Polanyi; 4) the Taylorian revolution (the 'scientific organization of labour') that installed consumerism and what Joseph Schumpeter would in 1942 call 'creative destruction'.

The period that was later called the 'Thirty Glorious Years', arising after the Second World War from both the Philadelphia Convention and the struggles waged throughout Western Europe, is also that of the triumph of the nation-states of the so-called free world, as (according to its advocates) the very embodiment of justice and reason. At the same time, however, the colonized territories set out on their long struggle for liberation.

From the 1970s, this model fell into 'crisis', initially caused by OPEC decisions, and the world would once again change profoundly. The 'nation-state' matrix began to decline while the technical system, particularly via what was being prepared with the first forms of digital and telematic networks, was initiating a new stage of globalization – all of the consequences of which would not unfold until the beginning of the twenty-first century.

## 76   The effects of proletarianization and the future of public authority in the Anthropocene

With proletarianization, the lack of recognition of knowledge within academic institutions themselves (initially the crisis of the school, now the crisis of the university), as well as the effects of the media on public debate, and, finally, the technospheric development of the technical system through its digitalization, bringing about an upheaval throughout all the dimensions of everyday life, along with the analytical systems of scientific activity – all this and numerous other things (under the pressure of the commercialization of every kind of service) have very deeply affected the conditions of the realization of a public authority and public decision-making, and therefore of the possibility of defining the common good. Furthermore, the integration of scientific research and academic activities into the aims of R&D in the service of an *inextricably economic and technological war* has progressively cast suspicion on science as well as on reason – and, eventually, on progress in general, whether scientific, technological or social, that is, on the very will for emancipation.

As we have seen, however, the sharing and recognition of knowledge *underpinned* the very idea of the nation as a political and state organization. What first presented itself, especially in France from the 1960s onward through what has been called 'French theory', as a *social critique of the state* – academic or activist – of which Marxism in general was the matrix elsewhere, and otherwise, and earlier, and of which 1968 was the protean and specifically juvenile (which does not mean errant, but profoundly new) manifestation, has thus become, since then and after the conservative revolution, *the popular rejection of a failed state* that has in turn provoked a regressive and disturbing nostalgia for the old and authoritarian forms of the nation-state.

Revisited by taking account of the analysis by Marcel Mauss, the questions of the *relation to the national scale*, and of the nature and *functions of public authority*, today require the *rearticulation of the questions of economics and politics to territorial localities and to the industrial technology that traverses and transforms them* – currently, by disintegrating them, and where their integration, as a source of wealth and not just of value,[32] requires locality itself to be integrated as a neganthropic function at the technospheric scale. Only a *political economy of the internation* that establishes its *relevance* at the national level as an organization of relations of scale makes it possible to hope for the rapid concretization (in the state of climate emergency) of the rearrangement advocated here – in particular with regard to the transition from the microeconomic and micropolitical level to the macroeconomic and macropolitical level, *and to the metapolitical and therefore supranational level*.

Let us call metapolitics what must be elaborated at the level of what we call the internation, by way of updating the Maussian outline. As for the macropolitical relevance of the national level, it is constituted as much in historical terms (as the legacy Mauss describes in *La nation*) as in terms of 'social physics', so to speak (see p.103), inasmuch as the *geophysical and geotechnical* contents of the relations between members of the same society cannot ignore: either 1) the social dimensions preserving the relative proximity that a territory forms, without which there is no sustainable functional solidarity; or 2) the technical and technological dimensions that are constantly re-dimensioning this proximity – and that are perfectly capable of anni-hilating it, this being what is happening at this very moment.

It is not our intention here to prescribe – in any way – the *types of reticulation* that can and must be carried out 'below' and 'above' the national level. We do posit, however – and in the same spirit as David Djaïz – that to want to dispense with this level, or to make it merely the organ for the sovereign functions of maintaining order and secu-rity, is to remain totally helpless in the face of the claims of platforms to functional sovereignty[33] or efficient sovereignty (which is a contra-diction in terms). We posit that because these are *based exclusively on calculation*, they are bound to lead to both the structural insolvency of economic circuits and the hyper-exponential growth of entropy in its various forms.

## 77  New supranationality and new sovereignty

It is a question of a *new supranationality*, respectful of national locali-ties, which are also democratic centres at the scale of the experience of social physics, which obviously need to be reinvented, and *re-credibilized*, and by *revalorizing all scales of locality directly linked with the economy*. Such a question must therefore be rethought, and at the same time so too must the nation be rethought, as a *synthetic and local level of a set of localities forming a territorial coherence*, and itself inscribed in a locality that is both biospheric and techno-spheric – a meta-local (and not 'global') level in which, as a prom-ise put constantly to the test, the individuation of a new sovereignty needs to take place.

As the key issue at stake in the construction of the European Union, the question of a new supranationality has until now been quite poorly posed. And the question of earlier forms of *supremacy*, in its various forms, as the diverse forms of superiority of higher complex exorgan-isms dominating the lower (from shamans to scientific authorities, via religious institutions), has been poorly studied from the standpoint of political philosophy – and insofar as it has long been, throughout his-tory, the theopolitical question.

In fact, if clans constitute tribes, which constitute ethnic groups, and vice versa (see §13), it is because the latter project the boundaries of what, for example in the Baruya world, passes through *dreaming*[34]

– through which a cosmology is configured. If for millennia so-called 'civilized' social organizations, in the sense of being composed of towns, cities and other sedentary urbanities, always articulated power and mystery,[35] it is because, in any sustainable social organization, a way of *projecting* that which constitutes the *incalculable* horizons of the future is required, *beyond* profane institutions. As for the meaning of this word, *profane*, it will change figuratively in the nineteenth century, designating the one who does not know what the scholars and scientists know, who know above all that science is *open*, unfinished and always fed by the experience of its non-knowledge, and as the limits of reason.

When philosophy arrives in the Modern Age, followed by industrial modernization, and finally by what Max Weber described as secularization, this higher or superior level, 'above', is imposed, for example, on 'enlightened monarchs' as the power of reason – which is then *in no way* reducible to the ratios and calculations that, nevertheless, spread into society from the Renaissance onwards as accounting techniques and the management of money and credit[36] by means of ratios, which involve the understanding. As for reason, it is what grants access to ends.

## 78   Rehabilitating reason and its mystery by restoring knowledge communities

The difference between lower complex exorganisms and higher complex exorganisms, a difference that we must know how to make,[37] raises the question of the highly 'mysterious' nature of this superiority and this difference. We say that this is and will always remain 'mysterious' because it is irreducible to any calculation whatsoever: superiority, which stems from this difference that can never be emancipated either from a necessary fiction or from an irreducible performativity, can obviously, and in the name of this 'superiority',[38] very quickly and very easily be transformed into an ethnocentrism and oppression of minorities, and more generally into the creation of scapegoats. This constitutes the *pharmacology of superiority*, which, while positing that superiority stems from what stands *beyond any locality*, and in this way *opens up* any locality, can always nevertheless be localized and institutionalized in dogma, whereby the noetic promise reverses its sign, and becomes betrayal.

For millennia, superiority took the form of the spirits of magical society, the deities of mythological society, or the one true God of monotheisms. We now posit that, in secularization, this superiority amounts to what opens societies to their future as neganthropic and anti-anthropic potential – as capacities for struggling against anthropy through knowledge, which has been progressively reduced in and by secularization to mere calculation, and, now, to probabilistic correlations. It is above all in this sense that we understand the need to *reconstitute a supranational dimension founded on communities of knowledge,* cultivating what makes all knowledge an *opening* to that which remains irreducible to mere calculation, a dimension that should be embodied in what Mauss called the internation, and that should take shape by supporting the laboratory territories whose creation we are advocating (see Chapter 4).

Modern superiority has been the superiority of *science,* long considered to be the specific feature of the West – underpinning the universality of its economic and political categories. The 'proof' of this superiority, that is, its recognition, then took the name of 'progress', so we said – whether this is interpreted in the sense of the liberal heirs of the Enlightenment or in the name of Marxism, all of these then recognizing in industry a fundamental positivity from which will arise a positivist current. The scientism to which this will lead, finding its *superior* form in what Albert Einstein will call a 'paradise lost',[39] will lead precisely to *inferiorizing* this supposed superiority, that is, to reducing it to pure efficiency, whether it is placed into the service of the military enterprise, as Paul Valéry, Edmund Husserl and Albert Einstein will deplore, or *disintegrated* by the *submission* of science and knowledge in general to economic war, knowledge finding itself precisely proletarianized in one way or another – on the basis of a founding axiom that posits that everything is reducible to *calculable* information.

## Notes

1   Marcel Mauss, *La nation ou le sens du social,* corrected edition (Paris: Presses Universitaires de France, 2018), pp. 385–404.

2   Immanuel Kant, 'Idea for a Universal History with a Cosmopolitan Purpose', *Political Writings,* trans. H. B. Nisbet, 2nd edition (Cambridge: Cambridge University Press, 1991).

3   Henry Kissinger, *Diplomacy* (New York: Simon & Schuster, 1994), p. 19.

4   Mauss, *La nation ou le sens du social,* p. 396.

5   David Djaïz, *Slow démocratie* (Paris: Allary, 2019).

6    Yuk Hui, *Recursivity and Contingency* (London and New York: Rowman & Littlefield, 2019), p. 269.

7    Mauss, *La nation ou le sens du social*, p. 389.

8    It is because of this coincidence between modern physics, modern metaphysics and the political construction of the nation-state that French theory undertook its critique of the state in the wake of Marxist and Leninist critique: metaphysics (in the Kantian and then the Heideggerian sense) was understood above all as the *illusion* of mastery, of which the Cartesian program of the mastery and possession of nature remains the clearest formulation.

9    See Bernard Stiegler, *Constituer l'Europe*, 2 vols (Paris: Galilée, 2005).

10   See Djaïz, *Slow démocratie.*

11   Which is always characterized by belonging to a territory by race, ethnic origin, the primacy of soil or blood, homogeneity and isolation.

12   Alberto Magnaghi, *The Urban Village: A Charter for Democracy and Local Self-Sustainable Development*, trans. David Kerr (London and New York: Zed Books, 2005), p. 194.

13   Ibid., p. 195.

14   See Elinor Ostrom, *Governing the Commons: The Evolution of Institutions for Collective Action* (Cambridge: Cambridge University Press, 1990); Benjamin Coriat (ed.), *Le retour de communs* (Paris: Les Liens qui Libèrent, 2015); Marie Cornu et al., *Dictionnaire des biens communs* (Paris: Presses Universitaires de France, 2017).

15   Djaïz, *Slow démocratie*, p. 18.

16   Ignace Meyerson, *Les Fonctions psychologiques et les oeuvres* (Paris: Albin Michel, 1995), p. 9.

17   Augustin Berque, *Écoumène. Introduction à l'étude des milieu humains* (Paris: Belin, 1987); Berque, *Thinking Through Landscape*, trans. Anne-Marie Feenberg-Dibon (London and New York: Routledge, 2013), pp. 55–61; Berque, 'Offspring of Watsuji's Theory of Milieu: Fûdo', *GeoJournal* 60 (2004), pp. 389–96; Watsuji Tetsuro, *A Climate: A Philosophical Study*, trans. Geoffrey Bownas (Japan: Government Printing Bureau, 1961).

18   Meyerson, *Les Fonctions psychologiques et les oeuvres*; Frédéric Fruteau de Laclos, 'Emile Meyerson et les sciences humaine', *Archives de Philosophie* 70 (2007), pp. 355–58.

19    Simone Weil, *The Need for Roots: Prelude to a Declaration of Duties towards Mankind*, trans. Arthur Wills (London and New York: Routledge, 2002).

20    Gilbert Simondon, *Individuation in Light of Notions of Form and Information*, trans. Taylor Adkins (Minneapolis and London: University of Minnesota Press, 2020), p. 5.

21    Etienne Balibar and Immanuel Wallerstein, *Race, Nation, Class: Ambiguous Identities*, trans. of Balibar by Chris Turner (London and New York: Verso, 1991).

22    See Claude Lévi-Strauss, *Tristes Tropiques*, trans. John Weightman and Doreen Weightman (Harmondsworth, Middlesex: Penguin, 1976), p. 543.

23    If we admit that this distinction can be made as early as the Upper Palaeolithic.

24    Clarisse Herrenschmidt, *Les Trois Écritures. Langue, nombre, code* (Paris: Gallimard, 2007).

25    Both by the constitution of printed libraries and by the formation of Protestant schools and academies, then by Jesuit colleges, in Europe and in its colonized territories, the rediscovery of the Greco-Latin sources leading to the break with scholasticism, which comes to 'crown', so to speak, this *transformation of superiority*, that is, of its consistence.

26    This is so, despite the fact that Machiavelli is taken to be the first theorist of the state, and the fact that, in France, the formation of the state in the modern sense is often attributed to Cardinal Richelieu.

27    This European 'national movement', unfolding contemporaneously with the industrialization of Europe, should not be confused with the 'question of nationalities' as it appeared during the dismantling of the Ottoman and Austro-Hungarian empires, which is more a matter of what Freud calls 'minor differences' and Derrida calls 'petty nationalism'. On the 'narcissism of minor differences', see Sigmund Freud, 'The Taboo of Virginity (Contributions to the Psychology of Love III)', in Vol. 11 of James Strachey (ed. and trans.), *The Standard Edition of the Complete Psychological Works of Sigmund Freud* (London: Hogarth Press, 1953–74), p. 199, and Freud, *Civilization and Its Discontents*, in Vol. 21 of Strachey, *The Standard Edition of the Complete Psychological Works of Sigmund Freud*, p. 114. On 'petty nationalism', see Jacques Derrida, in Derrida and Bernard Stiegler, *Echographies of Television: Filmed Interviews*, trans. Jennifer Bajorek (Cambridge: Polity Press, 2002), p. 80.

28    Such as, for example, in France – and after the 1794 National Convention had created the École normale supérieure – the

engineering schools under Napoleon, the École pratique des hautes études (EPHE) in 1868 on the initiative of Minister Victor Duruy, the Centre national de la recherche scientifique (CNRS) just before the Second World War, the École nationale d'administration (ENA) and the Commissariat à l'énergie atomique (CEA) after the Second World War.

29  With this modernization that the advent of the nation-state will always have been, the earlier and still religious forms that constituted the links between diverse societies become attenuated, to the point that in France the state and the church are kept separate by a specific law (1905) that was the subject of long struggle and whose effects have still not been extinguished, both positively (as a right to the diversity of opinion and religious belief) and negatively (as 'laïcism' that penalizes certain religions, in particular, today, the Muslim religion).

30  Central planning was, until the 1980s, also the privilege of the state in some countries that were neither communist nor socialist, such as France or Japan.

31  And let us never forget that Europe as a unified political entity should above all avoid new nationalist divisions.

32  See ch. 3, and Alain Supiot (ed.), *Le travail au XXIè siècle* (Ivry-sur-Seine: Atelier, 2019).

33  See §31 and Frank Pasquale, 'From Territorial to Functional Sovereignty: The Case of Amazon', *Law and Political Economy* (6 December 2017), available at: <https://lpeblog.org/2017/12/06/from-territorial-to-functional-sovereignty-the-case-of-amazon/>.

34  Itself harbouring the spirits that belong to what constitutes a noetic necromass, which is to noesis what the necromass is to the biomass. On this point, see Bernard Stiegler, *Qu'appelle-t-on panser? 2. La leçon de Greta Thunberg* (Paris: Les Liens qui Libèrent, 2020). On 'dreaming', see Maurice Godelier, *The Metamorphoses of Kinship*, trans. Nora Scott (London and New York: Verso, 2011), pp. 34–38; Barbara Glowczewski, *Desert Dreamers: With the Warlpiri People of Australia*, trans. Paul Buck and Catherine Petit (Minneapolis: Univocal, 2016).

35  As divination, divine filiation or the recognition of a higher theological spiritual power, for example in Christianity, where it gathers the lower localities of the earthly kingdoms.

36  And this is why, for example, for Descartes, the idea of God is the *condition*, as 'transcendental signified', of all meaning and all signification – something that Noam Chomsky completely ignores.

37   An operation of *making (the) difference,* the question of which is raised in Immanuel Kant, 'What Does It Mean to Orient Oneself in Thinking?', trans. Allen W. Wood, *Religion and Rational Theology* (Cambridge: Cambridge University Press, 1996).

38   Also called, still today, and in North America, *supremacy.*

39   Albert Einstein, 'Paradise Lost', *Ideas and Opinions,* trans. Sonja Bargmann (New York and Avenel: Wing Books, 1954), p. 3.

# 6   Internation and Institutions

*Michał Krzykawski, Edoardo Toffoletto, Bernard Stiegler*

## Third Stage of the Internation: Science

### 79   Evolutions of the process of the individuation of reference up until Einstein

In Chapter 2, and at the beginning of the previous chapter, we distinguished complex exorganisms from simple exorganisms, and we then distinguished two kinds of complex exorganisms, called lower and higher, inferior and superior. We have posited that these are always constituted in relation to an *extraterritorial process of the individuation of reference,* which nourishes and prescribes this 'superiority'. For millennia, this prescription was magical, mythological, dynastic or religious. It is only with modernity that the superiority of reference became secularized, identifying with the ideal of knowledge that, in Kant's eyes, Newtonian physics still represented[1] – the 'Republic of Letters' then constituting the new space of extraterritorial reference, thus initiating what Max Weber would describe as secularization.

Only a form of science integrating what Immanuel Kant, like Auguste Comte, could not yet have known, and, furthermore, a revaluated science integrating the questions raised by the irreducibly pharmacological dimension of exosomatization and by the reconstitution of noetic locality as the functional fabric of an economy of the struggle against entropy – only such a science bears the possibility of *reconstituting a prescription of reference* capable of opening localities up to one another at every scale, including national localities, synthesizing them within an internation that is united so as to overcome the limits of the Anthropocene era. Faced with the challenges of the absolute need to struggle against entropy, and against its anthropic forms, only a new union of nations based on the mutual recognition of the openness of science, and of its legitimacy regained through its commitment to this struggle, will make it possible to reopen prospects capable of mobilizing, at the same time, public opinion, younger generations of learners and researchers, economic investors and public institutions supporting laboratory territories that are candidates for territorial experiments in contributory research.

In the 'post-truth era', it is only in this way that the internation could reconstitute an exorganism of reference based on a leap and a rebound in scientific cooperation. In his article 'The International of Science', dated 1922, Albert Einstein pointed out that economic development was then largely based on intellectual work. In 1919, commenting on the founding of the League of Nations, he stated:

> Nowadays we are faced with the dismaying fact that the pol-
> iticians, the practical men of affairs, have become the expo-
> nents of international ideas. It is they who have created the
> League of Nations.[2]

Einstein was acutely conscious of how nationalist passions were destroying the 'community of the intellect' (*Gemeinschaft der Geister*), that is, the community of the 'men of learning' (*Wissenschaftler*), who are themselves representatives of national traditions. As a result, he was initially enthusiastic when the International Committee on Intellectual Cooperation was set up by the League of Nations in 1922:

> This commission was to be a strictly international and
> entirely non-political body, whose business it was to put the
> intellectuals of all the nations, who were isolated by the War,
> in touch with each other. It proved a difficult task; for it has,
> alas, to be admitted that [...] the artists and men of learning
> permit themselves to governed by narrow nationalism to a
> far greater extent than the men of affairs.

Einstein stressed that this task could not 'be achieved by treaties alone. The minds of the people must, above all, be prepared for it'.[3]

What he called the 'International of Science' was intended to bring about this spiritual change.

## 80   The New International of Science

While there are still artists and men of learning, particularly in Europe, who support nationalist-populist tendencies, or who are unable to follow an authentically international way of thinking, since that time there have emerged those who compromise with the 'universalism of the market' that subjects science to the imperatives of economic war – a compromise that reinforces the 'return of nationalism', including among some intellectuals. In other words, questions about the role of science in relation to politics and economics have changed – and this is suggested in particular by that scientific community represented by the IPCC and the debates that can be provoked within the scientific community itself concerning causal and risk factors, and therefore prevention.

Contrary to what the IPCC makes possible, the global problem with science, as a production function as well as a potential legitimization of what it is in the international that goes beyond local boundaries, is indeed that scientific activities have largely been subjected, through this economic functionalization, to the prescriptions of an industrial economy that produces massive amounts of entropy and is based on proletarianization. This entropic economy thus liquidates the singularities of which knowledge has always been composed, repressing the question of localities within science itself. Consequently, public authorities and local political institutions at every scale find themselves functionally delegitimized.

In 1939, Paul Valéry wrote:

> All these values that rise and fall constitute the great market of human affairs. Among them, the unfortunate value, *spirit*, continues to decline.[4]

The sacrifice of the theoretical ideas of science and the principles of scientific research to the short-term interests of a macroeconomic model that has become unsustainable and insolvent is the final stage in this *devaluation of science* as it engenders the post-truth era, a total loss of trust, and therefore a strong potential for violence in this context of mistrust, in which only a revalorization of knowledge can make it possible to hope that this state of affairs will be overcome – and that a new period of peaceful economic cooperation, respectful of localities, will enable us to reopen future prospects at the scale of the biosphere.

Einstein's proposal to set up a new International, that of science, must be rethought with a hundred years of hindsight, and with a view to putting science back in the service of the common good and on the scale of the biosphere – and not to abandon it to the particular interests of states or corporations, however powerful they may be. As Einstein stressed in his time, international intellectual exchange must become the reference point for the global struggle for peace, which nowadays involves the struggle against entropy in all its forms. But this also requires a reconsideration of the place of science in society – and a reconsideration of science as a whole, not just as a succession of disciplinary particularities.

The interests of science – to be understood here in a broad sense: from the human and social sciences (including philosophy and the humanities) to mathematics and the neurosciences – do not conflict with the interests of the economy. On the contrary, what science (starting with economic science) must once again be able to do for economic thought (for the thinking of economic actors, from the entrepreneur to the client, via the investor and the regulator) is to provide it with a *new rational basis*, irreducible to the 'irrational motives of rationalization' that André Gorz calls 'economicizing',[5] and rehabilitating reason, as Achille Mbembe recently proposed in Klagenfurt.[6] The interests of science run counter to the interests of what has become a diseconomy, and this situation will remain unchanged so as long as the macroeconomic model continues to be based on massively entropic economies of scale that are ruinous for knowledge and devastating for the environment – what Olga Goriunova and Matthew Fuller rightly call devastation.[7]

## 81  Concerning Europe and the performativity of narrative

In this respect, what we call the internation must represent the redefinition of the tasks of universities – in relation to what Kant defined as 'scientific societies' (*Societäten der Wissenschaften*), which form an independent organization propagating and developing knowledge for the good of societies,[8] and, in particular, in an industrial society where the economy has become the issue at stake in the very survival of the biosphere, where the aim must be to constitute a new economic rationality. This rationality can only be anti-entropic, that is, in this case, capable of shedding new light on nations as localities and on their fundamental role in the development of noodiversity.

The industrial revolution, which can be understood as one of the beginnings of modernity, was possible only on the basis of the discoveries made by Descartes, Leibniz, Newton, Humboldt and many other European thinkers, who provided us with a new representation of the world by breaking with ancient cosmology. What is now urgently needed is a noetic revolution based on new scientific advances that have invalidated a good number of modern assumptions. In making this revolution, however, which must be accomplished by forging new concepts rather than erecting barricades, it is necessary to take new technological challenges into account, and to reopen, between the sciences, an essential process of reflection beyond specializations, in relation to the humanities, and by facing the colossal challenges posed by the technological transformations tied to digital networks.

Ursula von der Leyen, the new president of the European Commission, argues that Europe must become the first climate-neutral continent and a leading 'exporter of knowledge, technology and best practice'. But this exciting and exhilarating challenge can be met only on the basis of a research program commensurate with such ambitions, which should be launched in close consultation with 'scientific workers' and 'intellectual workers',[9] and provide for political decision-making an incontestable intellectual basis, free from the short-termist limitations that have been imposed on all forms of research by the diktat of short-term efficiency.

It is in this sense that Jacques Derrida was able to say, in 2004, on the occasion of the fiftieth anniversary of *Le Monde diplomatique*, that 'we must fight for what of Europe remains irreplaceable for the world to come'.[10] The struggle to cultivate this 'irreplaceability' of Europe, and against its museification (result of what Achille Mbembe describes as the inescapable mourning of its pretention to centrality[11]), should continue within the internation through its localities and in dialogue with localities outside Europe. Europe, having lost its central geopolitical position in the process of the industrial development of the world, still has the means to contribute to a new public authority and a forum for deliberation with a view to realizing a new account of the industrial economy.

Meeting this economic challenge means revaluing the different forms of knowledge and recognizing them as the linchpin of a new industrial economy resolutely committed to deproletarianization (of designers and producers as well as consumers and regulators), as the *condition* of decarbonization. In her banquet speech upon receiving the Nobel Prize for Literature, the Polish writer Olga Tokarczuk stated:

> How we think about the world and – perhaps even more importantly – how we narrate it have a massive significance.

And as she also pointed out:

> Today our problem lies – it seems – in the fact that we do not yet have ready narratives not only for the future, but even for the concrete now, for the ultra-rapid transformations of today's world. We lack the language, we lack the points of view, the metaphors, the myths and new fables. Yet we do see frequent attempts to harness rusty, anachronistic narratives that cannot fit the future to imaginaries of the future, no doubt on the assumption that an old something is better than a new nothing, or trying in this way to deal with the limitations of our own horizons. In a word, we lack new ways of telling the story of the world.[12]

It is not the vocation of the internation to offer new narratives. Nevertheless, insofar as it could contribute to the emergence of a higher complex exorganism of reference appropriate to the vital issue of the struggle against entropy and anthropy, the internation, for which we propose a transitional and experimental constitution, can and must respond to these disruptive transformations of the world that Tokarczuk describes as ultra-rapid, and that are becoming destructive of this world. For this, it will be necessary to rely on the methods of contributory research and experiments in learning laboratory territories. Only in this way can the vastness of noetic space be reopened on territories from which new narratives for the future could thereby emerge, shared by these territories, and irreducible to the constructions of 'storytelling' pre-formatted by marketing.

## Fourth Stage of the Internation: Organology of Institutions and Internation

### 82   Institutions as complex exorganisms

The internation faces the challenge of encouraging the renewal of noetic forms of life, which can be developed only on a more or less local scale, and, as far as artistic, scientific, economic and juridical forms of noesis are concerned, can be maintained only by a process of deterritorialization (and dissemination). It is faced with this irreducible relationship between the noetic and the local that institutions must be thought anew, as international and national-local exorganisms. It is through the reticulation of these exorganisms that the internation can be constituted, and constituted in the spirit of what Einstein called the International of Science.

The widespread increase of entropy is characteristic of the Anthropocene. This state of affairs has arisen, to a significant extent, due to the crisis of institutions, especially at the supranational and national scales. Indeed, if supranational institutions have all too often become *agencies* of the macroeconomic model that tends to systemically weaken national-local institutions and to impose itself on all forms of authority without respecting them,[13] the recommendations given by international institutions, and in particular the UN, do not have the necessary impact on the reality of 'business as usual' and its impoverishing and literally exhausting short-term logic.

Moreover, these recommendations often appear too abstract or too general to be implemented by nation-states, which are systematically encouraged to compete with one another internationally, and so content themselves with actions that only simulate struggling against entropy, these simulations ultimately protecting their own short-term interests. This blatant disconnection of the international, national and local scales of instituted life is the main cause of public powerlessness and the inability to confront global problems or to recognize them as they are, without fleeing from reality. It is precisely in order to reconnect these scales that there is an urgent need to *rethink the institute starting from locality* and to reinvent the ways in which localities must be associated with one another through an open and working – that is, *active* – internation, on the scale of the biosphere-cum-technosphere.

Being an irreducibly 'exorganized' form of life, that is, conditioned and organized by its artificial organs, human life is impossible without institutions – from the shaman to the UN. In their current state, however, and faced with the challenges of the Anthropocene inasmuch as it amounts to an Entropocene, institutions appear less and less legitimate and credible, because they ignore the stakes of anthropy.

As a variety of organized states of matter, human life must be instituted in order to produce neganthropy. This is why the institutions that compose the internation as a higher complex exorganism of reference at its various scales can and must rediscover (urgently) their final and common cause, which is to struggle against entropy. Institutions, however, can effectively carry out this struggle only if they take account of the thermodynamic, organic and exosomatic constraints that must be observed.

## 83   Institutional metabolism

Such an *observance* – which should be read here starting from the religious connotation that it implies, but obviously without being confined to it, and taking account of change, as these thermodynamic constraints teach us[14] – obliges us to carefully distinguish between instituting and institutionalizing, as well as to rethink this distinction in this threefold context. Generally speaking, an institution is an organization instituted for an established purpose or practice. To institute this end and establish this practice necessarily implies their institutionalization. Today, the issues of the public good and the general interest observed at the scale of the technosphere consist in determining the conditions under which these institutionalized forms of life can maintain, in themselves, by themselves and through new relations with non-institutional actors, the ability to institute new principles and actions capable of giving rise to their own transformation.

Like all existing things, institutions are doomed to die. This is what is happening now, in this transitional period through which we are living. If this death is irreversible, it must not, however, provoke despair, and it can and even must always ultimately appear as a *chance*. As collectivities of living organisms endowed with artificial organs (what we call complex exorganisms), we are capable of deferring the advent of the irreversible by instituting and institutionalizing anti-entropic and anti-anthropic processes typical of collective life and its modes of organization (within higher complex exorganisms).

The death of institutions, from which we suffer as the development of anomie, and which confronts us with great dangers, obviously also contains something beneficial: it can and must enjoin us to redefine the final cause of their existence. To attempt this redefinition on the basis of thermodynamic, organic and exosomatic construction and the post-Newtonian framework it forms implies reviewing the question of stability in a new light, and overcoming it with the concept of metastability by redefining the relationship between necessary institutional sustainability and the irreversible and equally necessary temporary character of any institution.

Let us examine the phenomenon of instituting and institutionalizing collective life in the light of the arrow of time, which means that time always flows in the same direction, like a horizontal hourglass (oriented by entropy) and not just a vertical one (oriented by gravitation): once an institution is established, its entropy is bound to increase with time, this increase being irreversible. If we admit that an institution is an open system, we can see that it is through the exchange of information, prescriptions and actions (participating in the constitution of processes of the transindividuation of reference) that an institution maintains its negentropic power, such that it is capable of instituting new processes within itself (through what we call its anti-anthropy), and consequently of delaying its *hardening* (its sclerosis) through the continuous process of its own metamorphosis.

The dynamics driving these two processes of instituting ('founding') and institutionalizing (prescribing from this 'foundation') make it necessary to redefine institutions both intra-institutionally and inter-institutionally. These two planes amount to two sides of what might be called *institutional metabolism,* insofar as negentropic processes can be institutionally established only if both of these sides are taken into account *at the same time.*

An institution can preserve itself through its inter-institutional relations as it exchanges and composes with its milieu, itself composed of other institutions. In order for this exchange to be the operation of an inter-institutional transformation, however, an institution must be capable of adopting intra-institutional changes that allow it to maintain a high energetic potential (that is, a potential différance from individual and collective drive-based automatisms and transitional power in the sense of Donald Winnicott, forming knowledge that itself constitutes circuits of transindividuation) and to open (by working) new possibilities of inter-institutional exchange.

Openness on an *inter*-institutional and multiscalar level – on the scales of smaller localities, starting from the nano-locality that is the individual itself, and larger localities, the largest of which is the technospherized and exospherized biosphere[15] – can arise only from openness *practised* on the *intra*-institutional level. And the institutional deficiency that we have been experiencing since the Entropocene is due to the absence of such a double opening, and its scalability, as well as ignorance of the dynamics that make it effective, and a bearer of negentropy and neganthropy.

In the name of *efficiency*, platforms claim to fill this institutional malaise with calculation. This false road, which is a *calamitous impasse*, in the strict sense of the words 'calamity' and 'impasse', demobilizes institutions and their officials (those who assume such functions as were first laid down in ancient China and as scalabilities in that vast locality), and renders them powerless in the struggle against entropy. This is so because purposes in general and those of the 'functionaries' thanks to whom or because of whom an institution functions or dysfunctions (through its metabolism and its catabolism) are simply not reducible to efficiency.

## 84  Metabolism and anabolism in higher complex exorganisms: from Newton to Whitehead and Lotka

Calculation is not a response to institutional deficiency. On the contrary, it *aggravates* the calamitous effects of anthropic transformations of habitable environments, both for living things in general and for exorganic living things, whether natural or social. The challenge consists in reinventing institutions capable of anti-anthropic transformations, that is, institutions that act beyond calculation: only *deliberation* still allows hope for a 'shift' that is not completely chaotic.[16]

The institutional fact, like calculation, is a human fact – constitutive of any humanity that has not yet sunk into the inhuman. These human facts, however, must not lead to a deadening anthropization: they must encourage anti-anthropic flourishing. Opting for anti-anthropy in the context of the institutional organization of human life (non-inhuman life, which is *also* to say, capable of taking the interests of non-human life into account) implies, however, opening the question of collective individuation based on a transindividuation of singularities that are nourished – always on a more or less local scale – by those traces of human experience that form knowledge and accumulate as a noetic necromass composed of works (in Meyerson's sense).[17]

The question of collective individuation, therefore, amounts to the question of knowing under what conditions an institution can and must encourage this or that transindividuation through the transformations arising from the noetic necromass (which Simondon calls the preindividual fund), which becomes a germ for anti-anthropically organized forms of life (as the psychic individuation of singularities). The noetic necromass, however, is first and foremost composed of recordings and repetitions of all kinds (as objects, tools, fetishes, rituals, archives, writings, where the latter may be handwritten or printed manuscripts, whether ideographical or alphabetical), photo-graphs, phono-graphs, and so on, and finally 'data' of all kinds, fundamentally transformed into calculable information in a technosphere surrounded by an exosphere of satellites.

An institution is anti-anthropic insofar as it recognizes its local and therefore restricted condition, and that what it has is irreversibly temporary and therefore precarious. This is where the Newtonian manner of conceiving institutions and their sustainability becomes highly toxic and deficient. 'The duration or perseverance of the existence of things is the same, whether their motions are rapid or slow or null', Newton posited in his *Principia*.[18] From a *processual* standpoint, however, the opposite is true: the perseverance of things is due to their *movement*, itself generated in the process of their infinite transformations.

If these transformations occur in things that are finite, these are not, however, finite forms, insofar as, by transforming themselves, they become *other* than themselves – 'oneself as another', as Paul Ricoeur said.[19] And if they seem to constitute perceptible forms, these are only temporary states in the infinite process of their transformation. What remains indefinitely the same is that everything is constantly changing all together (this union constituting what Whitehead calls concrescence), while the sameness of this metamorphic process appears through temporary and infinitely differing forms that constitute, on the scale of exorganisms, their noodiversity.

Modern institutions, along with modern thought about institutions, have never recognized this temporary character – which is inherent to them and the very *condition* of their sustainability. Consequently, modern institutions, and our institutions are still modern, remain *conceptually disarmed* and prove to be incapable of *embracing irreversible change* as a vital constraint on the physical world and everything that emerges from it. It is therefore necessary to mobilize, at the level of institutional foundations, the concept of concrescence proposed in *Process and Reality*, together with Lotka's analysis in 'The Law of Evolution as a Maximal Principle'.

## 85   From Newton to Bergson: institutions as treatments for the aporias of the struggle against entropy

This disarmament becomes particularly striking with the advent of the conservative revolution, which amounts to a systemic attack on modern institutions belonging to nation-states, now paralysed by the imperative to *adapt* to the new global reality which was essentially that of economic warfare – soon to be doubled by technological warfare. Institutions have thus been deprived and in a way stripped of their potential to institute negentropic processes that would allow them to respond to this change by adopting it – instead of resigning themselves to adapting to it, and consequently 'losing their soul' as well as their *ēthos* (see Chapter 7).

Admittedly, to conceive institutional sustainability on the basis of change is a difficult, and above all counter-intuitive, task: as Newton describes it, duration always seems to us to start from stability – including as what we have the right to demand of our institutions. Change, on the contrary, especially when it is constant, presents itself as evidence of instability.

It must be said that modern common sense, as well as modern general culture, have failed to incorporate thermodynamic constraints – from entropy as conceptualized by Clausius to entropy as rethought by Schrödinger and Georgescu-Roegen in relation to, respectively, living organisms and the economic process, even if the ways they do so are limited. Only Bergson really took note of what fundamentally changes with respect to time and space reconsidered as dimensions of a process – and he did so by anticipating Lotka, defining intelligence as above all *fabrication* (*Homo faber*).

Entropy remains for us a 'prodigiously abstract' concept, as Poincaré said,[20] and seems to have little to do with matters that concern us 'down here' – even though the need to feed oneself, to 'clean up', to educate children, and so on (all these being diverse forms of economy), are daily and constant experiences of the need to counteract the increase of entropy, accelerated as it is by the appearance of life in the biosphere: there is no local increase of negentropy that does not come at the cost of a relative increase of entropy. This is why most of our theoretical approaches to economics, including those focused on the free market, politics, society, technology, nature, culture, nation and institutions, are based on assumptions that no longer hold in the face of the scientific achievements of the twentieth century, from thermodynamic physics and biology to technology and sociology.

The common sense [*bon sens*] – if not common sense [*sens commun*] as sought by Kant and Whitehead – that makes us associate duration with stability and change with instability, comes from the perception of objects, beginning much earlier than Newtonian mechanics. In fact, the distinction between stability and instability dates back to Eleatic (and Parmenidean, since Heraclitus says something quite different) antiquity. The Newtonian approach to time, space, place and movement was revolutionary because it showed that these quantities must be taken into account beyond the objects we perceive through the senses – as we saw with respect to inertia (see Chapter 1). Newtonian mechanics, however, did not question the ancient distinction between stability and instability, rest and movement. Consequently, the notion of equilibrium could be defined only in terms of stability, while instability refers to disequilibrium.

## 86   Fighting against breakage: the institution as metastabilization and disruption of disruption

Rethinking institutions by taking thermodynamic, organic and exosomatic constraints into account obliges us to review the dynamic between instituting (founding) and institutionalizing (transindividuating) on the basis of the notions of metastable equilibrium and phase transition, referring to physical properties as different states of matter that themselves call for overcoming the opposition between form and matter – what Gilbert Simondon calls the hylomorphic schema. As he showed, 'to define metastability, it is necessary to establish the notion of the potential energy of a system, the notion of order, and the notion of the increase of entropy'.[21] Taking these notions into account makes it possible to define a metastable state that is quite unlike a stable state inasmuch as its equilibrium is always precarious and constitutes a phase in a temporal process: if the equilibrium can be macroscopically maintained with weak perturbations, strong perturbations can induce a transformation of the state, which thereby becomes more stable or passes to another state of metastability.

With regard to living organisms or open exorganic systems such as institutions, their metastability must be recognized as their vital and more than vital condition (binding the generations on the basis of the continuity of the noetic necromass inasmuch as it bears the anti-anthropic potential for bifurcations). A metastable exorganism can maintain itself as 'alive' (that is, participating in the psychic and collective individuation of a set of exorganic individuals) as long as it retains the energetic (that is, anti-anthropic) potential that makes it capable of maintaining metastability in the process of transforming itself and the milieu within which this transformation takes places, and of which it is a performative occurrence. To struggle against entropy and anthropy is possible neither for stable institutions nor for unstable institutions. Institutions holding the promise of a future, that is, of neganthropy, must be metastable in order to adopt meta-morphic reality and contribute performatively to its concrescent realization. Here, adopting means adopting oneself through the other by transforming oneself into this alterity, and this implies metastabilizing oneself and remaining perpetually open to intra-institutional and inter-institutional alterations.

In this respect, metastability is a state from which to investigate the *responsibility* of institutions. If it proves incapable of maintaining its *metastable* equilibrium – which means that the logic of this maintenance has nothing to do with political or ideological conservatism: it calls for the constancy of change, and in this sense for the radicality of potential *bifurcations*, that is, for what Simondon calls major improvements, rather than the 'minor improvements' that constitute 'reform', however radical it may seem to be – an institution can be considered irresponsible, insofar as it does not respond to the increase of entropy and, consequently, works towards destabilization.

An unstable institution can be considered irresponsible in that it disregards the very principle of transformation and becomes an agent of entropic deformation, because it cannot inscribe the temporary into its physical temporality. Indeed, any transformation requires the existence of an old form – which can be defined as the past – to be transformed and renewed in a metastable equilibrium that opens the future. The temporary that is not inscribed in temporality cannot produce new institutions – be they organizations or established practices – because it contributes to the destabilization and decomposition of the state of things, rather than transforming it so as to give rise to new compositions.

It has today become urgent and crucial to respond with institutional metastability to disruption as a strategy of the technological giants, given that the latter are causing unprecedented social destabilization. This disruption is purely destructive, and this destruction is openly articulated in two famous Facebook slogans: 'Move Fast and Break Things' and 'Move Fast With Stable Infra[structure]'.[22] If breaking things and moving quickly are done without any relationship to the past, which excludes any real transformation and promises imminent chaos, stable infrastructure is what makes this über-closure absolute – and absolutely entropic – and brings no hope for the future inasmuch as the future is strictly and radically indeterminate, that is, incalculable, improbable and unknown.

However serious the chaotic threat posed by this hyper-closure may be, it has, to date, been fundamentally misunderstood or denied.

Confronting this threat means taking as a starting point the fact that the institutional challenge to be met in the years to come will be to produce a metastable institutional disruption, but so as to find a new metastable equilibrium on the scale of the technosphere, through which the institutional struggle against entropy would become not only possible, but obvious. This means that we must act rationally within metastable institutions and take care of things – instead of breaking them.

## 87 Five principles for metastable institutions nourished by transdisciplinary disputes

Metastable institutions must be *immediately* reinvented, if we are to truly 'change course by 2020' and 'avoid runaway climate change, with disastrous consequences for people and all the natural systems that sustain us', as António Guterres said in September 2018.[23] Of course, such a reinvention is beyond the capacities of our collective. If, however, we base ourselves on shared knowledge and scientific understanding, and if we admit, as is the rule in the field of reason, that solutions that are achievable in the short term but compatible with the long term in a thermodynamic, biological and exosomatic processuality can be elaborated only through *transdisciplinary disputes*, then we propose five principles, as a way of outlining a point of departure for a debate on institutions in the internation as a higher complex exorganism of reference, composed of multiple localities:

1   A neganthropic and anti-anthropic (see §§21–22) institution is a complex exorganism capable of transforming its form and structure, and of doing so in relation to its milieu, this transformation taking place in this milieu that itself metamorphoses in return. Such an institution makes it possible to invent new processes on the basis of already institutionalized forms.

2   The real power of a neganthropic and anti-anthropic institution comes from its energetic potential, which it knows how to conserve and save for new transformations allowing it to postpone irreversible institutional sclerosis. Such an institution recognizes transformation as its mode of existence. The capacity to transform should therefore become the object of a specific and primordial institutional care.

3   A neganthropic and anti-anthropic institution is sustainable only as an exorganism associated with other institutions,

and it recognizes that this associative relation constitutes the unsurpassable condition on the basis of which the institutional production of neganthropic and anti-anthropic processes is possible on the scale of the technosphere and as a world-making [*faire-monde*] rather than as befouling and de-worlding [*immondialisation*] that in turn provokes reactions of closure.

4 Whether large or small, international, national-local or infra-national, any neganthropic and anti-anthropic institution exists and is inscribed in different scales of locality. Local energy can be conserved, and can feed into anti-anthropic practices, only locally, and on the condition that it is valued beyond its own locality. That the institutional fact is irreducibly a local fact does not mean, however, that institutions on the scale of the biosphere are doomed to fail: the biosphere is itself a locality. Institutions on the biospheric and technospheric scale are necessary, and they must be capable of preserving their metastable equilibrium through neganthropic actions taken at more or less local scales – and respecting local specificities, which are always singular. The neganthropic 'global' can exist effectively only on the condition of being transformed locally.

5 Instituting and institutionalizing so as to produce neganthropy is possible only through deliberation, that is, through the co-production of rational argument, which must be functionally distinguished from competition as a power struggle. In this respect, neganthropic and anti-anthropic institutions must become the *bouleteriou* of the twenty-first century: in the cities of ancient Greece, the *bouleuterion* was the building where the assembled citizens met to deliberate, so as to open up the future within becoming, through an elaboration of the *boulē*.[24] On the threshold of the third decade of the twenty-first century, and faced with the global challenges of the Anthropocene, these *bouleteriou* should be rethought within a contributory general economy (in Georges Bataille's sense[25]). As a higher complex exorganism of reference, the internation encourages deliberation in its localized institutions at more or less local scales and recognizes that a common and internationalizable wish – to have 'something [...] (more) desirable'[26] in view when determining the *boulē* – can be realized and negotiated in its

multiple local variants, which are differentiated from one
another to such an extent that they transform the wish itself.

A lasting, amicable institution, open to life and respectful of thermodynamic, organic and exosomatic constraints, is one that is capable of putting itself into question, as well as recognizing itself as what
Jacques Derrida sometimes defined as a 'counter-institution'. For
Derrida, a counter-institution had to guarantee a place for 'expertise
and experimentation', as well as the 'incalculable'.[27] Derrida never
talked about metastability. Rethought in the light of phase transition,
however, the counter-institution can be understood today as the metastable institution. This is certainly not just a simple terminological
substitution. For Derrida, a counter-institution is of non-governmental origin, which suggests that its *raison d'être* is instead to be found
beyond the framework of established institutions. Today, however, the
institutional challenge consists in developing a new concept of governmentality as metastability, that is, the ability to maintain a metastable equilibrium in a process of infinite transformation.

## Notes

1   Ignace Meyerson, *Les Fonctions psychologiques et les oeuvres* (Paris:
    Albin Michel, 1995), p. 189: 'Science seems, in Kant, to be almost
    complete. He is "dazzled", as has often been said, by Newtonian
    physics [...], the essential has been acquired [...], the principles and
    frameworks cannot vary. Comte will still hold a similar position.
    The progress of physics and chemistry over the nineteenth century
    will destroy this dogmatism.'

2   Albert Einstein, 'Paradise Lost', *Ideas and Opinions*, trans. Sonja
    Bargmann (New York and Avenel: Wing Books, 1954), p. 3.

3   Einstein, 'The Institute of Intellectual Cooperation', *Ideas and
    Opinions*, p. 86.

4   Paul Valéry, 'Freedom of the Mind', in Jackson Mathews (ed.), *The
    Collected Works of Paul Valéry, Volume 10: History and Politics*,
    trans. Denise Folliot and Jackson Mathews (New York: Bollingen,
    1962), p. 190, translation modified.

5   André Gorz, *Critique of Economic Reason*, trans. Gillian Handyside
    and Chris Turner (London and New York: Verso, 1989), pp. 1–7;
    Gorz, *Farewell to the Working Class: An Essay on Post-Industrial
    Socialism*, trans. Michael Sonenscher (London and Sydney: Pluto
    Press, 1982).

6    Achille Mbembe, 'Bodies as Borders', *From the European South* 4 (2019), pp. 5–18, available at: <http://europeansouth.postcolonialita-lia.it/journal/2019-4/2.Mbembe.pdf>.

7    Matthew Fuller and Olga Goriunova, *Bleak Joys: Aesthetics of Ecology and Impossibility* (Minneapolis and London: University of Minnesota Press, 2019).

8    Kant, 'The Conflict of the Faculties', trans. Mary J. Gregor and Robert Anchor, *Religion and Rational Theology* (Cambridge: Cambridge University Press, 1996), p. 247.

9    Einstein, 'The International of Science', *Ideas and Opinions*, p. 83.

10   Jacques Derrida, 'A Europe of Hope', trans. Pleshette DeArmitt, Justine Malle and Kas Saghafi, *Epoché* 10 (2006), p. 410 (originally published in *Le Monde diplomatique* in 2004).

11   Achille Mbembe, *Critique of Black Reason*, trans. Laurent Dubois (Durham and London: Duke University Press, 2017).

12   Olga Tokarczuk, 'Nobel Lecture' (2018), trans. Jennifer Croft and Antonia Lloyd-Jones, p. 3, available at: <https://www.nobelprize. org/uploads/2019/12/tokarczuk-lecture-english-2.pdf>.

13   David Djaïz, *Slow démocratie* (Paris: Allary, 2019).

14   This means that taking these constraints into account is possible only through open dialogue, devoid of cynicism and beyond postur-ing, between the sciences, which can and must feed into each other's exchanges so as to work for social development and to develop a way in which these exchanges could be translated into concrete politi-cal decisions. We posit that it is through this dialogue that we must rethink what Einstein defined in 1930 as 'cosmic religious feeling' (Einstein, 'Religion and Science', *Ideas and Opinions*, p. 38).

15   On this question, see the 2017–2018 pharmakon.fr seminar: <https:// iri-ressources.org/collections/season-48.html>.

16   Anthony D. Barnosky et al., 'Approaching a State Shift in Earth's Biosphere', *Nature* 486 (7 June 2012), pp. 52–58.

17   See Bernard Stiegler, *Qu'appelle-t-on panser? 2: La leçon de Greta Thunberg* (Paris: Les Liens qui Libèrent, 2020), p. 17: 'The noetic necromass […] is as essential to noetic living things as the necromass formed by the humus resulting from the decomposition of vegetable and animal matter is essential to the plant and animal biomass.'

18   Isaac Newton, *The Principia: Mathematical Principles of Natural Philosophy*, trans. I. Bernard Cohen and Anne Whitman, assisted by Julia Budenz (Oakland: University of California Press, 1999), p. 56.

19   Paul Ricoeur, *Oneself as Another*, trans. Kathleen Blamey (Chicago and London: University of Chicago Press, 1992).

20   Henri Poincaré, *The Foundations of Science*, trans. George Bruce Halsted (Cambridge: Cambridge University Press, 2015), p. 151. See also Dominique Lecourt (ed.), *Dictionnaire d'histoire et philosophie des sciences* (Paris: Presses Universitaires de France, 2006), p. 418.

21   Gilbert Simondon, *Individuation in Light of Notions of Form and Information*, trans. Taylor Adkins (Minneapolis and London: University of Minnesota Press, 2020), p. 5.

22   See 'Facebook's Old Motto was "Move Fast and Break Things"', *Mind Matters* (19 October 2018), available at: <https://mindmatters. ai/2018/10/facebooks-old-motto-was-move-fast-and-break-things/>.

23   'Secretary-General's Remarks on Climate Change' (10 September 2018), available at: <https://www. un.org/sg/en/content/sg/statement/2018-09-10/ secretary-generals-remarks-climate-change-delivered>.

24   See Claude Romano, 'Will', in Barbara Cassin (ed.), *Dictionary of Untranslatables: A Philosophical Lexicon*, trans. Steven Rendall et al. (Princeton and Oxford: Princeton University Press, 2014), pp. 1234–35.

25   Or of what he tried to describe as an 'economy commensurate with the universe', which must, however, be rethought on the basis of thermodynamic, organic and exosomatic constraints. See Georges Bataille, 'L'économie à la mesure de l'univers', *Oeuvres complètes*, vol. 7 (Paris: Gallimard, 1976), pp. 7–16, Bataille, 'The Economy to the Proportion of the Universe', trans. Michael Richardson, in Bataille, *Georges Bataille: Essential Writings* (London: Sage, 1998), pp. 74–79, and Bataille, *The Accursed Share: An Essay on General Economy, Volume 1: Consumption*, trans. Robert Hurley (New York: Zone Books, 1988).

26   Bruno Snell, quoted in Romano, 'Will', p. 1234.

27   Jacques Derrida, 'The Philosophical Model of the Counter-Institution', trans. Jeffrey Mehlman, in Christopher Benfey and Karen Remmley (eds), *Artists, Intellectuals, and World War II: The Pontigny Encounters at Mount Holyoke College, 1942–1944* (Amherst: University of Massachusetts Press, 2006), p. 54.

**7**   Contributory Design and Deliberative Digital Technologies: Towards Social Generativity in Automatic Societies

*Anne Alombert, Vincent Puig, Bernard Stiegler*

> Design must become an innovative, highly creative, cross-disciplinary tool responsive to the true needs of men. It must be more research oriented, and we must stop defiling the earth itself with poorly designed objects and structures. [...] As socially and morally involved designers, we must address ourselves to the needs of a world with its back to the wall, while the hands on the clock point perpetually to one minute before twelve.
>
> *Victor Papanek[1]*

## I   Considerations

### 88   The new industrial context: from uses to practices

The industrialization of production (described by Marx in the second half of the nineteenth century) and the advent of consumer capitalism, that is, the creative destruction theorized by Joseph Schumpeter, have led to the proletarianization of ways of life, now prescribed by marketing campaigns, themselves prepared by market research.[2] These evolutions have tended to contribute to the replacement of *aesthetic experience*, which requires subjects to participate in the symbolic, with *aesthetic conditioning*, the aim of which is to capture, channel and standardize the attention of consumers in order to direct them towards consumption.[3] As Mauro Magatti and Laura Gherardi point out in their more recent analysis of contemporary capitalism, the negative consequences of the consumerist economic model are today showing themselves in all their power: 'individualized hyper-consumption', 'weakening of social bonds and shared meanings', 'anomie' and 'psychic suffering' are today all issues under the sociological microscope[4] – and they combine with the anxiety, anguish and sometimes suicidal acts caused by the ruinous effects of the acceleration of the Anthropocene.[5]

In his work on technology, Simondon already pointed out the risks inherent in the industrialization of production and the circulation of 'closed' technical objects on the market: users come to possess 'indecipherable' objects whose internal workings remain foreign to them, with which they cannot connect and through which they cannot individuate themselves.[6] The socialization of everyday objects, which traditionally occurred through the intergenerational transmission of *knowledge* and *practices,* now occurs through *uses* prescribed by standardized instructions and pre-programmed user guides, which thereby replace the singular and noodiversified arts of living that had hitherto been generated by local processes of collective individuation.

Despite the alternative potential afforded by the free software movement and related approaches, the way that environments and everyday objects (internet, web, smartphones, connected things and habitats) have been digitalized has to a large extent exacerbated this tendency – and apart from the production of highly professional software, free software itself has mostly been diluted into contributory models of open source production. This is how proletarianization intensifies as it develops in all dimensions of existence: through the diffusion of electronic objects whose functioning remains inaccessible to users. Without the development of the technical culture necessary to transform uses into practices, the technico-economic models that control the functioning of these digital systems (platform capitalism and the data economy) mainly aim to collect a vast set of traces and to control behaviour, leading to what Antoinette Rouvroy and Thomas Berns describe as 'algorithmic governmentality'.[7]

In recent years, the promise of digital networks has given way to profound doubt. Such doubts first emerged among hackers and 'hacktivists' (who are generally the best informed about technological developments), but now there is concern among the general public, as well as non-governmental organizations such as Amnesty International, who in a recent report highlighted how digital giants threaten fundamental rights.[8] This 'net blues'[9] is intrinsically linked to the evolution of digital media: as Geert Lovink has shown,[10] the transition from the web to platforms, along with the appearance of large 'social' networks, 'apps' and smartphones, means that 'link practices' are being degraded into an 'economy of likes', 'captology' and 'nudging', giving rise to various forms of social toxicity: individual profiling, information filter bubbles, the destructive economic exploitation of massively anthropized social relations and psychic resources, including in infants, for whom the consequences are extreme.[11]

As we have seen in previous chapters, from a geopolitical standpoint, the hegemony of platforms has led to the replacement of territorial sovereignties (urban, national, international) with a functional or efficient 'sovereignty',[12] subjecting populations to the control of the web giants and no longer to the authorities of political representatives. At the same time, localities are increasingly short-circuited, leading to concomitant increases in the rates of the various forms of entropy (thermodynamic, biological and informational).

## 89   Contributory design and digital studies

From the standpoint of design practice itself, these evolutions, which are anthropic in the sense put forward in Chapter 1, tend to replace the exercise of *invention* with the imperative of *innovation*: as Pierre-Damien Huyghe describes, design tends to be 'sloppy in the management of innovation', to the detriment of reflection on utility and caring about the forms that characterize it.[13] Hence designers, too, are subject to the process of proletarianization and that to which it gives rise: work without qualities.[14]

There is abundant research on specialized design, user experience design (UX), interface design (UI), 'design thinking', and so on, but research aimed at transforming methods and technologies in order to strengthen social ties and the production of practical value (in the sense we have established) is far less common. If it is a question of implementing 'design for the real world', however, that is, design in context and aware of its 'moral responsibilities',[15] then design cannot ignore either the contemporary digital technical milieu or its social function. The question thereby raised is how to take advantage of digital transformations so as to reinvent uses in everyday life, and, especially, to transform these (individual and standardized) uses into (singular and collective) practices.

We ourselves will refer here to contributory design, tied to contributory research, and in view of a contributory economy. This contributory economy must be political as well as mental: it must be, in a way, a general economy in the sense of Georges Bataille, which means that it is necessarily contributory. This entails the redefinition of the function of the multidisciplinary activity that is design, as part of what was first of all a socialization and consumption function, just as knowledge becomes a production function (see Chapter 4). As part of its social and political functions, in the context of the Anthropocene era and disenchantment with digital networks, design must fundamentally rethink the functioning of digital technologies,[16] if it is to be able to lay claim to the organization of new modes of collective life integrating the neganthropic function of reticular and scalar localities, and enabling inhabitants, through contributory technologies, to adopt new technical milieus – today characterized by the process of infrasomatization described by David M. Berry (see Chapter 2). It is therefore a question of encouraging the invention of new design practices (called 'practical organology' by the Digital Studies Network) associating inhabitants and enabling them to *locally prescribe* transformations of their everyday environments.

To do so, it seems necessary to accompany these practices with critical reflection based on digital studies, and to design, with theoretical computer scientists and software development engineers, new digital systems and devices (hermeneutic functionalities and deliberative social networks) to support and intensify contributory practices that can also be said to be *generative* in the sense proposed by Mauro Magatti, Chiara Giaccardi and Laura Gherardi. This chapter will therefore try to suggest two directions for design in hyper-industrial societies:

- the intensification of contributory design practices, involving inhabitants in the design and construction of their technical and urban environments through 'generative social actions';[17]

- the design and development of *contributory digital technologies*, allowing individuals to express themselves and to stage confrontations between points of view, thus generating processes of discussion, debate and collective deliberation, which are constitutive of collective intelligence.

It is a matter of initiating the development of a new technical culture (based on collective practices rather than individual uses) and a new industrial and technological politics (supporting the development of open, deliberative and contributory systems and caring and learning communities) – with a view to a contributory psychic and political economy.

## II  Open Cities and Contributory Design: Design that Serves 'Social Generativity'

### 90  Open city, territorial design and the ethics of cooperation

By making the unfinished or incomplete character of infrastructure a condition of possibility of the open city, Richard Sennett[18] invites us to consider the city as an open system, capable of being transformed over time and of hosting improbable events (unlike closed systems, characterized by their functional overdetermination, integration, homogeneity and predictability). Recall here that an open system is a negentropic living system in the general system theory of Ludwig von Bertalanffy – and that the city is here conceived as a complex exorganism in the sense proposed in Chapter 2.

According to Sennett, the design of the open city must make use of incomplete or unfinished architectural forms capable of being modified over time, according to the needs of the inhabitants and by these very inhabitants themselves: the forms must be able to change together with the functions of the buildings, thus becoming living, evolving structures. To this principle of incompleteness should be added the need for urban density and social and cultural diversity, which makes possible unexpected encounters and improbable bifurcations. Like Saskia Sassen, Sennett thus invites us to conceive borders (between cities, between neighbourhoods, between buildings) as membranes rather than as walls, or in other words as always porous boundaries, places of interaction and exchange.

Within such urban forms, it is necessary to develop what Sennett describes as an 'ethics of cooperation':[19] collective activities in which individuals come together in order to face the difficulties of everyday life. The design of the open city thus revives the participatory architecture projects developed in particular by Lucien Kroll, constituting knowledge communities (involving work knowledge, life knowledge, technical knowledge, theoretical knowledge) that are opposed to the individualistic and competitive tendencies of contemporary capitalist societies.

## 91   Social generativity

These rich and dynamic forms of collective life, over the course of which inhabitants confront problems, research solutions and explore unforeseen possibilities, also lie at the heart of what Magatti, Giaccardi and Gherardi describe as 'social generativity', which in their view is the only viable response to the crisis of hyper-consumerist societies. Social generativity is a form of self-realization – that is, individuation – in which the individual acts in a positive and creative way, thus contributing to the production of his or her milieu by promoting the realization of other individuals. Generative action is characterized by a threefold enrichment:

- capacitation, in Amartya Sen's sense;

- the satisfaction of the individual, who realizes an inner desire by exercising his or her creativity;

- the improvement of the social and technical context, of which individuals take care collectively and for the sake of future generations.

Generative social action is a dynamic collective process that unfolds in a variety of organizations, through which the group makes its original contribution to the world and leaves a trace of its passage. Such a process makes it possible to struggle against the entropic effects of institutionalization (see Chapter 6), producing novelty on the basis of shared enthusiasm. In this way, psychic individuals can discover that their own realization contributes to the realization of others: to their freedom – beyond any logic of control or domination. It is in this sense that Magatti, Giaccardi and Gherardi call for a 'generative society' that allows, builds and strengthens the infrastructure supporting collective care activities, the circulation of knowledge and the constitution of sustainable communities generating shared value:[20] this is how, in their vocabulary, a contributory political and psychic economy can be described.

   Shared value, which is here referred to more generally as practical value, goes beyond the market or purely financial accounting. On the economic level, the production of value comes from a relationship between contributors and their relationship to their environment, through which communities of neganthropic knowledge can be constituted (see §5). Shared value comes from the knowledge that circulates between individuals and enables them to take care of their common exosomatized milieus (which are complex exorganisms) by actively participating in the production of their everyday environments.

## III   The Hermeneutic and Contributory Web: Algorithms in the Service of Collective Intelligence

### 92   Social calculability and the destruction of noodiversity

In his contribution to the book *Digital Studies. Organologie des savoirs et technologies de la connaissance,* David Bates shows how, during the initial formulation of cybernetics, the models it produced and the reflections on the possibilities of artificial intelligence were far more cautious than is the case in the highly ideological computational cognitivism that has led to the transhumanist fable:

> Looking back at the very beginnings of the digital era, when what was to become the computer was beginning to be conceptualized, and when the idea of artificial intelligence was beginning to make its appearance, [...] the notion of computer science was not [...] entirely settled on the notion of automaticity. Primitive computers, as intellectual technologies, aspired to the characteristic flexibility of the brain [its plasticity], precisely because it suggested the possibility of creative intelligence that went beyond mere automatism.[21]

At that time, the notion of intelligence first and foremost meant the capacity for dis-automatization and tolerance for errors. The wish to eliminate error and to automate everything inevitably generates an anthropic tendency whose effects we are now witnessing in most aspects of everyday life.

Indeed, many studies now show the entropic effects (standardization, homogenization, synchronization) of the current functioning of digital technologies, in particular on social relations and language practices. These two essential dimensions of human political life are today subject to the market logic of the digital economy of attention or expression: social relations and language practices are systematically calculated, standardized, homogenized, 'dis-idiomatized' and 'de-historicized'. Algorithmic calculations applied to social relations or linguistic practices tend to eliminate the inherently singular and improbable dimension of social encounters and individual expressions.

First of all, this concerns social relations. While John L. Pfaltz shows that social networks tend to spontaneously produce stereotypical graphs and function according to entropic tendencies, Cléo Collomb, Igor Galligo and Filipe Pais show that social networks like Tinder, based on the quantification of 'likes' or 'matches', lead to an entropic dissemination of attention and a depletion of libidinal energy, which encourages the repetition of pre-programmed addictive uses rather than focusing on an object of desire, which is always singular, improbable and incalculable.[22] The process of idealization through which the object of desire is singularized is thus short-circuited by the functioning of real-time dating applications, which generate 'zapping' and hyper-solicitation effects, as well as a standardization of practices and profiles.

Second, it concerns linguistic practices. The work of Frédéric Kaplan on linguistic capitalism shows how Google's business model makes it possible to exploit user-generated linguistic material for commercial ends, by speculating on word searches.[23] In return, this new real-time linguistic market has effects on the evolution of language practices: autocompletion algorithms automatically transform user searches into statistically probable and economically profitable expressions. Google's algorithms thus tend to subject so-called 'natural' languages to the constraints of the global economy, eliminating the least calculable idiomatic forms that lie at the base of the diachronic evolution of languages, and therefore of their diversity and historicity, bypassing the localities within which idioms occur. These problems of 'dis-idiomatization' also arise with machine translation software, in particular because the 'pivot languages' used by algorithms impose the lexical and grammatical structure of English during the translation process, thus leading to a 'linguistic imperialism' based on denying the real diversity of languages.[24]

## 93  Thinking and generating meaning and signification beyond information theory: towards deliberative contribution platforms

These phenomena are described by Maël Montévil in terms of entropy.[25] Montévil describes Google Translate as a statistical machine that uses a database to determine the most probable translation. It is a machine that finds the statistically average translation according to the data at its disposal, but it is unable to introduce a new word into the target language, or, when necessary, to explain the meaning of a phrase rather than translating it. In short: it cannot *depart from* literal translation in order to better convey the meaning of the text.

Such practices, however, form the heart of the work of the translator. Translators seek, not the most probable translation, but the best translation for a particular context, occasionally choosing to invent a new word or to clarify the meaning without offering a word-for-word translation. They thus produce meaning in a dynamic, original and *improbable* way, amounting to a production of anti-entropy in the linguistic field. Antoine Berman brings decisive elements to bear on these questions in *The Experience of the Foreign*, and Yuliya Goncharova and Philippe Lacour develop original proposals with the TraduXio digital environment.[26]

Conversely, replacing the work of translation with a purely computational and statistical operation results in massive entropization of the linguistic field, manifested in a loss of meaning (creating meaning, unlike signification, always constitutes an event or a bifurcation that is highly improbable, and in this way anti-entropic). Montévil shows that these effects result from a problematic concept of translation, based on Shannon's information theory,[27] which considers translation to be a transmission of *information* without concern either for the *signification* or the *meaning* of the transmitted message, and in this way imposes algorithms possessing an irrelevant mathematical structure.

To avoid such entropic phenomena, it is necessary to design and develop algorithmic models that are not based on information theory alone, but take the effects of interpretation and meaning into account. Observations of this kind call for the design and development of, and experimentation with, alternative systems based on the contributions of reflexive subjects, making room for interpretive, deliberative and incalculable fields within data structures, and developing algorithms to assist with interpretation and deliberation, and not just the extraction and exploitation of statistical data. As Geert Lovink points out in his work on platform design, the centralization of networks, the hegemony of the web giants and the social destructiveness of the digital are not inevitable.[28] And Dominique Cardon's work shows that, far from being mere technical tools, algorithms are historical products that are bearers of political projects, constantly evolving, shaping uses and disrupting the traditional functioning of human societies.[29]

Digital technologies are indeed bearers of different modes of participation: participation can range from a simple production of navigational traces (the main object of the data economy and social networks), to contributory forms of editing, aggregation and discussion of contents (such as the online encyclopedia Wikipedia), editorialization and commentary (such as micro-reviews of films) or original publication (such as blogs). Such singular and contributory practices can be intensified, provided that we thoroughly rethink data architecture and the functioning of social networks – which so far and for the most part remain *functionally* anti-social.

## 94 Incalculable deliberations and interpretations within knowledge communities and the future of the World Wide Web

To struggle against the anthropy generated by the tracing and profiling of individuals, functionalities must be developed that cannot be reduced to simple calculations of probabilities: incalculable deliberative and hermeneutic fields must be constituted in the service of knowledge communities that are themselves deliberative. The principles underpinning this were laid out in Chapter 3 and the sections devoted to the Management Institutes of the Contributory Economy

(MICE). The expression of singular points of view, by nature irreducible to treatments that would reduce them to the status of particularities, already constitutes the horizon of much research in the field of the annotation and interpretation of textual, audio or visual files, leading to the comparing of contributions and deliberations within communities of amateurs, researchers or citizens. This work, however, remains marginal compared to the platforms that currently dominate digital networks.

To develop the contributory design of new territorialized platforms (where geographical information systems could be used for purposes very different from automated guidance), and, on this basis, territorialized contributory economies that are generative in the sense of Giaccardi, Gherardi and Magatti, systems must be created that do make use of algorithmic automatisms, but only in order to put them at the service of deliberation, which is also to say, the power to dis-automatize. Through successive consolidations, dis-automatization makes it possible to generate neganthropic practices – knowledge practices. These must themselves be based on anti-anthropic deviations that, by means of singular propositions that are irreducible to probable evolutions, introduce bifurcations that constantly fuel knowledge, its institutions and those who practise it. It is therefore a question of making the calculations of algorithms serve psychic and collective functions that escape all calculation, but which produce a constant enrichment of the social, economic, political, legal, artistic and scientific life of groups. From the epistemological standpoint introduced in Chapter 1, this means returning to the Kantian distinction between intuition, understanding, imagination and reason.[30]

In this sense, a new deliberative, hermeneutic and contributory web is needed to fight against anthropy. Such a revitalized web would revive the inaugural spirit of the World Wide Web launched in 1993, but cannot possibly be limited to the semantic web, as the latter currently functions on the sole basis of statistical calculations. A new web-based network,[31] on the contrary, requires the design of new architectures and structures of both data and algorithms, supporting new types of functions related to indexing, categorization, annotation, visualization, recommendation, editorialization and group-formation, and articulating these contributory functions with algorithmic data processing, as well as with the primary functions of a new kind of social network.[32]

Such platforms, which must emerge from communities of practical organology in the sense we have described, require theoretical computer science to be given a new foundation on a set of axioms and theorems based on the reconsideration of the faculties of knowing, desiring and judging – in Kant's sense – in the era of digital technologies. They must take note of the originally exosomatic dimensions of the cognitive faculties and functions, in particular with regard to categorical forms of the understanding (which continues the investigation of the questions begun by Durkheim in the late nineteenth century[33]). New publication systems must be developed, tested and practised in all spheres of everyday and urban life, as well as in academic and artistic communities, restoring to the digital technologies emerging from the World Wide Web the function of providing a space for disputation and public debate, which was their initial vocation before they became systems for the control and surveillance of populations.

## 95   Examples of contributory technology

### A Note-sharing and contributory categorization platforms

In all the systems tested at IRI since 2006 (and since 2001 at IRCAM, the theoretical foundations of which were developed and prototyped as early as 1993 as part of the BNF computer-assisted reading station – see http://www.enssib.fr/bibliotheque-numerique/documents/42680-la-lecture-assistee-par-ordinateur.pdf), the question of contribution has been approached starting from the figures of the 'amateur' and the researcher (see https://iri-ressources.org/themes/theme-7.html). Beyond 'participation' or even 'collaboration', contribution establishes a relationship of co-individuation between the participants in a project involving the production of knowledge (work knowledge, life knowledge, theoretical knowledge, aesthetic knowledge, practical knowledge and so on).

### A1 Example: Lignes de temps

The first empirical experiment with a contributory categorization protocol designed to encourage *transindividuation* was initiated at the Centre Pompidou's Institut de Recherche et d'Innovation. It was a note-taking system for lectures and conferences, first developed in 2009 as the Lignes de temps software (see http://ldt.iri.centrepompidou.fr), then the Polemic Tweet application in 2010 (see http://polemictweet.com), and finally IRI Notes in 2018.

The system works in three stages: 1) presentation of the protocol to explain to contributors that their notes will be published and synchronized with the recording of the course; 2) use of the note-taking interface, which is equipped with colour-coded metacategories (important, comment, problem, keyword) constituting tags and therefore vectors

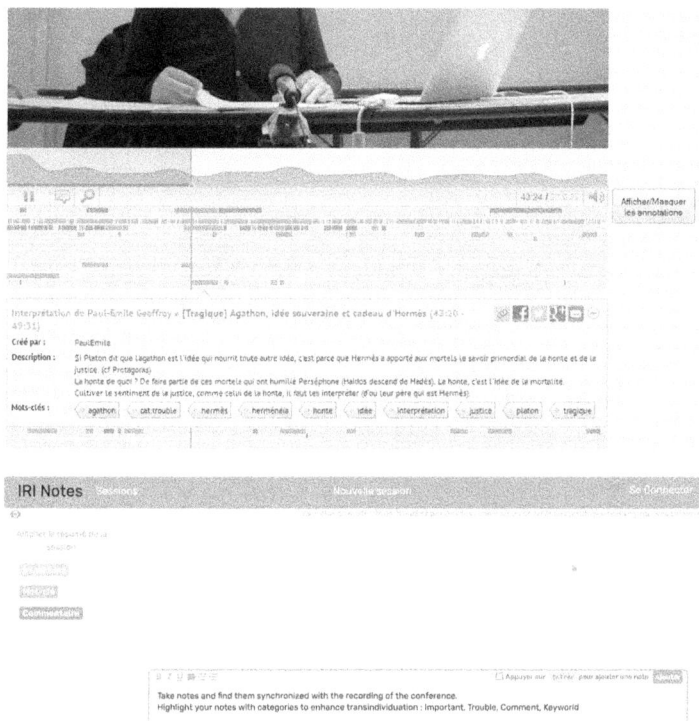

Figure 1. Visualization of convergences and divergences of interpretation in Lignes de temps and IRI Notes

for further discussions, debates and recommendations; 3) publication of the recording, indexed by categorized notes that have been taken, allowing direct consultation of the tagged units of meaning and the ability to use an intra-video search engine based on the content of the notes taken (see Figure 1).

The aim of such a system is to make *noetic processes traceable* by revealing both consensus and dissensus, sites of disputes and bifurcations that allow knowledge to evolve and transform. Subjects of consensus lead to the production of shared categories constituting a horizon of understanding, while subjects of dissensus are objects of deliberation on the basis of alternatives amounting to choices involving the future. *In contrast to statistical treatment that minimizes the standard deviation, the aim is instead to foster a diversity and differentiation of perspectives and interpretations.*

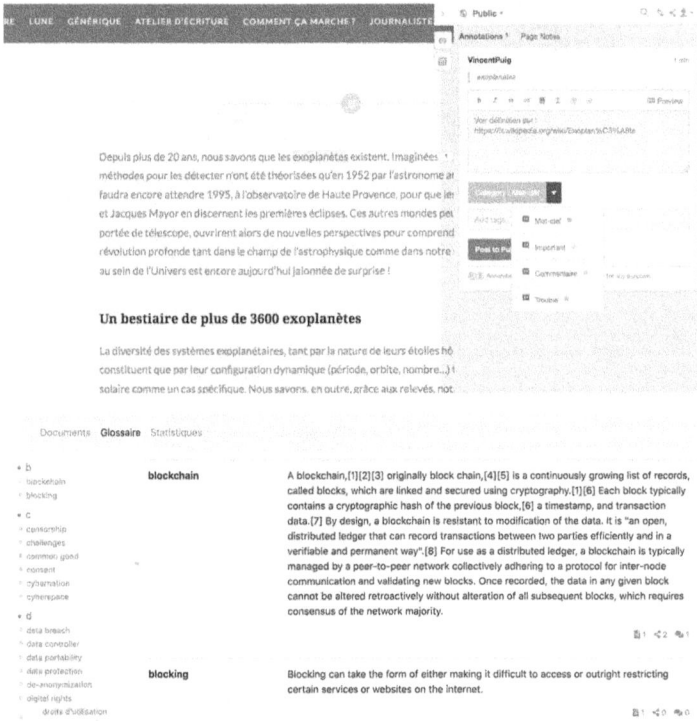

Figure 2. Annotation in Hypothes.is and glossary supplied by annotations

## A2 Example: Hypothes.is

The same principle of categorization is applicable to still images (with the IconoLab tool) or texts (the Hypothes.is tool). In this case, annotations in the margins constitute a dialogical space of interpretation, dispute and discussion (see Figure 2), but they can also contribute to the production of contributory glossaries (for each term, competing definitions can be proposed, different translations, occurrences of this term in the annotated documents, and so on).

## B Deliberative social networks

Research carried out by Harry Halpin and Yuk Hui[34] has shown that a social network like Facebook is built on the principle of Moreno's social graphs, that is, on the idea that the individual is the primary node in the network. Beyond this *techno-methodological individualism*, which tends to privilege the personalization of a profile based on equivalent parameters (the user becoming only a showcase of oneself among a multitude of others), Halpin and Hui propose an approach to social relations based on the group.[35] This tends to give value to the associated milieu[36] and therefore to functions that formalize sharing between members of the group.

What comes first is no longer the individual, but his or her relationship to the associated milieu: his or her belonging to one or more groups, his or her work on one or more projects, his or her contributions on this or that theme... In the framework of social networks of this kind, the function of algorithms is no longer the statistical processing of user data in order to predict behaviour, but rather qualitatively analysing annotations in order to identify interpretive convergences or divergences, and suggesting the formation of peer communities and the organization of disputes (around scientific, political or aesthetic arguments).

Such an approach also means offering network user-contributors greater room for manoeuvre with regard to the government and development of the network. Indeed, what characterizes a group is first of all its autonomy, that is, its ability to set its own rules: a group must be able to decide how the sharing of its contributions will be organized. This can result in the questioning of those metacategories that constitute the common language of annotation, or in decisions relating to the publication of collective work.

But this also means that the group must be able to transform its workspace by contributing to the open *co-design* of the categorization platform. A deliberative or contributory social network must thus be equipped with open systems, insofar as the editorial gesture inseparably implies mastery of both the tool and the content. In relation to this issue, and in order to develop this type of data structure and related algorithms on a 'scalable' level, it will be necessary to take inspiration from the specifiable models conceived according to the SGML standard and in terms of DTD (document type definition), which was at the origin of HTML and therefore of the World Wide Web.

## Notes

1    Victor Papanek, *Design for the Real World: Human Ecology and Social Change*, second edition (London: Thames & Husdon, 1985), pp. x and xiv.

2    Mark Hunyadi, *La tyrannie des modes de vie: sur le paradoxe moral de notre temps* (Lormont: Le Borde de l'Eau, 2015).

3    Bernard Stiegler, *Symbolic Misery, Volume 1: The Hyper-Industrial Epoch*, trans. Barnaby Norman (Cambridge: Polity Press, 2014).

4    Mauro Magatti and Laura Gherardi, 'Le capitalisme de la valeur contextuelle. La perspective de la générativité', *Revue de Mauss* 43 (2014), pp. 374–93.

5    See Jason Plautz, 'The Environmental Burden of Generation Z', *Washington Post* (3 February 2020), available at: <https://www.washingtonpost.com/magazine/2020/02/03/eco-anxiety-is-overwhelming-kids-wheres-line-between-education-alarmism/?arc404=true>.

6    Gilbert Simondon, *Sur la technique* (Paris: Presses Universitaires de France, 2014).

7    Thomas Berns and Antoinette Rouvroy, 'Gouvernementalité algorithmique et perspectives d'émancipation. Le disparate comme condition d'individuation par la relation?', *Réseaux* 177 (2013), pp. 163–96.

8    Amnesty International, *Surveillance Giants: How the Business Model of Google and Facebook Threatens Human Rights* (London: Amnesty International, 2019), available at: <https://www.amnesty.org/download/Documents/POL3014042019ENGLISH.PDF>.

9    Bernard Stiegler, *Automatic Society, Volume 1: The Future of Work*, trans. Daniel Ross (Cambridge: Polity Press, 2016), §14.

10   Geert Lovink, *Sad by Design: On Platform Nihilism* (London: Pluto Press, 2019).

11   B. J. Fogg and G. E. Fogg, *Persuasive Technology: Using Computers to Change What We Think and Do* (San Francisco: Morgan Kaufmann Publishers, 2003); Eric Singler, *Nudge Management: Applying Behavioural Science to Boost Well-Being, Engagement and Performance at Work* (Montreuil: Pearson, 2018); John L. Pfaltz, 'Entropy in Social Networks' (2012), available at: <https://arxiv.org/pdf/1212.2917.pdf>.

12   Frank Pasquale, 'From Territorial to Functional Sovereignty: The Case of Amazon', *Law and Political Economy* (6 December 2017), available at: <https://lpeblog.org/2017/12/06/from-territorial-to-functional-sovereignty-the-case-of-amazon/>.

13   Pierre-Damien Huyghe, interviewed by Tiphaine Kazi-Tani, 'À quoi tient le design: un entretien avec Pierre-Damien Huyghe', *Sciences du design* 2 (2015), pp. 71–81, available at: <https://www.cairn.info/revue-sciences-du-design-2015-2-page-71.htm>.

14   Richard Sennett, *The Corrosion of Character: The Personal Consequences of Work in the New Capitalism* (New York: W. W. Norton, 1998).

15   Papanek, *Design for the Real World*.

16   And it must do so with artists and scientists, but also with econo-
     mists and jurists, and of course with engineers, especially those who
     practise free software.

17   Magatti and Gherardi, 'Le capitalisme de la valeur contextuelle'.

18   Richard Sennett, 'The Open City', available at: <https://www.rich-
     ardsennett.com/site/senn/UploadedResources/The%20Open%20
     City.pdf>.

19   Richard Sennett, *Together: The Rituals, Pleasures and Politics of
     Cooperation* (New Haven and London: Yale University Press, 2012).

20   See Michael E. Porter and Mark R. Kramer, 'Creating Shared
     Value', *Harvard Business Review* 89 (2011), p. 65: 'The concept of
     shared value [...] recognizes that society's needs, not just conven-
     tional economic needs, define markets.' And see ch. 2, and David
     M. Berry, 'Against Infrasomatization: Towards a Critical Theory of
     Algorithms', in Didier Bigo, Engin Isin and Evelyn Ruppert (eds),
     *Data Politics: Worlds, Subjects, Rights* (London and New York:
     Routledge, 2019).

21   David Bates, 'Penser l'automaticité au seuil du numérique', in
     Bernard Stiegler (ed.), *Digital Studies. Technologies de la connais-
     sance et organologie des savoirs* (Paris: FYP, 2014), pp. 29–30.

22   Pfaltz, 'Entropy in Social Networks'; Cléo Collomb, Igor Galligo
     and Filipe Pais, 'Les algorithms du désir: enquête sur le design li-
     bidinal de Tinder', *Sciences du Design* 4 (2016), pp. 117–23.

23   Frédéric Kaplan, 'Vers le capitalisme linguistique. Quand les mots
     valent de l'or', *Le Monde diplomatique* (November 2011), available at:
     <https://www.monde-diplomatique.fr/2011/11/KAPLAN/46925>.

24   Frédéric Kaplan and Dana Kianfar, 'Google et l'impérialisme lin-
     guistique. Il pleut des chats et des chiens', *Le Monde diplomatique*
     (January 2015), available at: <https://www.monde-diplomatique.
     fr/2015/01/KAPLAN/51968>.

25   Maël Montévil, 'Entropies and the Anthropocene Crisis', *AI and
     Society*, forthcoming.

26   Antoine Berman, *The Experience of the Foreign: Culture and
     Translation in Romantic Germany*, trans. Stefan Heyvaert (Albany:
     State University of New York Press, 1992); Yuliya Goncharova and
     Philippe Lacour, 'TraduXio: nouvelle experience en traduction lit-
     téraire', *Traduire* 225 (2011), available at: <https://journals.openedi-
     tion.org/traduire/94>.

27   Claude Shannon, 'A Mathematical Theory of Communication', *Bell
     System Technical Journal* 27 (1948), pp. 379–423, reprinted in N.
     J. A. Sloane and Aaron D. Wyner (eds), *Claude Elwood Shannon:*

*Collected Papers* (New York: Institute of Electric and Electronics Engineers, 1993).

28   Lovink, *Sad by Design*.

29   Dominique Cardon, *À quoi rêvent les algorithmes, nos vies à l'heure des big data* (Paris: Seuil, 2015).

30   See Bernard Stiegler, 'The New Conflict of the Faculties and Functions: Quasi-Causality and Serendipity in the Anthropocene', trans. Daniel Ross, *Qui Parle* 26 (2017), pp. 79–99, and Stiegler, *Automatic Society, Volume 1*.

31   See Bernard Stiegler (ed.), *La toile que nous voulons: le web neguentropique* (Paris: FYP, 2017)

32   See Yuk Hui and Harry Halpin, 'Collective Individuation: The Future of the Social Web', available at: <https://digital-studies.org/wp/wp-content/uploads/2013/01/HuiYuk_and_HarryHalpin_FINAL_CollectiveIndividuation.pdf>.

33   Emile Durkheim, 'Introduction', *The Elementary Forms of the Religious Life*, trans. Joseph Ward Swain (London: George Allen & Unwin, 1915).

34   Hui and Halpin, 'Collective Individuation: The Future of the Social Web'.

35   This approach is inspired by the work of Gilbert Simondon on collective individuation, already discussed.

36   For Simondon, an individual is what can transform its *environment* into an associated milieu. Individuation is psychic *and* collective because the individuals never transform themselves on their own: the associated milieu is what is transformed to the extent that individuals transform themselves, and vice versa. See Gilbert Simondon, *On the Mode of Existence of Technical Objects*, trans. Cécile Malaspina and John Rogove (Minneapolis: Univocal, 2017).

# 8   Ēthos and Technology

*Michał Krzykawski, Susanna Lindberg (revised by David Bates)*


## 96   Reconsidering ethics from the perspective of the technosphere

This chapter will attempt to elaborate a general approach to ethics in which ethical life is understood in tandem with technics conceived as the set of technologies organizing noetic life in the technosphere. The technosphere is itself considered as the locality of twenty-first century hyper-industrial societies. The organization of noetic life is a technological question that should be discussed in ethical terms in that it obliges us to critically revise what we experience in our everyday life: human behaviour, duty and character are now shaped by automated artificial systems. In the current stage of exosomatic evolution, these artificial systems have become planetary exorganisms – both organized and organizing – within which and through which we live both as individuals and as political communities. As an unprecedented articulation of organic and inorganic matter that has now reached the technospheric stage, this exosomatic organization of life requires a profound reconceptualization of ethical life.

Talking about ethical life today is no easy task – that is, in the confrontation of life with the toxic effects of the Anthropocene era. The sense of ethical life has been distorted by the 'greenwashing' strategies of global corporations. Shamelessly refusing ethics insofar as, for the Greeks, *aidōs* (shame), along with *dikē* (justice), are the very conditions of ethical life, these companies exploit rising environmental concerns in order to protect, unchanged, their unsustainable business models.

When considering what ethical life can and should really mean in this situation, it seems that the question of ethics must be displaced from the sphere of personal choice to the sphere of the hyper-industrial organization of artificial systems. Since these systems do not just influence personal choices but also precede and outstrip them through the algorithmic infrastructure of the new data economy, where the latter evades social and political control, the fundamental ethical issue must relate to the hyper-industrial conditions in which an ethical life is possible. Addressing the question of ethics within these hyper-industrial conditions is possible only by questioning the current macroeconomic industrial model and the technological usage it imposes.

Ethical life can only be an illusion in a macroeconomic industrial model based on the systemic exploitation of increasing entropy
rates – for this is the principle of economic growth conceived on the
basis of GDP in its transformation of use value into exchange value.
In hyper-industrial societies that are plundering a burning biosphere,
the question of ethics is first of all a question of the organization of
the economic process – even though ethics is obviously not limited to
economics, unless we understand the latter with Georges Bataille as a
general economy and with Freud as libidinal economy.

A different organization of the economic process is needed to
breathe new life into ethics. It is possible to live well in the hyper-
industrial societies of the twenty-first century, provided that we
rethink and care [*repænser*[1]] – that is, take care of, theoretically and
practically – the question of the relationships between ethics, economics *and technology*. This is what we hope to do in this chapter, on
the basis of an interpretation of *ēthos*.

The chapter consists of six parts – the first two parts being intro-
ductory. The first part determines four conditions of possibility of
ethical life in the twenty-first century: these conditions are technological, technospheric, hyper-industrial and exosomatic. The second
part shows – through an examination of the problem of abstraction in
the field of ethics – why our general approach to ethics can be seen as
a critical extension of a normative/applied ethical approach. The third
and fourth parts are devoted to the notion of *ēthos*, reinterpreted in
the context of algorithmicization and automation. The fifth part, on
the vital link between *ēthos* and locality in the context of technodiversity, argues that the latter, as the very condition of technological
sustainability, and as the exosomatic condition of noodiversity, has
been endangered, as has the biosphere. Finally, the last part is devoted
to the ethical organization of life on Earth in relation to food production and animal-human relations in the Anthropocene.

## 97   Four conditions of possibility for ethics in the twenty-first century

The first condition of possibility for ethics in the twenty-first century
is technological – and an ethical question can arise only because exosomatic organs are not spontaneously beneficial. In arguing that the
question of ethics should be addressed *as* a technological problem,
however, it is first necessary to make a distinction between the French
term *technique* – which we can translate into English as *technics* (for
example, in translations of the works of Stiegler) and into German
as *Technik* – and what is commonly referred to as *technology*. If the

term 'technology' refers to technological equipment, technics encompasses all human actions based on knowledge. All human action has
something to do with *tekhnē*, which means that 'delimiting the field of
technics' is difficult.[2]

Unlike French, German, Italian, Finnish, Polish and other Slavic
languages, the English language makes a distinction between *technology, technique* and *technics*.[3] If the term 'technology' probably exists
in all languages, it generally refers to technological equipment rather
than to what Simondon described in terms of a metatheory of technics,
which would pave the way for the 'integration of technical reality into
universal culture'.[4] Consider, for example, that what Michel Foucault
described as *techniques de soi* has been translated into English as
*technologies of the self*.[5]

Using the term 'technology' in this way, however, can lead to some
confusion. With the advent of cybernetics in the 1950s, 'technology'
was also used to refer to high-tech systems, that is, organized inorganic matter,[6] and, more recently, the organizing inorganic[7] – but
these high-tech systems have nothing to do with what Foucault understood by *techniques of the self*, that is, practices aimed at taking care
of the self. Here, we will prefer the term *technique* to that of *technology*, not just to avoid terminological confusion, but to show that the
very possibility of taking care of the self must be carefully rethought
in relation to high technology.

Given that high-tech systems strongly (dis)organize the possibility
of an ethical life – and do so at lightning speed, leaving societies in a
state of disorientation – the distinction between technique or technics
and technology makes it possible to argue that:

1   technique must be addressed firstly as a local and localized
    form of knowledge of how to do [*savoir-faire*], how to live
    [*savoir-vivre*] and how to conceive and theorize;

2   technique, as a form of knowledge, must be reinvented
    starting from technological systems, these new artificial
    organisms both deforming and transforming techniques as
    human ways of making 'life worth living'.[8]

The second condition of possibility for ethics in the twenty-first
century is technospheric. The technosphere is not just a digital milieu
– where the latter is real and not virtual, as might have been thought
two or three decades ago.[9] It also constitutes a new system that, while
still requiring humans, nevertheless functions autonomously, and,
therefore, escapes human control[10] to the point of appearing inhuman. The technosphere, however, remains first and foremost a space

of human activity, characterized by the intervention of technological systems and technosciences into nature.

In the wake of Bonneuil and Fressoz, Latour, Bińczyk and many others, it is possible to define the technosphere as responsible for anthropogenic changes in the biosphere and the reorganization of social and biological structures.[11] In this regard, any ethical action should be taken or judged starting from 'technonature',[12] that is, from the perspective of a new living space on Earth where, on the one hand, the modern distinction between nature and technics seems to be porous, and, on the other hand, the metabolic system of the bio-sphere – which makes life on Earth biologically possible – is on the verge of collapse due to our use of industrial technology. Here, the ethical task is to *determine a new technospheric metabolism* in which life-sustaining processes can produce sustainable and anti-anthropic compositions of organic and inorganic matter/energy.

The third condition of possibility for ethics in the twenty-first century is hyper-industrial. Contrary to the analyses of Alain Touraine and Daniel Bell, the celebrated post-industrial society never appeared, unless the conception of industry is reduced to the presence of blast furnaces and coalmines.[13] We do not inhabit post-industrial societies, but rather hyper-industrial ones, in which everything 'has become subject to modelling and industrial activity – distribution, health, lei-sure, education, and so on'.[14] Absent a technology policy, this hyper-industry has ultimately led us to an increasingly disturbing era of surveillance, where it is 'human experience as free raw material for translation into behavioral data'[15] that has become subject to model-ling. In this unprecedented situation, any discourse on ethics must take this hyper-industrial fact into account: our data, as a new raw material in the service of old, obsolete, unsustainable and structurally unchanged economic models, is extracted from our daily activities.

In a very general way, capitalism in the industrial age is based on the exploitation of energy resources. Unlike the nineteenth-century capitalist model, however, which depended on the extraction of fossil fuels, and where this dependence certainly did not disappear in the twenty-first century, the economic model based on digital platforms additionally exploits the reserves of libidinal energy from which the extracted data originates. These two variants of systematically orga-nized extraction have the same destructive impact on forms of life: the human milieu – which can be developed through noetic activi-ties and the exchange of new forms of knowledge, rather than through algorithmized and controlled information exchange – is destroyed just as much as the environment. Yet only a well-cared-for human milieu can take care of the environment.

The hyper-industrial condition thus obliges us to develop a more complete assessment of the technosphere. Just as the biosphere appears to constitute a locality for all living organisms in the solar system, so too the technosphere must be understood as a planetary-scale locality for hyper-industrial societies and approached as a no less critical object of care. The future of the biosphere is *techno-logical*. Consequently, the technosphere must be preserved as our techno-*bio*-logical condition of life on Earth. This means that our relationship to technology must change along with changing the current macro-economic model, based as it is on the limitless exploitation of energy resources: natural and noetic, and, in a way, only techno-*physical*.

The fourth condition of possibility for ethics in the twenty-first century is exorganological, and it relates to what Alfred Lotka described as exosomatic evolution, that is, 'increased adaptation [of the human species] achieved by the incomparably more rapid development of "artificial" aids to our native receptor-effector apparatus'.[16] These artificial aids are exosomatic organs – from knives, arrows and cartwheels to autonomous cars; from the abacus to calculators, computers and 'clusters' – which develop outside the body and have an increasingly important impact on the organization of life on Earth.

Chapter 1 showed that exosomatic evolution is an extension of biological evolution, and that the economic process is a condition of exosomatic evolution. Nicholas Georgescu-Roegen builds on Lotka's observation:

> With the exosomatic evolution, the human species became addicted to the comfort provided by detachable limbs, which, in turn, compelled man to become a geological agent who continuously speeds up the entropic degradation of the finite stock of mineral resources.[17]

From an exorganological standpoint, ethics can accordingly be defined as a multiplicity of new techniques of the composition of life with artificial organs – organs on which noetic beings become more and more dependent during the course of biological-exosomatic-economic evolution. At the same time, they become more and more powerful, but this power necessitates knowledge-based economic, juridical, political and ethical regulations. This process and these regulations, however, threaten to be reversed by current production methods (and the use they make of these organs), which make life on Earth biologically unsustainable. It is only by taking these four conditions and their systemic interconnections into account that it is possible to formulate ethical proposals commensurate with the transition required by the current stage of the Anthropocene era.

## 98   Uses and abuses of abstraction

Under these conditions, the general ethical approach that we propose here can be seen as a critical extension of the normative/applied
approach to ethics used by experts on ethics and ethical committees,
whose role is to determine whether a new technological product is
good or bad for individual users, society, freedom, democracy and so
on. In 1991, observing how genetic engineering was being used to
increase the power and profits of the economic model, André Gorz
pointed out: 'To make "ethics" the preserve of experts is tantamount
to abstracting it from everyday life and culture, to preside over its
extinction.'[18] Given the growing impact of artificial intelligence technologies (brain-machine interfaces, hands-free computer control, the
use of algorithms more generally) on hyper-industrial societies, however, there does exist a need for ethical experts, provided that they
have the courage to firmly oppose short-term and short-sighted interests of global corporations, and are in this way able to pave the way
for a new understanding of public policy in the technosphere.

The recommendations of ethics experts and ethics committees cannot just go along with 'business as usual'. Experts and committees
cannot just rely on good intentions or wishful thinking while avoiding
the real problem by saying nothing about how these recommendations
could be implemented in a way that transforms them into effective
ethical principles. We need recommendations that are courageous,
and especially the kind of courage that dares to know (*sapere aude*),
which Kant made the spiritual principle of the Enlightenment – only
such courage responds to the now famous question addressed by Greta
Thunberg: 'How dare you?'[19] Only courage of this type will make it
possible to rebuild and reinvent public power as a milieu for ethical
action in the age of algorithms.

At the same time, however, and in the wake of Gorz, we must also
carefully rethink the dynamics of the relationship between abstraction and ethics – to see how the imposition of *general* ethical rules
abstracts them from the local circumstances in which authentic ethical actions, both individual and collective, take place. Jacques Derrida
has shown that by 'forces of abstraction' we should understand
'deracination, delocalization disincarnation, formalization, univer-
salizing schematization, objectification, telecommunication etc.'[20] If
these forces can also be defined as forces of evil or sickness ('the evil
of abstraction'[21]), it is because, when abstraction forgets the local circumstances of its origin, it becomes ineffective.

There is actually nothing abstract about Derrida's definition of the
machine and technics as 'sites of abstraction'. On the contrary, what

he is trying to tell us by his specific use of the term 'abstraction' is something very concrete, and relates to what we are living through in absolute terms:

1   on the one hand, technology tends to fashion a universal and homogeneous system;

2   on the other hand, the system tends towards totalization, which means that the more the system is developed, the more it is abstracted from local realities, which it transforms according to its own disruptive logic, and the more it frees itself from the control of these concrete and heterogeneous localities.

Moreover, and counter-intuitively, this tendency towards the universalization of the technical system makes it increasingly specialized.[22] Wherever it is that we have to live, according to the customs of our *plural singular* places, we are organized by the same totalizing system and condemned to let a small group of specialists design this system and decide how it functions.

## 99   'This is all wrong': abstraction, localities, noodiversity

Since the second half of the twentieth century, the internal logic of the technical system – inherent to the very 'nature' of technics – has been subjected to an economic process that has, in this way, become totalizing. Furthermore, economics, originally a social science and even an element of everyday life (as *oikonomia*), has been left in the hands of an equally small group of specialists. 'This is all wrong', as Greta Thunberg observed in September 2019 at the UN Climate Action Summit in New York. A substantial part of this hyper-industrial evil – this very old but constantly reinvented evil genius (*genius malignus*) using every effort (*omni sua industria*) to deceive us, to put it in Cartesian terms[23] – is due to the use made of abstraction in economic and technological processes (and here we continue David M. Berry's reflections on infrasomatization, discussed in Chapter 2). In this regard, an *irrevocably critical task of ethics* is to take the dynamics of abstraction into account.

If abstraction is always necessary for ethics to be able to define ethical rules for the technosphere, as well as for the technological macro-systems of which it is composed, abstraction is nevertheless also what can blind us to micro-levels and meso-levels. It is by starting from these levels, and distributed across these scales, that an ethically organized technosphere – as a complex set of reticulated open ethical systems, more or less local, but always localized in their histories – can and must be rethought.

A systemic change must be made in the common approach to ethics, as well as in the use made of it by experts and ethical committees working in hyper-industrial conditions, shaped by technoscience in tandem with the economic world. Seeking to determine whether a new technological product or service is good or bad for societies within the global techno-economic/techno-scientific system, which is itself headed in a bad direction, remains far too abstract an approach to be effective in relation to lives lived locally. *This irrevocably critical task of ethics*, therefore, is also a meta-task in the sense that it aims at determining the right place(s) for ethics and at adjusting the balance between the universal and the local, the totalized and the singular, the specialized and the common. In short, it is a question of rethinking ethics in the technosphere *on the basis of* those habitual or customary places that the Greeks called *ēthē* (plural of *ēthos*).

In this respect, a formal distinction between ethics and morality should be reintroduced in order to go beyond the restriction imposed by moral philosophy. In a word, ethical life, as long as it means acting well, is always conflictual. Acting well, doing the right thing, does not necessarily mean following what is defined as acceptable, right or just by moral philosophy. Morality is an abstraction as long as it is detached from mores, 'customs', that is, *ēthos* or *Sittlichkeit*. Redefining ethics consists in observing how *all of us* can and must speak about ethics through the multiplicity of European philosophies and languages as their material supports,[24] but also in discovering how this multiplicity can be aligned with non-European *ēthē* and work at the planetary level through the means of multilingual technological organs.

It is not strange that the reduction of technology to mere functionality goes hand in hand with the advent of a monolinguistic culture that affects local *ēthē* in the same way as agricultural monoculture affects biodiversity (see also §105). Breathing new life into ethics means recognizing that linguistic diversity is much more than something to be preserved through the logic of the cultural exception. Rather, it should be seen as the material condition of what Adam Smith described as the wealth of nations, and it is the essential condition of what we are here calling noodiversity. To rethink the wealth of nations from the perspective of general ethics, however, and going beyond the abstract/abstracting notion of growth, requires a deeper understanding of how ethical life is linked in an exorganic way to 'technical inventions as behaviors of the living',[25] and how this universal exorganological relationship is differentiated at local scales.

## 100 Ēthos and algorithms: ancient and modern meanings of ēthos

The word 'ethics' derives from the ancient Greek word ēthos, which originally meant *habitual site* and later meant *custom* or *habit*.[26] Ēthos is a particular *character*, belonging both to the community (customs) and to the individual (moral character) who displays his or her character in action and speech. As the particular character of a community, ēthos is manifested in its customs, habits and traditions: it is an unconscious and non-rational articulation of how things should be on the grounds that this is how they have 'always' been. In everyday life, the ethical character of individuals reflects the ēthos of their community: people follow the customs and beliefs that bring them together.

As Martin Heidegger shows in his 'Letter on "Humanism"', ēthos coincides with the *abode*, dwelling place, which appears as a *historical destination* that has guided the actions of people from time immemorial.[27] The force of the ēthos can be so great that a person who defends it is ready to stand up against public law, as was Antigone, the heroine of the eponymous tragedy of Sophocles, caught in a contradiction between the ēthos that orders her to act in a certain way and public law that forbids it. As G. W. F. Hegel shows in his interpretation of the ethical world in *Phenomenology of Spirit*, Antigone's ethical individuality, represented dramatically, is determined by her singular way of dealing with this contradiction.[28]

The force of ēthos does not mean that all inherited ēthos would be just, but only that it imposes itself, in the name of divine justice, *as if* it were. This is why ethical life is not just a question of following local traditions. On the contrary, ethical duty sometimes calls for challenging narrow-minded habits, repressive traditions and unjust laws, even if this can lead to heartbreaking tragedies. Ēthos is inseparable from conflict, shame and crime, and this is why ethical reflection often takes place in tragedy.

In the contemporary world, people's abodes are determined in a radically different way. Of course, custom and habit still play a role. But the ēthos of the contemporary world is increasingly marked by 'algorithmic life' and 'algorithmic governmentality', which condition ethical life itself.[29] This does not mean that algorithms would dictate ethical rules, but that the *social space in which ethical action can take place* is prearranged by algorithms. Such are the means of what Rouvroy and Berns call 'statistical governance': it does not control what is real, but structures what appears to be *possible*, while at the same time tending to suppress alternative virtualities.[30]

Some areas of statistical governance are conceived by public authorities.[31] Much larger areas, however, and their essential technological architecture, are created by large global corporations, which ultimately respond only to the needs of capitalism.[32] The world is not governed by an enormous self-aware mega-AI as in science fiction dystopias, but it *is* run by countless algorithmic systems that impersonally and automatically innervate social bodies. Why and how can algorithmic governance have an effect upon and even overdetermine the *ēthos* of the world in the most general sense?

## 101 *Ēthos*, algorithms and temporality

First, like classical *ēthos*, social algorithms frame social reality by determining who can do what. Ancient *ēthos* assigned different tasks to different types of people, for example, men were expected to wage war and women were expected to bury the dead. Contemporary social algorithms also indicate what different people can do, and, in principle, they can perform this role in a more sophisticated way than could ancient *ēthos*, because they can assign tasks to people according to their *personal* traits, and not just according to broad characteristics such as gender or race. Social algorithms can thus be used to select which people can obtain a loan, receive better health care, get a job or receive a place in a higher education institution. It has been shown, however, that instead of decreasing discrimination, they can in fact increase it: they tend to solidify the past, the state of fact, by locking people into their previous social positions.[33]

Second, like the classical *ēthos*, and as we have also seen with the process of infrasomatization, social algorithms govern social reality in a way that is unconscious and hence all the more difficult to challenge. Ancient *ēthos* was not questioned by the people: they observed the rules because their *ēthos* was 'ordained by the gods'. A social algorithm is not dictated by gods, but programmed by engineers, called 'data scientists', and by following the orders of their clients. But the people who are subject to it can neither know it nor question it. From their perspective, algorithms are impenetrable 'black boxes'. Moreover, with advanced machine learning, they evolve into black boxes *for the engineers as well.*

If *ēthos* thus controls life with the force of the unconscious (and of the superego within the unconscious), social algorithms govern with the force of the *unthought*, as N. Katherine Hayles has said.[34] This can happen, for example, if algorithms for selecting who gets access to higher education select some candidates and exclude others without the candidates ever being able to know why they were selected or rejected (either because the algorithm is a commercial secret or because it relies on undetectable datamining processes) – even if the law requires that a person can know and challenge the datasets and processes used in the assessment of his or her case.[35]

Social algorithms, however, are not of the same order as *ēthos*: they involve different temporalities. First of all, they have different relationships to the past. An *ēthos* has no definite origin: it is only a habit that has 'always' been there, and it remains valid only as long as people continue to repeat it. The algorithm has an origin, because a business or a corporation has set its objectives, a team of programmers has built it, and it limits itself to realizing its program. An *ēthos* is different from a social algorithm in that it is open to reinterpretation, reform and rebellion: it is valid only as long as people accept it. But a social algorithm, which can be updated by its programmers, cannot be modified by the people it governs: *one cannot say no to an algorithm*.

Furthermore, and as a consequence, an *ēthos* and a social algorithm have an utterly different relationship to the future – and the temporality of a machine is fundamentally different from human existential time: by physical and mathematical (probabilistic) necessity, technical systems function according to a causal logic by which past events *determine* future events (including as probabilities, and by exercising retroactive feedback loops). In a traditional computer program, this means running the program itself. Modern machine learning technologies seem to be different, in that they rewrite their rules according to patterns that are uncovered in the available data, so that they are based on recursivity rather than repetition[36] – and operate precisely through these feedback loops. Nevertheless, AI always functions through past possibilities (in the program or the data), and in this sense it is still *fundamentally different* from existential time, which develops by encountering impossibilities.

Existential time is capable of opening up to chance, which is the very foundation of human freedom, and this is what an algorithm cannot see. A social algorithm does not admit criticism, and it is not truly open to chance. In this sense, it leaves no room for existential choice, including the demands of justice, tragic action and finally ethical action itself. This is why it would be dangerous to allow social space to be completely saturated and overdetermined by social algorithms – precisely because they tend to become anti-social by substituting themselves for all ethical existence.

## 102 Automation and *ēthos* as 'a mode of relating to contemporality reality'

In 1984, Michel Foucault took up the notion of *ēthos* in relation to actuality, that is, in relation to contemporary reality. Commenting on Kant's famous text, 'An Answer to the Question: "What is Enlightenment?"', published two hundred years earlier on the threshold of what we call modernity, Foucault posited that the latter should be defined 'as an attitude rather than as a period of history'.[37] With the advent of modernity, *ēthos* as a habitual site underwent a transformation that would update its classical meaning. An ethical attitude then becomes 'a mode of relating to contemporary reality': to the now. If Foucault never stops referring to the ancient sense of *ēthos*, it is because the modern attitude always appears as a task, even if it is quite different from that of Antigone, for example. Positing that *ēthos* is always a 'voluntary choice', Foucault describes the modern ethical attitude as 'way of thinking and feeling; a way, too, of acting and behaving that at one and the same time marks a relation of belonging and presents itself as a task'.[38]

Let us try to develop this in order to understand this ethical transformation more clearly.

The immemorial, which is always given to us in the form of a law, must change in order to endure. We, however, who transform this law, if not we who go beyond it through a continuous task of reinterpreting its principles (*archai*), we are obliged to respect its immemorial character. And this task, one might add in the wake of Bergson, presents itself as an obligation, that is, as the irreducible condition of ethical life. Indeed, Bergson posits that obligation is not only one of the two sources of morality: it is also a social bond that 'links us to other members of a society, a bond of the same kind that exists between one ant and the others in an anthill, or the cells of an organism'.[39] Yet it is precisely by this ob-ligation that we are forced to go beyond Foucault's line of questioning, and to rethink what *ēthos*, as 'a mode of relating to contemporary reality' means *today*: in many respects, the actuality of the second decade of the twenty-first century is no longer what it was when Foucault wrote these lines.

Despite the fact that it is barely thirty-five years that separates us from Foucault's text, the fundamental difference between his world and ours is technological. In order to define the meaning of an ethical attitude, therefore, it is necessary to take note of the technological condition of our own 'mode of relating to contemporary reality'. On the one hand, an ethical attitude is governed by social algorithms from which it is difficult to escape, because they transform – if not annihilate – the very possibility of a social bond. On the other hand, an ethical attitude must recognize how it inevitably remains vulnerable to automation, which makes every ethical act *impossible,* if an ethical life involves making decisions (in relation to the ancient sense of *ēthos*) and, therefore, forges an attitude that results from this decision-making and remains voluntary (compared to the modern sense of *ēthos*).

In our present age, it seems urgent to rethink *ēthos* after 'automatic society',[40] in order to transform the immemorial (the archaic) and to determine the new conditions of possibility for ethics after automation. This is why the philosophical *ēthos* – which Foucault describes as 'a critique of what we are saying, thinking and doing, through a historical ontology of ourselves'[41] – needs once again to be transformed in order to become a technological *ēthos*. In brief, if the Foucauldian approach to critique as the foundation of *ēthos* is still valid today, it must nonetheless be rethought in relation to technology, which precedes ontology. An *ēthos* – such as a philosophical life, which Foucault theorized via Pierre Hadot and in the wake of his concept of way of life – would thus be taken as an experiment in technological life.

## 103 The techno-logical reinvention of ethics

An action can be considered ethical as long as the person who acts is responsible for what he or she does, and is capable of anticipating the consequences of those actions. It is for this very reason that an ethical act can never be automatic: it is always already singular in the sense that it calls for a decision that dis-automatizes the individual who makes it. Jacques Derrida often insisted on the impossible nature of this decision, which emerges from the profound meaning of the ethical or 'the ethicity of ethics'.[42]

Yet as soon as we take *ēthos* for an attitude or a 'way' – a way of being or acting, with regard both to oneself and to others – ethical life does not lead to the impossible, but becomes a question of techniques and technology, which encourages us to see it anew through the 'evolution of techniques of the self'.[43] For Foucault, techniques of the self, as modes of action, make us capable of taking care of ourselves, and, therefore, of interacting with others. Drawing from Greco-Roman philosophy and from the monastic principles typical of Christian spirituality at the beginning of the Roman Empire, Foucault distinguishes three types of techniques of the self: 1) writing letters to friends in order to reveal oneself; 2) examining oneself and one's conscience in order to assess what has been done; 3) acts of remembrance.

Consider an example: imagine that you are a monk living in the fourth century. Your monastery is located in some part of the Roman Empire. You speak Latin, which is the *lingua franca*, just as English is today, while Rome means – *urbi et orbi* – the whole world, in the same way that what we call globalization has, since the twentieth century, meant the whole world. You write a letter to your friend, in which you reveal yourself: examining what you have done, you undertake an act of remembrance, which takes effort on your part. But why make this effort to write? Why do you need a friend to know you, and why do you need to take care of yourself through this knowledge of the self that you obtain techno-logically?

Based on letters from the Stoics, interpreted during a seminar at the University of Vermont in 1982, Foucault would reply that it is through these techniques that you practise an ethical life: techniques allow you to access the truth about yourself, but also to 'transform truth into a permanent principle of action'.[44] It is this self-revelation that becomes *ēthos*, and this forms part of what the Greeks and after them Foucault called *tekhnē tou biou*.

The overwhelming majority of our contemporaries, however, are not monks. An attempt to transform the philosophical *ēthos* into a technological *ēthos* therefore also implies *popularizing* it, in the sense of enabling people to practise it in their everyday life and through the organizations and institutions they create. If it is true that techniques of the self, indispensable as they are for the leading of an ethical life, are subject to evolution, especially when technics becomes technology, then the same must be true for this life insofar as the conservation of the *ēthos* requires a meticulous transformation of immemorial ethical principles.

It is therefore a question of knowing how to lead an ethical life in the milieu of reticular digital technologies, inasmuch as they form a new type of associated milieu.[45] Under what conditions do these technologies – such as infrasomatic systems, platforms, devices, interfaces, functions, algorithms, formats and data structures – allow us to take care of ourselves, and under what conditions do they prevent it? How can we reinvent ethical life at a time when a large proportion of our actions have been automated?

If these blunt questions are necessary, it is not possible to answer them in a serious way without questioning the hyper-industrial organization of these new technologies, which consists in extracting data beyond any control. As long as the absence of a technological politics ensures the continuation of this extraction, talking about ethical life will be an occupation for philosophers without consequence for society. It is possible to free *ēthos* from what it contains that is obsolete, however, only if it is transformed so that it remains a 'progressive consideration of self, or mastery over oneself',[46] in the data age.

Without being able to intervene in the becoming and future of the data we share in everyday life, and faced with the abuses perpetrated by the technological giants, the possibility of achieving such mastery is in many respects illusory. This is why opening the epoch of technological *ēthos* consists first of all in regaining control over our data by redefining its very structures, and by making it a key question for a new political economy, in order that it serve new modes of social organization that will once again make it possible to act ethically.

## 104 *Ēthos*, locality, principles and values

Characterizing techniques of the self, and remembering his earlier works, Foucault explains:

> It is one of my targets to show people that a lot of things that are a part of their landscape – that people think are universal – are the result of some very precise historical changes.[47]

How are we to understand these changes in *our* age, in 2020, given that our landscape is shaped by a quasi-universal technological system, and that it is composed of 'things' that are increasingly standardized according to the tendency towards totalization and unification typical of new technologies? How can we organize an ethical technospheric landscape, and why is the relationship between the landscape and the technological *ēthos* so vital for this organization? How can we redefine knowledge of life so that a digital society worthy of being called a society can emerge from it?

The tendency to totalization and unification characteristic of technology forces us to rethink the irreducible character of *ēthos*, as well as the relationship between the universal and the particular. The latter must be seen in compositional rather than oppositional terms, this composition defining the ethical ecosystem. An *ēthos* is local *precisely because* it is a character that is localized in *a habitual site*. Yet it would be wrong to reduce this local appearance of an *ēthos* to the notion that 'small is beautiful'.

What we call locality appears on different scales, and continuously varies from one specific locality to another. And it is precisely this variation, articulating localities through their singularities, that can be considered universal. The one can appear only through its multiple – more or less local – appearances. And conversely, if each of these forms can be said to be universalizable, it is because they all repeat themselves in their multiple variants, while belonging to different places. This *dynamic relation between the one and the many* lies at the heart of the ethical ecosystem composed of open localities and delimited by porous borders.[48] This openness is not the result of an ethical choice. It is the vital condition of any so-called open system (in Bertalanffy's sense[49]), just as porous borders are indispensable for such a system, because they allow exchanges at the universal scale.

What we define as an *ēthos* can be conserved (and localized) only in a more or less local open system. In fact, a universal or global *ēthos* does not exist, which also means that so-called universal values do not exist: all values belong to a particular local landscape. And if ever such values are proclaimed as universal, this proclamation is made by or on behalf of a privileged group – white middle-class males, Western states, multinationals, and so on[50] – who defend their political interests on the back of this claim to universalism. This is why it is all too often only a seditious pretext to silence, stigmatize or attack those who are too readily accused of not respecting such a claim.

In the current period of transition that calls for global responses, we must more than ever be wary of those who invoke universal, immemorial or atemporal values: it is this false universalism that prevents us from thinking about transformation. Nevertheless, the ethics that we are trying to conceive here is not particularist: it is *situated*, and for this reason it is *responsible*. It relates less to values than to principles, and to the organization that makes it possible to uphold these principles, allowing citizens to form and transform their own values – through their everyday ethical practices, and at different scales of locality.

## 105 Technodiversity

If the totalizing, unifying and globalizing technical system constitutes a threat to ethical life, it is because it tends to destroy localities by means of standardization, and to degrade the complexity of the habitual bonds that allow ethical life between and within localities. Taking account of the way technology has evolved – from technical objects to the technological mega-exorganism in which we live – shows that the totalizing and unifying tendency of technology results from the logic of its evolution. And if it never ceases to surprise us, or even to outstrip us to the point of seeming inhuman, it is because technology takes the form of a unifying and totalizing system long before the people who believe it is they who are using technological devices realize that they are in fact the ones governed by that which they are using. This is because each innovation that occurs in the course of technological evolution also generates both increasingly advanced specialization and a diversity of uses.[51]

Because the technical system in which we live is global, we need global ethical rules for the design, production and commercialization of the elements of technical systems – particularly in relation to the application of artificial intelligence. As long as regulations stem from so-called universal ethical values, however, the ethics of technics will serve the interests of technology companies for which technology remains reduced to pure functionality, dictated by imperatives coming from a macroeconomic model that is economically and environmentally unsustainable, as well as ethically unsustainable: it destroys localities as sites of the practise of *ēthos*, as well as neganthropic generativity.[52]

It is clear that technologies have functions that make economic life possible. We must, however, see technology in a different light, beyond these functionalities, in order to free ourselves from the global techno-economic trap and to bring about a technological *ēthos* as 'a way of relating to contemporary reality'. With its current tendency towards unification and totalization, as well as specialization and personalization, technology appears almost as a quasi-universal: human animals are specifically human because they use technics in a way that is incomparably more developed than non-human animals.

Anthropology *is* technology insofar as the techno-logical condition of human existence can be defined as universal. What remains to be discovered is that this technological fact appears in 'particular cosmologies'[53] and the multiple localities of which they are composed. The challenge is then to rethink technics on the basis of the category of diversity – which we so often evoke under the pretext of defending culture (cultural diversity against the cultural homogenization resulting from globalization) or the environment (biodiversity against monoculture).

Ethical life is unsustainable independently of technodiversity. It is precisely for this reason that technodiversity must be protected, in order to save localities and to make their inhabitants capable of transforming them technologically, and, therefore, capable of preserving their *ēthos*. It may be that what is needed is not to fight against the totalizing and unifying force of technologies: they constitute what makes us human, all too human – but also inhuman. What is needed is *to think and take care [panser] of this inhuman aspect of ourselves and our technologies*, in order to struggle with them for a diversified distribution of technological power, respecting local open systems as sites of the practise of ethical life.

## 106  How can we live well with animals while feeding ten billion people in 2050?

The development of human technology in industrial capitalism, especially since the 'great acceleration', has led to unimaginable animal suffering. Ethology brings us increasing evidence of near-human levels of consciousness in vertebrates, and of cognitive processes possessed by animals in their habitats. Yet the animal condition has never been more tragic than it is today.

Whether we like it or not, from an ethical standpoint this fact is becoming an increasingly heavy burden to bear: the process of meat production in intensive farming can well engender what Primo Levi has described as 'the shame at being human'.[54] In the context of the animal industry, this inhuman power of human technologies – those human industrial machines that exploit animals in search of a constantly greater return at lower cost, which excludes any possibility of animal ethics – perhaps hits home here more than it does elsewhere, even if we prefer to turn away from it. 'The relations between humans and animals *must* change', declares Derrida, adding that this duty is as much ethical as ontological.[55]

These relations must change not just with respect to the moral consideration of animals: the consideration of non-human species *must* transform our *ēthē*, that is, our ways of life, standardized as they are in terms of what we eat.[56] These relations must also change because the industrial degradation of animal life, which we must learn to recognize as existences,[57] has become a threat to humanity. Not enough attention is given to the fact that human consumption in general and the industrial production of meat in particular have a major impact on climate change (as carbon production), on the sixth mass extinction, and on the health of the inhabitants of industrial societies. The current system of food production and distribution is largely anthropic, and is one of the factors contributing to the increase of thermodynamic entropy (concentration of greenhouse gases in the atmosphere) and biological entropy (agricultural monoculture destroying biodiversity: forests, animal habitats and local human ways of life). Given this state of affairs, the question that must be asked is whether the production and distribution of industrial food can be anti-anthropic.

Can industry in general and the food industry in particular encourage anti-anthropic behaviour towards our animal friends and anti-anthropic eating habits, taking account of the fact that they have radically changed during the development of industrial capitalism, and particularly after the advent of the great acceleration?[58] According to UN estimates, the world's population is expected to increase from

7.7 billion today to 9.7 billion in 2050 (see https://population.un.org/
wpp/). Feeding ten billion people, 70% of whom will be urban dwellers, will not be possible unless we invent new industrial food production and distribution methods.

The urbanization of the planet, responsible for the shrinking of
rural areas[59] and the emergence of megacities, notably in developing regions, is one of the most striking features of the Anthropocene.
Faced with this situation, a transformation of food production and distribution systems now appears to be the very condition of sustainable
urbanization. In fact, this unprecedented global urbanization forces
us to raise the question of eating beyond individual food preferences.
In order to combat the anthropic impact of intensive farming, concerted political action must be taken to change the questions we ask
about population health, local economies, environmental protection,
the interests of producers and those of animals.

In an effort to anticipate the future consequences of global urbanization, we argue that the transformation of urban culinary practices
can be seen as an opportunity and a means to produce change in the
Anthropocene era, rather than being simply a matter of giving up the
pleasure of eating *well*. Vegetarian cuisine has great urban potential:
it is capable of transforming local culinary practices and, therefore,
of preserving them, while contributing to the development of new
knowledge of how to do, make and live. The ethical imperative formulated by Jacques Derrida – we must eat *well* – implies that we should
today take the food industry as an object of critique within the framework of a new political economy. With the advent of the global expansion of the 'total market',[60] the giants of the food industry have not
only destroyed local ways of life: through marketing strategies and
the programming of consumer choices, they have also changed the
eating habits of Western societies while extending the Western food
model to countries whose traditional cuisine contained less meat.[61]

This is why the question of food in hyper-industrial societies must
be raised not just in relation to the global system of meat production
and consumption, and as a threat to life, including human life, in the
biosphere. A sustainable food production/consumption system must
also be reinvented: it should be focused on localities and their culinary practices in order to combat an insipid monoculture, that is, one
devoid of knowledge, *savoirs*, and therefore of flavour, *saveurs*: the
vital link between food and diversity must be reopened in a way that
fits with our now urbanized planet.

It will not be possible to leave the Anthropocene without asking
how to live *together with* animals, whose welfare is a major ethical

issue. Hyper-industrial societies capable of recognizing the interests of animals will in fact be those capable of taking care of themselves.

On the cusp of the third decade of the twenty-first century, the ethical question must be raised as that of the organization of life in hyper-industrial societies, rather than as that of values. Faced with the planetary disorientation produced by technological disruption, ethical thought is above all a question of critical thinking. The challenge to be taken up in the epoch of algorithms and generalized automation is to determine the conditions under which ethical acts are possible through everyday practices at more or less local scales and on the basis of a territorialized contributory economy, based on the ethical, practical and economic valuing of more or less local knowledge (from the domestic nanoeconomy to biospherically-situated scientific knowledge).

## Notes

1   Bernard Stiegler, *Qu'appelle-t-on panser? 1. L'immense régression* (Paris: Les Liens qui Libèrent, 2018).

2   Bernard Stiegler, *Technics and Time, 1: The Fault of Epimetheus*, trans. Richard Beardsworth and George Collins (Stanford: Stanford University Press, 1998), p. 94.

3   Susanna Lindberg, 'Technics of Space, Place and Displace', *Azimuth* 10 (2010), pp. 27–44.

4   Gilbert Simondon, *On the Mode of Existence of Technical Objects*, trans. Cécile Malaspina and John Rogove (Minneapolis: Univocal, 2017), p. 159.

5   Michel Foucault, 'Technologies of the Self', in Paul Rabinow (ed.), *The Essential Works of Michel Foucault, 1954–1984, Volume One. Ethics: Subjectivity and Truth*, trans. Robert Hurley et al. (London: Penguin, 1997).

6   Stiegler, *Technics and Time, 1*, p. 26.

7   Yuk Hui, *Recursivity and Contingency* (London and New York: Rowman & Littlefield, 2019), p. 28.

8   Bernard Stiegler, *What Makes Life Worth Living: On Pharmacology*, trans. Daniel Ross (Cambridge: Polity Press, 2013).

9   Yuk Hui, *On the Mode of Existence of Digital Objects* (Minneapolis and London: University of Minnesota Press, 2016), pp. 47–48.

10 Peter Haff, 'Humans and Technology in the Anthropocene: Six Rules', *Anthropocene Review* 1 (2014), pp. 126–36.

11 Christophe Bonneuil and Jean-Baptiste Fressoz, *The Shock of the Anthropocene*, trans. David Fernbach (London and New York: Verso, 2016); Bruno Latour, *Down to Earth: Politics in the New Climatic Regime*, trans. Catherine Porter (Cambridge: Polity Press, 2018); Ewa Bińczyk, *Epoka człowieka. Retoryka i marazm antropocenu* (Warsaw: PWN, 2018); Vladimir I. Vernadsky, 'Scientific Thought As a Planetary Phenomenon: The Biosphere and the Noosphere', in Paul. R. Samson and David Pitt (eds), *The Biosphere and Noosphere Reader: Global Environment, Society and Change* (London and New York: Routledge, 1999), and Vernadsky, *The Biosphere*, trans. David B. Langmuir (New York: Copernicus, 1998).

12 Susanna Lindberg, *Techniques en philosophie* (Paris: Hermann, 2020).

13 Alain Touraine, *The Post-Industrial Society. Tomorrow's Social History: Classes, Conflicts and Culture in the Programmed Society*, trans. Leonard F. X. Mayhew (New York: Random House, 1971); Daniel Bell, *The Coming of Post-Industrial Society: A Venture in Social Forecasting* (New York: Basic Books, 1973).

14 Bernard Stiegler, *States of Shock: Stupidity and Knowledge in the Twenty-First Century*, trans. Daniel Ross (Cambridge: Polity Press, 2015), p. 228, n. 24.

15 Shoshana Zuboff, *The Age of Surveillance Capitalism: The Fight for a Human Future at the New Frontier of Power* (New York: PublicAffairs, 2019), p. 8.

16 Alfred J. Lotka, 'The Law of Evolution as a Maximal Principle', *Human Biology* 17:3 (1945), p. 188.

17 Nicholas Georgescu-Roegen, *Energy and Economic Myths: Institutional and Analytical Economic Essays* (New York: Pergamon Press, 1976), p. xiv.

18 André Gorz, *Capitalisme, socialisme, écologie. Désorientations, orientations* (Paris: Seuil, 1991), p. 109 (note that this sentence was not included in the English translation of this book – *trans*.).

19 During her speech delivered to the United Nations in New York on 23 September 2019.

20 Jacques Derrida, 'Faith and Knowledge: The Two Sources of "Religion" at the Limits of Reason Alone', trans. Samuel Weber, *Acts of Religion* (New York and London: Routledge, 2002), p. 43.

21 Ibid.

22   Hui, *Recursivity and Contingency*, p. 21.

23   René Descartes, 'Meditations on First Philosophy', *Selected Philosophical Writings*, trans. John Cottingham, Robert Stoothoff and Dugald Murdoch (Cambridge: Cambridge University Press, 1988), p. 79: 'some malicious demon [...] has employed all his energies in order to deceive me'. It is also a question of seeing, by referring to evil in privative terms, that is, by tying evil to sickness or malaise, the way in which the evil genius today appears technologically, rather than theologically. In French, the adjective *malin* (*malignus* in Latin) can be considered the equivalent of *smart* in English. We should beware this old-new intelligent genius and all its efforts, so much more powerful, rapid, automated and convergent in the hyper-industrial age, in the context of 'real smart cities' (see ch. 2). In this regard, the relationship between religion and theology sketched out by Jacques Derrida (although he did not thematize it clearly), must be rethought, particularly in relation to what transhumanist discourse describes, completely erroneously, as the technological singularity.

24   Barbara Cassin, Marc Crépon and François Prost, 'Morals/Ethics', in Barbara Cassin (ed.), *Dictionary of Untranslatables: A Philosophical Lexicon*, trans. Steven Rendall et al. (Princeton and Oxford: Princeton University Press, 2014), p. 691: '"Morals" (from the Latin *mores*, "customs") and "ethics" (from the Greek êthos [ἦθος], "character"), like their equivalents in the other modern languages, generally refer to the rules that make up the norms of human behavior. They are distinguished, both within one language and from one language to another, in terms of two types of problem. The first is the problem of the subject and its conduct, whether as an individual or as a community. The second concerns the nature of what "morals" designate: as a simple description, the designation "morals" refers to nature and to history; as a prescription, it dictates laws, and establishes values, whether good or bad. How these four dimensions (individual and collective, descriptive and prescriptive) are linked constitutes the arena in which the differences between languages are played out.'

25   Georges Canguilhem, *Knowledge of Life*, trans. Stefanos Geroulanos and Daniela Ginsburg (New York: Fordham University Press, 2008), p. 95.

26   On the relationship between *ēthos* and algorithms, see also Susanna Lindberg, 'Just Machines: On Algorithmic Ethos and Justice', in Susanna Lindberg and Hanna-Riikka Roine (eds), *The Ethos of Digital Environments: Technology, Literary Theory and Philosophy* (New York and London: Routledge, 2021).

27    Martin Heidegger, 'Letter on "Humanism"', trans. Frank A. Capuzzi, *Pathmarks*, ed. William McNeill (Cambridge: Cambridge University Press, 1998).

28    Georg Wilhelm Friedrich Hegel, *Phenomenology of Spirit*, trans. A. V. Miller (Oxford: Oxford University Press, 1977), p. 284.

29    Éric Sadin, *La vie algorithmique. Critique de la raison numérique* (Montreuil: L'Échappée, 2015); Antoinette Rouvroy and Thomas Berns, 'Le nouveau pouvoir statistique. Ou quand le contrôle s'exerce sur un réel normé, docile et sans événement car constitué de corps "numérique"…', *Multitudes* 40 (2010), pp. 88–103.

30    Antoinette Rouvroy and Thomas Berns, 'Détecter et prévenir: de la digitalisation des corps et de la docilité des normes' (2009), available at: <http://works.bepress.com/antoinette_rouvroy/30>, and Frédéric Neyrat, 'Avant-propos sur les sociétés de clairvoyance', *Multitudes* 40 (2010), pp. 104–11.

31    Philip Alston, *Extreme Poverty and Human Rights*, a report to the United Nations General Assembly (11 October 2019), available at: <https://undocs.org/A/74/493>.

32    Shoshana Zuboff, 'Big Other: Surveillance Capitalism and the Prospects of an Information Civilization', *Journal of Information Technology* 30 (2015), pp. 75–89, and Zuboff, *The Age of Surveillance Capitalism*.

33    See Cathy O'Neil, *Weapons of Math Destruction: How Big Data Increases Inequality and Threatens Democracy* (London: Penguin, 2017).

34    N. Katherine Hayles, *Unthought: The Power of the Cognitive Unconscious* (Chicago and London: University of Chicago Press, 2017).

35    See Cédric Villani et al., *For a Meaningful Artificial Intelligence: Towards a French and European Strategy*, report to the French Parliament (16 November 2018), available at: <https://ec.europa.eu/knowledge4policy/publication/meaningful-artificial-intelli-gence-towards-french-european-strategy_en>, and Tambiama André Madiega, *EU Guidelines on Ethics and Artificial Intelligence: Context and Implementation*, European Parliament Think Tank (19 September 2019), available at: <https://www.europarl.europa.eu/thinktank/en/document.html?reference=EPRS_BRI(2019)640163>.

36    See Hui, *Recursivity and Contingency*.

37    Michel Foucault, 'What is Enlightenment?', trans. Catherine Porter, in Paul Rabinow (ed.), *The Essential Works of Michel Foucault,*

*1954–1984, Volume One: Ethics*, trans. Robert Hurley et al. (London: Allen Lane, The Penguin Press, 1997). p. 309.

38   Ibid.

39   Henri Bergson, *The Two Sources of Morality and Religion*, trans. R. Ashley Audra and Cloudesley Brereton, with W. Horsfall Carter (Westport: Greenwood Press, 1974), p. 73, translation modified.

40   Bernard Stiegler, *Automatic Society, Volume 1: The Future of Work*, trans. Daniel Ross (Cambridge: Polity Press, 2016)

41   Foucault, 'What is Enlightenment?', p. 315.

42   Jacques Derrida, 'Passions: "An Oblique Offering"', *On the Name*, trans. David Wood, John P. Leavey, Jr. and Ian McLeod (Stanford: Stanford University Press, 1995), p. 16, and François Raffoul, 'Derrida and the Ethics of the Im-possible', *Research in Phenomenology* 38 (2008), pp. 270–90.

43   Foucault, 'Technologies of the Self', p. 225, translation modified.

44   Ibid., p. 239.

45   In the sense of Gilbert Simondon, *Individuation in Light of Notions of Form and Information*, trans. Taylor Adkins (Minneapolis and London: University of Minnesota Press, 2020), p. 50.

46   Foucault, 'Technologies of the Self', p. 238.

47   Michel Foucault, 'Truth, Power, Self: An Interview with Michel Foucault', in Luther H. Martin, Huck Gutman and Patrick H. Hutton (eds), *Technologies of the Self: A Seminar with Michel Foucault* (Amherst: University of Massachusetts Press, 1988), p. 11.

48   In this, locality corresponds to Richard Sennett's definition of an open city as a porous city. It does not function as an open door, but it does have membrane-borders that are necessary for it to function well. See Richard Sennett, *Building and Dwelling: Ethics for the City* (London: Penguin, 2018).

49   Ludwig von Bertalanffy, *General System Theory: Foundations, Development, Applications* (New York: Braziller, 1968).

50   See Susanna Lindberg, Mika Ojakangas and Sergei Prozorov (eds), *Europe Beyond Universalism and Particularism* (Houndmills, Basingstoke: Palgrave Macmillan, 2014).

51   See Jacques Ellul, *The Technological System*, trans. Joachim Neugroschel (New York: Continuum, 1980), and Hui, *Recursivity and Contingency*, p. 21.

52   In the sense of 'neganthropy' discussed in the introduction and ch. 1; in the sense of generativity discussed via the work of Mauro Magatti, Laura Gherardi and Chiara Giaccardi.

53   Hui, *Recursivity and Contingency*, p. 265.

54   Quoted in Gilles Deleuze, *Negotiations*, trans. Martin Joughin (New York: Columbia University Press, 1995), p. 172.

55   Jacques Derrida, in Derrida and Elisabeth Roudinesco, *For What Tomorrow...A Dialogue*, trans. Jeff Fort (Stanford: Stanford University Press, 2004), p. 64.

56   Corine Pelluchon, *Éthique de la considération* (Paris: Seuil, 2018).

57   Florence Burgat, *Une autre existence. La condition animale* (Paris: Albin Michel, 2012).

58   Although the belief that animal proteins are necessary for a balanced diet is deeply rooted in popular consciousness, the explosion in meat consumption is a historical fact. It took place in the 1950s in Europe, and its exponential growth was spurred by marketing strategies and the development of television. On this point, see Éric Baratay, *Le point de vue animal. Une autre version de l'histoire* (Paris: Seuil, 2012), p. 295. This disruption in our food 'preferences' is the corollary of a no less radical change in human-animal relations. See Michał Krzykawski, 'Re-animalizing Animals, Re-animating Humans', in Chiara Mengozzi (ed.), *Outside the Anthropological Machine: Crossing the Human-Animal Divide and Other Exit Strategies* (London and New York: Routledge, 2021).

59   Today, the most urbanized regions are found in North America (with 82% of the population living in urban areas in 2018), Latin America and the Caribbean (81%), Europe (74%) and Oceania (68%), with the level of urbanization in Asia reaching 50%. By contrast, Africa remains considerably rural, with 43% of the population living in urban spaces. See '68% of the World Population Projected to Live in Urban Areas By 2050, Says UN', *UN Department of Economic and Social Affairs* (16 May 2018), available at: <https://www.un.org/development/desa/en/news/population/2018-revision-of-world-urbanization-prospects.html>.

60   Alain Supiot, *The Spirit of Philadelphia: Social Justice vs. the Total Market*, trans. Saskia Brown (London and New York: Verso, 2012).

61   Florence Burgat, *L'Humanité carnivore* (Paris: Seuil, 2017), p. 9.

# 9 Planetary Detox and the Neurobiology of Ecological Collapse

*Gerald Moore, Nikolaos A. Mylonas, Marco Pavanini, Marie-Claude Bossière, Anne Alombert*

> We as a civilization are too much like someone addicted to a drug that will kill if continued and kill if suddenly withdraw.
> *James Lovelock[1]*

## I Introduction

### 107 Addictogenic society and adaptation to stress

To the surprise of commentators worldwide, in his 2006 State of the Union Address, George W. Bush began a call for investment in climate change solutions with the assertion that 'America is addicted to oil', and, moreover, that 'the best way to break this addiction is through technology'.[2] The claim was met with dismay by critics who, insisting on the need to differentiate between economic necessity and the euphoria of uncontrolled consumption, saw the 43rd president as legitimating hyperbole usually identified with the political left. Others have sought to demonstrate that the metaphor is not metaphorical: 'Just as the consequences of alcohol abuse, from DUIs to cirrhosis, are symptoms, global warming is a symptom of oil addiction.'[3]

The tension between the two positions can be resolved by loosening the etiological criteria of addiction in line with contemporary research. In this context, it makes more sense to speak of our increasingly pathological attachment to the world of technological *pharmaka* enabled by oil, rather than being directly addicted to the black stuff itself – whether oil or carbon in general (see Chapter 10). Our focus is therefore less on a narrow definition encompassing only the stereotype of far-gone, destitute, and seemingly irrecuperable abusers of a small range of traditionally recognized addictogens, like alcohol and heroin, and more on what the social psychologist Bruce K. Alexander terms 'addiction$_3$': a category that admits the prospect of consuming more or less anything to the extent of consequential 'overwhelming involvement' (shopping, eating, video games, pornography,...), and

which for the most part sustains the appearance of normality by denying the potentially 'fatal consequences' of our actions.[4]

If, as Alexander claims, addiction is a 'substantial and growing
danger in the 21st century',[5] this is, contrary to myth, not because
we have been seized by uncontrollable hedonism (we have known for
close to thirty years that the neural mechanisms for craving are bound
up with but not identical to those of pleasure[6]). Rather, it is because of
the short-term therapeutic role addiction continues to play in facilitating our adaptation to the stressful environments of contemporary living, however detrimental it proves to be beyond that.

## 108 Addiction, entropy and microworlds

Foreshadowing Bush, and with a greater emphasis on the simultaneous curativity and toxicity of technology than we find in his eulogiza-
tion of ecotech, in 1977 Nicholas Georgescu-Roegen wrote of 'mankind's addiction' to the 'comfort offered by the exosomatic organs'.
This addiction, he continued,

> which is completely analogous to that of the first fishes
> which evolved into air-breathing reptiles and thus became
> irrevocably addicted to air, now constitutes a predicament
> because the production of exosomatic organs became from a
> certain moment on dependent on the use of available energy
> and available matter stored in the bowels of the earth.[7]

The analogy risks being unhelpfully simplistic if read as diluting the
concept of addiction to the point where even air is seen as addictogenic. But Georgescu-Roegen's argument seems more refined if we
link it back to his work on the use of technology to stave off entropy
– and what the psychologist Mihaly Csikszentmihalyi terms 'psychic
entropy, a disorganization of the self that impairs its effectiveness
[...] to the point that it is no longer able to invest attention and pursue
its goals'.[8]

Through the technological organization of our local milieus, we
construct our own little ecological niches, or microworlds, and create our own interiority in the process. This is what Bernard Stiegler
calls the anti-entropy of 'work', in strict opposition to the entropic,
or 'anthropic', exhausting, forces of 'labour'.[9] This sense of work is
fundamentally related to what Csikszentmihalyi famously calls the
vitalizing, 'transcendent' happiness of 'flow', or immersion in a self-
contained and autotelic world of one's own making, oblivious to the
distractions of competing external stimuli. It is what he refers to as
'being in the zone'. Csikszentmihalyi also sees, however, that flow

experiences, from watching television to performing surgery, can be powerfully addictive, providing zones of calm focus in the midst of bewildering transformation.[10]

Subsequent research, most notably by the addiction anthropologist Natasha Dow Schüll, has shown that the gap between therapeutic work and toxic addiction may be imperceptibly narrow. Technologies from gambling machines to smartphones, often designed explicitly with addictogenesis in mind, serve as substitutes for world- and self-creation, a means of restricting the turmoil-afflicted mind with goals and direction, alleviating stress and anxiety – in other words, psychic entropy – for those otherwise unable to achieve flow states.[11]

### 109  Dysregulation of the dopaminergic system, delocalization and consumption

Proponents of 'entropic brain theory' in neuroscience similarly posit that stability-reinforcing patterns of activity associated with addiction (as well as OCD and depression) 'could be functional in […] working to resist a more catastrophic collapse' into the regression they identify with 'primary', or elevated-entropy, states of consciousness.[12]

Yet regardless of the relative health, or capacity for withstanding environmental perturbation, afforded by these zones, a potentially explosive problem results from the way that local sites of anti-entropy tip out entropy into their surrounding environments, be they individual bodies or the societies that house them. Mental stability comes at a price, and one that becomes all the costlier when the stress produced by the labours of our ever-expanding technosphere goes hand-in-hand with exosomatosis, or the spiralling doses of technology needed to prop up our ailing biology and planet. This ailing has become all the more acute of late, on account not just of climate change, but moreover because of a mooted 'evolutionary mismatch' between the anthropic forcings and pressures exerted on us by our technologically organized milieus and the ability to accommodate them afforded by our evolved ('endosomatic') physiology – most notably, an overburdened and increasingly dysregulated dopamine system.[13]

The central contention of this chapter is that the two phenomena are indissociable: we cannot hope to combat the collapse of our planetary ecosystems if we do not first address the 'functional uncoupling'[14] of *Homo sapiens* from the delocalized global spaces to which we are ever-increasingly pushed to adapt. At the very heart of ecological catastrophe is a chronic-systemic crisis of our psychological and social habitats, caused by populations who consume to dangerous excess as the only available strategy for coping with the pressures of exploitation to which contemporary society exposes us.

## II   The Entropocene as Limbic Capitalocene

### 110  What the words *pharmaka, anthropy* and *health* mean here

It is a fundamental premise of this book that 'Technology', in the words of John Stewart, paraphrasing Stiegler, 'is Anthropologically Constitutive'.[15] We cannot grasp what it means to be human without reference to the technical prostheses that regulate our experience of time, desire and attention, not to mention our ability to participate in the expected norms of society. Our tools are as vital to social life and the life of the (noetic) mind as oxygen is to our physiological existence. For our evolved physiology to be continually reinvented by our technics, however, there needs to be a biological correlate that explains our plasticity; one that allows for who we are to be transformed by what we use to navigate the world.

The latest suggestion attributes the enlarged cerebral cortex of members of the genus *Homo* to a 'dopamine dominated stratum', which differentiates us from earlier hominid ancestors by accounting for enhanced sensitivity to social and environmental cues, as well as diminishing aggression in favour of sociality and cooperation.[16] The dopamine system thus constitutes the neurobiological interface through which the human organism learns from and adapts to its surroundings, governing our responsiveness to external stimuli.

While it has long been understood that certain pharmaceutical substances, like alcohol or nicotine, exert a decisive modulatory effect on dopaminergic activity, and correspondingly on our behaviours, it is now becoming increasingly apparent that our experience of the world is continually rewritten, via the brain, by the technical objects that organize our lifeworlds. There is no hard and fast distinction, in other words, between pharmaceuticals and the simultaneously toxic and curative *pharmaka* that are technologies.

From ritual drinking and smoking, to the ever-larger and more energy-demanding cars needed by commuters (Georgescu-Roegen's example), to the takeaway coffees and smartphones that now serve as unavoidable entry-points into the contemporary world of work, whose very necessity disinclines us to acknowledge the extent to which we are automated to accommodate their present, our social and mental lives are habitually structured around the legitimation of certain modes of addictive, up-dosed technology consumption. But just as breathing oxygen is a principle cause of carcinogenesis, the life created or sustained by our exosomatic organs is also inseparable from what, following Stiegler, we are here calling *anthropy* and the deterioration of our artifactual environments. In a vicious circle of consumption, leading to environmental destabilization and to further, more pathological, consumption, the greater the stress placed on us by those environments, the more we become reliant on the therapy provided by the very technologies that do so much to cause the stress in the first place, and at ever greater cost to the planet.

The impact of some of this dependence is already well established and, indeed, being tackled, for instance, in the commitment of the United Nations Sustainable Development Goals to reducing deaths from 'non-communicable' diseases by one third. The WHO's report on *Health in 2015: From Millennium Development Goals to Sustainable Development Goals* devotes two whole chapters to NCDs: one focusing on mental health, dementia and substance abuse; and another on maladies stemming from poor lifestyle and preventable, *anthropically-caused*, environmental conditions including cancer, chronic respiratory problems, and so-called 'diseases of poverty' and 'despair' like cardiac illness and diabetes.[17]

The report remains conspicuously silent, however, on what can be identified as the underlying dopaminergic and ecological – and above all, economic – causes that link the two chapters, and has just as little to say about newer forms of environmental illness tied to the excessive consumption of more recent technologies. The effects of excessive screen-time on childhood development, and of social media on the health of our democracies,[18] are only now becoming the object of emerging scientific knowledge. The recourse to digital tablets by exhausted parents, who for respite use them to pacify small children, has led to diagnoses of attentional deficiency and linguistic and emotional under-development often confused with autism.[19]

### 111 A dopaminergic history of industrial capitalism and proletarianization

In another indication that the fallout of technological intoxication calls for an understanding of addiction that takes us beyond conventional ideas about the scale and social impact of problematic consumption, connections have been made between election-hacking in the United Kingdom and United States, and digital media consumers' craving for a 'buzz value' that trumps the veracity of online content.[20]

Luca Pani is the progenitor of the aforementioned theory of an 'evolutionary mismatch' between 'current environmental conditions in industrialized countries' and the 'completely different' ones 'in which the human central nervous system evolved'. One 'remarkable example' of this uncoupling of the human organism from its habitat, he argues, is the development of ever more powerful delivery mechanisms of drugs into the brain, the cumulative effect of which is to

> interfere with the global adaptation of an individual to its environment, producing not only an impairment in his/her hedonic capacities, but also a more disruptive effect on the cognitive and emotional abilities that are necessary for an effective interaction with the external world.[21]

The claim is made specifically in relation to hypodermic needles, crack pipes and the organic solvents often sniffed by addicts. But it also lends itself readily to a reading of the increasing potency of everyday technologies across the whole history of capitalism, which should no longer be separated into distinct producer- and consumer-led phases.

What began with the trade in spices and sugar, proceeds through tobacco, opium and caffeine on the way to pornography, pop music, modified corn starch and carfentanyl. The portable screen as a route of administration for the intoxications of ubiquitous gambling and fake news is just the latest stage in this history, and needs to be understood ecologically, in relation to the environmental stresses that push people in their direction, most notably the proletarianization of world-building, which the industrial production of craving, if not pleasure, seeks to offset. The passage to commodity-harvesting of comparatively mild psychoactives previously used only for medicine coincides with the early-modern onset of what the environmental historian Jason W. Moore calls 'Cheap Nature', referring to the un(der)paid toil extracted by merchants who would credit themselves for the industry of slaves, not to mention that of plant matter and the progressively depleted soil of the plantations.

This concept of Cheap Nature, encompassing 'Cheap Food', 'Cheap Energy', 'Cheap Raw Materials' and 'Cheap Labour', all priced in a way that ignores the long-term consequences of systemic overwork, takes us to the heart of what Moore reclassifies as the 'Capitalocene'.[22] But there's also another, vital, 'cheap' at stake, here: one that cuts across the binary of nature and culture, forcing us to see the collapse of planetary ecosystems in terms of the degradation of our social-technological environments, and the undue stress that this places on our biological functioning. Let us call it Cheap Desire, or Cheap Attention, in reference to a will that the climate-change-disavowing mentality of business-as-usual needs to be infinite. The *exhaustion* of this will, both individually and collectively, is bound up with increased reliance on the manufacture of habitual and frequently addictive consumption as a coping strategy.

## 112  The Anthropos of the Anthropocene

The long-standing but increasingly explicit elicitation of dopamine release in the human limbic system functions as the under-acknowledged engine of contemporary economics, not least because it constitutes the flipside of our enforced adaptation to the disadjusted environments in which we consume. Biologists have been warning for years of the risk posed to our health and intelligence by endocrine-disrupting pollutants,[23] but the reciprocal reinvention of humans and the technosphere is yet more profound than even this warning implies.

The *Anthropos* of the Anthropocene is one whose biochemistry is undergoing constant modulation by extractive technologies that engineer consumptive habits to maintain the waning levels of demands around which global order is organized. In the words of Bruce Alexander, addiction has been 'globalized' through the exploitation of the very nervous system via which we interact with and learn from our surroundings. This 'dopamining' is, in turn, inextricable from capitalism's production of 'psychosocial dislocation'[24] and our corresponding attempts to withdraw from what David Graeber has called the 'dead zones' of our traumatized working habitats.[25]

When Jason W. Moore speaks of the 'Capitalocene', he does so to avoid holding the planet's various populations equally responsible for an ecological catastrophe caused vastly disproportionately by the 'developed' capitalist economies of the prevailing world system.[26] In so doing, he runs the risk of unduly divorcing us from complicity, as if capital is somehow distinct from the people who continually remake and enact it; hence our (Stieglerian) stated preference for Anthropocene, with its echo of *Entropocene*.[27]

A more nuanced assignation of responsibility comes from reframing the problem of causality in relation to habit-creation and the manipulation of the pleasure circuitry of the brain. The American historian David T. Courtwright has coined the expression 'limbic capitalism' to describe the coupling of the entrepreneurial exploitation of the 'evolved drives' of our neural infrastructure of reward, with the provision of goods and services designed 'to cope with the damage' inflicted by free markets on the psychosocial structures that enable us to absorb the shock of change.[28] Limbic capitalism has been brought to the fore by the combination of relentless labouring under conditions of mounting precarity and deficient social support systems, which places the burden of coping firmly on the side of individuals whose only survival mechanisms become the panoply of cures-for-sale offered up for consumption by the market.

Recent research into the social psychology and neurobiology of addiction suggests that this process should no longer be framed around the idea of the brain being irreversibly 'hijacked' by substances that destroy its natural chemical composition.[29] But there is a legitimate question of our complicity in the surrender of an agency that is only ever fragile. We willingly, albeit passively, submit to bombardment by ever more refined forms of stimulation to distract us from the perturbations of a market system that – be it via workplace deregulation, or through the imposition of structural adjustment programs on developing countries – systematically dissolves the capacity of communities to employ collective niche construction in the service of vitality, that is, to participate actively in the formation and modification of their living environments.

## 113 Anaesthesia and destruction

Bringing together Moore and Courtwright enables us to see that the 'Entropocene' is also a 'limbic Capitalocene': an epochal disaster encompassing not just the planet and human civilization, but one moreover rooted in a retreat into oblivion that Alexander describes as a 'rational', 'adaptive' response to the entropic climate in which we labour.[30] Ecological catastrophe is less about a surfeit of human ecosystem-engineering than its absence: the surrender of agency to an automation of the nervous system by technologies that think and feel in our place.

The result is a vicious cycle of excess, where climate change is biochemically intertwined with the overworking of the dopamine system, produced by the ever more efficacious doses of intoxicants we consume to anaesthetize ourselves against the impact of social breakdown. And this means that attempts to deal with climate change will only be treating its symptoms, and doing so in vain, unless they also engage with the addictogenic, 'hyperdopaminergic society' that lies at its origin. By the same measure, the solution will not reside in implementing consumption abstention, 'dopamine fasting', or a global 'Twelve Steps' programme either.

We cannot do without our *pharmaka*, and nor can we simply eliminate their constitutive toxicity through some fantasized process of purification that preserves only their curativity. But we can aim for an organization of society that curbs their toxic power by generating alternative forms of therapy. Such a reorganization would aim to lessen those stresses, which leave us in such need of noetic bandages and treatments [*pansements*] that we find ourselves consuming these intoxicating *pharmaka* to pathological, destructive excess. Understood in these terms, the project of planetary detox intersects felicitously with the philosophico-political aims of the internation: to cultivate locality and a restoration of depleted social bonds as a means to recapacitate the agency that we have surrendered to the compulsion to consume.

## II  Dopaminergic Animals in a Hyperdopaminergic Society

### 114  Culture, dopamine and attention

The crux of what looks like our collective pathology revolves around the relationship between culture and the neurotransmitter, dopamine, whose functions include bonding, the facilitation of experiential learning (through acquiring what we have throughout this book called retentions), habituation and anticipation (as what we have called protentions). The principal role of dopamine concerns its involvement in the seeking out of novel information and the encoding of repeat behaviours that prove initially rewarding, or 'salient'. To put this in the recent language of Yuk Hui,[31] it works to absorb contingency into a routine, by bringing us to crave the stability of habitual repetition.

The process begins at birth: one currently dominant idea builds on the attachment theory of John Bowlby to argue that the limbic system is responsible for the formation of social bonds between mother, child and the extended family.[32] Bowlby observed that young children starved of maternal attention quickly adapt to their environmental instability by becoming withdrawn and emotionally detached, reacting more to the novelty of new toys than to the unfamiliar adults who bestow them.[33] These changes are now understood in relation to neuroplasticity, meaning the ability of the neuronal organization of the brain to be dopaminergically moulded by the stimuli of its surroundings. Rat studies have shown that contact between mother and child influences not only the development of dopaminergic circuits in the newborn's brain, but also conditions the parents' emotional and physical attentiveness, by bringing them to suffer the absence of their offspring through craving more familiarly recognized as love. Pups reared in prolonged isolation demonstrated 'elevated baseline dopamine levels and increased dopamine release in acute stress in adulthood'.[34]

The dopamine system, in other words, compensates for the lack of a familial anchor point by facilitating the creation of stabilizing habits in the face of stress. Through it, we reach out and latch on to anything able to create an emotional impact, with our neuronal circuitry reorganizing to become more responsive to the source of reward, pruning away synaptic relations linked to the decreasingly necessary wider orbit of attention, in the process. This mechanism for coping with the absence of a social bond proves highly adaptive, equipping us to live through anxiogenic periods of instability.

But it is also linked to 'enhanced sensitivity to psychostimulants such as cocaine' and 'may lead to increased vulnerability to addiction'.[35] Addiction thus 'shared a common neurobiology' with attachment,[36] in an identity that explains the scientific recognition that love bears all the neurobiological and psychological hallmarks of substance dependence. It should also, therefore, be seen as a kind of substitute for social investment – a way, we might say, of fabricating (ontological) ground, there where its absence becomes most apparent. The effect cuts both ways, with addiction characterized by a retreat from the social relations for which it substitutes. Looking at the tightly knit networks of companionship that often exist among street users, we can also see how it functions as a complicated attempt to create social attachments where they are found wanting.[37]

## 115  The biology of attachment and the dopaminergic genesis of the mind

The biology of attachment is one way of making sense of Bernard Stiegler's claim that addictions are not solely pathological, but simultaneously toxic and curative.[38] It likewise sheds light on an established, but debatably successful, therapeutic tradition of seeking to replace toxic addictions (heroin, smoking, alcohol) with 'better' ones (to God, methadone, vaping, AA meetings and running, for instance).[39]

Catherine Malabou is another recent exemplar of this tradition, arguing that 'addictive processes have in large part caused the Anthropocene, and only new addictions will be able to partly counter them.'[40] We need to be careful not to conflate 'better' with toxicity-free, or next-generation technological quick fixes, intended to facilitate consumption, however. The looming future of geo-engineered skies, seeded with a shield of aerosol phosphates to protect the planet from the solar heat building up behind it, has already been compared to enabling alcoholism, as the 'dialysis that allows the patient to continue drinking'.[41]

The release of the dopamine neurotransmitter is at the heart of our capacity to adjust to environmental change, and its relation to managing uncertainty, in particular, explains why it has arguably played a vital role in both making and now unmaking the modern globalized world. Writing in *The Dopaminergic Mind in Human Evolution and History*, the psychologist Fred H. Previc argues that the story of human ecological history is one of increasing dominance of dopamine in the brain, which he links, in turn, to the rise of 'abstract intelligence, exploratory drive, urge to control and conquer', as well as acquisitiveness, goal- and future-directedness, long-term planning and the pursuit of religious and scientific truth.[42] The emergence of the dopaminergic mind is developmental rather than evolutionary, a product of ecological shifts inducing neurochemical, but not genetic, change. It begins with prehistorical alterations in diet before intensifying around 6,000 years ago, alongside the growing need to compete for resources and ensuing calculations of settled societies.

Here, Previc's argument resonates with major evolutionary-anthropological claims about the inability of our cognitive architecture comfortably to manage large numbers of social relationships and the breakdown of our sense of communal belonging and motivation to participate in the life of the collective, once a certain scale threshold is passed.[43] We can identify Neolithic sedentarization and, in particular, the ensuing rise of cities (see Chapter 2) as a significant source of this growth of competition, because they removed people from the familiar, small-scale networks of extended family life and transplanted them into 'depersonalized'[44] urban settlements where they had to 'suppress suspicion of others', negotiate cultural politics and 'adapt to densely crowded neighbourhoods' of complete strangers: '*unfamiliarity* became the measure of human relations'.[45]

The result of this heightened stress, Previc contends, was neurochemical imbalance, triggered by the depletion of serotonin and norepinephrine relative to dopamine. The next stage of his argument corroborates Peter Sloterdijk's identification of early-modern European expansionism with the rise of 'risk-taking', 'disinhibited' subjectivity.[46] Previc posits that the reorganization of society around dopamine was a decisive factor in colonialism, the growth of capitalism and the Enlightenment – and has become even more pronounced since the second, 'hyperdopaminergic', half of the twentieth century.

## 116  Neoliberalism as a hyperdopaminergic system

'Hyperdopaminergic society' describes the neoliberal era of enforced adaptation to the demands of free markets; the ideology of 'disruption'; and the proliferating use of dopamining techniques to colonize what has elsewhere been termed the 'available brain time' of consumers.

> A highly dopaminergic society is fast-paced and even manic, given that dopamine is known to increase activity levels, speed up our internal clocks and create a preference for novel over unchanging environments.[47]

Previc reels off a list of 'hyperdopaminergic disorders', including depression, obsession-compulsion, autism, schizophrenia, Tourette's, Alzheimer's and Parkinson's. We can also add ADHD to this list, though it is also, ironically, linked to traits that can thrive in hyperdopaminergic conditions.

The D4 dopamine receptor is believed to have evolved around forty thousand years ago, at a time when the enhanced susceptibility to stimulation it confers would have proved adaptively advantageous for ancestors who took risks to explore new territories in search of food. Nowadays, the allele is thought prevalent in sufferers of attention deficit disorders, who end up being pathologized by the absence of unexplored Palaeolithic landscapes in the cramped and understimulating conditions of contemporary urban living.[48] Homogenized, metric-heavy and greenspace-poor classrooms would be foremost examples of environments to which holders of the gene now risk being maladapted.[49]

The attempt to diminish this maladaptation, by increasing our margins of tolerance for the 'inconstancies of the environment' (to borrow a phrase from Georges Canguilhem[50]), is a major cause of addiction, which should be recognized as another hyperdopaminergic disorder; perhaps even the most prevalent one. Its inclusion within this category of stress-related illness need not presuppose the classical and now, it is argued, outdated 'disease model', which treats dependence as a neurobiological disorder of the dopamine system, routinely said to be triggered when the brain is 'hijacked' by a limited range of corruptive intoxicants. If this model offers an all-too-easy mechanism for separating out problem drinkers, junkies and pornography users from mere model consumers, contemporary research is moving in the opposite direction, disentangling addiction from threshold-surpassing quantities of specific substances to focus more on the hyperdopaminergic setting that occasion an increasingly universal culture of obsessive consumption.

Addiction is now increasingly located at the intersection of the neuroplastic brain with the instability of what the clinician Jean-Pierre Couteron, a former president of France's Fédération Addiction, has baptized 'addictogenic society'.[51] Pathology no longer resides solely in the addict, but is learned, stemming from the viciously circular moulding of synaptic circuits around manufactured intensities that substitute for the social bonds we are losing the luxury of forming. As our surrounding environments become more hyper-competitive and antisocial, ever higher doses of supply-maximized stimulus respond to both rising baseline levels of dopamine and the desensitization that follows from the brain's adjustment to habituation.

## III   Adaptation and Encapsulation

### 117   Capitalism and dependence

Addiction as a strategy for managing ecological stress is what we saw with the 'Gin Craze' of anomic, industrializing London, and in the gambling and opium dens through which the dislocated peoples of dopaminergic society absorbed the disadjustments of the eighteenth and nineteenth centuries. Phenomena like 'white morbidity'[52] and the current American opioid crisis combine with the 'soaring' non-medical recourse to Tramadol in parts of Africa and Asia,[53] to say nothing of the ubiquity of staring vacantly at the screens of our digital devices, as instances of what Bruce Alexander describes as capitalism's contemporary 'globalization of addiction'.

There is nonetheless a difference between earlier, historical, epidemics and those that mark our hyperdopaminergic present. Patterns of abuse appear alongside periods of rapid technological change – the evolution of distillation and techniques, or instruments, of stimulation delivery – as new sources of stimulus overwhelm the social norms organized around older forms of technology.

But there is reason to think the organization of culture can prove highly effective in regulating consumption. One post-millennial rereading of China's Opium Wars emphasizes the success of traditional Chinese smoking rituals in absorbing the massive increase in supply and facilitating the management of functional habits. Frank Dikötter attributes much of received wisdom regarding opiate-addled Chinese people to colonialist-biological stereotypes of evolutionarily weak-willed Orientals, which resurgent nationalism also exploited. Far more destructive, in terms of eliminating the social shock absorbers of 'backward' imperial culture, were the nationalists' politics of prohibition and the emergence of the disease model of addiction, which rewrote history to cast opium as wholly and singularly toxic: a destroyer of agriculture, work ethic and national character.[54] Fredric Jameson has written that 'the postmodern, or late capitalism, has at least brought the epistemological benefit of revealing the ultimate structure of the commodity to be that of addiction itself'.[55] But this was perhaps already apparent from the time of the Opium Wars, with opium's change in status coinciding with its commodification.

In any case, as has been argued elsewhere, historical addiction epidemics have tended to fade out as affected societies readjust their educational norms and social organization to accommodate hitherto disruptive technologies.[56] Bernard Stiegler has argued that, in our present age of the economics of 'disruption', the historical pattern of innovation leading to a 'readjustment' of society around new technologies, breaks down.[57] It comes as no surprise that global consumption has skyrocketed over the last thirty years, during the very period when knowledge of climate change might have suggested that we would be taking actions to curb it.

## 118  The conservative revolution of consumer capitalism

Since the conservative revolution of the 1980s, relentless waves of technological change have combined with labour market reforms intended to reduce the welfare safety net and spur us on to adapt to a more aggressively competitive, Darwinian way of life, dressed up as creative destruction. There is no time for systems of social support and integration to catch up with the disintegrations created by waves of technological-stimulatory overload. Coupled with the built-in obsolescence of technological devices designed for shortness of lifespan, these changes make chasing to keep up with the rest of society our default mode of existence.

It is in this context that the contemporary pattern of consumption is to have multiple, overlapping addictions, overlain on a metanarrative of unending adaptation, which leaves us struggling to create curativity with intermittent, 'hormetic' doses.[58] A constant state of excitation has become the ideological rule, irrespective of the longer-term damage this inflicts on our capacity for life-building.

Previc also suggests that, while posing potentially 'the greatest threat to mental health' in the industrialized world, the prevalence of dopaminergic disorders is 'much rarer or at least less severely manifested in non-industrial societies'.[59] Emerging research on the serious under-diagnosis of mental illness in the developing world raises questions about the latter part of this claim.[60] So, too, should the continuity of ecological factors behind the rise of addictogenic societies. We can read the adaptationist economics underpinning the manufacture of dependence in the West as a direct continuation of the policies of dependence-inculcation trialled and imposed on Africa and Latin America, first through colonialism and then through the 'structural readjustment' programs of the IMF and WTO. The effect of both has been sustained disadjustment, where consumption comes to substitute for community-led vitality and social support systems.

### 119  Colonialism, opium war and forced adaptation

Between the seventeenth and early twentieth centuries, the British East India Company imposed organizational reforms on Indian agriculture that, in addition to causing massive starvation and cata-lysing the Opium Wars, also set the tone for the whole of the lim-bic Capitalocene. Prior to colonization, subsistence farming on com-munal land had been the norm. A traditional system of grain storage and reciprocal, mutual support enabled farmers to stave off the worst of climatic instability. But the British enclosed the commons and compelled the sale of grain reserves to drive up agricultural pro-ductivity, forcing the replacement of subsistence crops with those, including opium, specifically cultivated for export. The same opium was dumped on China to create habits and a demand that would be financed by the sale, hitherto refused, of Chinese tea to a British pub-lic newly enraptured by caffeine.[61]

Similar stories of enforced adaptation come from Latin America, where the carefully managed diversity of indigenous agriculture gave way, under duress, to the dominance of calorie- and dopamine-boost-ing sugar for export, which, in turn, freed up European labour to focus on urban industrialization.[62] Later, postcolonial efforts to overturn industrial underdevelopment and the dependence of the developing world on Western industrial technologies were battered into submis-sion by Western loans, distributed in the manner of a dealer looking to snare new clients, which merely reinforced relations of patronage. The conditions of loan receipt, and eventually also of their forgive-ness and restructuring, went further in necessitating the destruction of techniques of social readjustment deemed to be constraints on the free functioning of the market.[63]

'Resilience' came to denote the very opposite of how the philoso-pher of medicine, Georges Canguilhem, understands health: not the

capacity to reinvent one's milieu in the face of environmental perturbation, but relentless adaptation to the demand to open up domestic
economies to international competition. The proletarianizing effect
of dependence on licensed Western technologies is redoubled by the
active inhibition of local forms of community vitality.

## 120  Globalization and dopamine

Dopamine is linked to globalization, on the one hand, by its contribution to abstract spatialization, exploration, conquest and the pursuit of
stimulation; on the other hand, by its links to the destruction of locality to which we are now bearing witness. If the history of dopaminergic society is coextensive with that of the stresses and seductions
of the city, with the latter now collapsing from the centre outwards,
the two may yet also prove coterminous. Much recognisably modern
state-building was also born of the pressures of urban intoxication.
Well into the nineteenth century, cities were plagued by cholera-
infested water, the pernicious effects of which were diminished by the
'antidiarrheal properties of narcotics and the antimicrobial properties
of alcohol'.[64] According to Courtwright the building of waterworks
and public fountains provided both hygiene and alternative sources of
much-needed stimulation.

Public parks and spaces worked to similar counter-stimulatory
effect. Their ongoing disappearance is already recognized as a contributory factor in the rise of the ADHD that has been described as
the other 'side of the same mental coin' as addiction,[65] due to the
way in which both conditions habitually entail a compulsive switch-
ing of focus away from socially preferred objects of attention, and
towards more potent, distracting, sources of stimulus like screens and
video games.

One of the great problems of the digital stage of dopamining, on
this note, is that the conventional organization of our lives and analogue living spaces routinely provides little in the way of sufficiently
attractive alternatives to coax those who have withdrawn from society
back into it. If the city just about survives as a commercial entity, that
is surely in large part because its high streets have been colonized by
outlets furnishing the very objects of addiction and heightened stimulus, like smartphones, electronic cigarettes, coffee and alcohol, that
push us away from it. As a site of ritual coming together and localized
point-of-retreat, it is ceding its place to the delocalized, virtual micro-
spheres of Amazon, Netflix and social media.

Hence, more broadly, the irony of our unfurling planetary crisis: it corresponds to the fracturing of the world, understood in the

Heideggerian sense of an ecology of possibility. Bruno Latour has recently analysed the politics of climate change disavowal around the idea of the 'absence of a *common world* we can share'.[66] Faced with the choice between sacrificing their way of living, or maintaining business-as-usual at the price of condemning vast swathes of the globe to devastation, Latour argues, governing elites have retreated from the aspiration to rule in the interests of the many, and simply seek to sequester themselves away in privatized niches, from which they can ride out the Apocalypse.

## 121 Spheres, bubbles, foam

Latour's argument works equally as a description of a much greater spectrum of limbic Capitalocenic behaviour, insofar as disavowal – a classic symptom of addiction – has become the default mode of experience; insofar as we are all seemingly engaged in a process of withdrawal from the universal public spaces formerly characterized by joint attention, collective projects and what Jacques Rancière would call a 'common aisthesis', or unifying experience of what amounts to the same place.[67] In dopamined, addictogenic society, the shared world succumbs to fragmentation into the hermetically self-contained bubbles of private islands, gated communities and internet echo chambers in which one can escape the feelings of stressed-out hopelessness.

The reference to bubbles, here, recalls not only the filter bubbles of Web 2.0 evoked by Eli Pariser,[68] but also the social and psychological structures of immunity, the 'capsule architectures' and 'foam' of Peter Sloterdijk: 'In foam worlds, the individual bubbles are not absorbed into a single, integrative hyper-orb',[69] but remain separate. The limbic Capitalocene reveals itself as just the latest stage of the foaming of the world into self-contained capsules.

According to the psychiatrist Daniel Casriel, this search for insularity and 'safe spaces' is exactly what is at stake in addiction. Casriel understood 'encapsulation' as a third way out for those maladapted for 'fight or flight' to 'anesthetize' the feeling of being unable to cope.[70] And his generation of drug therapists sought to counter the tendency towards withdrawal by recreating a bridge between the addict's zones of retreat and the public sphere by reabsorbing individual bubbles of foam into a communal milieu.

Their project of detox through a reintegration of addicts into the public sphere was derailed by a combination of rehab consumerism – that is, of treatment models that reinforce the very proletarianizing tendencies they are supposed to combat – and the shift of policy-making towards the 'War on Drugs'. But proponents of this re-synthesis of the public also ran up against the complexities of seeking to replace toxic forms of dependence with others deemed beneficial. Even during the 1970s, therapeutic communities of the kind pioneered by Phoenix House were accused of functioning as 'encapsulated addict worlds',[71] where addicts were allowed to live without thought for their reinsertion into the shared space from which they had withdrawn through addiction.

## IV Towards a Psychosocial Ecology of Detoxification

### 122 The symptomatic effects of worldwide withdrawal

If climate change is a problem of the limbic Capitalocene, which is to say, a phenomenon of addictive consumption induced by generalized proletarianization, then what would that mean for how we treat it? Interestingly, there is a parallel argument present both in the dominant paradigm of addiction treatments and partly also in the discourses of climate change. Its main logic consists in emphasizing the necessity of a radical break with existing patterns of consumption.

We owe to Daniel Ross the observation that, in an image much exploited by the industries of climate denial, the public imagination is dominated by visions of carbon cuts leading to enforced cold turkey: abrupt withdrawal from a way of life organized around technology-led consumerism, followed by the misery of endless abstinence, planet-wide 'counting the days', and slip-ups where we indulge in fracking 'just one more time'. In the best-case version of this scenario, we might manage to get by as 'functional' addicts, carefully allowing ourselves a few minutes of internet, oil and shopping for plastic per day, but only in the strictly controlled doses already (ineffectually) advised in the small print of greenwashed society. Anything to avoid the intolerability of withdrawal symptoms that would be experienced both individually and collectively: perhaps not the vomiting and diarrhea induced by discontinuing opioids, but certainly anxiety, irritability and fatigue. And who knows how these would scale up at the level of politics and society?

Distaste for such symptoms, not to mention conviction in their absolute unviability, has already been circularly deployed to proscribe the diagnosis of addiction in relation to pathological digital media consumption.[72] Environmental writers have been equally quick to insist that abstention from technology consumption is simply not an option.

Saving the world, it is routinely argued, will require more and greater technological modernity, not a reversion to 'collective sacrifice'.[73]

The dubious advantage of framing ecological collapse in terms of the intolerable price of cold turkey, and more broadly of clinging to a disease model of addiction that allows us to distance climate change from pathological consumption, is that it exonerates us from taking preventive climate action until it's effectively too late – until, that is, we hit the mythical, iceberg-free, point of 'rock bottom'.

### 123  To touch or not to touch the (rock) bottom

Most famously spelled out in the second of AA's Twelve Steps, 'rock bottom' is the moment where we supposedly, finally, take the crucial measure of admitting 'hopelessness' and 'complete defeat' in the face of a 'mental obsession so subtly powerful that no amount of human willpower could break it'.[74] It dawns on us once the object of addiction becomes so all-consuming as to exclude everything else we hold dear from the increasingly narrowed orbit of attention. According to this logic, the typical alcoholic is so selfish and lacking in care that they will only be roused to action when it becomes a matter of literal life or death. Only having lost their job, their money, their family, their health and perhaps even their home – and now their planet – will they recognize the need to replace their own defective willpower with the motivation provided by AA, through God.

We should note a degree of wiggle-room in the original formulation of the *Twelve Steps*. AA co-founder Bill W refers to some early success in recruiting 'young people who were scarcely more than potential alcoholics', and even states one aim of the nascent society as being to spare them hell by 'rais[ing] the bottom the rest of us had hit to the point where it would hit them' sooner. That ambition was ultimately abandoned and he concedes that 'few people will sincerely try to practice the AA program unless they have hit bottom'.[75]

The rock-bottom doctrine has since hardened into a cornerstone of the rehab industry, in spite of doubts over its basis in evidentiary science. According to the addiction writer Maia Szalavitz,[76] the consecration of hitting bottom is due in part to a judicial system that legitimates the counterproductively punitive treatment of addicts, not least by dressing up retribution as tough love. Writing in *The Sober Truth: Debunking the Bad Science Behind 12-Step Programs and the Rehab Industry*, the Harvard clinician and psychiatrist Lance Dodes is similarly critical. For Dodes, it is a myth that constitutes the ultimate form of marketing for a defective cure we are encouraged to consume all the more fervently when it emphatically doesn't work.[77]

The continued success of the commercialized rehab industry cannot be divorced from the way that its failures are routinely explained away through reference to clients who, having yet to hit the nadir required to spur them towards committed sobriety, just don't want 'it' badly enough. The typically neoliberal emphasis on deficient personal responsibility conveniently covers over more compelling accounts of rehab's production of relapsing recidivists: namely, its replication of the paralysis and enforced adaptation to the very kind of (institutionally imposed) stressful circumstances that push people towards addiction in the first place.

Fortunately, however, abstention is no longer the shibboleth it once was in therapeutic circles. The majority of the 'addiction treatment industry is based on a defective model that has been unchanged since the 1930s', namely one built on the reification of the Twelve Steps into the kind of doctrinally rigid and proletarianizing, mass-produced consumerist model never envisaged by the Kropotkinian forefathers of Alcoholics Anonymous. Ideological dogmatism and the marketing of abstractly universal and ultimately branded modes of therapy have rendered many therapeutic institutions incapable of the self-transformation they preach, unwilling to share and create knowledge with 'rival' providers, and unwilling to devolve decision-making autonomy to patients who are frequently there by coercion, court-mandated to undergo rehab as an alternative to prison, and with no option but to comply with inflexible regimes imposed on them from above.[78]

## 124  The origins of the Alcoholics Anonymous movement – contributory therapy

But 'there is also significance evidence' of 'empathetic and empowering approaches that let patients set their own goals'[79] yielding greater success than those that ultimately reproduce the environmental dislocation underpinning recourse to addiction. An emerging panoply of alternatives to the dominant one-size-fits-all programs of rehab includes elements of a return to the roots of AA in the anarchist theory of 'mutual aid'.[80] Previous chapters in this volume have sketched out how localities might be revitalized around the use of digital platforms to cultivate participatory, citizen-led, research, as per the territorial experimentations being undertaken in the Plaine Commune Contributory Learning Territory. In a clear nod to the ethos of self-organizing and spontaneously-emerging community support, their potential is to provide groups and networks of groups with their own means of generating self-knowledge, which enables them, in turn, to transform and revitalize through their own efforts the toxic environments that make hyper-consumption a therapeutic response to disadjustment.

One pioneering experiment of this nature is Plaine Commune's 'Clinique Contributive' (see recherchecontributive.org/clinique-contributive/), which, under the auspices of the child psychiatrist Marie-Claude Bossière, brings together researchers, healthcare professionals and parents of young children diagnosed as suffering from the effects of overexposure to the distractions of digital technologies. Its aim is to combat screen addiction by creating a locality in which parents can learn from one another in a non-judgmental setting and generate shared knowledge about the developmental impact on their children of both parties' excessive consumption. The clinic also provides the basis for recreating the extended care networks whose erosion has made often isolated, tired and stressed-out adults cling to the comfort of their smartphones in the absence of better psychosocial integration. In exploring the connections between fatigue and the sustained use of sleep-impoverishing devices, they discover alternative forms of invigoration to digital overstimulation.

Contributory therapy thus becomes a technique for inventing forms of emotional and social connection that transcend commercialized individualism, new forms of *philia* tied to the pursuit of the common good, echoing the kind evoked by Aristotle in Books VIII and IX of the *Nicomachean Ethics*. We can also see it as a form of work (not labour – see Chapter 3) and as a process of 'capabilization' (see Chapter 4) in which the contribution to knowledge allows people to become what they are 'able to do and be'.[81]

### 125 The therapeutic group – *therapeia* and *philia*

The therapeutic potential of contributory research can also be understood through the insights into human development of the Russian psychologist Lev Vygotsky. Vygotsky's conviction was that human action is a transformational process where individuals, *Homo sapiens* as a species, and tools, exist in a network of mutual co-creation. In an essay on 'The Collective as a Factor in the Development of the Abnormal Child', Vygotsky characterized the social dimension of development as a 'function of collective behaviour, as a form of cooperation or cooperative activity'.[82] He borrowed from city-planning the concept of a 'zone of proximal development' to articulate how, with the help of peers, or of another more competent individual, the child becomes able to do things that she was not previously capable of doing.[83] Vygotsky saw this phenomenon occurring especially in playful situations, where the 'child always behaves beyond his average

age, above his daily behaviour; in play it is as though he were a head taller than himself'.[84] Development, he argued, emerges from a social, relational context in which the individual and the group grow into something different, by creating new norms in their relationship with the environment.

One of the few attempts to transfer this perspective into practice took place in the East Side Institute in New York, where, in the 1970s, the therapists Fred Newman and Lois Holzman combined Vygotskian conceptualizations of development with Wittgenstein's work on language to create the psychotherapeutic method of 'Social Therapy'.[85] Social Therapy starts from the premise that individuals 'are forced to adapt to conditions which increasingly and more and more obviously are against not only their own interests but those of the human species as a whole',[86] with drugs and homelessness being part of a wide range of failed attempts at adaptation. And it understands the group as a 'unit of transformation/change/growth/learning' through which individuals can be transformed without a specific focus on 'fixing the problems' of its members.[87]

The group becomes both a method and a result, its activities serving as an *emotional zone of proximal development*. This volume's chapter on 'social sculpture' outlines a similar 'transindividuation' of individuals within a collective through knowledge-sharing. Despite criticizing the rigidity of the Alcoholics Anonymous, Dodes likewise reinforces the value of this kind of localized therapeutic community, suggesting that 'groups would be a highly valuable component' in the treatment of addiction 'If they were designed to help patients [...] to experiment with new ways of relating'.[88]

## 126 The mother of all critical situations

From this perspective, the function of addiction is to facilitate the co-creation of forms of life hitherto impossible to imagine. And the relationship between what constitutes the possibility and impossibility of future development should be considered one of the most important steps in a therapeutic endeavour.

In his book, *The Psychology of Experiencing: The Resolution of Life's Critical Situations*, another Russian, Fyodor Vasilyuk, sought to investigate

> just what a person does when there is nothing to be done, when he or she is in a situation that renders impossible the realisation of his or her needs, attitudes, values, etc.[89]

Such moments are 'critical situations' in which the individual is unable to 'cope with the existing external and internal conditions of life'.[90] The same encounter with a metaphorical brick wall is addressed in DeYoung and Krueger's understanding of psychopathology as a 'persistent failure [...] to generate effective new goals, interpretations, or strategies when existing ones prove unsuccessful'.[91]

The Anthropocene presents us with the mother of all critical situations, one that threatens the very habitability of the planet, over and above exposing as ineffective the existing norms around which our lives are organized. Yet it therefore also offers an opportunity for the abandonment of old norms that are making us ill, and an overdue end to hyperdopaminergic society. Hence its paradoxical promise of renewed vitality.

## Notes

1    James Lovelock, *The Revenge of Gaia* (Harmondsworth, Middlesex: Penguin, 2007), p. 8.

2    George W. Bush, 'State of the Union Address' (31 January 2006), available at: <https://georgewbush-whitehouse.archives.gov/stateoftheunion/2006/>.

3    Stephen Healy, 'Psychoanalysis and the Geography of the Anthropocene: Fantasy, Oil Addiction, and the Politics of Global Warming', in Steve Pile and Paul Kingsbury (eds), *Psychoanalytic Geographies* (New York: Routledge, 2014), p. 181.

4    Bruce K. Alexander, *The Globalization of Addiction: A Study in the Poverty of Spirit* (Oxford: Oxford University Press, 2007), pp. 35–37.

5    Ibid., p. 37.

6    Terry E. Robinson and Kent C. Berridge, 'The Neural Basis of Drug Craving: An Incentive-Sensitisation Theory of Addiction', *Brain Research Reviews* 18 (1993), pp. 247–91.

7    Nicholas Georgescu-Roegen, 'Inequality, Limits and Growth from a Bioeconomic Viewpoint', *Review of Social Economy* 35 (1977), p. 363.

8    Mihaly Csikszentmihalyi, *Flow: The Psychology of Happiness* (London: Rider, 2002), p. 37.

9    Bernard Stiegler, *L'emploi est mort, vive le travail! Entretien avec Ariel Kyriou* (Paris: Mille et une nuits, 2015).

10   Mihaly Csikszentmihalyi, 'Reflections on Enjoyment', *Perspectives in Biology and Medicine* 28 (1985), pp. 489–97.

11   See Natasha Dow Schüll, *Addiction by Design: Machine Gambling in Las Vegas* (Princeton: Princeton University Press, 2012), and Louis Leung, 'Exploring the Relationship Between Smartphone Activities, Flow Experience and Boredom in Free Time', *Computers in Human Behaviour* 203 (2020), pp. 130–39.

12   Robin L. Carhart-Harris, et al., 'The Entropic Brain: A Theory of Conscious States Informed by Neuroimaging Research with Psychedelic Drugs', *Frontiers in Human Neuroscience* 8 (2014), p. 15.

13   See Luca Pani, 'Is There an Evolutionary Mismatch Between the Normal Physiology of the Human Dopaminergic System and Current Environmental Conditions in Industrialized Countries?', *Molecular Psychiatry* 5 (2000), pp. 467–75, and also Pani, A. Porcella and G. L. Gessa, 'The Role of Stress in the Pathophysiology of the Dopamine System', *Molecular Psychiatry* 5 (2000), pp. 14–21.

14   Pani, 'Is There an Evolutionary Mismatch?', p. 473.

15   John Stewart, *Breathing Life into Biology* (Newcastle: Cambridge Scholars, 2019), p. 132.

16   Mary Ann Raghanti et al., 'A Neurochemical Hypothesis for the Origin of Hominids', *PNAS* 115 (2018), p. E1111.

17   World Health Organization, *Health in 2015: From MDGs, Millennium Development Goals, to SDGs, Sustainable Development Goals* (December 2015), available at: <https://www.who.int/gho/publications/mdgs-sdgs/en/>, chs 6–7. For overviews on diseases of poverty and despair, see Michael Meit, Megan Heffernan and Erin Tanenbaum, 'Investigating the Impact of the Diseases of Despair in Appalachia', *Journal of Appalachian Health* 1:2 (2019), pp. 7–18, and Jonathan McGavock, Brandy Wicklow and Allison B. Dart, 'Type 2 Diabetes in Youth is a Disease of Poverty', *The Lancet* 390 (2017), p. 1829.

18   See, for example, David Runciman, *How Democracy Ends* (London: Profile, 2018), pp. 124–26.

19   Daniel Marcelli, Marie-Claude Bossière and Anne-Lise Ducanda, 'Plaidoyer pour un nouveau syndrome "Exposition précoce et excessive aux écrans"', *Enfances & Psy* 79 (2018), pp. 142–60. See also Morgane Balland, Delphine Bizeul, Carole Guillet and Marie-Claude Bossière, 'Les effets des écrans sur les tout-petits: Syndrome ou symptom? Hypothèses sociétales et psychomotrice', *Enfances & Psy* 80 (2018), pp. 157–67.

20  Gerald Moore, 'Automations, Technological and Nervous: Addiction Epidemics from Athens to Fake News', *New Formations* 98 (2020), pp. 119–38.

21  Pani, 'Is There an Evolutionary Mismatch?', pp. 469 and 471.

22  Jason W. Moore, *Capitalism in the Web of Life* (London: Verso, 2015), pp. 114–18 and 171–73.

23  See, for example, A. C. Gore, R. T. Zoeller et al., 'EDC-2: The Endocrine Society's Second Scientific Statement on Endocrine-Disrupting Chemicals', *Endocrine Reviews* 36 (2015), pp. E1–E150.

24  On 'dopamining', see, for example, Gerald Moore, 'Dopamining and Disavowal: Addiction and Digital Capitalism', in Vanessa Bartlett and Henrietta Bowden-Jones (eds), *Are We All Addicts Now? Addiction and Digital Capitalism* (Liverpool: Liverpool University Press, 2017); Gerald Moore, 'The Pharmacology of Addiction', *Parrhesia* 29 (2017), pp. 190–211. On the 'globalization of addiction', see Alexander, *The Globalization of Addiction*, pp. 250–64.

25  David Graeber, 'Dead Zones of the Imagination: An Essay on Structural Stupidity', *The Utopia of Rules: On Technology, Stupidity, and the Secret Joys of Bureaucracy* (New York: Melville House, 2015).

26  Jason W. Moore, 'Anthropocene or Capitalocene? Nature, History, and the Crisis of Capitalism', in Jason W. Moore (ed.), *Anthropocene or Capitalocene: Nature, History and the Crisis of Capitalism* (Oakland: Kairos, 2016), p. 81.

27  See also Bernard Stiegler, *Qu'appelle-t-on panser? 2: La leçon de Greta Thunberg* (Paris: Les Liens qui Libèrent, 2020), pp. 108–11.

28  David T. Courtwright, 'Mr ATOD's Wild Ride: What Do Alcohol, Tobacco and Other Drugs Have in Common?', *Social History of Alcohol and Drugs* 20 (2005), p. 121. See also David T. Courtwright, *The Age of Addiction: How Bad Habits Became Big Business* (Cambridge, Massachusetts: Belknap, 2019), pp. 6–12.

29  See, for example, Sally Satel and Scott O. Lilienfeld, 'Addiction and the Brain-Disease Fallacy', *Frontiers in Psychiatry* 4 (2014), pp. 1–11.

30  Alexander, *The Globalization of Addiction*, p. 64.

31  Yuk Hui, *Recursivity and Contingency* (London and New York: Rowman & Littlefield, 2019).

32  See Lane Strathearn, 'Maternal Neglect: Oxytocin, Dopamine and the Neurobiology of Attachment', *Journal of Neuroendocrinology* 23 (2011), pp. 1054–65; see also Thomas R. Insel, 'Is Social

Attachment an Addictive Disorder?', *Psychology & Behaviour* 79 (2013), pp. 351–57.

33  John Bowlby, *Attachment and Loss, Volume 1: Attachment* (London: Pimlico, 1997), pp. 27–28.

34  Strathearn, 'Maternal Neglect', p. 1060.

35  Ibid., p 1058.

36  Insel, 'Is Social Attachment an Addictive Disorder?', p. 351.

37  Jesse Proudfoot, 'Drugs, Addiction, and the Social Bond', *Geography Compass* 11 (2017), p. 2.

38  Bernard Stiegler, *The Lost Spirit of Capitalism: Disbelief and Discredit, Volume 3*, trans. Daniel Ross (Cambridge: Polity Press, 2014), p. 86.

39  See Gerald Moore, 'Philosophy and Other Addictions: On Use and Abuse in the History of Life', in Oliver Davis and Colin Davis (eds), *Freedom and the Subject of Theory: Essays in Honour of Christina Howells* (Oxford: Legenda, 2019), p. 185.

40  Catherine Malabou, 'The Brain of History, or the Mentality of the Anthropocene', *South Atlantic Quarterly* 16 (2017), p. 47.

41  Eli Kintisch, *Hack the Planet: Science's Best Hope – or Worst Nightmare – for Averting Climate Catastrophe* (Hoboken: John Wiley & Sons, 2010), p. 9.

42  Fred H. Previc, *The Dopaminergic Mind in Human History and Evolution* (Cambridge: Cambridge University Press, 2009), pp. 149–50 and 162.

43  R. I. M. Dunbar, 'Coevolution of Neocortical Size, Group Size, and Language in Humans', *Behavioral and Brain Sciences* 16 (1993), pp. 681–735; Dieter Claessens, *Das Konkrete und das Abstrakte* (Frankfurt am Main: Surhkamp, 1993), pp. 93–144.

44  On the 'depersonalization of life', see Daniel Casriel, *A Scream Away from Happiness* (New York: Grosset & Dunlap, 1974), p. 126.

45  Monica L. Smith, *Cities: The First 6,000 Years* (London: Simon & Schuster, 2019), p. 8.

46  Peter Sloterdijk, *In the World Interior of Capital: Towards a Philosophical Theory of Globalization*, trans. Wieland Hoban (Cambridge: Polity Press, 2013), pp. 50–51 and 57–58.

47  Previc, *The Dopaminergic Mind in Human History and Evolution*, p. 150.

48    Thomas Armstrong, *The Power of Neurodiversity: Unleashing the Power of Your Differently Wired Brain* (Philadelphia: DaCapa, 2011), p. 36; see also Gerald Moore, 'De la neurodivérsité à la noodiversité: Pour construire des niches numériques dans la ville stupéfiée', in Bernard Stiegler (ed.), *L'Intelligence des villes et la nouvelle révolution urbaine* (Paris: FYP, 2020).

49    Armstrong, *The Power of Neurodiversity*, pp. 41–42; see also Jaak Panskepp, 'Attention Deficit Hyperactivity Disorders, Psychostimulants, and Intolerance of Childhood Playfulness: A Tragedy in the Making?', *American Psychology Society* 7:3 (1998), pp. 91–92.

50    Georges Canguilhem, *The Normal and the Pathological*, trans. Carolyn R. Fawcett with Robert S. Cohen (New York: Zone Books, 1991), p. 197.

51    Jean-Pierre Couteron, 'Société et addiction', *Le Sociographe* 39 (2012), pp. 10–16.

52    Anne Case and Angus Deaton, 'Rising Morbidity and Mortality in Midlife among White Non-Hispanic Americans in the 21st Century', *PNAS* 112 (2015), pp. 15078–83.

53    United Nations Office on Drugs and Crime, *World Drug Report 2018*, 'Executive Summary: Conclusions and Policy Implications' (June 2018), available at: <https://www.unodc.org/wdr2018/pre-launch/WDR18_Booklet_1_EXSUM.pdf>, p. 1.

54    Frank Dikötter, Zhou Xun and Lars Laamann, *Narcotic Culture: A History of Drugs in China* (London: Hurst & Co., 2004), pp. 88–91.

55    Fredric Jameson, 'The Politics of Utopia', *New Left Review* 25 (2004), p. 52. See also Fredric Jameson, 'An American Utopia', in Slavoj Žižek (ed.), *An American Utopia: Dual Power and the Universal Army* (London: Verso, 2015), pp. 89–92.

56    Moore, 'Automations, Technological and Nervous', pp. 137–38; Moore, 'Philosophy and Other Addictions', p. 186.

57    Bernard Stiegler, *The Age of Disruption: Technology and Madness in Computational Capitalism*, trans. Daniel Ross (Cambridge: Polity Press, 2019), §8.

58    Courtwright, *The Age of Addiction*, pp. 226–27.

59    Previc, *The Dopaminergic Mind in Human History and Evolution*, p. 151.

60    Tina Rosenberg, 'Busting the Myth That Depression Doesn't Affect People in Poor Countries', *The Guardian* (30 April 2019), available at: <https://www.theguardian.com/society/2019/apr/30/

busting-the-myth-that-depression-doesnt-affect-people-in-poor-countries>.

61    Jason Hickel, *The Divide: A Brief Guide to Global Inequality and Its Solutions* (London: Windmill, 2017), pp. 86–93.

62    Ibid., p. 76.

63    Ibid., pp. 150–53.

64    Courtwright, *The Age of Addiction*, pp. 98–99.

65    Susan Greenfield, *Mind Change: How Digital Technologies Are Leaving Their Mark on Our Brains* (London: Rider, 2014), p. 188.

66    Bruno Latour, *Down to Earth: Politics in the New Climatic Regime*, trans. Catherine Porter (Cambridge: Polity Press, 2018), p. 2.

67    Jacques Rancière, 'Ten Theses on Politics', trans. Rachel Bowlby and Davide Panagia, *Theory & Event* 5:3 (2001).

68    Eli Pariser, *The Filter Bubble: What the Internet is Hiding from You* (New York: Penguin, 2011).

69    Peter Sloterdijk, *Spheres, Volume 1: Bubbles. Microspherology*, trans. Wieland Hoban (Los Angeles: Semiotext(e), 2011), p. 72. See also Peter Sloterdijk, *Spheres, Volume 3: Foams. Plural Spherology*, trans. Wieland Hoban (South Pasadena: Semiotext(e), 2016).

70    Casriel, *A Scream Away from Happiness*, pp. 58 and 64. See also Claire D. Clark, *The Recovery Revolution: The Battle Over Addiction Treatment in the United States* (New York: Columbia University Press, 2017), p. 83.

71    Clark, *The Recovery Revolution*, p. 92.

72    Sherry Turkle, *Alone Together: Why We Expect More from Technology and Less from Each Other* (New York: Basic Books, 2010), p. 293.

73    See, for example, Michael Shellenberger and Ted Nordhaus, 'Evolve: The Case for Modernization as the Road to Salvation', in Michael Shellenberger and Ted Nordhaus (eds), *Love Your Monsters! Postenvironmentalism and the Anthropocene* (Washington, D.C.: Brookings Institute, 2011).

74    Alcoholics Anonymous, *Twelve Steps and Twelve Traditions* (New York: Alcoholics Anonymous World Services, 1953), p. 22.

75    Ibid. pp. 23–24.

76    Maia Szalavitz, *Unbroken Brain: A Revolutionary New Way of Understanding Addiction* (New York: St. Martin's Press, 2016), pp. 180–82.

77    Lance Dodes and Zachary Dodes, *The Sober Truth: Debunking the Bad Science Behind 12 Step Programs and the Rehab Industry* (Boston: Beacon, 2014), p. 135.

78    See, for example, Allison McKim, *Race, Gender and Drugs in the Era of Mass Incarceration* (New Brunswick: Rutgers University Press, 2017), p. 13.

79    Szalavitz, *Unbroken Brain*, p. 183.

80    Robin Room, 'Alcoholics Anonymous as a Social Movement', in B. S. McCrady and W. R. Miller (eds), *Research on Alcoholics Anonymous: Opportunities and Alternatives* (New Brunswick: Rutgers Center of Alcohol Studies, 1993), pp. 167–87.

81    Martha Nussbaum, *Women and Human Development: The Capabilities Approach* (Cambridge: Cambridge University Press, 2000), p. 69.

82    Lev S. Vygotsky, 'The Collective as a Factor in the Development of the Abnormal Child', in Robert W. Rieber and Aaron S. Carton (eds), *The Collected Works of L. S. Vygotsky, Volume 2: The Fundamentals of Defectology*, trans. Jane E. Knox and Carol B. Stevens (New York: Kluwer/Plenum, 1993), p. 192.

83    Lev S. Vygotsky, 'Thinking and Speech', in Robert W. Rieber and Aaron S. Carton (eds), *The Collected Works of L. S. Vygotsky, Volume 1: The Problems of General Psychology*, trans. Norris Minick (New York and London: Plenum, 1987), p. 198.

84    Lev S. Vygotsky, *Mind in Society: The Development of Higher Psychological Practices* (Cambridge, Massachusetts: Harvard University Press, 1978), p. 102.

85    For a brief and not uncritical review of Newman and Holzman's work, see Morten Nissen, Erik Axel and Torben Bechmann Jensen, 'The Abstract Zone of Proximal Conditions', *Theory and Psychology* 9 (1999), pp. 417–26.

86    Fred Newman and Lois Holzman, *Lev Vygotsky: Revolutionary Scientist* (London: Routledge, 1993), p. 157.

87    Lois Holzman, '"Vygotskian-izing" Psychotherapy', *Mind, Culture, and Activity* 21:3 (2014), p. 188.

88    Dodes and Dodes, *The Sober Truth*, p. 79.

89    Fyodor Vasilyuk, *The Psychology of Experiencing: The Resolution of Life's Critical Situations* (New York: Harvester Wheatsheaf, 1991), pp. 6–7.

90    Ibid., p. 35.

91    Colin G. DeYoung and Robert F. Krueger, 'A Cybernetic Theory of Psychopathology', *Psychological Inquiry* 29:3 (2018), p. 121.

## 10 Carbon and Silicon: Contribution to an Elemental Critique of Political Economy

*Daniel Ross*

### 127 Introduction: aporia of sustainability and the blind-spot

We are confronted in the twenty-first century with an array of serious problems but among them two immense challenges stand out: on the one hand, those problems presented by *carbon technologies*, and, on the other hand, those posed by *silicon technologies*. While it may seem that nothing can trump the planetary threat of climate change, in fact both of these challenges involve existential threats and dangers amounting to what is sometimes called 'extinction risk', not least because these two challenges are absolutely inextricable.

What follows is an attempt to outline the stakes of this situation in an age that has come to be known as the Anthropocene. An idea of the conditions within which those stakes are unfolding can be illustrated by juxtaposing two recent official declarations:

1   On 8 October 2018, the Intergovernmental Panel on Climate Change (IPCC) published a special report on *Global Warming of 1.5°C*: the 'Summary for Policymakers' argues for the urgent necessity of aiming to limit global temperature increases to no more than 1.5°C, stating that keeping climate change at or near this limit can today be achieved only if global net anthropogenic $CO_2$ emissions are reduced by 45% (from 2010 levels) by 2030 and are reduced to zero by 2050, which can be achieved, according to the IPCC, only with rapid, far-reaching and unprecedented transitions in energy, land, urban, infrastructure and industry systems, far beyond what would be possible under the current nationally-stated mitigation ambitions.[1]

2   One month after this declaration by the IPCC, on 5 November 2018, President Xi Jinping of the People's Republic of China (PRC) spoke at the opening of the China International Import Expo in Shanghai, reportedly stating that 'China is a big market of over 1.3 billion people' and that he 'would turn his country of 1.3 billion into global consumers'[2] by increasing imports to USD$45 trillion over the next fifteen years, as well as continuing to pursue

economic policies aimed at a correspondingly large increase
in the domestic consumption of *domestically* manufactured
consumer products.

The IPCC claims with 'high confidence' that there are 'a wide
range of adaptation options that can reduce the risks of climate
change'. Furthermore, the PRC shows evidence of understanding the
seriousness of global warming and at least some commitment to pursuing climate policies that encourage the development of renewable
energy resources, the transition away from fossil fuel-based transport
and so on.[3] Despite these positive signals and efforts, we nevertheless
believe that throughout the world there is a fundamental disconnection between discourses and policies on *ecology* and discourses and
politics on *economics*: can commitments to *large decreases in global
carbon emissions* really be maintained while at the same time maintaining commitments to *large increases in global consumption and
manufacturing?* We believe that the disconnection if not irreconcil-
able contradiction between these discourses and commitments ultimately reflects what could be called an *aporia of sustainability.*

In other words, contemporary geopolitics seems marked by the
virtual impossibility of finding a viable macroeconomic pathway out
of the contradiction between economic imperatives founded on the
existing 'perpetual growth' global macroeconomic model and ecological imperatives founded on the discoveries by climate science
about the effects of anthropogenic atmospheric emissions. More than
that, we contend that the difficulties involved in the attempt to resolve
this aporia are greatly exacerbated by technological processes of other
kinds, processes presently giving rise to what Bernard Stiegler has
recently termed an 'immense regression'.[4]

With respect to the last of these questions, we believe that there is
a widespread intellectual and political *blind-spot* about the economic,
political, psychological and sociological significance of the vast technological transformation that has unfurled across the past quarter
of a century. More specifically, it is today crucial to understand the
complex and fundamental ways in which the economic and ecological poles of this aporia of sustainability relate to and are compounded
by the transformation of computation, information and network technologies, and the algorithmic technologies that link them all together.[5]

The elimination of this blind-spot should therefore be an urgent
priority, and the combination of the aporia of sustainability and the
unfolding of a process of immense regression incontestably amounts
to a global crisis. If so, then this situation, like any crisis, calls for
a critique, on the basis of which alone it is possible to make good

decisions. In that light, what follows can be considered as a preliminary contribution to what we propose calling an 'elemental critique',
that is, a new critique of political economy founded on the respective
technologies of *carbon* and *silicon*.[6]

## 128  On the notion of an 'elemental' critique

Before attempting to identify the content of any such critique, some
words concerning the term 'elemental' may be advisable.

1. The focus on 'carbon' and 'silicon' indicates that this is indeed a
matter of the crucial place of the sixth and fourteenth atomic elements
of the periodic table in the technological transformations of the nineteenth, twentieth and twenty-first centuries, the span of time covered
by the so-called Anthropocene era. To this extent, the 'elemental'
character of the critique we are proposing means that it does not forget the fundamentally 'material' character of these transformations,
even if this is always and everywhere a question of what these materials can be *organized to do* and what they can organize *us to do, in
terms of both supporting and undermining the possibility of individual
and collective autonomy.*

We could also relate this notion to Whitehead's account of mathematics as a 'primordial element' in the history of thought that, combined with today's physical understanding, suggests the possibility
of 'some new doctrine of organism which may take the place of [...]
scientific materialism'.[7] For us, however, this element is not just scientific but technical, and the 'organism' under the microscope is not just
organic but, in Stiegler's terms, 'organological'.[8] In the case of silicon
technologies, digital and computational technologies have also made
it possible to analyse, isolate and manipulate the atomic elements of
the periodic table, as well as the genetic elements of which DNA is
composed, giving rise to new and powerful technologies combining
and recombining these elemental materials in ways that can be both
beneficial and monstrous.

2. More importantly, however, by 'elemental' is meant the
Aristotelian notion that, for sensible beings, each of the senses has its
own 'element'. The distant echo of this can be heard, for instance, in
the quotidian English expression according to which those who find
themselves in circumstances to which they are very well-suited can
be defined as being 'in their element' (a professional swimmer in a
swimming pool, for instance, or a river[9]).

For Aristotle, the element is what suffuses the milieu of a sensible
being, *through* which perception operates (in the case of vision, for
example, it operates not through light but, more primordially still,

through 'the transparent'[10]). This element itself, however, is very difficult for the sensible being to perceive: as Stiegler has often mentioned, Aristotle offers the example of the fish, which, according to Aristotle, 'would not notice that the things which touch one another in water have wet surfaces'.[11]

The element of the fish, water, is so *intimate* to its existence as to escape perceptibility (with the possible exception of the *flying* fish, who may have an *intermittent* experience of this element, in briefly *leaving* it). One of the most recent formulations of this idea by Stiegler is the following:

> A change of technical system always initially entails a disadjustment between this technical system and what Bertrand Gille called the social systems, which had hitherto been 'adjusted' to the preceding technical system, and which had therein formed, *along with it*, an 'epoch' – but where the technical system as such fades into the background, forgotten as it disappears into everydayness, just as, for a fish, what disappears from view, as its 'element', is water.[12]

In the case of the elemental critique being proposed here, this does not mean that we have no *awareness* of the suffusion of carbon and silicon technologies in our surroundings: the thick anthropotechnical film of automobiles, electrically-powered devices, smartphones and internet devices that covers the Earth and surrounds our existence is *transparently* obvious to everyone. Rather, what is meant by the quasi-imperceptibility of the element is that there is something about our *entanglement* with these technologies, and in particular with silicon technologies, that we find very difficult either to pinpoint or to grasp.

This is so precisely *because* of this suffusion and because there is no positive prospect of any *disentanglement* (other than through a shift towards some *post*-silicon technologies, which are likely in any case to bear many of the same characteristics as silicon technologies in terms of being digital, networked, algorithmic and so on). This is the issue at stake in the proposals outlined in Chapter 4 concerning the design, development and implementation of deliberative technologies (and for a precise description of these technologies, see Chapter 7).

Contemporary technologies, and especially silicon technologies, are so difficult to perceive because, although they consist in nothing but external devices (or the possibility of *internal* devices such as those of neurotechnology), they are nevertheless always and constantly *occupying us and within us*, almost *haunting us*. Technics is the spectral element that constitutes 'the transparent' for *noetic* beings:

our attention perpetually operates *through* such technologies but is only intermittently attentive *to* such technologies.

3. 'Elemental' has a third sense, indicated for instance in Sigmund Freud's description of the fate of microscopic organisms in a petri dish:

> An infusorian, therefore, if it is left to itself, dies a natural death owing to its incomplete voidance of the products of its own metabolism. (It may be that the same incapacity is the ultimate cause of the death of all higher animals as well.)[13]

What Freud describes here amounts to the entropic consequences for any kind of being occupying a closed system in which it lacks the means to eradicate the toxicity brought by its own waste products, throwing the system into uncontrollable disequilibrium and ultimately leading to its collapse. In the case of the 'metabolism' with which we are dealing for the 'higher animal' that we ourselves form, a being that in Aristotle's terms is not just sensible but 'noetic', which is to say a *being that knows*, this 'metabolism' is not just biological but fundamentally and irreducibly psychological, sociological and technological.

The 'metabolic' productions of the technical, knowing beings that we ourselves are also contain the possibility of exposing our 'element' to potentially fatal toxicity, when we lose the intergenerationally transmitted capacities of knowledge and care required to take care of life in any particular technical system. But when this becomes a matter of our 'noetic element', the entropic consequences entailed by this 'self-poisoning' are no longer just thermodynamic or biological but psychic and social. All technical systems are localized, but the locality of today's technical system has reached the scale of the biosphere itself (this is what, throughout this work, has been called the technosphere): in such circumstances, where there is effectively no 'outside', the risks of toxicity are that much greater.

## 129 The division of twenty-first century technologies

Some remarks are necessary about the attempt we are pursuing here to distinguish carbon technologies from silicon technologies. The first is that this is neither an absolute distinction nor an opposition: in the world in which we live today, almost every internal combustion engine that is manufactured for an automobile is also a computer, with the ICE powering the CPU and the CPU governing the rhythms of the pistons and so on. Even more obviously, every digital device is powered by electrical energy, a high proportion of which is produced through carbon combustion of one kind or another.

These specific examples point to a far more general characteristic: just as *we* are inextricably entangled with the technical milieu we have constructed across the entire biosphere, so too are the various kinds of technologies inextricably entangled with each other (and with us), thereby forming what Bertrand Gille called a technical system. It is a 'structural' or synchronic system in the sense that each technical artifact finds its possibility only in relation to a plurality of others which it cannot do without.

The second thing to say is that these names, carbon and silicon, are to some extent an abstraction in the sense that we are creating a very broad categorization that is in some way just a useful fiction. In practice, they could be construed in a more inclusive way as referring to technologies lying outside the strict (atomic) bounds of these 'elemental' characteristics. There exists a complicated relationship between the dominant technologies involved in the technical system of a particular epoch and the form of thinking that is possible in that epoch. Norbert Wiener, writing at the midpoint of the last century, argued that the 'thought of every age is reflected in its technique',[14] and he delineated the shifts of technical system from the eighteenth to the nineteenth to the twentieth centuries in a way that is congruent with the division we are proposing here:

> If the seventeenth and early eighteenth centuries are the age of clocks, and the later eighteenth and the nineteenth centuries constitute the age of steam engines, the present time is the age of communication and control.[15]

Wiener associates the first of these epochs, that of Newton and Huyghens, with the age of navigation made possible by precision instruments, opening up a new scale of maritime commerce based on 'the engineering of the mercantilists', while from the nineteenth century and 'almost to the present time', the Newcomen engine and its heirs would give rise to all those large-scale industries based on thermodynamics and irreversible processes, and most recently the communication age, based on a 'split between the technique of strong currents and the technique of weak currents', has led to a proliferation of electronic instruments opening onto the age of the 'automatic computing machine'.[16] The range of technologies included in each of the very broad categorizations we are describing here is thus quite large. Furthermore, it is always the result of local and historical processes that can both begin and end, where the end is not determined in any teleological way by the beginning, and where there is nothing permanent or eternal about this distinction.

Nevertheless, thirdly, our contention is that, in *this* epoch, an account of these particular abstractions can nevertheless be *fruitful*. In the technical system of the twenty-first century, or at least of its first two decades, it is indeed possible to *make* this distinction between two vast technological categories. For example, *a high proportion of the largest global companies measured by revenue are based on carbon technologies,*[17] while *a high proportion of the largest global companies measured by market capitalization are based on silicon technologies*[18] (these two facts also indicating something about the relationship between the present and the future, as perceived by investors). More than that, it is *necessary* to make this distinction in order to elucidate fundamental questions of political economy that have thus far tended to be avoided in most theoretical or policymaking considerations with respect to the consequences generated by our own metabolic products.

For these reasons, we will now outline what is intended by each of these categorizations respectively, in relation to their genesis, function and fate.

## 130 Carbon technologies: Palaeolithic fire in the Anthropocene era

Hominins acquired the ability to create and use fire as early as the Lower Palaeolithic and the controlled use of carbon combustion became common in the Middle Palaeolithic. From that moment, the beings that would become ourselves found themselves within a fiery element defined by the capacity for artificial, controllable energy production and consumption founded on the flammability of organic materials. From the moment cooking was invented, this capacity was a matter of the potential to produce and consume energy in order to do work, thereby opening the possibility of 'ways of life', or what Marx called a 'mode of consumption':

> the hunger that is satisfied by cooked meat eaten with knife and fork differs from hunger that devours raw meat with the help of bands, nails and teeth.[19]

Both dangerous and beneficial, controllable within the risks of being extinguished or turning wild, this first symbol of technics was also the first object of *care*, long before the Neolithic Revolution. In addition to warmth and cooking, the development of the controlled use of carbon combustion gave rise to other technologies, such as smelting, forging and gunpowder.[20]

But the *modern* history of carbon technologies obviously begins with the invention of heat engines powered by hydrocarbons derived from fossilized organic matter. More specifically, it begins with the external combustion engine, and more specifically still with the industrial (or thermodynamic) revolution that was set off by the steam engine envisaged by the University of Glasgow repairman James Watt, which he patented in 1781 and which was to transform manufacturing and rail and maritime transport throughout the nineteenth century.

In the twentieth century, fossil fuel power plants linked to electricity grids would further vastly transform both production and consumption, and automobiles equipped with internal combustion engines would transform road transport and make possible the rise of global aviation. The combustion of hydrocarbons, however, inevitably releases a significant level of 'metabolic products': while for the ten thousand years prior to the industrial revolution the global atmospheric $CO_2$ concentration was 280 parts per million, in 2018 it stood at 410 ppm, with annual emissions and concentrations continuing to increase.[21]

### 131  Silicon technologies

Turning to the history of silicon technologies, the first integrated circuit was produced in 1958, the first CPU in 1971, the Apple II and Commodore PET home computers entered the market in 1977, the Microsoft Windows 'operating environment' was first released in 1985, the World Wide Web was opened to the general public in April 1993, Amazon was founded in July 1994, the domain name google. com was registered in September 1997, the Tencent and Alibaba conglomerates were founded in 1998 and 1999 respectively, the Facebook social network was made universally open in September 2006 (with active users rising from 100 million in August 2008 to two billion in June 2017), the capacitive multi-touch smartphone known as the iPhone was launched in June 2007 and Uber's mobile app and transport services were officially launched in July 2009.

It is notable that this timeline of significant dates increasingly focuses on *consumer*-based silicon technologies, reflecting the vast entrance of these transformational technologies into the consumer market over the past forty years. It is also notable that we have chosen to end it in 2009, reflecting that the last decade has seen a period of *consolidation* and *monopolization* of the silicon economy in the hands of a small number of super-giant corporate players.

Today, it has become *transparently* clear to everyone that silicon technologies have transformed *every* aspect of production and consumption,[22] along with scientific and technological research of every kind, and this is especially so in the quarter of a century that has transpired since the internet became public and global. All of this amounts to a vast 'disruption' of the technical system, along with every other psychosocial and institutional system.

This history is obviously familiar, and its facts are moreover available to anyone anywhere with a smartphone and internet access. Compared with the history of carbon technologies, however, which have existed in one form or another for hundreds of thousands of years, the silicon technologies just listed have a history lasting just a few decades. On what basis can this amount to some vast and fundamental division, or does their rapid ascent and ubiquity generate a kind of illusion of exaggerated significance? In fact, silicon technologies must be inscribed into a much older genealogy, even if still not quite as long as the history of the acquisition and use of fire. But this is possible only if we consider these technologies not in terms of their atomic or molecular composition but in terms of their elemental function.

## 132  Retentional technologies and the industrial capitalism of production

If the elemental function of carbon technologies fundamentally consists in the production of chemical energy in order that it can then be transformed into mechanical or electrical energy and consumed as work, then the elemental function of silicon technologies fundamentally consists in the production of an artificial *memory* that, too, can be put to work in manifold ways. Silicon technologies are *retentional* technologies (to borrow a term from Husserlian phenomenology). In Stiegler's work, this very long history of retentional technologies (and especially of what he calls *hypomnesic* technologies, those technologies that are *purposely* rather than *accidentally* retentional) has been explored in detail and with respect to a wide variety of dimensions.

If we here prefer to refer to *silicon* technologies – while keeping in mind the mnemotechnical history that extends through cave painting, the invention of writing systems (including alphabetization, which remains an almost unchanged standard from the Roman Empire to the Digital Leviathan), the printing press, the phonograph, the radio, cinema, analogue television and the becoming-digital of everything that we now see unfolding with silicon technologies strictly speaking – if we refer to *silicon* technologies, therefore, it is only because the proliferation of uses, services and functions associated with this latest stage of memory technology seems so greatly to exceed the mere ability to 'record the past'. And yet, this is precisely the *basis* of all of them.[23]

The industrial revolution whose possibility we previously ascribed to Watt's steam engine could never have occurred without retentional technologies of a kind we have hitherto failed to mention: those technologies by which the complex and continuous gestures of workers of all kinds were broken down analytically into their discrete elements, in order to be then programmed back into machines powered by the heat engines of Watt and his successors. The paradigmatic case of such a machine is *Jacquard's loom*, but a thousand examples could no doubt be cited.

The basis of this analytical process is what Stiegler refers to as 'grammatization', the process of turning something temporal (like speech) into something spatial (like writing), by turning the continuous into the discrete, on the basis of which it can be analysed and reproduced. The noetic, political and economic consequences of grammatization can be to support new forms of knowledge, but grammatization can also lead to what Stiegler calls 'proletarianization' (drawing on Gilbert Simondon's reading of the *Grundrisse*'s 'fragment on machines'). If proletarianization has in traditional Marxist discourse been understood to refer to the systematic separation of workers from the means of production, Stiegler's use of the term draws attention to the way in which those means first of all consist in the *knowledge* possessed by workers and transmitted intergenerationally.

It is this knowledge that is literally removed from the minds of weavers and programmed into Jacquard's loom and a thousand other machines, dispossessing the workers of their knowledge and literally destroying the intergenerational transmission of all manner of skills and crafts. In addition to the ownership of the energy-production capacities of the heat engine, what in fact made the rapid acceleration of the industrial revolution possible was thus the ability of the capitalist to dispossess the worker of the knowledge of how to *make* things, knowledge that was then turned into information and recorded and exploited in the retentional technologies of machines: it is here that the history of industrial automation and artificial intelligence truly begins.

*Industrial capitalism based on production* thus arises from the concentration of carbon technologies in the hands of capital, but *equally* from the capitalist acquisition of retentional technologies through which workers, systematically dispossessed of knowledge, become labourers, that is, servants of the machine. From this vast process is born that great division between capital and proletarianized labour on the basis of which Marx and Engels would construct a revolutionary politics.

In fact, of course, this founding moment of the industrial revolution was only the first step of a history that would continue through many chapters, including ones that Marx could never have anticipated: one key way in which to understand this set of chapters is as the unfolding of the epochs of grammatization. To pursue this history in terms of the distinction between carbon and silicon, it is worthwhile returning to the recent proclamation by the Chinese president concerning his country's ambition to produce 1.3 billion 'global consumers'.

### 133  On the vision of a nation of 1.3 billion 'global consumers'

An issue that has been raised many times by many commentators, with potentially very significant global macroeconomic consequences, is the wage pressure in China that seems bound to result from the enormous rise of Chinese prosperity. This prosperity has been generated by clever and concerted development policies, and by the so-called 'opening up' of China to the world, but what was *primarily* made available through this opening up was the vast army of low-cost labour that China was able to supply to domestic and foreign manufacturers of all kinds. In this way, the consumers of the industrialized democracies became able to purchase low-cost consumer goods, corporations became able to inexpensively mass produce products and thus maintain profitable businesses, and China was able to attract an increasingly large proportion of the global manufacturing sector to the mainland, together driving an economic transformation not just of the economy and society of the PRC but of the whole global economy.

Increasingly, of course, and by design, this is not a one-way street: exports *into* China are themselves increasingly profitable for foreign manufacturers, and likewise the enormous rise in Chinese prosperity opens up new opportunities for domestic producers. Hence President Xi's declaration. His quantification of import levels is of course highly conditional upon global and Chinese economic conditions that could easily and unexpectedly shift (with the vagaries of what is wrongly called the economic 'cycle'). Beyond that, however, China's economic rise inevitably leads to pressure for the *redistribution* of the wealth that has been generated, ultimately including to the millions of subsistence labourers in Chinese factories. As this wage pressure becomes increasingly difficult to resist, even for an economy that is still subject to strong centralized control, the very basis of that *generation* of wealth is potentially threatened.

None of this would in any way count as news for President Xi. But if it is not news, then what is his strategy for dealing with this pressure? What are the implications of his statement that he wants to produce a country of 1.3 billion global consumers, especially given that he is also asserting the PRC's capacity for *long-term* planning, at least compared with the government of his American 'rival' (who could argue?)? It is hard to avoid the conclusion that behind such a pronouncement is the thought that the solution to this dilemma lies in a transformation of manufacturing through which a high proportion of these labourers will become dispensable. In other words, to build this market of global consumers, a very great number of these labourers will, in the medium term at most, need to be replaced, not by some *new* army of cheap human labourers, but by automation and AI, that is, by a process of robotization.

Such a transition obviously implies other questions concerning the need for a new *basis* for redistribution to replace the disrupted wage labour (and welfare) model that has been the engine of the Keynesian model for many decades. Such questions are difficult and fundamental, amounting to the question and the *challenge* of what Stiegler has called 'automatic society': in a world where *labour* requires fewer and fewer human beings to operate machines, what is the future of *work* (where we are thus *distinguishing* work from proletarianized labour, and where it is only the worker and not the labourer who has the possibility of transforming his or her conditions *through* such work) and what is the basis of the distribution of the *income* without which these 'consumers' will be unable to consume?[24] It is ultimately these questions that are implied by the declaration of an intention to create a market of 1.3 billion Chinese global consumers, along with those ecological questions implied by the aforementioned aporia of sustainability.

The vision that lies behind such a declaration, therefore, bears some resemblance to that described by Marx and Engels in *The German Ideology*: a vision of a society that no longer forces me to constrain my existence to a fixed, limited role in order to subsist, and instead

> makes it possible for me to do one thing today and another tomorrow, to hunt in the morning, fish in the afternoon, rear cattle in the evening, criticise after dinner.[25]

For Herbert Marcuse in 1969, this 'early Marxian example' did indeed sound 'embarrassingly ridiculous', but only because the vision it offers in fact refers to merely 'a stage of the development of the productive forces which has been surpassed'.[26] With 'the development of the productive forces beyond their capitalist organization', he suggests, a transformation may well be accomplished in which the 'quantitative reduction of necessary labor could turn into quality (freedom)' and 'the stupefying, enervating, pseudo-automatic jobs of capitalist progress would be abolished'. But Marcuse argues that this will *also* require a transformation of the noetic beings that we ourselves are: it 'presupposes a type of man with a different sensitivity as well as consciousness'.[27]

Today, this vision might be reinterpreted as one in which the *revolutionary* expansion of automation and artificial intelligence opens up prospects for the emergence of new forms of autonomy (ignoring, for the moment, the question of what it would mean to go 'beyond capitalist organization'). In such an interpretation, it would be as if the technological system becomes a new kind of 'preindividual milieu' (in Simondon's terms), simply supplying the background conditions from out of which, liberated from the enervating toil of proletarianized labour, new noetic beings will crystallize.[28] But in 2018, President Xi's concern does not seem to be with how to produce new forms of autonomy or noesis: by this statement at least, he wants to create neither new kinds of workers nor new kinds of citizens but 'global consumers'. The possibility of raising the latter prospect without considering the former challenge, we argue, is symptomatic of a failure to address the real stakes of silicon technologies in the twenty-first century.

Rising prosperity may well be bound by economic law to lead to rising consumption, but the manner of the correlation is dependent on numerous other factors. In China and Asia generally, for example, there is a well-known tendency to save rather than spend (compared with Western consumers), with overall macroeconomic effects on investment and consumption, not to mention the 'global savings glut' diagnosed by Federal Reserve Chairman Ben Bernanke in 2005, which is to say, a potentially unstable tendency in which savings are favoured too greatly over investment (from the standpoint of the existing macroeconomic model). In short, 'global consumers' are artificial beings, not natural ones: *con*-sumers must be *pro*-duced – they must be *made*.

### 134 Protentional technologies and the hyper-industrial capitalism of consumption

The twentieth century can be understood as the age of the global *cinesphere*.[29] The pharmacological (which is to say, both entropic and negentropic) character of this cinesphere can be discerned by conjoining two statements that appear in the first episode of Jean-Luc Godard's *Histoire(s) du Cinéma*: first, that cinema replaces our gaze with a world that conforms with our desires, and second, that for fifty years, in the dark, we burned imagination (that is, libidinal energy) in order to heat up reality.[30]

That consumers must be produced through cinespherical means was precisely the realization that came to capitalist producers at the beginning of the twentieth century. For Marx, the spread of machines (powered by carbon technologies and programmed by retentional technologies of mechanical grammatization) amongst the capitalist class was bound to make it increasingly difficult for any one capitalist to maintain an edge over others, leading to his diagnosis of a tendency of the rate of profit to fall. Economists ever since have disparaged this analysis, above all on the grounds that it is not what is observed in the economic history that has unfolded since it was described by Marx, 'natural' boom-and-bust 'cycles' notwithstanding. Indeed, this history does not seem to confirm Marx's analysis. But this may be the result less of analytical error than of a fundamental transformation of capitalism resulting *from* this tendency: in short, what Marx could not *imagine* was the development of a capitalist *imagination* capable of solving this dilemma, even if this solution is itself only a *postponement* of this tendency.

The essence of this 'solution' was the realization that it is possible to create new markets, not just by geographical expansion, but through the possibility of manipulating consumer desire and therefore consumer behaviour. If capitalism is a perpetual economic competition giving rise to perpetual technoscientific innovation, this is not just a matter of R&D and production: it is also a matter of the socialization of that innovation – all those processes through which new products are taken up by consumers, by which they are *adopted*.

The shift to a *hyper-industrial capitalism of consumption* was in part a matter of the new organization of consumption that arose when Henry Ford realised that the wages he was paying to those employed on his assembly lines could in turn be used by them to purchase the very products they were producing. But the large-scale investment required to achieve the productivity gains to be realised from mass production was feasible only if consumer behaviour could be more or less reliably predicted, which is to say, *produced*: for this new consumer market in transport vehicles powered by internal combustion engines to succeed, it was necessary to invent public relations, or in other words, marketing.

As Stiegler has shown on many occasions, this invention was made possible not just by the discovery of this 'idea', but by the development of new forms of grammatization, and specifically the 'grammatization of the sensible' inaugurated with audiovisual technologies such as radio, cinema and television. It is not technological change as such that Marx could not anticipate, but the significance of the new analytical and programming possibilities opened up by these new retentional technologies (Guglielmo Marconi patented his wireless telegraphy system in 1896, Marx having died in 1883). With these powerful new tools that could be used to access and influence the minds of potential consumers on an *industrial scale,* it became possible to completely transform the basis of profit-making in industrial capitalism, by constantly *manufacturing the market* for the new products that could then be constantly introduced and updated.

By accessing consciousness and targeting the unconscious, marketing and its associated technologies and techniques have progressively learned how to make consumer behaviour *controllable,* by interpolating (in the literary sense) tertiary retentions into the stream of consciousness. The basis on which it can do so, however, depends on *reducing* desire as much as possible to a *calculable* phenomenon, which is to say, *grammatizing* the relationship to the future. In other words, this amounts to a grammatization of *protention,* Husserl's term for my immediate expectation, but expanded here to include every form of motive, reason, expectation, dream and desire.

This in turn involves a *detachment* of desire from everything *in*calculable, incomparable and *long*-term (including every form of education and inter-generational transmission), inducing a *regressive* tendency that aims instead only at the finite and short-term goals of the consumer behaviour required by the market. But this ultimately risks being self-destructive for the consumerist model itself, setting up a tendency for the *libidinal* economy (on which the macroeconomic 'perpetual growth model' fundamentally depends) to collapse, as libidinal *energy* is depleted: the ability to stimulate the perpetual increase in consumption required by the consumerist economy is thereby threatened. It is ultimately for this reason (along with the aporia of sustainability) that consumerist capitalism can be nothing but a postponement of Marx's diagnosis with regard to the rate of profit.

### 135  Silicon technologies
### and the ultra-industrial capitalism of algorithmic platforms

The protentional grammatization technologies of the twentieth century had only limited means of accessing the information and data that is necessary in order to calculate and predict the relationship between, first, *grammatized content* (for example, a television commercial that, in Husserl's terms, amounts to a kind of *industrial* temporal object), second, *protentional conditioning,* and third, *consumer behaviour:* the clearest indicator was ultimately the success or otherwise of a marketing campaign. But with the introduction of silicon technologies that now dominate the twenty-first century, this question is fundamentally transformed, because the consumers of such grammatized content are ceaselessly and immediately sending data *back* to producers. On the basis of such data, producers can ever more finely calculate the relationship between particular content and particular responses from particular 'kinds' of users.

The extreme speeds at which these processes occur in contemporary algorithmic silicon systems means that it is also possible for these producers to *adjust* content in a very rapid and targeted way that was simply impossible in the twentieth century. This speed *exceeds* that of noetic processes themselves, and this rapid exchange and algorithmic control of vast amounts of user data gives rise to a kind of informational and protentional shock wave, analogous at the noetic level to the 'sonic boom' produced at flight speeds above Mach 1.[31]

Every major consumer platform today utilizes ultra-powerful algorithmic techniques of this kind in order to absolutely maximize their ability to performatively influence consumer behaviour. Furthermore, global 'platforms' such as Alphabet and Facebook are now among the largest corporations on the planet and have become so through the *new market* they have created for the vast amounts of data generated by their users.

If the capitalism of analogue audiovisual technologies was already hyper-industrial and performative (in Austin's sense), then the new market of platform capitalism based on silicon technologies, user profiling and social networking is *highly* performative and can thus be considered an *ultra-industrial capitalism of algorithmic platforms*.[32] But this only intensifies the deleterious effects of such processes on the libidinal economy of consumers. And this in turn is bound to intensify the self-destructive tendencies of the consumerist macroeconomy, since it ruins the very basis of its 'success': the control of desire.

## 136 The anti-politics of ultra-industrial populism in the Entropocene

Behind this highly paradoxical intention to *produce consumers* lies the even more paradoxical belief that this mass of consumers can continuously drive the engine of the global economy like a perpetual motion machine, and drive it to ever new heights. But perpetual motion is a myth based on the notion of an abstract machine that is *thermodynamically impossible,* and the 'heights' to be reached are in this case transparently at odds with the unambiguous imperatives declared by the IPCC. But in addition to that, the billions upon billions of bytes of data gathered from consumers by producers and platforms, fed into increasingly powerful and increasingly intelligent automated algorithms designed to calculate and control behaviour according to the imperatives not of the IPCC but *solely of the market*, has an extremely *ruinous* effect on the psyches of the individual consumers of whom this market is composed (who are today targeted almost from birth, if not from before birth), giving rise as it does to an infernal spiral of consumerist addiction.

Evidence abounds throughout the industrialized democracies of the political consequences towards which this ruination tends. And these consequences are intensified by the fact that all these performative techniques are applied also in the *political* realm. If, as Stiegler suggests, this entails the replacement of the adoptive performativity of 'democracy' with the adaptive performativity of 'telecracy',[33] where the *demos* no longer finds itself in possession of any *kratos*, then the algorithmicization of this telecracy via the silicon technologies of platform capitalism is already exposing the utter vulnerability of 'representational' political systems to a thoroughgoing disintegration at the hands of the 'owners' of this data and the manipulators of these algorithms.

This can be described as an *ultra-industrial political regression* (a new form of what is often called 'populism') to which ultra-industrial capitalism tends to give rise. But regardless of the degree to which the leading industrial populists imagine they can cynically keep hold of the reins of power as they exploit the fears and irrationality of the crowd, the enormous risk that they are precipitating is of hubristically engendering processes that will completely run out of all control. All of this is what first began to get going with the shift from an industrial capitalism of production to a hyper-industrial capitalism of consumption a century ago, for which the immensely destructive wars of the twentieth century stand as testament, and it is all this that *remains* at stake in the wish to create a society of global consumers in an ultra-industrial capitalism of algorithmic platforms.

## 137  On crystallization and crystal palaces

For Marcuse, as we have already mentioned, the reduction of the need for labour made possible by automation opens up the prospect of a new age of autonomy. Such autonomy, however, is by no means a guaranteed outcome: it 'presupposes a type of man with a different sensitivity as well as consciousness'. Marcuse himself describes what this means only rather abstractly as involving a 'union between

causality by necessity and causality by freedom', which he problem-
atically understands in terms of an 'instinctual transformation'.[34]

In Simondonian terms, we might say that, in the age of silicon technologies, the invention of a new noetic milieu is in principle *entirely*
possible (and, what's more, that there is no future for knowledge,
understood in the broadest possible sense, *other than through* silicon technologies, all knowledge always being a possibility for noetic
beings that is only ever opened up *intermittently, technically, reten-
tionally and protentionally*). But this possibility of a new noetic *element* is realizable only provided that the arrangement between the
technical and the psychosocial is re-organized so as to *foster* (rather
than undermine) psychic and collective individuation processes giving rise to the new sensitivity and consciousness (new noesis) for
which Marcuse calls.

Simondon's first, 'physical' model for the emergence of individuation from out of a preindividual milieu is the way that crystals emerge
from out of a parent liquid possessing just the right molecular composition for a process of crystallization to be catalysed by a germ. But as
the artist Robert Smithson pointed out (via the work of the physicist
Percy Bridgman), the crystals produced by this process run counter to
the commonly-held layman's conception of entropy as always leading
from states of order to states of disorder:

> But I think nevertheless, we do not feel altogether com-
> fortable at being forced to say that the crystal is the seat of
> greater disorder than the parent liquid.[35]

The crystal *seems* to be *organized*, because it appears to our eyes to
be order*ly*. In fact, as a perfectly ordinary thermodynamic process, it
complies with the 'arrow of time' and corresponds to a lower state of
potential energy: the *regularity* of the crystal gives rise to the *illusion*
of what only seems to be a counter-entropic organizational process.

Genuinely counter-entropic processes are possible at the biological and noetic levels – even if these counter-entropic tendencies, too,
can only ever be *localized* and *temporary*. For exosomatic beings,
such processes depend on the accumulation of past noetic wealth, the
improbable memory of which they cultivate and transform in order
to maintain the rich cohesion of a particular locality on a particular
scale, and to produce new improbable futures.

Contemporary disruption and regression are, however, precisely a
kind of illusion of counter-entropy of the sort produced at the molecular level by crystallization. This is not just a question of the crystal
palaces of industrial capitalism but also of the silicon crystal palaces
that form the exo-techno-cine-spherical tertiary layers of algorithmic

and ultra-industrial capitalism. They may be highly ordered and regularized, but beneath this deceptive surface they are thoroughly entropic for noetic processes, precisely because they fail to cultivate and draw upon this wealth of knowledge, instead destroying it and replacing it with the dictates of the market of calculable information.

For Smithson, writing in the 1960s and 1970s, it was a question of thinking thermodynamic entropy beyond the pleasure principle:

> There's a certain kind of pleasure principle that comes out of a preoccupation with waste. Like if we want a bigger and better car we are going to have bigger and better waste productions. So there's a kind of equation there between the enjoyment of life and waste. Probably the opposite of waste is luxury.[36]

Smithson's raising of the question of entropy also extended beyond the relationship between thermodynamics and the death drive already suggested by Freud. Hence his call for an 'attempt to formulate an analog between "communication theory" and the ideas of physics'.[37] Unfortunately, how far he may have been led by these speculations will remain forever unknown, thanks to his untimely death in a plane crash in 1973.

## 138  Reinventing economics as the science of struggling against entropy in exosomatization

Carbon technologies are thermodynamic: their function is to contribute to the struggle of noetic, technical (that is, exosomatic) life against its irreducible entropic conditions. But in utilizing these technologies to pursue anti-entropic ends, and given that all negentropic systems are *localized* systems that are bound to remain entropic in an *overall* sense, we inevitably produce entropic consequences *elsewhere*. And when those systems have extended across the entire biosphere, cinesphere, technosphere and exosphere, then this 'elsewhere' remains precisely *here*, and the toxicity they produce is unavoidably self-poisoning, ruining its biospheric element just as does the infusorian in Freud's petri dish.

Silicon technologies are informational: their function, too, is to contribute to the struggle of exosomatic life against its irreducible entropic conditions. But in this case, the toxicity they produce pollutes not the biosphere but the noetic element of the knowing, technical beings who must nevertheless find the noetic *resources* to address *all* of these self-poisonings, whether carbonic or noetic, and to do so by *making good collective decisions*. It is this *division* between two kinds of entropic toxicity, and the necessity of recognizing the *gravity* of informational entropy, that we here seek to highlight.

Most economic theory (like most philosophy) has, to its detriment, remained rooted in a mechanistic physical conception that predates the discovery of the second law of thermodynamics, at least if we believe the economic historian Philip Mirowski.[38] This means that economic systems are not truly viewed as dynamic processes in perpetual struggle against entropic tendencies but are instead understood as involving one or another kind of static or cyclical equilibrium making possible the fantasy of perpetual growth.

From the work of the physicist Erwin Schrödinger, the mathematical biologist Alfred J. Lotka and the economist Nicholas Georgescu-Roegen, however, it becomes possible to see biological (endosomatic) evolution as precisely involving manifold processes amounting to so many struggles against entropy, where these struggles are always localized – at the scale of the cell, the organism, the species, the ecosystem or the biosphere. And it also becomes possible to see that *economic* processes are what replace these evolutionary tendencies when life becomes technical (exosomatic), still always localized – at the scale of the tribe, ethnic group, society, nation or global economic system.

Mirowski's work has focused largely on the history of economics in the twentieth and twenty-first centuries, and more specifically on the way in which the history of neoliberalism has interacted both with the notion of information and with the integration of computation into economic theory and practice.[39] From Hayek's argument in 1945 that the 'decentralized' market makes better use of knowledge in society than do 'centralized' authorities and bureaucracies, the history of neoliberalism has amounted to the history of the notion of 'the Market' as a vast 'information processor'. In the unfolding of this history, the market-*qua*-information-processor is found by neoliberal economists to depend less and less on the 'rational agents' of neoclassical economics, as the concept of (economic) knowledge is reduced more and more to calculable information that may escape the level of the individual altogether.

In turn, economists take advantage of this conception by redefining their function less as scientists and advisers and more as engineers and designers of markets, whether the market is being designed to facilitate the sale of the electromagnetic spectrum, to mitigate carbon emissions or to find market-based solutions for the market-induced problems of the global financial crisis.[40] This, however, entails a contradiction: setting out from an idea of 'the Market' as the best and most efficient guarantor of correct outcomes, if not as a transcendental and universal processor of truth, neoliberal economists then start to manufacture diverse and specific markets. But the good outcomes promised by the purveyors of these markets (in competition with purveyors of other markets) absolutely depend on the initial conditions set by economists, who are able to do so, they claim, thanks to their 'expertise', which they then market to governments, institutions and other economic actors, including at the highest levels, arguing that this is the only way to ensure positive outcomes, since there is no such thing as the market *itself*.

The contradiction is thus between an absolutized, 'universal' conception of 'the Market' and a localized (but still informational and computational) conception of specific but highly artificial markets, where the assertion of this universality in fact ends up authorizing the elimination of the wealth of actual knowledge embodied in institutions of exchange of all kinds. Furthermore, the *consumer* market, as we have already seen, is *premised* upon *systemically* depriving these consumers of knowledge in a way absolutely at odds with the conception of an economy of 'rational actors' contributing to some market-based information processor. Mirowski's work makes clear that the dangerous turn of recent macroeconomic history – characterized by neoliberalism, financial crisis and proletarianization (in Stiegler's sense) – has everything to do with the failure of economic theory to incorporate an understanding of entropic and counter-entropic processes, at both the thermodynamic and informational levels. The implicit question it raises is how to reinvent economic theory and practice by incorporating such an understanding from its founding premises.

## 139 For a general theory of entropy

This in turn raises the question of the necessity of a *theory of general entropy*. Such a theory would on the one hand seek to juxtapose and articulate the thermodynamic notion of entropy with the informational notion, and to exceed the limitations especially of the latter.[41] And it would also be in this way an account of the relationship between every kind of anti-entropic system, which is to say every kind of *localization and de-localization* process that *works against* the tendency towards the elimination of improbabilities, which is to say the elimination of the past (as what, for any noetic system, opens the possibility of a *future*). But as Smithson's association of entropy with both waste and *luxury* already suggests, this also bears upon Georges Bataille's 'notion of expenditure' and 'general economy' (not forgetting that for Bataille, expenditure beyond subsistence is not a question merely of waste but of an irreducible necessity *of life*).

What this implies, ultimately, is that any such theory is compelled to integrate difficult mathematical, scientific, economic, anthropological and technological questions with others that exceed these divisions between fields of knowledge, in the first place because what is at stake is the anti-entropic function of knowledge itself. Stiegler has indeed begun a project to open up this question of entropy in terms of its thermodynamic, biological, informational and noetic dimensions (in all of its 'exorganological' dimensions, in Stiegler's recent terms), drawing on the work of Vernadsky, Georgescu-Roegen and Lotka, among others, and in discussion with scientists such as Giuseppe Longo, but in truth it is extraordinarily complex and requires large-scale transdisciplinary contributory research projects to be established involving scholars across a wide variety of fields. Despite this apparent daunting complexity, it is the conclusion of this 'elemental critique of political economy' that, in the context of the Anthropocene, such a theory of general entropy has today become an urgent necessity.

*Why* is such a theory necessary? Because what is ultimately at stake in the complex field that is unfolding between carbon technologies and silicon technologies in the *Entropocene* is the need to completely reinscribe old values in new terms, where values are what supply the criteria on the basis of which decisions are taken and resources invested in order to generate *wealth* (as distinct from narrowly calculable economic 'value' or 'prosperity'). Investment must here be understood in every sense and in a *general* sense as that 'putting in reserve' – that *work* – that alone is capable of opening the possibility of another future. Every question of investment is in this way a question of struggling to differ and defer entropy *in general,* in the movement of what Derrida called différance (but where this is also a differentiation beyond the limits of Derrida's formulation).

In a context in which the globalized systems of consumerist capitalism are reaching their limits, and in the process dragging many other systems past their limits, including geophysical systems such as the climate system, and also including the noetic systems through which alone good collective decisions can ever hope to be made – in such a context, where a cascade of catastrophic system failures seems entirely possible if not highly probable, it is solely on the basis of such a theory that anti-entropic investment prospects with the potential to bifurcate away from such a globally dangerous and monstrous situation can be identified, imagined, invented and *realised*. Such a bifurcation, and the general theory on which it can be established, will presuppose a reconsideration of the very basis and division of fields of knowledge, but it will also require a complete reorganization of silicon technologies at least as profound as the elimination of carbon technologies called for by the IPCC, and on a comparably short timespan.

## 140 For a new critique of global governance

Finally, for all the seeming 'straight talking' by the IPCC, it remains captive to the institutional conditions it is compelled to occupy. If the questions raised by this body concern not just scientific understanding but policy and action (in relation to which the term 'mitigation' is entirely inadequate), then this too is a question of the conditions of making good collective decisions. In truth, if the IPCC is to be something other than a diarist of the downfall, then it (or some related body) cannot avoid the question of the relationship between policy recommendations and the *conditions* of actual decision-making and actual transformation (or 'transition'), including the conditions of will, belief and expectation, or alternatively of apathy and nihilism. In that case, it is also obvious that the question of the future of the noetic element cannot avoid confronting the question of the future of international decision-making, and vice versa – the question, precisely, of the wealth and diversity of *elemental* conditions required for neganthropic choices to be made and actions to be taken.

The United Nations is a body composed of a General Assembly whose individual autonomous members have a commitment to addressing the issues of carbon technologies that can be described as patchy at best, and subject to a Security Council with even less resolve, not least because of the economic *fear* generated by the aporia of sustainability. This General Assembly and Security Council are themselves premised on the sovereignty of nation-states, whose political systems, whether representative or otherwise, are entirely subject to what we have called 'telecratic' tendencies. Furthermore, what ecologists and the IPCC must not avoid reckoning with, without denying the processes of psychosocial and economico-institutional denial that are also clearly operative, is the possibility that the fear generated by the aporia of sustainability is in many ways *legitimate*, and that this fear is itself a very significant threat in terms of the possibility of becoming a *panic*, even if it is also true that the paralysing consequences of such fear and panic in turn catastrophically seal the fate of the biosphere.

In short, it is a question of the possibility of dealing noetically with the aporia of sustainability. But the fact is that this society of nations is *also* composed of members almost *none* of whom have *any* effective analyses or policies with respect to silicon technologies that reflect any true weighing of the stakes of the immense transformations such technologies have wrought and are continuing to bring. Yet these technologies are well on the way to destroying the local conditions for the flourishing of noetic and exosomatic life (at all scales of locality), just as carbon technologies are well on the way to destroying the local conditions for the flourishing of biological and endosomatic life (at all scales of locality).

What this ultimately suggests is that a critique of the political economy of silicon technologies cannot avoid a critique of the character and institutions of decision-making at every level of locality from the sub-national to the international and global, as well as of the elemental conditions in which they operate. And the purpose of such a critique can only be the reformulation and reconstruction of these institutions and bodies on the basis of new values legitimating new criteria for investment to be derived from the kinds of considerations whose first steps we have tried to outline in this chapter, and whose ultimate basis must lie in a theory of general entropy and anti-entropy (see Chapters 5 and 6). For in the case of international governing and advising bodies such as the IPCC and the United Nations, these organizations, too, form a sometimes almost imperceptible aspect of the global element.

## Notes

1   IPCC, 'Global Warming of 1.5°C: An IPCC special report on the impacts of global warming of 1.5°C above pre-industrial levels and related global greenhouse gas emission pathways, in the context of strengthening the global response to the threat of climate change, sustainable development, and efforts to eradicate poverty: summary for policymakers' (6 October 2018), available at: <http://report.ipcc. ch/sr15/pdf/sr15_spm_final.pdf>.

2   Gerry Shih, 'Xi tells the world China will boost imports while swiping at Trump's "law of the jungle"', *Washington Post* (5 November 2018), available at: <https://www.washingtonpost.com/world/asia_ pacific/xi-tells-the-world-china-will-boost-imports-while-swiping- at-trumpslaw-of-the-jungle/2018/11/05/c9b61f9c-e0bc-11e8-a1c9- 6afe99dddd92_story.html>.

3   It goes without saying that much hangs on the degree of that commitment. See for example the following article, which implies that China's current mitigation strategies would, if taken as a global

benchmark, produce catastrophic warming of 5.1°C by 2100: Yann Robiou du Pont and Malte Meinshausen, 'Warming Assessment of the Bottom-Up Paris Agreement Emissions Pledges', *Nature Communications* 9 (16 November 2018), available at: <https://www.nature.com/articles/s41467-018-07223-9>.

4    Bernard Stiegler, *Qu'appelle-t-on panser? 1. L'immense régression* (Paris: Les Liens qui Libèrent, 2018).

5    Many of the extremely worrying trends in contemporary global politics, for example, can clearly be viewed as in large part symptoms of decisions taken and not taken with respect to the manner in which this transformation has proceeded.

6    It should be noted that the division between carbon technologies and silicon technologies we will elaborate in these pages is essentially a slightly simplified and modified reinterpretation of Bernard Stiegler's distinction between *carbon-time* and *light-time*.

7    Alfred North Whitehead, *Science and the Modern World* (New York: Macmillan, 1925), p. 41.

8    Stiegler's general organology is an account of the processes involved with beings (such as ourselves) whose somatic and psychic (bodily and mental) organs are inadequate for life unless they are supplemented with artificial and prosthetic (technical) organs such as tools (but where the ensemble of such technical organs forms a technical system). Because these technical organs are in no way 'natural', however, they require knowledge and care in order to prevent their productive effects from becoming destructive, and this knowledge and care is contained in social organizations. General organology thus posits three inextricably-tied organological levels dynamically unfolding together over the course of proto-human and human history: the individual, the collective and the technical.

9    For Heidegger, swimming was the example through which he raised the epistemological question of how we can *know* our element (which for Heidegger is the element of thinking, given that we are, in Aristotelian and Stieglerian terms, *noetic* beings), and the more-than-epistemological question of how we can *respond* to what we know of our element. See Martin Heidegger, *What is Called Thinking?*, trans. J. Glenn Gray (New York: Harper & Row, 1968), p. 21: 'We shall never learn what "is called" swimming, for example, or what it "calls for", by reading a treatise on swimming. Only the leap into the river tells us what is called swimming. The question "What is called thinking?" can never be answered by proposing a definition of the concept *thinking*, and then diligently explaining what is contained in that definition.'

10  Aristotle, *On the Soul*, 418b–419a. 'The transparent' is the usual translation of *diaphanēs*, alluded to by Joyce, who refers to the 'ineluctable modality of the visible' in order to evoke the 'limits of the diaphane' and Aristotle's being 'aware of them bodies before of them coloured'. James Joyce, *Ulysses. Annotated Student Edition* (London: Penguin, 1992), p. 45.

11  Aristotle, *On the Soul*, 423a33–34. See Bernard Stiegler, *Acting Out*, trans. David Barison, Daniel Ross and Patrick Crogan (Stanford: Stanford University Press, 2009), pp. 13–14.

12  Bernard Stiegler, *The Age of Disruption: Technology and Madness in Computational Capitalism*, trans. Daniel Ross (Cambridge: Polity Press, 2019), p. 13.

13  Sigmund Freud, *Beyond the Pleasure Principle*, in Volume 18 of James Strachey (ed. and trans.), *The Standard Edition of the Complete Psychological Works of Sigmund Freud* (London: Hogarth, 1953–74), pp. 48–49.

14  Norbert Wiener, *Cybernetics, or Control and Communication in the Animal and the Machine*, second edition (Cambridge, Massachusetts: MIT Press, 1961), p. 38.

15  Ibid., p. 39.

16  Ibid., pp. 38–39. With this, it is important to note that automation does not begin with computers, and that Wiener himself describes a genealogy of automation (and more particularly of the automaton as 'a working simulacrum of a living organism') that itself follows the delineation of technical systems he describes across the last three centuries: 'In the time of Newton, the automaton becomes the clockwork music box, with the little effigies pirouetting stiffly on top. In the nineteenth century, the automaton is a glorified heat engine, burning some combustible fuel instead of the glycogen of the human muscles. Finally, the present automaton opens doors by means of photocells, or points guns to the place at which a radar beam picks up an airplane, or computes the solution of a differential equation' (pp. 39–40).

17  See the Wikipedia list available here: <https://en.wikipedia.org/wiki/List_of_largest_companies_by_revenue>. As of January 2020, seven out of the top ten are energy companies, along with two automobile manufacturers, and rounded out (at number one) by Walmart.

18  See the Wikipedia list available here: <https://en.wikipedia.org/wiki/List_of_public_corporations_by_market_capitalization>. As of January 2020, seven out of the top ten are internet or computing companies (Microsoft, Apple, Amazon, Alphabet, Facebook, Alibaba, Tencent).

19 Karl Marx, *Contribution to a Critique of Political Economy*, trans. S. W. Ryanzanskaya (Moscow: Progress Publishers, 1970), p. 197.

20 Gunpowder was invented or discovered during the Tang Dynasty in China, giving rise to the long history of fire weapons and guns, which were initially technologies of external war but also of internal social control.

21 Daily atmospheric $CO_2$ concentration totals recorded at Mauna Loa Observatory, along with all-time highs, are available here: <https://www.co2.earth/daily-co2>.

22 On 11 November 2018, that is, the tenth anniversary of Alibaba's promotion of so-called 'Singles Day' as a kind of consumerist festival, their Tmall shopping platform recorded sales totalling ten billion yuan (US$1.44 billion) *in the first two minutes and five seconds of the day's trading*. This possibility, involving the processing of *hundreds of thousands of transactions per second*, exposes the true meaning of automation in the current macroeconomic model (even if, in this particular case, many of these transactions may have been 'preordered'). See He Wei, 'Singles Day Achieves New Record', *China Daily* (12 November 2018), available at: <http://www.chinadaily.com.cn/a/201811/12/WS5be881a3a310eff303287e8d.html>. It has also been suggested that these annual 'records' are in fact engineered, evidence for which would be the smoothness of the curve showing year-to-year growth.

23 Once again, carbon technologies and memory technologies are inextricably entangled together throughout their history. To give a seemingly minor example, if writing is a memory technology, the paper on which one writes is a carbon technology (and one producing a significant environmental impact). Or more obliquely: the very possibility of carbon technologies lies in the fact that fossilized organic material still retains traces of the molecular complexity of the organisms of which it is composed – this molecular complexity in the form of hydrocarbons is the source of the potential energy that is liberated in combustion (thereby reducing these hydrocarbons to much *less* complex molecules). Such complexity ultimately derives from the organizational characteristics of organic material, characteristics that are constructed and maintained on the basis of the genetic molecule, which is itself a kind of biological memory. And, on the other hand, every fabricative technology has an *accidental* retentional capacity (a prehistoric flint tool *records* the gestures of the hand that made it): what we are here calling retentional technologies are those in which this memorial function is deliberate rather than accidental.

24 See Bernard Stiegler, *Automatic Society, Volume 1: The Future of Work*, trans. Daniel Ross (Cambridge: Polity Press, 2016).

25   Karl Marx and Friedrich Engels, *The German Ideology: Students Edition*, trans. William Lough, Clemens Dutt and Charles Philip Magill (London: Lawrence and Wishart, 1974), p. 54.

26   Herbert Marcuse, *An Essay on Liberation* (Boston: Beacon Press, 2000), p. 20.

27   Ibid., p. 21. And we should note that in *our* terms, this sensitivity and consciousness are *both* aspects of the *noetic* being, whose *way* of being sensitive is always inscribed in a becoming-symbolic.

28   Ibid., p. 22.

29   The notion of the 'cinesphere' is borrowed from a work of science fiction: Charles Eric Maine, *The Man Who Couldn't Sleep* (Philadelphia and New York: J. B. Lippincott, 1956), published in England under the horological title, *Escapement*. Here we use it in a way that sees the conjunction of the process of globalization with the process of what, using Husserlian terms, Stiegler calls the 'becoming-temporal-object of everything "that happens", through the operation of media and, beyond them, through the omnipotence of the new programmatology producing space-light-time's weave of rhythms'. Bernard Stiegler, *Technics and Time, 2: Disorientation*, trans. Stephen Barker (Stanford: Stanford University Press, 2009), p. 188.

30   In 'Toutes les Histoires' (1988), the first episode of *Histoire(s) du Cinéma* (directed by Jean-Luc Godard, 1988–98). Note that the first of these statements also appears in Godard's *Contempt* (1963), attributed to André Bazin, but it actually comes from a 1959 article by Michel Mourlet in *Cahiers du cinéma*. See also Bernard Stiegler, *The Neganthropocene*, trans. Daniel Ross (London: Open Humanities Press, 2018), pp. 163–64, and Daniel Ross, 'Moving Images of the Anthropocene: Rethinking Cinema Beyond Anthropology', *Screening the Past* 44 (2019), available at: <http://www.screeningthepast.com/2019/03/moving-images-of-the-anthropocene-rethinking-cinema-beyond-anthropology/>.

31   In fact, the speed at which information circulates in the silicon memory of a computer is 200,000 km per second (two thirds of the speed of light), which is more than 500,000 times quicker than a plane flying at Mach 1 (that is, 0.34 km per second, or 20 km per minute).

32   Note that this distinction between a *hyper*-capitalism of consumption and an *ultra*-capitalism of algorithmic platforms deviates from Stiegler's own terminology. The sense of 'ultra' here is that of 'the furthest possible', 'the ultimate'.

33   See for example Bernard Stiegler, 'Telecracy Against Democracy', trans. Chris Turner, *Cultural Politics* 6 (2010), pp. 171–80.

34 Marcuse, *An Essay on Liberation*, pp. 21. For a critique of Marcuse on these questions, see Bernard Stiegler, *The Lost Spirit of Capitalism: Disbelief and Discredit, Volume 3*, trans. Daniel Ross (Cambridge: Polity Press, 2014), part 2, 'The Automatization of the Super-Ego and the Passage of Desire as Original Diversion of Libidinal Energy'.

35 Percy Bridgman, *The Nature of Thermodynamics*, quoted in Robert Smithson, 'Entropy and the New Monuments', *Robert Smithson: The Collected Writings* (Berkeley: University of California Press, 1996), p. 20.

36 Smithson, 'Entropy Made Visible', *Robert Smithson: The Collected Writings*, p. 303.

37 Smithson, 'Entropy and the New Monuments', p. 17.

38 Philip Mirowski, 'Philosophizing With a Hammer: Reply to Binmore, Davis and Klaes', *Journal of Economic Methodology* 11 (2004), p. 500. And see Philip Mirowski, *More Heat Than Light. Economics as Social Physics: Physics as Nature's Economics* (Cambridge: Cambridge University Press, 1989).

39 Philip Mirowski, *Machine Dreams: Economics Becomes a Cyborg Science* (Cambridge and New York: Cambridge University Press, 2002).

40 Philip Mirowski and Edward Nik-Khah, *The Knowledge We Have Lost in Information: The History of Information in Modern Economics* (New York: Oxford University Press, 2017).

41 Information theory has always been premised on a de-substantialized, de-materialized and de-functionalized conception of information. But in addition to its irreducible materiality (which forms, furthermore, the retentional basis of all anti-entropy), information must be reconceptualized in terms of its tensional and protentional dimensions (in Simondon's sense of tension, and in and beyond Husserl's sense of protention). It is on the basis of this pro-tending outwards to the new and unexpected that a renewed concept of information within a theory of general entropy will be able to think the possibility of *bifurcation* to which we refer below.

# Afterword: The Territorial Inscription of Law[1]

*Alain Supiot*[2]

In legal terminology, the notion of space was not, until recently, some Cartesian abstraction that might be applied to any sort of place. Its use was reserved for those parts of the world that cannot be occupied on a lasting basis because they have no discernible limits and are unfit for long-term human habitation: the seas and the oceans, the skies and interstellar space. In their current use, juridical notions of air space and outer space, maritime space and oceanic space, are always defined in opposition to the Earth. The Earth is not conceived by the law as an abstract space, but rather as a mesh of territories, domains (public or private), regions or countries, jurisdictions and sometimes sites or zones (subject to overriding clauses). It was the European Union that first defined itself in legal terms as an 'area of freedom, security and justice' (in French, an '*espace* de liberté, de sécurité et de justice'), without discernible limits, rather than as a territory or group of territories with clearly identified borders. Significantly, it was only with the creation of a 'single market' that the notion of space began to be used to refer to the land and not only to the skies or the seas. This indifferentiation of places goes hand in hand with the emergence of global law, which will assert its independence with respect to territorially based legal systems.[3]

One may wonder about the meaning and future of this contemporary aspiration for a spatial legal order that would be free from any territorial grounding. The place of civilization, in the primary legal sense of the word 'civilized' (subject to the rule of civil law), has until now never been the inherently formless space of the sea or the skies, but always the *terra ferma*. Civilizing space has always meant referring it to terrestrial dimensions that give it both a being and a form. *Forma dat esse rei* ('the form gives being to the thing'[4]): this old adage of Roman law already registers the inaugural gesture by which all mythologies mark the birth or rebirth of the world, by making the 'higher waters' of the Heavens rise up from the face of the waters, whereupon between the Heavens and the ocean there emerges dry land. This founding gesture is normative, assigning the world its first limits and hence making possible the measure of all things. Limiting and measuring are the two inseparable sides of the activity of the jurist as of the geometer, these two figures coming together in the figure of the surveyor who, in measuring the land, delimits what is due to each and what is common to all.

This is how the world becomes *habitable*, in the multiple senses of this word derived from the Latin *'habere'* (to have, to hold).[5] To inhabit the world is to have a safe place in it, fit for *habitation*. For this, it is necessary to give form to it, to make it into a human *habitat*, through the words by which we name even the tiniest parcel of land and through the acts by which we fashion our landscapes. We must also conform to shared *habits* that govern the lives of inhabitants and take account of their ecological milieu. A habitable world is a world in which the human relationship to the land is instituted in rules that assign to each a place fit for living.

In the Western tradition, these rules are part of what we call the law, which encompasses penal and administrative law as well as civil law. Like all civilizations that have emerged from the religions of the Book, this tradition contains the ideal of a superhuman, atemporal and universal Law, which would apply to every person in every place and could ignore territorial diversity. But modern law is built on abandoning this ideal in favour of a territorial inscription of law. Implicitly responding to Pascal's quips about the geographical limits of human laws ('Odd kind of justice that is bounded by a river! Truth on this side of the Pyrenees, error on the other'[6]), Montesquieu affirmed that laws are necessarily relative in the introduction to *The Spirit of the Laws*:

> They should be related to the physical aspect of the country; to the climate, be it freezing, torrid, or temperate; to the properties of the terrain, its location and extent; to the way of life of the peoples, be they plowmen, hunters, or herdsmen; they should relate to the degree of liberty that the constitution can sustain, to the religion of the inhabitants, their inclinations, their wealth, their number, their commerce, their mores and their manners.[7]

In modern times, the territorial inscription of law is linked to legal systems in which the State crowns the institutional edifice. The world becomes a mosaic of sovereign States in competition with each other over borders, control of the seas and colonization overseas. But each acknowledges the other's right to lay down the law within its own national territory. Carl Schmitt theorized just such an international order in his *The Nomos of the Earth*, while also diagnosing its gradual decline.[8] But his Nazi sympathies prevented him from seeing the deeper causes of the crisis affecting this State-based organization of the world. He attributed it to the rising power of the United States and the abstract pacifism of the founders of the League of Nations, and failed to notice the return to a belief in universal and timeless law, which was the hallmark of the major contemporary ideologies, including the National Socialist theory of *Lebensraum*. These ideologies were based on scientistic certainties, and tended to deny any idea of limit or human measure. 'Law', said Hitler, 'is a human invention. Nature knows neither the notary nor the surveyor. God knows only force.'[9]

If one can talk here of the *return* of a belief in superhuman laws, it is because, like divine laws, laws that appeal to science do not accept the borders defining States and their dominion transcends any territorial limit. Just as the Catholic Church proclaims that it knows no territory,[10] so it is that the truth claimed by the 'laws' of economics, biology or history covers the whole surface of the globe. However, unlike the religious laws that unified Medieval Europe, the universal laws invoked today are immanent and not transcendent. They do not appeal to the Heavens but to the nature of things and human nature. It is biology, economics and history that are summoned to affirm their authority over the terrestrial world. While this scientistic normativity was already present in the nineteenth century (particularly with Comte or Marx theoretically, and on the political level with the colonial enterprise), it flourished in the twentieth century in the guise of racial biology and historical materialism, along with their respective political by-products: racism, social Darwinism and the class struggle. What distinguishes these modern variants of scientism from religious proselytism, however, should not be forgotten: faith in these laws without a Legislator leads not to conversation but to 'abolishing the parasitic sections of society',[11] to be treated like refuse[12] destined for the 'rubbish heap of history'.[13] This is undoubtedly the specific mark of the insane massacres that accompanied the various imperial enterprises that dominated the history of the past century.

These empires have now fallen, and the countries they once ruled over have all donned the garments of the nation-state. Today the State crowns the legal edifice, both internally and internationally, and it is under the aegis of the State that today man inhabits the Earth (I). But no one can ignore that this institutional edifice is coming apart and that an imperial logic is still at work. This logic no longer assumes the guise of a localizable power bent on extending the territorial scope of its laws, but instead takes the form of a deterritorialization of law, carried out in the name of the globalization of the world (II). This deterritorialization of law has no more future than does nostalgia for a purely inter-state legal order. The only thing of which we can be certain is that man is an earth-bound animal who must discover anew a sense of measure by which to redraw a liveable world (III).

## I Inhabiting the World: The Institution of Territories

Just as all cosmogonies show the birth of the Heavens and the Earth from the cosmic Ocean, so too they all affirm the earthly substance of the human being. Adam, the first man in the religions of the Book, derives his name from the red earth (*adama*) with which God fashioned him, and *l'homme* itself, man, comes from the Latin *humus* (damp earth): *Homo* is the one who comes from the earth and is destined to return to it, to be inhumed.[14] Although born of the earth, man is endowed with a divine spirit that entitles him to take possession of it, to fashion it in his image and to make it fruitful by his labour.[15] This second aspect – the 'taking of land',[16] taking possession by labour or force – has been dominant in the modern Western world, at the cost of repressing how humans belong to the land. This lop-sided vision, whose religious origins we can only surmise,[17] sees nothing but the imprint of humans upon the Earth and remains blind to the imprint of Earth upon humans.

In order for our sight to be fully restored, we should turn to the civilizations that have not yet been blinded to the earth-bound dimension of man.[18] Black Africa has without a doubt remained most sensitive to what humans owe to the land,[19] and it is on this continent that one can find the most subtle institutional manifestations of the complexity of this relationship. Thus, in all West African countries, there are two distinct and complementary authorities that preside over land relations: the village chief and the 'master of the land'.[20] The village chief parades the signs of his power and never walks barefoot. He embodies 'the fate of one who, in his relationship to the surrounding world, would have chosen no form of relation other than that between hunter and prey'.[21] The master of the land, by contrast, lives humbly and walks barefoot, and his 'essential task is to ensure that each person and the whole village have a viable relation to the land'.[22] He presides over rituals designed to ensure the land's fertility and settles disputes relating to its use or distribution. Compared to the predatory figure of the chief, he incarnates the authority of the forefathers and the stability of territorial connections.

African civilizations thus invite us to make a distinction within our own institutions between: 1) what connects someone to the land; and 2) what gives them control over it.

1 In the legal sphere, *a person's connection to the land* continues to inform decisions on two fundamental issues: the determination of his or her identity and the laws which he or she must observe.

The question of identity concerns the status of persons, and connection to a territory is at work in what is today called nationality law. 'Nationality' is related etymologically to the verb *naître*, 'to be born', and it situates each of us, from birth, at the intersection of a territory and a lineage. Consequently, nationality law combines, in varying ways depending on the country, considerations of the place of birth (*jus soli*) with that of the nationality of the parents (*jus sanguinis*), to which should be added the possibility of acquiring one or more other nationalities later and hence of adopting new homelands. Nationality, which is an element of identity in the legal sense, is the source of personal status, that is, of a non-negotiable set of rights and duties towards the State or States of which one is a national.[23] This status can limit or even prevent the movement of a person beyond the territory to which he belongs.[24] The weightiest duty, however, is to defend the national territory and hence run the risk of 'dying for one's country'.[25] It was on the basis of such a duty that motherlands devoured their children by the millions in the last two World Wars.[26]

A person's connection to a territory can be seen in a different light when the question is no longer who he is but by what law he is governed. Are people always and everywhere bound by the laws of their nation or must they obey the laws of the place in which they happen to be? In the West, the answer to this question has evolved over hundreds of years. In Europe, the invasion and dislocation of the Roman Empire led to populations living together while obeying different laws. The new barbarian masters followed their various customs while the descendants of the subjects of the Empire (and the Church) remained subject to a greatly adulterated version of 'Roman law'. In this system, which lasted from the fifth to the eleventh century, each person lived by the law of his origins, that is, of his ethnic group.[27] This principle, which was called the personality of laws, was undermined by the mingling of populations and the rise of feudalism, which led to the same local or regional customs, the same territorial law (*lex loci*), being applied to all the inhabitants of the same seigniory. This is how the principle of the territoriality of the laws gained currency, and its progress accompanied that of the nation-state.[28]

The world thus came to look like a jigsaw of separate legal regimes, with each State having sovereignty over the laws to be applied on its territory. But since the borders between them were not watertight, it was necessary to decide what judge was entitled to adjudicate and what law was to be applied in situations involving a foreign element. The objective rules laid down for this constituted what is called Private International Law, which, despite its name, was until recently largely internal and differed from one State to the next. In all countries, however, the degree of territorial purchase of national law varies according to the situations it is a matter of governing: it has greatest territorial purchase in the fields of immovables, liability in tort and public security, and the least purchase in the context of international transactions, which by definition are associated with different territories.[29]

2   *Man's hold over the land* takes two distinct but complementary forms in modern law: sovereignty and property. Both establish an exclusive relationship between the sovereign or owner and the lands governed or possessed. This exclusivity is completely new in the long history of law and could well be only a passing phase. For if we take a comparative historical view of land laws, man's rights in the land have at almost all times and places been a function of the bonds between men or with the gods.[30] This stems from a deeply rooted sense that the human being, an earthly and mortal creature, cannot seriously lay claim to exercise sovereign power over natural elements. The power man *holds* over the land is always derived from another: from a master or a god who has granted man use of it but who may take it back.

In the history of Western law, this notion of *tenure* is linked to feudal structures, which, to varying degrees (in France more than elsewhere[31]), dominated the Medieval period.[32] In the feudal world, it was the bonds of dependence between people that determined their rights over land. This was true of political power (which the suzerain exercised only indirectly over the territory of his vassals) and also of economic power, which was divided (with the exception of allodial land) between the *dominium eminens* of the lord and the *dominium utile* of the vassal or tenant. Tenure, whether in its noble form (the fief) or common form (censive tenure), was always *tenure-service*, a concession granted in return for dues, leading to a division of rights between several people over one piece of land.

Yet this type of legal arrangement was not restricted to
Western feudalism, and there are other, more recent examples. In the Ottoman Empire, rights were divided between
those who cultivated the land and thus had certain rights
over it (provided they did so fruitfully), regional administrators who collected taxes on the produce, and lastly the
imperial treasury, which had ultimate tenurial superiority.[33]
Another example was studied by Jacques Berque: irrigated
and cultivated terraces in the valleys of the High Atlas in
Morocco, where each family has tenurial superiority over
its plot, which is handed down from generation to generation, and can always demand to buy back the land from its
present occupier.[34] One of the common features of these
variants is that several people may exercise different rights
simultaneously in the same property, which itself remains
indivisible.

With the advent of the modern right to property, the situation was reversed: land was no longer perceived as the
site of relations between people but was treated as a thing
submitted to the will of one person alone. The far-reaching
consequences of this reversal could not fail to have considerable impact on how human environments were shaped,
corresponding in the legal sphere to what, from a geographical perspective, Augustin Berque called the 'freeze
on the object'.[35]

As Louis Dumont has shown, economic ideology implies
that relations between people are subordinated to relations
between people and things.[36] Moreover, the market economy needs goods fit for exchange, that is, cleansed of any
trace of personal bonds. In the Napoleonic Code the direct
relation between persons and things (treated in Book II)
forms the basis of the contractual relations between persons
(treated, with successions, in Book III). The equivalent of
this development in the political order was the establishment of the figure of the sovereign, incarnated in the State
as guarantor of respect for private property. Public and private were no longer interlinked as they were in feudalism,
but sharply differentiated: the public domain of national
territory was controlled by the State and seamlessly[37] jux-
taposed with private domains subject to the sovereign
will of their owners. The *dominium eminens* of the State
has not disappeared completely, however. Legislation provides for the expropriation of land for public use in return

for compensation,[38] and, in the absence of legal claimants, property still escheats to the State. More generally, the right to property must be exercised in conformity with the law.[39] Exercising this right assumes the existence of a sovereign State to guarantee that the property of each is respected by all. When this condition no longer applies, the fiction of a direct and exclusive legal bond between people and things is no longer tenable and the relations of dependence between people once again come to the fore.[40]

## II Globalizing the World: The Deterritorialization of Law

The terms 'globalization' or 'mondialisation' are slogans more than concepts, since they encompass a heterogeneous set of phenomena which should be carefully differentiated. The abolition of physical distances through the circulation of signs between people is a structural phenomenon enabled by new digital technologies. By contrast, the globalization of trade in things is a conjunctural phenomenon that stems from reversible political decisions (lifting trade barriers) and the temporary over-use of non-renewable natural resources (keeping transport costs artificially low). It is the combination of these two different phenomena that reduces the heterogeneity of signs and things by referring them to a single monetary standard, that is, by transforming them into 'liquidities'.[41]

Of course, territory does not escape this process of 'liquidation'. It ceases to be seen as a place from which one comes and to whose laws one is subject, existing only as object of property and as such submitted to laws that transcend its singularity. This process of uprooting laws from their territorial grounding has clearly not come to an end (nor can it, without an apocalyptic liquidation of the entire world). But it has led to the dislocation of territorial legal systems due to the dual pressure of: 1) personal laws undermining them from within; and 2) universal laws dismantling them from without.

1   The *personality of laws* first reappeared in Western legal systems with colonization, when the colonizers enjoyed a different status to that of the colonized.[42] It then reached Europe when certain States began to base personal status on racial characteristics. Nazi Germany was obviously the main actor in this biologization of the juridical condition of human beings. It certainly had no monopoly on biologism or racial discrimination,[43] but it took these to their most extreme consequences in its programmed extermination of the Jews and the massacre and enslavement of Slavs living

in the *Lebensraum,* which it wanted to annex. The monstros-
ity of these acts, together with the independence progressively gained by colonized countries, explain why the idea
of personal status was thoroughly discredited in the immediate post-War period. However, it is reappearing today in
different forms, but, instead of being imposed, it is actually
claimed in the name of individual liberties. And it is no longer by racial biology but by genetics, referred to in certain
legal provisions, that people are today being governed.

Today, the *free choice of one's status* is in full swing,
both economically and personally. In terms of economic
exchange, the freedoms associated with free trade (freedom
of establishment, to supply services and to put goods and
capital into circulation) have been invoked to allow investors and firms to dodge the legislation of the country in
which they operate in favour of one with more favourable
laws. Flags of convenience, which used to be confined to
the law of the sea, have been hoisted on dry land in the form
of 'law shopping', which treats national law as a product
competing on an international market of norms.[44]

This approach has been actively promoted in Europe by
the Court of Justice of the European Communities, which
upheld a company's right to avoid the rules of the State
in which it is operating by registering in a State with less
restrictive rules.[45] In order to facilitate such law shopping,
the World Bank's 'Doing Business' programme regularly
ranks 178 countries (renamed 'economies') according to
their tax and welfare legislation – the least stringent first.[46]
The legal representation of the world implicit in these developments is that of a market of norms in which free individuals may choose to adopt the law that is most profitable
for them. This sort of market will gradually eliminate the
normative systems least capable of satisfying the financial
expectations of investors.[47]

This free-market version of the personality of laws is not
restricted to the economic field. The notion of personal law,
which was reinvented in the nineteenth century in the context of colonialism, has found a new lease of life through
the vast numbers of people in Western countries who have
been imported to work there for next to nothing or have
been driven from their homes through the destruction
of their traditional ways of life. Faced with this phenomenon, Western countries have opted for one of two policies:

assimilation or multiculturalism. Assimilation means upholding the territoriality of laws by subjecting all citizens to the same personal status. Multiculturalism reintroduces the personality of laws so that new citizens may conserve their former legal status. This kind of multiculturalism, however, in contrast to older forms of coexistence between communities (such as indigenous status under colonialism or the Ottoman *millet* system[48]), claims to act in the name of human rights and the freedom of the individual to choose his or her personal status. The Chief Justice of England and Wales, Lord Chief Justice Phillips, recently relied on the freedom of the parties to submit their agreements to a law other than English law (law shopping) in order to defend the idea that jurisdiction could be given in his country to Islamic or Rabbinical courts.[49]

In this context, claims shift from the realm of having to that of being, from the socio-economic to identity – and it is not only groups but individuals who want to become their own law-givers. On the collective level the 'right to difference' has been invoked by various minorities – ethnic, sexual and religious – which stake their claim as victims in order to have a special status attributed to them and hence to limit the scope of the law that applies to all the inhabitants of the same territory.[50] On the individual level, the right to privacy is invoked in order to erode the principle of the inalienability of civil status so that each person may determine his or her own identity.[51]

As always in the history of law, the re-emergence of older legal structures does not imply a return to the past, but contributes to the construction of new categories. The personality of laws, in its individualist form of 'a law for me' and 'myself as law', is the legal expression of the potentially devastating narcissism that is characteristic of this latest stage in Western culture,[52] of which Islamism is in many respects only an inverted image, as evidenced by the so-called *fatwamania* in Sunni countries and the claim of any imam to be able to set himself up as a legislator.[53] This narcissism is devastating because it involves the impasse described by Pierre Legendre:

> Forcing the subject to act as the Third towards himself is no liberation; it crushes him, transforming social relations *politically* into a free-for-all concealed

beneath a discourse of generalized seduction. What is implicit in the new management-inspired legal initiatives can be revealed for all to see, and I would summarize it as follows: *good luck to you.*[54]

The emergence of a *biological status* is the other facet of this contemporary version of the personality of laws. The idea of grounding private property in land on biological inequalities is as old as economic liberalism itself.[55] It was used to justify the colonization of peoples who persisted in seeing their land as an oecumene[56] and not as a commodity, long before racial biology supplied 'scientific' arguments. 'We shape the life of our people and our legislation according to the verdicts of genetics', said the Nazis,[57] thus expressing a conviction which today has become a commonplace: that the only laws really binding on man are those revealed by science. Population genetics may have given way to biomolecular genetics over the last half century, but explanations based on the genome have simply replaced racial ones, within a discourse whose dogmatic structure has remained unaltered.[58] Nowadays biotechnology enables us to ascertain the genitor of any mammal. Consequently, complex institutional mechanisms, which used to refer every human being to a territory as much as to a filiation – and that filiation itself to a familial status rather than to a 'genetic truth' – seem suddenly outdated.

Indeed, the last thirty years have seen the idea of a 'biological truth' of filiation gain ground, to varying degrees, in the legislation of European countries.[59] In countries like Germany, where *jus sanguinis* was already the cornerstone of nationality, this produced little resistance.[60] In countries attached to the *jus soli*, however, like France, people were less keen to let test tubes decide on a person's identity[61] but the pressure to do so was strong. The bill on the use of genetic testing to monitor immigrant family reunion programs, which had been thrown out in 1987, was adopted in 2007, with the approval of the Constitutional Council.[62] Moreover, the highest echelons of the French State make no secret of their belief that human behaviour is genetically determined, which would justify screenings and preventive measures.[63]

A similar faith inspires the economists who look to biology for the ultimate laws governing their vision of the

world. It is a world peopled by hordes of contracting par-
ticles whose behaviour could be explained and monitored
by analysing their genes or cerebral cortex.[64] Biological
identification is even set to supplant civil status in border
controls, through the progressive extension of biometrics,
by which cosmopolitan elites entitled to circulate across the
entire globe may reliably be distinguished from migrants
driven out by penury, who are to be turned back or selec-
tively passed according to manpower needs.[65] Inhabiting
the global world in these two extreme ways – as winners or
as losers – should not be confused with the ancient figure of
the nomad. Nomadism is not defined by moving from place
to place; the nomad is not without a territory but simply
does not settle on any part of it.[66] This doubtless makes him
unassimilable to categories derived from Roman law, which
all emanate from the idea of attributing to each his own.
By contrast, insofar as biometric methods of identification
extract identity from any territorial reference, they are ideal
for controlling nomads (or what remains of them) as well
as sedentary peoples, migrants and transnational managers.

2   The belief in *universal laws* is the second factor in the dislocation of territorial laws. Today it takes the form of the economic dogma of globalization. Unlike classical economic
liberalism, which viewed the legal system as the institutional basis for the production and distribution of wealth,
this new *credo* views it simply as an instrument in the
service of the supposedly immanent laws of the economy.
This dogma was systematized in the West in the *Law and
Economics* doctrine, which tallies with the Marxist creed
of law as the 'reflection' of the economic base. It could
therefore serve to justify combining capitalist and communist systems in the development of what the Chinese
Constitution calls the 'communist market economy'.[67] In
this hybrid system, the free market has contributed the competition of all against all, free trade and maximizing individual utilities, while communism has contributed 'limited
democracy', the instrumentalization of the legal system,
an obsession with quantification and the abyss separating
the lot of the rulers from that of the ruled. This system is
not specific to China and it has gained ground, in different guises and to varying degrees, in Eastern and Western

Europe.[68] It has contributed to the deterritorialization of law in two different ways.

The first and most obvious effect has been the dismantling of any sort of legal limit that might hinder the circulation of goods and capital or the provision of services internationally. The system's ultimate goal is a Total Market encompassing all of humankind and all the products of the planet, within which each country would abolish its trade barriers in order to exploit its 'comparative advantages'. Such a programme was clearly spelled out in the Preamble to the Marrakesh Agreement establishing the World Trade Organization (WTO). The growth in quantifiable economic indicators – employment levels, a large and steadily growing (sic) volume of income and demand; increased production of and trade in goods and services – is presented in this text as an end in itself, to be attained by means of 'the substantial reduction of tariffs and other barriers to trade and the elimination of discriminatory treatment in international trade relations'.

Such a policy entails reducing the diversity of national legal systems, which are summoned to rid themselves of any rules liable to hinder the free circulation of goods and capital.[69] Dismantling trade barriers in this way has significant environmental effects,[70] which are not addressed by the high-profile condemnation of countries that forbid the importation of goods whose mode of production does not conform to their own environmental legislation.[71] This economic dogma is even applied to land itself, which is assimilated to a commodity and so must be open to investment or real estate speculation. According to the European Court of Justice:

> Whatever the reasons for it, the purchase of immovable property in a Member State by a non-resident constitutes an investment in real estate which falls within the category of capital movements between Member States. Freedom for such movements is guaranteed by [the] Treaty.[72]

It is in the context of this metamorphosis of land into an asset into a liquid value on a global market that the notion of space, which was previously restricted to the law of the sea, has now been extended to the 'law of the earth'. The European Union, for example, no longer defines itself as a single territory or a group of discrete territories but as an 'area without internal frontiers' or an 'area of freedom, security and justice'[73] designed to include an indeterminate and indeterminable number of new member States.

This dissolution of the singularity of territories into an abstract, measurable and negotiable space encounters strong resistance in some countries and has not yet taken place at a global level as completely as it has in the European Union.[74] More generally, the process of globalization cannot of course ignore the concrete diversity of landscapes, human environments, modes of life, languages, cultural treasures and intellectual riches. Unlike commodities (and what the market economy assimilates to commodities, like work, land and money), their value has no market price, which is why their preservation and renewal should in principle be governed by the *lex loci*.

Yet the global market still considers them as resources to be taken into account when evaluating the comparative advantage of a country or a region of the globe. This is why new techniques designed to quantify and measure the relative value of these non-market goods and find a universal accounting image for them have emerged. Such *scoring* techniques are applied today in fields as diverse as scientific research, comparative law (for the purposes of 'law shopping' mentioned above) and 'human development'. Geographical elements such as towns, nations and territories are treated like competing trademarks, from which the notion of *nation branding* has emerged, based on quantitative indicators of 'local identity capital'.[75] This presupposes that local identity can be broken down into a normalized list of features, which may be evaluated (landscape, climate, public infrastructures, public safety, cuisine, etc.) and that local political and economic 'players' are enlisted to vie with each other in 'territorial competitiveness'.[76]

Here the law applicable to a territory gives way to a new type of normativity claiming to be based on the observation of fact and no longer on legal imperative. This is a final avatar of the positivist temptation to dissolve law into the immanent laws revealed by science, such that the political headaches and uncertainties of *governing* a territory may be swept away thanks to the techniques of good *governance*. The attempt to transform any and every singular quality into a measurable quantity launches us into a speculative loop in which belief in quantitative representations gradually supplants any real contact with the realities to which these representations are supposed to refer. Typical of the communist market economy, territorial performance indicators are founded on the same dogmas as Soviet planning and produce the same effects: public initiatives target quantitative objectives rather than concrete results, and the real situation of the economy and society is concealed from a governing class disconnected from the lives of those it governs. Quantified representations of the world, which today determine how private and public affairs are managed, imprison international organizations, States and companies in an autism of quantification that increasingly cuts them off from how people really live.[77]

## III Redrawing the World: A Sense of Measure

The market economy is not a state of nature. In order to turn the market into a general principle regulating economic life, it was necessary to behave *as though* land, work and money were commodities, which clearly is not the case.[78] The market economy is based on legal fictions, but fictions which are not the stuff of novels: they can be *sustainable* only if they are humanly liveable. From this perspective, environmental law could be defined as the set of rules that sustain the fiction of nature-as-commodity, just as labour law could be defined as the rules that sustain the fiction of work-as-commodity. These legal supports were established at the national level and are being eroded by the process of globalization. When the rules of the free market are no longer subtended by anything, their grounding in the diversity of territories and people collapses, which is bound to lead to ecological, social or monetary catastrophe.

Making competition into the only universal principle of the organization of the world leads to the same impasse as the totalitarianisms of the twentieth century, the common feature of which was precisely the subordination of the legal form to supposed laws of competition (between races or classes). Stating this, and predicting that such a doctrine is bound to generate insanity and violence, is not dictated by some political or moral stance. Rather, it stems from one of the rare certainties that the 'science of Law' may bring: namely, that since egoism, greed and the struggle for life are well and truly present in this world as it is, they must be contained and channelled by a common reference to the world as it should be. By contrast, making universal

struggle into the founding principle of the legal system denies the latter's very possibility and sets humanity on the road to disaster.

The West shows some signs of becoming aware of these risks. The
dangers entailed by the disappearance of public space are at last being
recognized in the countries most 'advanced' along the path towards
'to each his own law'.[79] It is also becoming more difficult to ignore the
systemic risks to the planet incurred by a real economy that is disconnected from the potential of our biosphere (ecological risk), from its
monetary representation (financial risk) and from minimal standards
of social justice (social risk). But this awareness of diffuse dangers
has not as yet led to any genuine challenge to the economic dogma
governing globalization. One can only hope that the rising economic
powers will use the resources of their own cultures to avoid embark-
ing along the same calamitous paths.

In this respect China is eminently well placed. Confucianism is of
course one such resource, with its emphasis on the close links between
the cosmic and the social order. But the Legalist School, introduced
to French jurists by the work of Léon Vandermeersch, is another.[80]
In many respects, the Legalists of the *Fa-kia* School can be seen as
precursors of Western utilitarianism. Two thousand years before the
English political philosophers, the Legalists saw man as an egotistical
being driven by self-interest alone. They had no notion of civil law
and were also the first to develop a technocratic conception of law –
with efficiency as the measure of legitimacy – and to use law purely
as an instrument for exercising power. But unlike utilitarian philosophy, they had the pessimism of intelligence and considered man's egoism and greed as a threat and not as a benefit from which the common
good would spring spontaneously. They would not have dreamed of
making the calculation of individual utility into the supreme universal norm. On the contrary, they viewed egoism as an energy, which
the law should take into account, but in order to channel it so that
it would serve the general interest. In this respect, they were jurists
in the fullest sense, and the lessons we can draw from them can still
today assist us in civilizing globalization.

## Notes

1    Originally published in French as Alain Supiot, 'L'inscription ter-
     ritorial des lois', *Esprit* 11 (2008), pp. 151–70. *Translator's note*:
     An earlier English translation was originally published in Gralf-
     Pieter Calliess, Andreas Fischer-Lescano, Dan Wielsch and Peer
     Zumbansen (eds), *Soziologische Jurisprudenz: Festschrift für*

*Gunther Teubner zum 65. Geburtstag* (Berlin: De Gruyter, 2009). What is printed in these pages has been modified, but still owes a great deal to Saskia Brown's earlier translation, for which we give sincere thanks here.

2    Institut d'études avancées de Nantes. I would like to thank the Société des amis de Qufu, which gave me the opportunity to discuss the first version of this text at the colloquium 'Space and Civilization', organized at Qufu in the Confucius Research Institute, 31 May–2 June 2008.

3    See especially Gunther Teubner (ed.), *Global Law Without a State* (Brookfield: Dartmouth, 1997).

4    On this adage, which comes from the commentators on the *Digest* (35, 2, 80), see Henri Roland and Laurent Boyer, *Adages du droit français*, 3rd edition (Paris: Litec, 1992), no. 137, p. 278.

5    Charlton T. Lewis, Charles Short and William Freund, *A Latin Dictionary* (Oxford: Clarendon Press, 1958), 'Habeo', pp. 833–35.

6    Blaise Pascal, *Pensées*, ed. and trans. Roger Ariew (Indianapolis and Cambridge: Hackett, 2004), p. 19.

7    Montesquieu, *The Spirit of the Laws*, ed. and trans. Anne M. Cohler, Basia C. Miller and Harold S. Stone (Cambridge: Cambridge University Press, 1989), p. 9.

8    Carl Schmitt, *The Nomos of the Earth in the International Law of the Jus Publicum Europaeum*, trans. G. L. Ulmen (New York: Telos Press, 2003).

9    Adolf Hitler, *Libres propos sur la guerre et sur la paix, recueillis sur l'ordre de Martin Bormann* (Paris: Flammarion, 1952), p. 69. *Translator's note*: For some reason, these lines are not included in the English translation of this book: cf., H. R. Trevor-Roper (ed.), *Hitler's Table Talk, 1941–1944: His Private Conversations*, trans. Norman Cameron and R. H. Stevens (New York: Enigma Books, 2008), p. 55.

10   See Pierre Legendre, *Dominium Mundi. L'Empire du management* (Paris: Mille et une nuits, 2007), p. 21.

11   V. I. Lenin, 'Declaration of Rights of the Working and Exploited People', trans. Yuri Sdobnikov and George Hanna (written 3 January 1918; first published 4 January 1929 in *Pravda* and *Izvestia*), available at: <https://www.marxists.org/archive/lenin/works/1918/jan/03.htm>.

12   Hitler, in Trevor-Roper (ed.), *Hitler's Table Talk, 1941–1944*, p. 51: 'War has returned to its primitive form. The war of people against people is giving place to another war – a war for the possession

of the great spaces. Originally war was nothing but a struggle for pasture-grounds. To-day war is nothing but a struggle for the riches of nature. By virtue of an inherent law, these riches belong to him who conquers them. [...]. That's in accordance with the laws of nature. [...]. The law of selection justifies this incessant struggle, by allowing the survival of the fittest. Christianity is a rebellion against natural law, a protest against nature. Taken to its logical extreme, Christianity would mean the systematic cultivation of the human failure.'

13   It was Trotsky who first used this expression to designate opponents of the Bolshevik party within the Congress of Soviets.

14   Lewis, Short and Freund, 'Homo' and 'Humus', *A Latin Dictionary*, pp. 859–60 and 870–71.

15   In Mesopotamian mythology, the creation of man (out of earth mixed with the blood of a sacrificed god) is attributed to the fact that the lesser gods, weary of working, came out on strike. See Jean Bottero and Samuel Noah Kramer, *Lorsque les dieux faisaient l'homme. Mythologie mésopotamienne* (Paris: Gallimard, 1989), p. 526. Cultivating the land was the first way in which it was made fruitful by human labour. Cultivating the land implied that one possessed it, and the Enlightenment philosophers were unanimous in considering cultivation to be the first title deed. See John Locke, 'The Second Treatise of Government', ch. 5, 'Of Property', *Two Treatises of Government* (Cambridge: Cambridge University Press, 1988).

16   According to Carl Schmitt, the taking of land (*Landnahme*) is the same as the *Nomos* of the land, that is, the 'primeval act in founding law' (Schmitt, *The Nomos of the Earth*, p. 45).

17   Christianity is the religion both of a divine Father without a woman and of a man-god on Earth.

18   This dimension was of great importance in European Antiquity. See Johann Jakob Bachofen, *An English Translation of Bachofen's Mutterrecht (Mother Right). A Study of the Religious and Juridical Aspects of Gynecocracy in the Ancient World*, trans. David Partenheimer, 5 vols (Lewiston: Edwin Mellen, 2003–2007): 'As the Ocean faces the Land, so man faces woman.'

19   See Odile Journet-Diallo, *Les créances de la terre. Chronique du pays Jamaat* (Brepols: Publications de l'École Pratique des Hautes Études, 2007).

20   See the case of Kasena country in Burkina Faso, in Danouta Liberski-Bagnoud, *Les Dieux du territoire. Penser autrement la généalogie* (Paris: CNRS Éditions/Éditions de la Maison des Sciences de l'Homme, 2002).

21    Ibid., p. 100.

22    Ibid., p. 206.

23    According to the Court of Justice of the European Communities
      (henceforth CJEC), the bond of nationality is founded on 'a par-
      ticular relation of solidarity with respect to the State and recipro-
      cal rights and obligations' (CJEC 3 June 1986, Case C-307/84,
      Commission of the European Communities v French Republic,
      European Court Reports 1986, 1725; CJEC 16 June 1987, Case
      C-225/85 Commission v Italy, European Court Reports 1987, 2625;
      CJEC 30 May 1989, Case C-33/88 Allué and Coonassu v Universita
      degli studi di Venezia).

24    Numerous institutions in the history of law oblige peasants to stay
      on the land they cultivate (see, for example, the Roman colonus sys-
      tem or later serfdom, in: Paul Frédéric Girard, *Manuel élémentaire
      de droit romain*, 5th edition (Paris, Rousseau, 1911), p. 132); also
      Charles Revillout, Étude sur l'histoire du colonat chez les romains
      (Paris: A. Durand, 1856); Fustel de Coulanges, *Recherches sur
      quelques problèmes d'histoire*, vol. 1 (Brussels: Culture et civilisa-
      tion, 1964), pp. 3–186. This obligation to remain on a particular ter-
      ritory has not disappeared (see, for example, the residence require-
      ments accompanying certain jobs) but it tends today to involve a
      prohibition on entering or remaining on other territories rather than a
      prohibition on leaving one's own.

25    See Ernst H. Kantorowicz, '*Pro Matria Mori* in Medieval Political
      Thought', *American Historical Review* 56 (1951), pp. 472–92.

26    The number of soldiers killed during the First World War is estimat-
      ed at 7.8 million. In the Second World War, the number of civilian ca-
      sualties of both sexes rose dramatically. Half of all the human losses
      on the European continent were sustained by the USSR alone, with
      21 million dead (11% of its population), of which 13.6 million were
      soldiers and more than 7 million were civilians. See Alan Bullock,
      *Hitler and Stalin: Parallel Lives* (London: HarperCollins, 1991).

27    See Louis Stouff, *Étude sur le principle de la personnalité des
      lois depuis les invasions barbares jusqu'au XIIe siècle* (Paris:
      Larose, 1894).

28    This principle is only apparently straightforward, since it has re-
      ceived different interpretations in international law. See Pierre
      Mayer and Vincent Heuzé, *Droit international privé*, 9th edition
      (Paris: Montchrestien, 2007), no. 49; Dominique Bureau and Horatia
      Muir Watt, *Droit international privé* (Paris: Presses Universitaires
      de France, 2007), vol. 1, no. 329.

29 See Article 3 of the French Civil Code: 'Statutes relating to public policy and safety are binding on all those living on the territory. Immovables are governed by French law even when owned by aliens. Statutes relating to the status and capacity of persons govern French persons, even those residing in foreign countries.'

30 C. M. Hann applies a concept developed by Karl Polanyi to property, and talks of the 'embeddedness of property'; see C. M. Hann (ed.), 'Introduction', *Property relations: Renewing the Anthropological Tradition* (Cambridge, Cambridge University Press, 1998), esp. p. 9ff.

31 Adhémar Esmein, *Cours élémentaire de droit français* (Paris: Larose, 1898), pp. 185ff.); Jean-François Lemarignier, *La France médiévale. Institutions et sociétés* (Paris: A. Colin, 1970), p. 161.

32 See Marc Bloch, *Feudal Society*, 2 vols, trans. L. A. Manyon (London and New York: Routledge, 2004–2005).

33 See Marth Mundy and Richard Saumarez Smith, *Governing Property, Making the Modern State: Law, Administration and Production in Ottoman Syria* (London and New York: IB Tauris, 2007), p. 11).

34 Jacques Berque, 'Documents anciens sur la coutume immobilière des Seksawa', *Revue africaine* 93 (1948), pp. 363–402.

35 Augustin Berque, *Écoumène. Introduction à l'étude des milieu humains* (Paris: Belin, 2000), p. 69.

36 See Louis Dumont, *From Mandeville to Marx: The Genesis and Triumph of Economic Ideology* (Chicago and London: University of Chicago Press, 1977).

37 This leads to the issue of the legal regime applicable to the public face of private property. The question arose, for example, of whether the owner of a building had rights over the image of its façade (the French courts ruled that the owner did, but this was subsequently annulled by the Court of Cassation, 7 May 2004). See Yves Strickler, *Les biens* (Paris: Presses Universitaires de France, 2006), no. 12; pp. 36ff.

38 See the *Declaration of the Rights of Man and of the Citizen* (1789), article 17: 'Since property is an inviolable and sacred right, no one shall be deprived thereof except where public necessity, legally determined, shall clearly demand it, and then only on condition that the owner shall have been previously and equitably indemnified.'

39 See the French Civil Code, art. 544: 'Ownership is the right to enjoy and dispose of things in the most absolute manner, provided they are not used in a way prohibited by statutes or regulations.'

40  As Macfarlane notes: 'The dissolution of the state is not a good ba-
    sis for modern private property, which is ultimately underpinned,
    as Locke and his successors recognized, by powerful, if largely in-
    visible, state power.' Alan Macfarlane, 'The Mystery of Property:
    Inheritance and Industrialization in England and Japan', in Hann
    (ed.), *Property Relations*, p. 115.

41  A debt or a debt-claim is termed 'liquid' when it can be converted
    into a determinate quantity of money. Liquidating an asset means
    making it fungible, converting it into monetary rights. In every-
    day language, French 'liquide' refers both to ready money (cash)
    and to an aqueous medium; see Gérard Cornu (ed.), *Vocabulaire ju-
    ridique* (Paris: Presses Universitaires de France, 1987), entries on
    'Liquidation' and 'Liquide'; in English, the terms 'liquidities' and
    'liquid' communicate in a similar way.

42  In the French colonies, for example, indigenous status (French *in-
    digénat*) combined the original personal status with a restricted
    French nationality. Citizenship was reserved for those who were
    'native French' and, in Algeria, was extended to indigenous Jews
    by the Crémieux Decree in 1870, and later to non-Muslim (that is,
    European) foreigners in 1889. Similar solutions were adopted in the
    English colonies (see, on India, Ved P. Nanda and Surya Prakash
    Sinha (eds), *Hindu Law and Legal Theory* (Aldershot: Dartmouth,
    1996), p. xiv ff.). Far from contributing to reducing the diversity of
    personal statuses, colonization helped anchor them in the legal cul-
    ture of the country: after Algerian independence, being a Muslim
    became a condition for attribution of Algerian nationality.

43  See the useful summary by André Pichot in *La société pure. De
    Darwin à Hitler* (Paris: Flammarion, 2000), and Pichot, *Aux origi-
    nes des théories raciales. De la Bible à Darwin* (Paris: Flammarion,
    2008). On Vichy legislation, see Dominique Gros, 'Le Droit anti-
    sémite de Vichy contre la tradition républicaine', *Le Genre humain*
    28 (1994), pp. 17–27.

44  For an overview and a substantial bibliography, see Horatia Muir
    Watt, 'Aspects économiques du droit international privé', in
    *Collected Courses of the Hague Academy of International Law* 307
    (2004), and Muir Watt, 'Concurrence d'ordres juridiques et conflits
    de lois de droit privé', Bertrand Ancel (ed.), *Le droit international
    privé: esprit et méthode. Mélanges en l'honneur de Paul Lagarde*
    (Paris: Dalloz, 2005).

45  CJEC, 9 March 1999, *Centros*, Case C-212/97, *European Court
    Reports* 1999, I, 1459 concl. La Pergola. For a similar conclusion, see
    CJEC, 11 Dec. 2007, *Viking*, Case C-438–05 (which deduced from
    the freedom of establishment the right to use flags of convenience).

46 See <www.doingbusiness.org>, and particularly a map of the world represented as a space of competition between legislations ('Business planet mapping the business environment').

47 On the ideological origins and logical insufficiencies of this normative Darwinism, see Alain Supiot, 'Le droit du travail bradé sur le marché des normes', *Droit Social* 12 (2005), pp. 1087–1096.

48 On this form of exercise of imperial power, see Robert Mantran, 'L'Empire ottoman', in Hélène Ahrweiler and Maurice Duverger (eds), *Le concept d'empire* (Paris: Presses Universitaires de France, 1980).

49 See Patrick Wintour and Riazat Butt, 'Sharia Law Could Have UK Role, Says Lord Chief Justice', *Guardian* (4 July 2008), available at: <https://www.theguardian.com/uk/2008/jul/04/law.islam>.

50 For the United States, see Michael J. Piore, *Beyond Individualism* (Cambridge, Massachusetts: Harvard University Press, 1995); for Canada (and using the same notion of 'minority' to refer to the Inuits, homosexuals and women), see Andrée Lajoie, *Quand les minorités font la loi* (Paris: Presses Universitaires de France, 2002).

51 For this shift towards laying claim to a self-determined personal status in the name of the right to privacy, see Muir Watt, *Droit international privé*, p. 43ff.; Daniel Gutmann, *Le sentiment d'identité. Étude de droit des personnes et de la famille* (Paris, LGDJ, 2000), p. 340ff.; Jean-Louis Renchon, 'Indisponibilité, ordre public et autonomie de la volonté dans le droit des personnes et de la famille', in Alain Wijffels (ed.), *Le code civil entre ius commune et droit privé européen* (Brussels: Bruylant, 2005).

52 Christopher Lasch, *The Culture of Narcissism: American Life in an Age of Diminishing Expectations* (New York and London: Norton, 1979).

53 See Y. Habib, 'Halal, haram, sport panarabe', *Le Temps* (Algeria, 19 September 2008).

54 Pierre Legendre, *Les enfants du texte. Étude sur la fonction parentale des États* (Paris: Fayard, 1992), p. 352.

55 Locke, 'The Second Treatise of Government', §§ 27 and 32.

56 Berque, *Écoumène*, p. 14: 'The oecumene is the totality and the condition of human environments in their properly human, but no less ecological and physical, dimension.'

57 *The Nazi Primer*, quoted in Hannah Arendt, *The Origins of Totalitarianism*, 2nd edition (Cleveland and New York: Meridian, 1958), p. 350.

58   See André Pichot, *Histoire de la notion de gene* (Paris: Flammarion, 1999); also Pierre Legendre, 'L'attaque nazie contre le principle de filiation', in Alexandra Papageorgiou Legendre and Pierre Legendre (eds), *Filiation: fondement gnénéalogique de la psychanalyse* (Paris: Fayard, 1990).

59   See Catherine Labrusse-Riou, *Écrits de bioéthique* (Paris: Presses Universitaires de France, 2007), esp. pp. 49 and 327.

60   See Rainer Frank, 'La signification différente attaché à la filiation par le sang en droit allement et en droit français de la famille', *Revue internationale de droit compare* 45 (1993), pp. 635–55, available at: <https://www.persee.fr/doc/ridc_0035-3337_1993_num_45_3_4730>.

61   See articles 16–10 of the French Civil Code, which set stringent conditions on the examination of the genetic particulars of a person.

62   French Constitutional Council, Decision no. 2007–557 DC, 15 November 15 2007 ('Act relating to the control of immigration, integration and asylum').

63   Their belief goes under the banner of scientific truth, as illustrated for example by Nicolas Sarkozy's declarations when he was Minister of the Interior on the existence of genes for paedophilia and suicide (Sarkozy interview with Michel Onfray, *Philosophie Magazine* 8 [2007]). Likewise his programme for early detection of children genetically predisposed to delinquency. This programme set out to give legislative expression to the results of a report by the National Institute for Health and Medical Research (INSERM), which maintained that 50% of 'Oppositional Defiant Disorders' were genetically determined and which also recommended screening for these disorders as early as the creche or nursery school; INSERM, *Troubles des conduites chez l'enfant et l'adolescent* (September 2005), available at: <http://ist.inserm.fr/basisrapports/trouble-conduites.html>.

64   See Gary S. Becker, *The Economic Approach to Human Behavior* (Chicago and London: University of Chicago Press, 1976), esp. the final chapter, 'Altruism, Egoism, and Genetic Fitness: Economics and Sociobiology'. The most recent trend is called neuroeconomics and refers to neurology rather than genetics to explain economic behaviour. See Paul W. Glimcher, *Decisions, Uncertainty, and the Brain: The Science of Neuroeconomics* (Cambridge, Massachusetts and London: MIT Press, 2003); also Colin Farrell Camerer, George Loewenstein and Drazen Prelec 'Neuroeconomics: How Neuroscience Can Inform Economics', *Journal of Economic Literature*, 43 (2005), pp. 9–64; and Jean-Pierre Changeux and Christian Schmidt 'La refondation de l'analyse du risque à la lumière des neurosciences', *Risques* 71 (2007).

65   According to an agreement signed between the United States and
     some thirty (mostly Western) countries, holders of biometric pass-
     ports do not have to obtain a visa to enter the USA. A PARAFES
     file of biometric data on air passengers has recently been created
     in France (PARAFES: 'Automated fast track crossing at Schengen
     external borders' (Passage Automatisé Rapide Aux Frontières
     Extérieures Schengen), in order to 'improve border police controls
     of air passengers and enable [Schengen area] external borders to
     be crossed more rapidly' (Decree no. 2007–1182 of 3 August 2007,
     Journal Officiel of 7 August 2007, p. 13203).

66   Gilles Deleuze and Félix Guattari, *A Thousand Plateaus: Capitalism
     and Schizophrenia*, trans. Brian Massumi (Minneapolis and
     London: University of Minnesota Press, 1987), ch. 12, 'Treatise
     on Nomadology – The War Machine', cited by Altan Gokalp,
     'Palimpseste ottoman', in Alain Supiot (ed.), *Tisser le lien social*
     (Paris: Éditions de la Maison des Sciences de l'Homme, 2004).

67   The exact phrase (which can be found in Article 15 of the
     Constitution of the People's Republic of China) is *shehuizhuyi
     shichang jingji*, which translates literally as 'socialist market econo-
     my'. In order to avoid confusion with the sense which 'socialist' has
     acquired in French politics (the idea of a mixed economy, which the
     Socialist Party espoused for a time), I have preferred the translation
     'communist market economy'.

68   Alain Supiot, 'L'Europe gagnée par « l'économie communiste de
     marché »', *Journal du Mauss* (30 January 2008), available at: <http://
     www.journaldumauss.net/?L-Europe-gagnee-par-l-economie>.

69   Article 56E of the EU Treaty prohibits 'all restrictions on the move-
     ment of capital [or on payments] between Member States and be-
     tween Member States and third countries'.

70   For example, the removal of customs duties on imports into the
     European market of American oilseeds and related animal-feed
     proteins in 1962 led to intensive soil-less culture in Brittany which
     caused massive pollution to the region's entire hydrographic system.
     See Louis Lorvellec, 'GATT, agriculture et environnement', *Écrits
     de droit rural et agroalimentaire* (Paris: Dalloz, 2002).

71   See the famous cases of tuna or shrimp fished with nets which de-
     stroy dolphins and sea turtles; or the condemnation of Europe's
     refusal to import American hormone-treated beef. On the rul-
     ings, see Robert Howse and Donald Regan, 'The Product/Process
     Distinction – An Illusory Basis for Disciplining "Unilateralism"
     in Trade Policy', *European Journal of International Law* 11 (2000),
     pp. 249–289.

72   CJEC, 13 July 2000, *Alfredo Albore*, Case C-423/98, European Court Reports 2000, page I-05965.

73   Preamble and art. 2, 29, 40 and 61 of the Consolidated Treaty (Official Journal of the European Union, 29. 12. 2006). Absent from the Treaty of Rome signed in 1957, the notion of *'espace'* (or area) was introduced into the 1986 Single European Act.

74   In China, 'Decision 171' of 11 July 2006 limited the access of foreigners to the property market and reserved real estate investment to legal persons under Chinese law. Poland has a scheme whereby non-Community nationals require authorization to acquire land, and in Turkey foreigners may not purchase areas of more than 6.2 acres (2.5 hectares).

75   See Luigi Doria, 'La qualità totale del territorio: verso una fenomenologia critica', *Archivio di studi urbani e regionali* 80 (2004), pp. 11–56; and Doria, 'Managing the Unmanageable Resource: Multiple Utility and Quality in the EU Policy Discourses on Local Identity', in Doria, Valeria Fedeli and Carla Tedesco (eds), *Rethinking European Spatial Policy as a Hologram* (Aldershot: Asgate, 2006).

76   See Doria's analysis (in 'Managing the Unmanageable Resource') of the European Commission's LEADER programme. It received 2 billion euros for 2005/2006, with a remit to 'help rural actors consider the long-term potential of their local region': <http://ec.europa.eu/agriculture/rur/leaderplus/index_fr.htm>.

77   See Robert Salais, 'On the Correct (and Incorrect) Use of Indicators in Public Action', *Comparative Labor Law & Policy* 27 (2006), pp. 237–256.

78   Karl Polanyi, *The Great Transformation: The Political and Economic Origins of Our Time* (London: Victor Gollancz, 1945), ch. 6.

79   See the debates in Quebec on 'reasonable accommodation', which gave rise to the establishment of a Consultation Commission on Accommodation Practices Related to Cultural Differences: <www.accommodements.qc.ca>.

80   Léon Vandermeersch, *La formation du légisme: recherche sur la constitution d'une philosophie politique caractéristique de la Chine ancienne* (Paris: École française d'Extrême-Orient, 1987).

# Appendix: Mission of the Association of Friends of the Thunberg Generation

Greta Thunberg calls on adults to take their responsibility. In so doing, she poses the problem of a kind of generalization of irresponsibility that seems to have taken hold in various ways in much of the world, if not all of it.

The causes of this state of affairs are numerous, and have been interpreted in various ways. There is no doubt, however, that intergenerational relations, which themselves seem to be fundamentally challenged by the most recent developments in industrial societies, play an essential role in this great civilizational malaise.

This situation poses enormous problems for parents and, more generally, educators, while the younger generations find themselves seriously harmed, all the more so given that their future is in far greater question than was their parents' generation – a situation that oftentimes leads to a feeling of abandonment that can prove devastating, even fatal.

We have heard Greta Thunberg's various appeals, and the appeals she has inspired in her generation around the world, particularly through Youth for Climate, and we wish to respond to Greta Thunberg and to the movements she has inspired. We have therefore taken the initiative to create the Association of the Friends of the Thunberg generation, to contribute to the establishment of a dialogue between the generations, building first and foremost on the work of scientific authorities.

It is not a question of organizing public meetings and media events, but of creating, wherever possible and expected, working groups to deal with well-defined questions, documented in advance, and with a view to producing, on the basis of this work, memoranda to be published when the participants in these working groups consider them to be worthwhile.

In the face of the factual weakening of responsibility, Greta Thunberg and Youth for Climate call above all for rationality. Nothing is more precious, and we must encourage them.

### Founding Members

Yves Citton, professor of literature, Université Paris VIII

Victor Chaix, student, independent journalist and member of Extinction Rebellion (UK)

Michel Deguy, writer, philosopher

Hidetaka Ishida, professor of philosophy, University of Tokyo

Jean-Marie Le Clézio, writer, Nanjing University

Susanna Lindberg, philosopher, University of Helsinki

Giuseppe Longo, mathematician, École Normale Supérieure, Paris

Virgile Mouquet, geography student, Université de Bordeaux Michel de Montaigne and member of Youth for Climate, Bordeaux

Hans Ulrich Obrist, curator and director, Serpentine Galleries

Stéphane Paoli, journalist

Saskia Sassen, sociologist and urbanist, Columbia University and London School of Economics

Richard Sennett, sociologist, New York University and London School of Economics

Carlos Sonnenschein, doctor, biologist, Institut d'Études Avancées de Nantes and Tufts University

Ana Soto, biologist, Tufts University and École Normale Supérieure

Bernard Stiegler, philosopher, Institut de Recherche et d'Innovation, Paris, and Nanjing University

Yann Toma, artist, Université Paris I

Marie Chollat-namy, doctoral student in oncology, Université Paris-Saclay, member of Extinction Rebellion, Paris Centre

Esther Martin, high school senior, Lycée Richelieu Rueil-Malmaison and member of Youth for Climate, Paris-IDF

# Lexicon of the Internation: Introduction to the Concepts of Bernard Stiegler and the Internation Collective

*Anne Alombert, Michał Krzykawski*

> We do not lack communication. On the contrary, we have too much of it. We lack creation. [...] The creation of concepts in itself calls for a future form, for a new earth and people that do not yet exist [...]. Becoming stranger to oneself, to one's language and nation, is not this the peculiarity of the philosopher and philosophy, their 'style', or what is called a philosophical gobbledygook?
> *Gilles Deleuze and Félix Guattari[1]*

## Anthropocene/Entropocene

The term Anthropocene was introduced by the Nobel Prize-winning chemist Paul Crutzen. It describes the geological era that commenced when human activities began to have a significant global impact on the Earth's ecosystem and the future of planet Earth, to the point of bringing into question the continued possibility of human life on Earth. This new era began at the end of the eighteenth century with the industrial revolution. One debate that has arisen about the term Anthropocene, however, concerns the proposal for an alternative concept, Capitalocene, put forward in order to emphasize the role of the capitalist economic system in ecological disaster. According to the philosopher Bernard Stiegler and the Internation Collective, however, the Anthropocene must also, and in a more general way, be characterized as an Entropocene, insofar as this period corresponds to a massive increase in rates of entropy, which must be conceived and theorized at all possible levels: physical (dissipation of energy), biological (destruction of biodiversity), informational (reduction of knowledge to information) and psycho-social (destruction of cultural and social diversity).

### Supplement: from the Anthropocene to the Neganthropocene

Most researchers in Earth system science refer to the Anthropocene epoch and tie its advent to the start of 'the Great Acceleration', a period referring to the 1950s, when the human impact on the structure of the Earth and its ecosystems became undeniable, due in particular to the development and intensified integration of science and technology, the phenomenon of globalization and the fact that atmospheric nuclear detonation left traces that are detectable across the terrestrial surface. The upheavals of the biosphere resulting from these transformations have given rise to the argument that a new name is required to describe an epoch that succeeds the geological epoch known as the Holocene (itself referring to a 'wholly new' phase of the geological timescale corresponding to the rising human impact that began with the Neolithic revolution), because the impact of the human species on geology and ecology has now become, not just significant, but decisive for the future of the biosphere.

Stiegler refers to the Anthropocene *era*: in so doing he does not mean to question the achievements of Earth system science, but rather to emphasize that our present time is an 'epoch of the absence of epoch', reflecting that it corresponds to 'the possibility of the end of everything (of everything that makes human life possible)',[2] but *also* to the seeming impossibility for our contemporary existence to cohere into a sense of dwelling within a shared 'world': for Stiegler, one can refer to an epoch only if individuals and groups develop knowledge (the knowledge of how to do, how to live and how to theorize) that enables them to adopt the transformations of their technical or exosomatic milieus. Stiegler argues that the 'non-epoch' characteristic of the Anthropocene era results from an immeasurable acceleration in the evolution of exosomatic organs. Becoming more and more complex, these organs are transformed so quickly that the knowledge required for their fruitful adoption does not have time to develop. Therefore, what is truly new in the Anthropocene era (the suffix *-cene* means new[3]) stems from a new relationship with non-living organs that did not exist during the Holocene, and from the explosion of technical evolution that occurred with the industrial revolution and intensified once again in the second half of the twentieth century.

The term Neganthropocene was introduced by Stiegler to designate a new era that could and must succeed the Anthropocene: in the face of the massive increase in entropy rates (at the physical, biological, informational and psycho-social levels) characteristic of the Anthropocene, to open a path to the Neganthropocene involves implementing one or more economic models, based on the systemic valorization of anti-entropic production. This is the ambition of the contributory economy, which aims to be anti-entropic by fostering contributory or capacitating activities, corresponding to the practice and production of a diversity of knowledge (technical knowledge, practical knowledge, existential knowledge, as well as the knowledge of how to do, how to live and how to conceive), serving to readjust the 'disadjustment' between the technical system and social systems characteristic of the Anthropocene.

## Anthropy/Neganthropy/Anti-Anthropy

*See also: Entropy/Negentropy/Anti-Entropy*

In geography or ecology, the term anthropization refers to the transformation of landscapes, ecosystems or environments under the effect of human activities. Anthropogenic forcing refers to the disturbance of certain dynamic systems due to human activities (for example, the disturbance of climate systems by greenhouse gas emissions or that of ecosystems by deforestation). Anthropy, an almost homophonous variation on entropy, can thus be understood as referring to the production of entropy (disturbance, disorganization, dissipation of energy, depletion of resources) by human societies, that is to say, through the techno-economic processes of production and consumption.

The concepts of anthropy, neganthropy and anti-anthropy are used by Bernard Stiegler to designate the production of entropy, negentropy and anti-entropy at the level of exosomatic life, which is to say of the technical, psychological and social life that is commonly known as 'human' life. Stiegler argues that it is now necessary to rethink this 'human' life in strict relation to the 'passage from the organic to the organological', organology being Stiegler's term for a form of life that involves the inextricable entanglement of three levels – the individual, the collective and the technical, understood as the three 'transductive' processes of individuation characteristic of exosomatic life. With artificial selection replacing natural selection, this passage to the organological, constituting the very history of the exosomatization process, 'displaces the play of entropy and negentropy'.[4] It is thus a question of underlining the ambivalence of this process that comes to organize life 'by means other than life'.[5]

*Supplement: anthropy, neganthropy and anti-anthropy in exosomatic life*

According to Bernard Stiegler, unlike the endosomatic or biological organs of living beings, which are always local and temporary producers of negentropy (organization and diversification), exosomatic or technical organs are ambivalent. On the one hand, they can accelerate the production of entropy (through the process of combustion and energy dissipation that technological production involves, and through industrial standardization that homogenizes and standardizes behaviour). On the other hand, exosomatic organs can produce new, improbable and singular (social, artistic, cultural and technical) forms of organization and diversification, provided that these are successfully adopted by humans, through collectives that share and practise knowledge.

The production of knowledge thus corresponds to the production of neganthropy (organization and diversification on the psychic, technical and social levels). In other words, if a living organism is able to organize itself to produce anti-entropy through its biological organization, by temporarily and locally delaying entropy, human beings can and must organize themselves on the neganthropic and anti-anthropic level, by practising knowledge and constituting social organizations, in order to postpone the anthropogenic effects inevitably entailed by the production of exosomatic organs, which have now become industrial and digital.

Neganthropic organizations, however, tend to themselves become anthropic: knowledge tends to rigidify (in the form of dogmas) and social institutions tend to close. Anti-anthropy refers to the ability to refresh knowledge and institutions by transforming them diachronically, that is, by causing them to evolve or bifurcate towards new horizons.

## Capacities/Skills

The development of capacities or capabilities is distinct from the acquisition of competences or skills.

Skills precede the individual who is supposed to acquire them and correspond to predetermined behavioural standards to which the individual is required to conform. An individual who has acquired skills applies pre-established rules and repeats learned behaviours, but does not produce anything new. Two individuals may individually acquire identical skills, in which case they become interchangeable on the labour market. Employment is based on the use of previously acquired skills, and skills are acquired for the sake of employability.

Capacities, on the contrary, correspond to each individual's singular possibilities of existence. These possibilities can be exercised and actualized only when individuals individuate themselves collectively and when they practise and share knowledge with other individuals, and thus 'capabilize' themselves: capacities are expressions of the singularity of individuals. It is true that, in order to be developed, capacities require the acquisition of skills or automatisms, yet what they require above all is the ability to dis-automatize acquired automatisms, through which improbable and singular practices may be invented, by making internalized rules bifurcate.

In this sense, the process of capacitation can be understood as the development of what the economist Amartya Sen and the philosopher Martha Nussbaum define as 'capabilities', which increase the power of individuals to act as they individuate themselves within the group and which are the core of 'human development'.

## Contributory Economy

The thesis proposed by the contributory economy model consists in arguing that the productivity increases made possible by automation could free individuals from a certain number of proletarianizing jobs, and thus open new fields of capacitating and contributory activities based on the practice of knowledge. The goal of such an economy is to take advantage of the gains in time enabled by automation in the productive sphere, in order to develop processes of capacitation and contribution that make possible the production and sharing of the new knowledge necessary to face ongoing technological evolution (and its psychic, social, political and ecological impacts). Such an economic model is based on redistributing the time saved by automation to citizens, who may thus spend less time in employment but acquire the means to develop work activities that are both sustainable for the biosphere and desirable for populations, and producing anti-entropy and anti-anthropy in this sense. The contributory economy is therefore based on a systemic valuation of anti-entropic and anti-anthropic activities: for this reason, it implies the implementation of new indicators of value.

*Supplement: practical value, exchange value and use value*

Whereas the market economy is concerned with the producer in terms of maximizing profit and the consumer in terms of the utility function, the contributory economy is characterized by the fact that economic actors are no longer separated into producers and consumers: 'contributors' are neither producers nor consumers, because they share and produce different kinds of knowledge.

For an activity to be 'contributory' requires:

- the choice by individuals to participate in an empowering activity involving the practice of knowledge;

- the socialization of the knowledge thus practised, through the sharing or transmission of this knowledge with society.

The value produced by contributors is not fully monetizable: it cannot be reduced to exchange or use value because it does not increase with scarcity and does not wear out over time. Indeed, the value of knowledge increases as it is shared and practised, and for that reason it tends to gain in richness. Knowledge is built gradually and over the long term: the individuals who exchange it mutually enrich each other, by transforming and diversifying their ways of living and by improving the quality of their environment and their daily lives – in short, by expanding their possibilities of existence. In this sense, they are producers of practical or societal value. A contributory economy does not, however, necessarily exclude other ways of producing and exchanging, but goes hand in hand with them: for the short and medium term at least, it accepts the rules of the game of monetary exchange and is concerned with investment choices (particularly those that lead to the production of public goods).

### Contributory Income and Intermittent Contributory Employment
*See also: Contributory Economy*

The role of the contributory economy model is to equitably distribute among citizens the time made available by the automation of production, and to put this time at the service of the capacitation of inhabitants and their contribution to the anti-anthropic development of the region. Fundamental to the notion of a contributory economy is the idea of intermittent contributory employment, that is, intermittent employment in projects designated as contributory. This involves two dimensions:

- setting up a contributory income scheme designed to remunerate the capacitation time of individuals (during which they collectively share, practise and produce knowledge);

- individuals can, however, receive such income only if the knowledge and capabilities developed in this way are intermittently used in the context of casual employment in projects designated as contributory for the region.

The functioning of the proposed contributory income scheme is inspired by the longstanding scheme set up in France for casual workers in entertainment and the performing arts [*intermittents du spectacle*]: the financing of preparatory capacitation activities is conditional upon the return of the fruits of this work to society in the form of employment in designated projects.

Contributory income is distinct from universal basic income (UBI), although it can be complementary to it: it may indeed be possible to understand contributory income as a right, but it is nevertheless conditional upon participation in the contributory economy as it is inscribed in the region. Because it requires acquired knowledge and capabilities to be utilized in the service of projects designated as contributory or anti-anthropic by and for the region, it assumes the development of institutions authorized to designate such projects, institutions that will themselves involve collective deliberation and decision-making about the anti-anthropic, contributory or societal value of an activity.

## Disruption

Disruption refers to the upheaval of social organizations and institutions (from the family to government via businesses, languages, law, economic regulation, taxation, etc.) through the highly rapid development of new technologies. Disruption results from the fact that the evolution of the technical system is occurring far quicker than the evolution of social organizations. This is not a new phenomenon. Bertrand Gille described it as disadjustment between the evolution of the technical system and the evolution of social systems, arguing that disadjustment is typical of the industrial revolution.[6] Gilbert Simondon defines this phenomenon as a phase shift between technical reality and cultural content.[7] Lastly, Jacques Derrida refers to the dislocating effects resulting from technological acceleration.[8] Today, however, these technical transformations occur so quickly that they leave the political and social realms behind, as well as public power in general, so that no new viable model of long-term social and economic development can emerge. Under the regime of radical and permanent innovation, regulation, legislation and knowledge always arrive too late: the resulting constant expansion of legal vacuums and theoretical vacuums seems to be without historical precedent.

## Entropy/Negentropy/Anti-Entropy

The production of entropy corresponds to the tendency towards disorganization, destructuration and disorder. Taken in its broadest sense, and not just as it is understood physically in thermodynamics, an entropic process is one that involves the tendency of a system to exhaust its dynamic potentials and its capacity for conservation or renewal. It can also be understood as the tendency for the probable to eliminate the improbable.

Anti-entropy refers to a tendency occurring in the opposite direction than the production of entropy – a tendency towards organization, structuration, diversification and the production of novelty or improbability. Although anti-entropy can never eliminate the inevitable increase of entropy, it can locally delay or defer this increase. As a generalized concept, anti-entropy is intended to describe anything that tends to create difference, choice or novelty – everything in the development of a system that tends to self-conservation, renewal or transformation towards improvement.

### Supplement: entropy and anti-entropy as transversal concepts

The concept of entropy appeared in the nineteenth century in the field of thermodynamic physics and was coined by Rudolf Clausius. Initially arising from the need to engineer more energy-efficient steam engines, this 'second law of thermodynamics' was a way of describing the irreversible dissipation of energy. By recognizing that the entire universe could be understood as a closed system, the concept of entropy led to the nineteenth-century hypothesis of the eventual heat death of the universe. The philosopher Henri Bergson considered the second law of thermodynamics to be 'the most meta-physical of the laws of physics since it points out [...] the direction in which the world is going'.[9]

In the 1950s, the theory of entropy was taken up in the field of information theory (in particular through the works of Claude Shannon[10]) and in cybernetics (in particular through the work of Norbert Wiener[11]). Despite referring to a completely different process than that which is described by the second law of thermodynamics, the name 'entropy' was used to describe the degree of uncertainty contained in a message, because the form of the equation turned out to be identical in both physics and computation. The significance of this has been much debated, but a fundamental reason for this identity lies in the fact that in both fields the equation can be seen to arise from a division of systems into statistically calculable microstates.

Of even greater importance, however, is the physicist Erwin Schrödinger's effort to mobilize the notion of entropy in biology, in order to show that life entails a kind of 'negative entropy' or negent-ropy, that is, a tendency that runs counter to the overall entropic pro-cess.[12] Living organisms are endowed with a metabolic capacity to reduce the increase of thermodynamic entropy by exchanging mat-ter and energy with the environment, thus maintaining their life. It remains the case, however, that the very phenomenon of life is irre-ducibly linked to the production of entropy: the living organism can fight against its own entropy only by continuing to add to the over-all production of entropy in the universe. No living thing escapes the global entropic tendency, but organisms are engaged in a local and temporary struggle against the dissipation of energy and the result-ing disorganization. The process of biological evolution can thus be understood as the differentiation of organs, functions and species that occurs in the course of this negentropic postponement. Hence Norbert Wiener refers to living organisms as 'local and temporary islands of decreasing entropy in a world in which the entropy as a whole tends to increase'.[13]

More recently, and unlike Wiener, who seems to conceive 'anti-entropy' as a possibility common to biological organisms and machines, the philosophers and mathematicians Giuseppe Longo and Francis Bailly[14] have developed a notion of 'anti-entropy' to describe the specific characteristics of the living state of matter, that is, of biologically organized matter: they argue that life, unlike the machine, can arise only as a dynamic and historical process capable of maintaining and differentiating the 'multilevel entangled structure' of living organisms. The high level of correlation of parts and whole involved in biological organization amounts to an 'extended critical situation' where the integration and regulation of the various levels of this organization is the crucial anti-entropic process of life.

### Exorganisms (Simple and Complex/Lower and Higher)
*See also: Exosomatization*

The notion of an exorganism (exosomatic organism) was put forward by Bernard Stiegler, and is further divided between simple and complex types. A *simple exorganism* is an exosomatic organism whose survival depends upon equipping itself with technical or prosthetic organs external to its own body (human beings are simple exorganisms in this sense, because there is no human being anywhere who is not so equipped in one way or another). The notion of exorganism makes it possible to go beyond the analogy between organism and machine, which had been the source of many debates in philosophy and which is at the heart of cybernetic literature. The organism and the machine do not constitute two distinct terms that could be compared to one another: on the contrary, they must be considered as a relational unit, as a whole to which the simple exorganism (traditionally called an 'individual' and conceived as the union of body and soul, but which is here understood as the coupling between a living organism and its technical organs) precisely amounts.

Simple exorganisms, however, cannot survive on their own: they need to exist in groups, which are *complex exorganisms*, that is, a grouping of several simple exorganisms sharing a technical environment and exosomatic organs. These complex exorganisms can be formed at various scales and take various forms: the family, the tribe, the ethnic group, the city, the nation are examples of complex exorganisms, but we could also cite the crew of a boat or the members of a factory, a company or an institution.

Among complex exorganisms, it is necessary to distinguish *lower* complex exorganisms and *higher* complex exorganisms. Some complex exorganisms are said to be 'lower' because they are subject to the rules or laws of other complex exorganisms, which are thus called 'higher': for example, a company (lower complex exorganism) is subject to the laws of the state (higher complex exorganism) in which it is located, and the state is itself in principle subject to international law and to that extent constitutes a lower exorganism compared to an institution such as the UN, for example (although the legal and practical reality is more complicated than this example might suggest).

*Supplement: exorganisms, territoriality, sovereignty and superiority*

According to Stiegler, higher complex organisms are vectors of a 'process of the transindividuation of reference', that is to say, they support a set of meanings or significations shared by all lower complex exorganisms, allowing them to communicate and exchange (for example, a national language or an international law). It is this process of the transindividuation of reference that gives higher exorganisms their authority, their sovereignty and, therefore, their superiority.

Traditionally, a complex exorganism was always territorialized, that is, located in a given territory, although in fact it is also possible for a complex exorganism to be significantly delocalized (for example, a multinational corporation). The current era is nevertheless characterized by the emergence of complex planetary and extraterritorial organizations: indeed, the exospheric platforms that constitute the infrastructures of giant tech companies (GAFAM) are extraterritorial. These planetary complex exorganisms take advantage of their delocalization to bypass the rules of territorial complex exorganisms (notably sovereign nations and states, but also other social organizations), thus dispossessing the latter of their sovereignty, their authority or their superiority. This phenomenon leads to what Antoinette Rouvroy and Thomas Berns describe as 'algorithmic governmentality'[15] and to what Frank Pasquale describes as the 'functional sovereignty'[16] of platforms.

Nevertheless, such planetary exorganisms do not produce any process of the transindividuation of reference: they exploit the natural resources of the territories and the psychic resources of individuals outside of any common law capable of limiting their toxicity. This is why their sovereignty is only 'functional': it is a matter of *de facto* efficiency without legal authority. This process leads complex exorganisms of all kinds to a situation of disorder and instability, which is symptomatically revealed through the coming to power of authoritarian and nationalist governments, which can appear as reactions to the short-circuiting of national legal authorities through the efficiency of extraterritorial platforms.

It thus seems necessary to reconstitute a process of the transindividuation of reference at the planetary level, which can be done only through the constitution of a new international higher complex exorganism (here referred to as the internation). To avoid the pitfalls of globalization and of what jurist Alain Supiot calls the 'total market',[17] such an inter-national higher complex exorganism should nevertheless respect, value and cultivate the singularities of the various localities constituting the biosphere (these singular localities are precisely what computational capitalism today tends to liquidate, through the elimination of local knowledge).

## Exosomatization

Exosomatization refers to the technical externalization of living beings, that is, the production of non-biological organs by biological organisms. Exosomatic organs (usually described as technical or artificial organs) are organs that develop outside of the body or organism ('exo' and 'soma' meaning respectively 'outside' and 'body' in Latin). By contrast, endosomatic organs (usually referred to as biological or natural organs) are organs belonging to the body or organism ('endo' meaning 'within').

Those living beings usually described as 'human' are exosomatic organisms: they can survive only on the condition of producing artificial organs, which not only constitute their environment, but may also have effects on their minds and bodies. Exosomatic organs can become destructive for biological organisms, if they are not practised collectively according to shared rules. The function of social organizations is to produce therapeutic arrangements between endosomatic organs (human psychosomatic organisms) and exosomatic organs (technical objects), by regulating and socializing the use of the latter.

*Supplement: exosomatization in the age of the Anthropocene and transhumanism*

The concept of exosomatization was introduced by the bio-mathematician Alfred Lotka[18] to refer to the production of technical organs by living organisms. We must therefore distinguish two types of organogenesis (organ production): endosomatic organogenesis and exosomatic organogenesis. Paleoanthropologist André Leroi-Gourhan[19] has shown that in the process that led to the human species, the evolution of exosomatic organs took precedence over that of endosomatic organs and therefore continued to accelerate: with the process of exosomatization, the diversification of species thus gives way to the ethnic and technical diversification of societies. The bio-economist Nicholas Georgescu-Roegen[20] concludes that the evolution of human societies is no longer regulated by biological principles (evolution by 'natural' selection, the organogenesis and physiology of 'natural' endosomatic organs) but rather by economic principles (innovation, production, functioning and exchanges of exosomatic organs, that is, 'artificial' selection and 'artificial' organs), in turn governed by cultural rules and legal and political principles.

Unlike the production of biological organs, which allows a local decrease in entropy, the production of exosomatic organs is ambivalent: it can just as easily accelerate the entropic tendency (exploitation of resources, disorganization and standardization) as it can intensify the anti-entropic tendency (renewal of resources, organization and diversification). To become producers of anti-entropy at the psychosocial level, exosomatic organs must be adopted by living beings through the constitution of collective organizations and through the transformation of knowledge.

Throughout the Anthropocene, the entropic aspect of the exosomatization process has become visible everywhere, now that it has been 'disembedded' from any scientific, legal or political structure, subjected to economic deregulation and market automatisms: once this disembedding of exosomatization has occurred, it threatens to lead to the destruction of the very possibility of the existence of complex life forms on Earth, eliminating the localities of endosomatic life (biological niches) and exosomatic life (technical milieus and social organizations). In this context, it seems necessary to rethink the questions raised by artificial intelligence and transhumanism no longer as possibilities of 'enhancement' but as a profoundly ambivalent step in the process of exosomatization.

### Hermeneutic Web and Deliberative Social Networks

A hermeneutic web enables individuals to practise active interpretations and singular expressions, unlike current platforms that operate on the basis of capturing data and treating it through intensive computing. A deliberative social network enables the constitution of peer groups, and rational deliberation and debate between these groups,[21] unlike the dominant model that links individuals to other individuals according to their data and profiles, thus isolating them within fragmented and hyper-personalized informational environments ('filter bubbles').

The design and implementation of a hermeneutic web and deliberative social networks would have the function of putting digital platforms at the service of the creation of knowledge communities and no longer of capturing attention and exploiting data. Digital technologies would then become the supports of anti-entropic processes of co-individuation, rather than agents of psycho-social entropy.[22]

*Supplement: the functionalities of the hermeneutic web*
*and deliberative social networks*

The creation of a hermeneutic web and deliberative social networks entails rethinking network architectures and data formats, in order to introduce new contributory and interpretive functions into current web formats and already existing tools.

For example:

- graphical annotation and shared categorization functions allowing active users to compare note-taking and content interpretation;

- data-analysis algorithms based on qualitative recommendation through the analysis of annotations enabling the constitution of groups of interpretations or affinities;

- new types of social networks founded on linking groups rather than isolated individuals, enabling the conflict of interpretations, disputation and reasoned discussion, all of which are essential to the exercise of public debate and to the constitution of knowledge.

## Internation

The internation designates an agreement, a consensus and a network between various open localities (nations, regions, metropolises), united by the common concern to design and experiment with new anti-entropic and anti-anthropic economic models – that is to say, economic models that take care of the biosphere and promote local knowledge and arts of living. The aim of the internation is to become a new kind of higher complex exorganism at a planetary scale, based on reticulated localities and constituting a new public power on the basis of a new law.

*Supplement: the internation, the reticulation of localities faced with globalization*

The notion of the internation was proposed by Marcel Mauss in 1920,[23] when the internationalist movement was emerging in the post-war world: according to Mauss, the internation is diametrically opposed to nationalism (which ideologically and economically isolates the nation), but it does not for all that deny the nation ('inter-nation' is opposed to 'a-nation'). According to Mauss, the ideal of internationalism should not lead to a 'supranation' that absorbs all nations, but should instead constitute the pillar of an internationalism aimed at uniting nations rather than erasing them.

One hundred years later, it seems necessary to rethink this ideal of the internation, distinguishing it from superficial notions of international cosmopolitanism, and considering its implications in the context of the Anthropocene and the 'functional sovereignty' of digital platforms. The current context indeed corresponds to a planetary industrial development that threatens the entire biosphere and is characterized by a new 'functional sovereignty' established by extraterritorial technological companies and their supranational economic organizations, disintegrating local public powers (including national public power) and leading to the revival of nationalist and reactionary tendencies. As Jacques Derrida explained,[24] the withdrawal of territories into national identities and the closing of national borders are reactions to the effects of dislocation generated by the global 'teletechnological' acceleration.

In this context, the function of the internation is to open up an alternative path to both nationalism and globalization. Instead of producing a viable, liveable and desirable world for the majority of living organisms, globalization has become 'de-worldization':[25] it is therefore a question of re-worldizing (of re-creating 'worlds') through the reconstitution of sustainable, solvent and diversified localities and through the cultivation of different forms of local knowledge, which always emerge from local potentialities. The localities reticulated through the internation aim at inventing and experimenting, in a collective way, with various economic models capable of producing anti-entropy (at the thermodynamic, biological, psychic, and social levels): that is to say, new ways of living, working and inhabiting that are ecologically sustainable, economically solvent and collectively desirable.

The constitution of the internation therefore requires the implementation of technological infrastructures allowing the opening of localities to one another and their reticulation, in particular through the circulation of knowledge, always localized, but always susceptible to being deterritorialized, through the confrontation, sharing and enriching of this knowledge. The internation then has the chance to implement a new process of the transindividuation of reference at a planetary scale, and therefore to constitute a new higher complex exorganism, based on noetic exchanges between anti-entropic localities at different scales.

## Knowledge

All forms of knowledge (from the knowledge of how to do and how to live to existential knowledge, as well as formal and theoretical knowledge of every kind) may be described as a 'transindividual' process: knowledge exists only if it is transmitted, practised and transformed by a group of individuals who share a certain number of common rules, themselves transmitted from generation to generation and transformed over time. By practising a form of knowledge, individuals transform themselves along with the knowledge they practise: inscribing singular bifurcations into knowledge, that is, dis-automatizing the rules of this knowledge, they invent new ways of doing, living and thinking. In this regard, the practice of knowledge involves a normative capacity in a positive sense.

*Supplement: knowledge and anti-anthropic processes of care*

Knowledge is always social and collective, and always requires a technical milieu through which it can be shared and practised. This technical milieu serves as a memory support and allows psychic individuals to be connected with one another: groups collectively invent new norms (for example, new ways of producing, cooking, educating, inhabiting, living together, counting, measuring, etc.) through which they take care of themselves, of others and of their artificial environment, developing their capacities and cultivating social, transindividual and transgenerational relationships. For this reason, the Internation Collective argues that the wealth of a society is constituted by the practice of knowledge: knowledge produces practical or societal value by increasing collective memory, by strengthening social cohesion and by making possible the dynamic evolution of societies. At both the general social level, and at the level of the formal knowledge produced by communities of peers, academic institutions and scholarly publication, the practice of knowledge thus has an anti-entropic function that in one way or another contributes to cultural and social renewal and diversification (socio-diversity or 'noodiversity').

## Proletarianization

Proletarianization refers to a process that deprives individuals and communities of their knowledge. An individual is proletarianized when he or she fails to reappropriate/re-interiorize knowledge that has been exteriorized (and often automated) in a technical support. Indeed, transmitting or acquiring a form of knowledge always presupposes that the knowledge that has been psychically interiorized by some individuals (those who transmit it) is technically exteriorized (in a medium, a memory-support). This knowledge can then be psychically re-interiorized by other individuals (those who learn), who internalize it, collectively frequenting the supports on which this knowledge is conserved. 'Proletarianization' occurs when the re-interiorization of knowledge exteriorized by psychic individuals in technical supports is made impossible – it occurs when memory supports are not socialized or practised. Individuals are then subordinated to the procedures exteriorized in apparatus [*dispositifs*], instead of using these supports to transmit and share different forms of knowledge.

### Supplement: from the proletariat to generalized proletarianization

It can be argued that the problem of proletarianization was already an issue for Plato, as evidenced by the fact that Socrates described writing as a '*pharmakon*' possessing the capacity both to aid memory and to undermine it, and that Plato's or Socrates's concern arose at a time when the spread of writing was creating new social classes capable of both generating new knowledge and exploiting its destruction. In the middle of the nineteenth century, this question of the externalization of knowledge in technology was raised in *The Communist Manifesto*. Karl Marx and Friedrich Engels argued that 'the proletariat is recruited from all classes of the population', and that this is possible because the 'specialized skill [of the workers] is rendered worthless by new methods of production': due to 'the use of machinery and division of labor', the latter becomes indifferent to the worker and loses 'all individual character, and, consequently, all charm for the workman'. The proletarianized worker then becomes 'an appendage of the machine, and it is only the most simple, most monotonous, and most easily acquired knack, that is required of him'.[26]

A century later, in *On the Mode of Existence of Technical Objects*, Gilbert Simondon will take up Marx's analyses in order to insist on the epistemic dimension of the alienation of workers.[27] According to Simondon, alienation derives not only from the fact that workers are dispossessed of the means of production, but also from the ignorance and incomprehension of workers and owners alike in the face of machines. As a result, workers must subordinate themselves to the internal norms of the machine instead of being able to participate in its evolution (by repairing or improving it), just like users who can only consume or damage technical objects whose functioning they are not able to understand or alter.

Drawing upon Marx and Simondon, Stiegler broadens the concept of proletarianization in order to show how processes that destroy knowledge are manifested in the twenty-first century.[28] Stiegler distinguishes three stages in the evolution of proletarianization, corresponding to three stages in the history of capitalism:

- in the nineteenth century, the proletarianization of the knowledge of how to do work, which occurred through the development of industrial machinery and the implementation of the scientific organization of labour (productivist capitalism);

- in the twentieth century, the proletarianization of the knowledge of how to live, which occurred through the development of cultural 'programme' industries and of mass media such as radio, cinema and television (consumerist capitalism);

- in the twenty-first century, the proletarianization of the knowledge of how to conceptualize, which is occurring through the development of digital and algorithmic technologies, and of what is referred to as 'artificial intelligence' (computational capitalism).

In the nineteenth century, the development of industrial machinery, which marked the beginning of the Anthropocene, generated the first process of capitalist proletarianization: the first individuals affected by proletarianization were workers, and what they were deprived of was their knowledge of how to make and do, exteriorized and automated in machines (supports of mechanical knowledge), to which labouring bodies are subordinated in the functions of production.

During the twentieth century, however, what is proletarianized is not only the producer's knowledge of how to make and do: it is also the citizen-cum-consumer's knowledge of how to live. Indeed, marketing and the advertising industry (based on mass media and analogue technologies) tend to replace ways of life with 'lifestyles', by capturing attention and by standardizing behaviour: individuals find themselves increasingly unable to invent their own singular modes of existence, while the arts of life are progressively replaced by consumer behaviour – shopping and 'brands'.

In the twenty-first century, which corresponds to the development of digital and network computer technologies, it is also designers, researchers and decision-makers who are proletarianized, through the application of high-performance computing to massive amounts of data (big data), which short-circuits the time for reflection and theoretical elaboration, or through computer programs providing 'automated decision support systems', which short-circuit processes of deliberation, interpretation and decision-making.

Rather than each new stage replacing the previous one, these three stages build upon and reinforce the proletarianization that came before. Therefore, what we are witnessing today amounts to a process of generalized proletarianization that can be overcome only if the practice and production of all types of knowledge is systemically valorized.

## Work/Employment

Leaning on the Greek distinction between *ergon* and *ponos*, work must here be distinguished from labour, insofar as it constitutes not only an expenditure of force or physical energy, but an investment by the individual or group in the production of (a) work. While work involves the practice of knowledge and self-realization, and therefore the production of practical value, employment is based on the transformation of labour power into exchange value.

A work activity implies the transmission, circulation and transformation of all forms of knowledge (which are always collective practices), during which the individuals 'individuate' (capacitate or transform) themselves through the transformation of their working environment and through a process of co-individuation with 'peers'. By working, individuals organize themselves collectively through sharing knowledge, each individual developing his or her singular capacities and thus participating in the transformation of knowledge itself.

In this sense, work can be considered an anti-entropic activity at the psycho-social level (because it produces organization, differences and novelty). Employment activities, on the contrary, are mostly based on the repetition of tasks or on the application of specific procedures requiring the controlled implementation of acquired skills. In this sense, employment activities (jobs) tend to lock the employee into pre-established and standardized behaviour. Employment thus tends to prevent the production of novelty and to promote the repetition of the same: in this sense, it can be considered an entropic and prole-tarianizing activity, isolating individuals and dispossessing them of their knowledge.

### Supplement: work, employment and automatization

As André Gorz[29] showed in the 1980s, with the advent of industrial modernity, work in the philosophical or anthropological sense (under-stood as an activity through which the subject realizes him- or herself through what he or she creates or produces, by objectifying him- or herself in the world) has become 'work-employment', that is, a 'job that we have' rather than 'work that we do'. Work has thus lost its function as a place of identification or a time of personal development for the majority of worker-employees, who sell their time by perform-ing tasks that often seem meaningless and unnecessary. Far from allowing the liberation of time that it should have made possible, the exponential development of automation has only worsened, through the generalization of what David Graeber describes as 'bullshit jobs',[30] which Richard Sennett refers to as low-quality work.[31]

This is so because the (standardized and repetitive) activities mobilized in the context of bullshit jobs are easily automated: they are based on the repetition of programmed tasks that can be formal-ized and implemented in a mechanical or algorithmic automatic sys-tem. By contrast, the (singular and evolving) activities mobilized through activities of work can hardly be automated, since they imply the capacity to dis-automatize acquired automatisms and to produce unpredictable novelty, through the practice and the transformation of transmitted knowledge.

In a context of constant technological innovation, and according to the accelerating development of artificial intelligence and robot-ics, we can foresee the automation of a considerable number of jobs in many sectors and activities. This automation is not limited to just a particular sector (industry, service, education, health): any job that does not imply the exercise of knowledge and the production of nov-elty can by definition be automated. To cope with this gradual auto-mation of jobs, which is putting the Fordo-Keynesian model of redis-tribution (based on wages) into crisis, a solvent economy will have to encourage the development of work activities and the production of different forms of new knowledge. This is the aim of the contributory economy, which proposes to take advantage of the time freed up by automation in order to develop work activities implying the practice of different types of knowledge.

## Notes

The entries of this lexicon were originally published in French as 'Vocabulaire de l'Internation. Introduction aux concepts de Bernard Stiegler et du collectif Internation', *Appareil* (published 3 February 2021), available at: <http://journals.openedition.org/appareil/3752>.

1   Gilles Deleuze and Félix Guattari, *What is Philosophy?*, trans. Hugh Tomlinson and Graham Burchill (New York: Columbia University Press, 1994), pp. 108–10.

2   Bernard Stiegler, *Qu'appelle-t-on panser? Volume 2. La leçon de Greta Thunberg* (Paris: Les Liens qui Libèrent, 2020), p. 15.

3   Ibid., p. 108.

4   Bernard Stiegler, *Automatic Society, Volume 1: The Future of Work*, trans. Daniel Ross (Cambridge: Polity Press, 2016), p. 14.

5   Bernard Stiegler, *Technics and Time. Volume 1. The Fault of Epimetheus*, trans. Richard Beardsworth and George Collins (Stanford California: Stanford University Press, 1998), p. 17.

6   Bertrand Gille, *The History of Techniques*, 2 vols, trans. P. Southgate and T. Williamson (New York: Gordon and Breach, 1986).

7   Gilbert Simondon, 'Psychosociologie de la technicité', *Sur la technique* (Paris: Presses Universitaires de France, 2014), pp. 25–129.

8   Jacques Derrida and Bernard Stiegler, *Echographies of Television: Filmed Interviews*, trans. Jennifer Bajorek (Cambridge: Polity Press, 2002).

9   Henri Bergson, *Creative Evolution*, trans. Arthur Mitchell (New York: Henry Holt and Company, 1911), p. 243.

10  Claude Shannon, 'A Mathematical Theory of Communication,' *The Bell System Technical Journal* 27 (July, October 1948), pp. 379–423 and 623–56.

11  Norbert Wiener, *Cybernetics, or Control and Communication in the Animal and the Machine*, second edition (Cambridge, Massachusetts: MIT Press, 1961).

12  Erwin Schrödinger, *What is Life?*, in *What is Life?, with Mind and Matter and Autobiographical Sketches* (Cambridge: Cambridge University Press, 1992).

13  Norbert Wiener, *The Human Use of Human Beings. Cybernetics and Society* (London: Free Association of Books, 1989), p. 36.

14  Francis Bailly and Giuseppe Longo, 'Biological Organization and Anti-Entropy', *Journal of Biological Systems* 17 (2009), pp. 63–96.

15  Thomas Berns and Antoinette Rouvroy, 'Gouvernementalité algorithmique et perspectives d'émancipation. Le disparate comme condition d'individuation par la relation?', *Réseaux* 177 (2013), pp. 163–96.

16  Frank Pasquale, 'From Territorial to Functional Sovereignty: The Case of Amazon', *Law and Political Economy* (6 December 2017), available at: <https://lpeblog.org/2017/12/06/from-territorial-to-functional-sovereignty-the-case-of-amazon/>.

17  Alain Supiot, *The Spirit of Philadelphia: Social Justice vs. the Total Market*, trans. Saskia Brown (London and New York: Verso, 2012).

18  Alfred J. Lotka, 'The Law of Evolution as a Maximal Principle', *Human Biology* 17:3 (1945), pp. 167–194.

19  André Leroi-Gourhan, *Gesture and Speech*, trans. Anna Bostock Berger (Cambridge, Massachusetts, and London: MIT Press, 1993).

20  Nicholas Georgescu-Roegen, *The Entropy Law and the Economic Process* (Cambridge, Massachusetts, and London: Harvard University Press, 1971).

21  See Yuk Hui and Harry Halpin, 'Collective Individuation: The Future of the Social Web', available at: <https://digital-studies.org/wp/wpcontent/uploads/2013/01/HuiYuk_and_HarryHalpin_FINAL_CollectiveIndividuation.pdf>.

22  John L. Pfaltz, 'Entropy in Social Networks' (2012), available at: <https://arxiv.org/pdf/1212.2917.pdf>.

23  Mauss Marcel, 'Complément à La Nation', in *La nation ou le sens du social*, corrected edition (Paris: Presses Universitaires de France, 2018), p. 396.

24  Derrida and Stiegler, *Echographies of Television*, pp. 79–81.

25  Alain Supiot (ed.), *Mondialisation ou globalisation? Les leçons de Simone Weil* (Paris: Collège de France, 2019).

26  Karl Marx and Friedrich Engels, *Manifesto of the Communist Party*, trans. Samuel Moore (1848), available at https://www.marxists.org/archive/marx/works/1848/communist-manifesto/.

27  Gilbert Simondon, *On the Mode of Existence of Technical Objects*, trans. Cécile Malaspina and John Rogove (Minneapolis: Univocal Publishing, 2017), pp. 133–35.

28  Bernard Stiegler, *States of Shock: Stupidity and Knowledge in the Twenty-First Century*, trans. Daniel Ross (Cambridge: Polity Press, 2015).

29  André Gorz, *Reclaiming Work: Beyond the Wage-Based Society*, trans. Chris Turner (Cambridge: Polity Press, 1999), and André Gorz, *Critique of Economic Reason*, trans. Gillian Handyside and Chris Turner (London and New York: Verso, 1989).

30  David Graeber, *Bullshit Jobs: A Theory* (New York: Simon & Schuster, 2018).

31  Richard Sennett, *The Corrosion of Character: The Personal Consequences of Work in the New Capitalism* (New York: W. W. Norton, 1998).

www.ingramcontent.com/pod-product-compliance
Lightning Source LLC
Chambersburg PA
CBHW020824270326
41928CB00006B/432